Global Logistics and Supply Chain Management

Global Logistics and Supply Chain Management

John Mangan,
Chandra Lalwani and Tim Butcher

John Wiley & Sons, Ltd

Other Wiley Editorial Offices

John Wiley & Sons Inc., 111 River Street, Hoboken, NJ 07030, USA

Jossey-Bass, 989 Market Street, San Francisco, CA 94103-1741, USA

Wiley-VCH Verlag GmbH, Boschstr. 12, D-69469 Weinheim, Germany

John Wiley & Sons Australia Ltd, 42 McDougall Street, Milton, Queensland 4064, Australia

John Wiley & Sons (Asia) Pte Ltd, 2 Clementi Loop #02-01, Jin Xing Distripark, Singapore 129809

John Wiley & Sons Canada Ltd, 6045 Freemont Blvd, Mississauga, ONT, L5R 4J3

Wiley also publishes its books in a variety of electronic formats. Some content that appears in print
may not be available in electronic books.

Library of Congress Cataloging-in-Publication Data

Mangan, John, 1968-
Global logistics and supply chain management / John Mangan, Chandra
Lalwani and Tim Butcher.
    p. cm.
  Includes bibliographical references and index.
  ISBN 978-0-470-06634-8 (pbk. : alk. paper)
1. Business logistics. I. Mangan, John II. Lalwani, Chandra.   III. Butcher, Tim.   IV. Title.
  HD38.5.M3637 2008
  658.7–dc22   2007044544

A catalogue record for this book is available from the British Library

ISBN: 978-0-470-06634-8(P/B)

Typeset in 10/12 Optima by Thomson Digital, India
Printed and bound in Great Britain by CPI Antony Rowe, Chippenham, Wiltshire

Dedication

Maeve, Cathal, Eibhlín and Eoghan
Mohini, Nikita and Nishant
Brenda

Contents

Foreword   ix

Preface   xi

About the Authors   xv

About the Contributors   xvii

Acknowledgements   xix

PART ONE – LOGISTICS AND SUPPLY CHAIN CONTEXT   **1**
  1. Introduction   3
  2. Globalisation and International Trade   19
  3. Supply Chain Strategies   35
  Part One Case Studies   **53**
    Dell: High Velocity, Focused Supply Chain Management   53
    The Medical Devices Company   56

PART TWO – LOGISTICS AND SUPPLY CHAIN OPERATIONS   **57**
  4. Logistics Service Providers   59
  5. Procurement and Outsourcing   75
  6. Inventory Management   89
  7. Warehousing and Materials Management   111
  8. Transport in Supply Chains   131
  9. Information Flows and Technology   149
  10. Logistics and Financial Management   165
  11. Measuring and Managing Logistics Performance   185
  Part Two Case Studies   **205**
    Deutsche Post/DHL   205
    Gate Gourmet: Success Means Getting to the Plane on Time   211
    Managing Supply Chain Information at HBOS   217
    Supplier Evaluation at EADS   223

PART THREE – SUPPLY CHAIN DESIGNS   **227**
  12. Supply Chain Vulnerability, Risk, Robustness and Resilience   229
  13. Integration and Collaboration   249
  14. Sustainable Logistics and Supply Chain Systems   267
  15. New Supply Chain Designs   281

Part Three Case Studies   **295**

Humanitarian Aid Supply Chains   295

*Good Distribution Practice and Pharmaceutical Supply
Chain Management*   299

Dubai Logistics City: A Quantum Leap in Logistics   303

*Morning365: An Online Bookstore's Strategy to Grow
in the Constantly Changing Market*   317

SCM: The Past is Prologue   335

Glossary   **345**

Index   **357**

Foreword

Over the past few decades there have been many new ideas, tools and frameworks advanced to enable organisations become both more efficient and more effective. However, few of these have had as much impact on actual business practice and performance as what we now term logistics and supply chain management. The idea that the processes by which we serve customers and fulfil demand are critical may seem obvious, and yet only recently have we seen these concerns elevated to a strategic level in the business.

Today, leading companies now see their supply chains as a potential source of competitive advantage. The transformation in the way in which organisations design and manage the processes of value delivery has been truly revolutionary. Rather than thinking of the business as a set of loosely connected 'vertical' functions, it is increasingly recognised that the goal has to be to break down the walls between those functions and instead to manage 'horizontal', customer-facing processes.

This new way of thinking and working is reflected in the focus of this present book. It recognises the central role of logistics and supply chain management in enhancing competitiveness both through cost reduction and value enhancement. While in the future there are always going to be better ways of doing things as today's best practice becomes tomorrow's baseline, the guidelines provided in these pages will enable both students and practitioners to better understand the possibilities and the challenges.

Professor Martin Christopher
Cranfield University, School of Management
November 2007

Preface

This book has its origin in the University of Hull Logistics Institute where all three authors are based. The Institute is located near to the Humber Estuary, the largest (in freight volume terms) port complex in the UK, and an area of intense logistics activity. It is thus a useful location for teaching and researching logistics. Two of the authors (Mangan and Lalwani) have worked together for many years on joint research and teaching activities. In 2005 they joined the faculty of the University of Hull where they met the third author (Butcher). All three authors teach on the University's Masters programme in logistics and supply chain management, a programme that attracts students from all over the world. It was while working together on this programme that we realised the need for a comprehensive book which would have the following key characteristics:

- *Be concise* – logistics is a very pragmatic subject and it has been our intention throughout to 'stick to the point'. We hope that you the reader will appreciate this. Notwithstanding such intended brevity, we have endeavoured to cover both practical and strategic aspects of the subject matter. The book is neither a 'how to' cook book, nor is it a high level strategy book with little relevance to practice. The aim of the book is to convey to both advanced students and practitioners of logistics and supply chain management the diverse operational and strategic content of the subjects of logistics and supply chain management.

- *Truly global, up-to-date perspective* – the world is changing daily and the typical 'Western' worldview no longer necessarily dominates. As we will see in the book, logistics is a key driver of globalisation and facilitator of international trade and development. We have thus endeavoured to reflect these characteristics by adopting a truly global perspective and hope that the book will appeal to students regardless of what geography they are located in.

  The context of logistics is constantly shaped by emerging trends and new technologies and we have tried to ensure that the book is as up to date as possible and takes cognisance of these trends and technologies. Sadly, despite much progress, today's world still contains many divisions, tensions and inequalities. We have attempted to take cognisance of these while fully embracing a neutral and nonpolitical perspective.

- *Pedagogical approach* – we have endeavoured to use a variety of pedagogies in this book, which we hope will create a fertile learning platform for you the reader. Both long(er) and short(er) case studies are included and are intended to highlight key issues in a focused manner. Key points are detailed in separate boxes and this should also help with revision. Italics are used within the text to emphasise specific issues. Various terms are in bold when first used to indicate that explanations are given in the glossary at the end of the book. We hope you find these various features useful. There are two other features of our pedagogical approach which we believe are especially important.

Firstly, the three authors named on the cover (Mangan, Lalwani and Butcher) are not the only people to have contributed to this book. We are also very fortunate to have contributions from various experts in specific areas of logistics and supply chain management. They have written chapters and case studies based on their specific areas of expertise and which we believe add to the richness of this book over and above what we could have achieved working on our own. This multidisciplinary approach has allowed us to draw in not just logisticians, but also people from backgrounds as diverse as, for example, military and accounting.

The second pedagogical feature we wish to highlight is the mix of qualitative and quantitative content in this book. We are of the view that many logistics books tend to occupy one of two opposite positions, either containing a large share of quantitative material, or else none at all. We believe that a certain level of quantitative aptitude and knowledge is an important feature of most logistics and supply chain managers' jobs (for example, in the areas of logistics costs and inventory management). Many such managers, however, do not routinely engage in sophisticated mathematical analysis, this is usually the domain of operations researchers, engineers and management accountants. We thus aim to convey the necessary quantitative features of logistics and supply chain management, while at the same time not excessively burdening the reader with quantitative analysis.

These various characteristics and perspectives adopted in the book are discussed further in Chapter 1. The book itself is divided into three parts, again this is discussed, and the content of each part elaborated, in Chapter 1.

Book companion website

Our text is also supported by additional teaching and learning resources, which are available on the companion website at **www.wileyeurope.com/college/mangan**. They include PowerPoint slides, suggested answers to end of chapter questions and case teaching notes for lecturers. Students will also find an online glossary and multiple choice quizzes.

Relationship to other disciplines, especially operations management

Chapter 1 details the various factors that have led to the evolution of logistics and supply chain management. Figure 1 outlines the various disciplines which we believe logistics and supply chain management are closely linked to. In fact it is

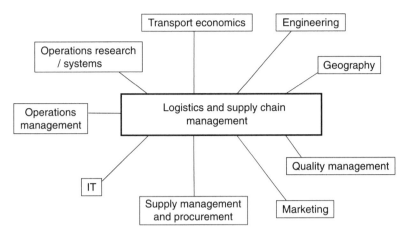

Figure 1 Links to other disciplines

only in recent years that third level courses and explicit career paths have emerged in logistics and supply chain management. It is thus often the case that many practitioners today will have backgrounds in one or other of the disciplines illustrated in Figure 1. Various issues pertaining to some of these disciplines are discussed in this book.

Perhaps the discipline to which logistics and supply chain management is most often closely linked is *operations management*. As we will see in Chapter 1, supply chains involve three interdependent flows: material, information and resources. We discuss these flows in depth throughout the book. The study of operations management is also concerned with these flows. We are in fact of the view that this book could also be effectively used for teaching more general operations management courses, and especially those with a particular emphasis on logistics and supply chain issues. It is becoming increasingly apparent that many operations managers today are engaging more and more in wider supply chain management activities. As processes become increasingly automated and simplified, the focus of many operations managers is shifting to service issues beyond core manufacturing, and to flows and interactions along the supply chain. All of these issues are discussed in this book.

Logistics and supply chain management are ever changing and demanding disciplines, but provide attractive and rewarding opportunities to people who wish to work in these areas. The purpose of this book has been to equip you, the reader, regardless of whether you are a student or a practitioner, with the necessary knowledge and skills to allow you to work more effectively in these areas. We hope you enjoy working with this book and find it of benefit.

John Mangan, Chandra Lalwani and Tim Butcher

About the Authors

John Mangan is Director of the University of Hull Logistics Institute where he also holds the Peter Thompson Chair in Logistics. A native of Ireland, he holds the following qualifications: BSc (National University of Ireland), Higher Diploma (Maynooth University, Ireland), MA (Lancaster University, UK), MSc (Cranfield University, UK), and PhD (Cardiff University, UK). Prior to entering academia, he worked in Aer Lingus (the Irish national airline) and in the Irish Civil Service. John's teaching and research is largely focused in two areas: global and maritime logistics, and management development in logistics and supply chain management (SCM). Prior to his appointment at Hull, John lectured first at University College Dublin, Ireland, and then at the Trinity IMI Graduate School of Management in Dublin, Ireland. He also spent time as a Fulbright Scholar at Boston College, USA. In addition to his current teaching and research commitments at the University of Hull, John also regularly teaches operations and logistics on University of Hull MBA programmes in both the Middle East and Asia.

Chandra Lalwani is Professor of Supply Chain Management and Director of the Centre for Logistics Research at the University of Hull Logistics Institute. He holds a BEng in Electrical Engineering, an MEng in Control Systems and another MEng in Systems Engineering. He obtained his PhD from the University of Wales in 1978 based on his research on the dynamic modelling of commodity flow systems. Prior to joining the University of Hull he taught at Cardiff University Business School and was responsible for doctoral research in logistics and operations management. Professor Lalwani was a Deputy Director and Co-investigator at Cardiff Business School on the Cardiff University Innovative Manufacturing Research Centre, and Principal Investigator on one of its three flagship research projects on sustainable logistics. Chandra's teaching and research focus is in supply chain management, retail logistics, logistics and transport modelling, and integration of transport in supply chains. With his research in transport in supply chains, he has worked closely with the retail and distribution industry in the UK.

Tim Butcher is a Lecturer in Operations and Project Management at the University of Hull Logistics Institute where he is the MSc Logistics and Supply Chain Management Programme Director. He holds the following qualifications: BEng(Hons) (University of Liverpool, UK), MSc (Cranfield University, UK), and EngD (Cranfield University, UK).

Prior to entering academia, he completed a technical engineering apprenticeship and worked as a maintainability engineer for Westland Helicopters. Tim's teaching and research is largely focused in two areas: human factors and new technologies in logistics and SCM. In addition to his current teaching and research commitments at the University of Hull, Tim also regularly teaches project management on University of Hull MBA programmes in the Middle East.

About the Contributors

Chuda Basnet (Chapter 6) is an Associate Professor at the University of Waikato, New Zealand. He has received a Bachelor's degree in Mechanical Engineering, a Master's degree in Industrial and Management Engineering, and a PhD in Industrial Engineering and Management. He teaches in the areas of operations management and supply chain management. His research interests are in the areas of manufacturing modelling, supply chain management and decision support systems. He has published papers in *Decision Support Systems, Journal of the Operational Research Society* and *Annals of Operations Research*.

Paul Childerhouse (Chapter 6) is an Associate Professor at the University of Waikato. He obtained his PhD in 2002 whilst a member of the Logistics Systems Dynamics Group at Cardiff University for his research into supply chain integration and market-orientation. His major research interests are in supply chain change management and the development of methods to enable supply chain integration and market-orientation. He is practitioner focused and enjoys auditing and advising organisations on how to improve their supply chain practices. This focus has resulted in a great deal of first-hand industrial knowledge especially in the automotive, aerospace, dairy, construction and retail sectors. He has published over 20 articles in quality journals including: *Journal of Business Logistics, Journal of Operations Management, International Journal of Physical Distribution and Logistics Management, International Journal of Production Research* and *OMEGA*.

Noel McGlynn (Chapter 11) is employed by Microsoft as a Senior Logistics Manager, and is currently working on a range of performance improvement initiatives within the company's European Operations Centre based in Ireland. He previously has held a role of Business Relationship Manager for Hewlett-Packard in Ireland, where he had specific responsibility for managing third-party logistics providers. He also worked for Irish Express Cargo/Flextronics Logistics in a range of logistics related roles in Europe, the USA and Asia. He holds a Bachelor's degree in Commerce and a Master's degree in Business Studies, both from the National University of Ireland, Dublin.

Helen Peck (Chapter 12) is a Senior Lecturer in Commercial & Supply Chain Risk in the Resilience Centre, Department of Defence Management and Security Analysis (DDMSA) at Cranfield University, Shrivenham. She joined the University in 1983, having previously worked for a major UK clearing bank. Initially employed within the University's library and information service, Helen transferred to the academic staff of Cranfield School of Management in 1988, working in the Marketing & Logistics Group where she completed her PhD as a first degree. Today Helen teaches on graduate programmes and short courses at the DDMSA and guest lectures at a number of other universities in the UK. She has led Cranfield University's government-funded programme of research into all aspects of supply chain related risk and resilience since its inception in May 2001. She is author of numerous academic papers and practitioner journal articles, co-editor and author of several books, and an award-winning writer of management case studies. Her research and consultancy interests span mainstream commercial, defence and other public service contexts. Helen is a regular speaker at academic, business and defence conferences around the world.

Mike Tayles (Chapter 10) is Professor of Accounting and Finance and Director of the Centre for International Accounting and Finance Research at Hull University Business School. He is also Visiting Professor of Management Accounting, University Pompeu Fabra, Barcelona, Spain and European Editor of the *Managerial Auditing Journal*. Mike is a Chartered Management Accountant with approximately 10 years' experience in industry and commerce, some of this at a senior level. His first degree is in economics and statistics and his PhD involved a study of contemporary management accounting practices. Since 1990 he has produced almost 100 publications in academic and professional journals, research monographs, textbook chapters and conference presentations. He has experience of and publications from both survey and case study research. Mike has worked in the food processing, light engineering and textile industries and has consulting and research experience in various manufacturing, service and not-for-profit businesses.

Acknowledgements

Many people have helped us on our journey to produce this book. First and foremost, the book would not exist but for the continuing support and advice received from many people at John Wiley & Sons Ltd. These include Sarah Booth (Executive Commissioning Editor), Deborah Egleton (Development Editor), Emma Cooper (Project Editor) and Anneli Mockett (Assistant Editor). We thank them for their professionalism and patience. We would also like to thank the various anonymous reviewers for their helpful comments.

The University of Hull, where we work, has been tremendously supportive of our endeavours. In particular we would like to mention Professor Mike Jackson, Dean of the University's Business School and one of the world's foremost management systems scholars, whose vision led to the establishment of the University of Hull Logistics Institute (UHLI). We thank our colleagues at UHLI for their support and collegiality. Special thanks are also due to Professor Martin Christopher of Cranfield University and to Dr Peter Thompson OBE LLD JP for their continued support of our endeavours.

Certain specific elements of the book were generated from funded and/or collaborative research undertakings. In this regard we would like to extend our thanks to: Engineering and Physical Sciences Research Council; European Union IT&C Programme; Chartered Institute of Logistics and Transport; Department for Transport; Mr John Perera of Royal and Sun Alliance; Robert Mason, Dr Steve Disney and Dr Andrew Potter (Cardiff University); Professor Janat Shah (Indian Institute of Management, Bangalore); and Professor Kulwant Pawar (Nottingham University Business School). We would also like to thank Dr Raymond Swaray (University of Hull) for his comments on Chapter 2. We are also very grateful to various copyright holders for allowing us to use certain material.

We sincerely thank the various chapter contributors whose expert inputs have added considerably to our own endeavours: Dr Chuda Basnet and Dr Paul Childerhouse (Waikato University), Mr Noel McGlynn (Microsoft), Dr Helen Peck (Cranfield University), and Professor Mike Tayles (The University of Hull). We would like to also thank the various case contributors for agreeing to the inclusion of their insightful cases: Mr Ciaran Brady (PLS Pharma Logistics), Dr Marc Day (Henley Management College), Mr Lars Eiermann (European Business School), Dr Jean-Noel Ezingeard (Kingston Business School), Mr Tom Ferris, Mr Graham Heaslip (Institute of Technology, Carlow), Professor Bowon Kim (Korea Advanced

Institute of Science and Technology), Roger Moser (European Business School), and Prof Dr Stefan Walter (European Business School).

Finally, a special word of thanks to one of the pioneers of logistics and supply chain management, Professor Donald Bowersox, for agreeing to allow us to include his excellent, insightful article 'SCM: The past is prologue' from CSCMP's *Supply Chain Quarterly*.

PART ONE

LOGISTICS AND SUPPLY
CHAIN CONTEXT

Introduction

INTRODUCTION

This chapter lays the foundations of the textbook and explains the origins and application of logistics and supply chain management, as well as giving descriptions of key concepts. A framework for the textbook is developed and this illustrates where each chapter fits in the overall schema of the book, while the various perspectives adopted by the authors when writing this book are also described.

The chapter comprises six core sections:
- The evolution of logistics and supply chain management
- What is logistics?
- What is supply chain management?
- Distinguishing logistics and supply chain management
- Applications to manufacturing *and* services
- Book framework

LEARNING OBJECTIVES

- Explain the origins of logistics and supply chain management.
- Define both terms and outline how logistics and supply chain management differ from each other.
- Highlight the importance of these areas in both manufacturing *and* services contexts.
- Identify how best practice logistics and supply chain management can yield both cost reduction *and* value addition.

THE EVOLUTION OF LOGISTICS AND SUPPLY CHAIN MANAGEMENT

Both logistics and supply chain management (SCM) are fascinating and exciting areas that touch all of our lives. Just think of the many different products that are purchased and consumed each day – how do they reach the customer and at what cost? Although logistics and SCM are areas that have only come to widespread prominence since the mid 1980s, the reality is that they have roots which run much longer than that. Not only are they key aspects of today's business world, but they are also of importance in the not-for-profit and public sectors. In addition, while the origins of much logistics thinking and practice are in a manufacturing context, we are witnessing increased and highly successful application of logistics and SCM principles in a services context also (just think of the efficiencies that have been driven into many service based activities such as banking and hospitals where the emphasis has shifted to serving more customers, better, faster, cheaper).

> The commonly accepted abbreviation for supply chain management is SCM, so that abbreviation will be used in the remainder of this book.

The terms logistics and SCM, although often used interchangeably, are distinct and will be defined later in the chapter. First, however, it is appropriate to examine how some key developments have shaped the evolution of these important areas. In fact, five separate and important developments, each of which evolved largely independently, can be identified and are now detailed.

Reduced transport intensity of freight

In the past, international trade was dominated by bulky raw materials. Times have changed however, and in-process and finished products, not raw materials, now play a much greater role in world trade. Some simple examples illustrate this clearly. Compare the value of the various computer products currently being shipped around the world daily with the bulky, low value, agricultural produce shipped around the world a hundred years ago. Agricultural produce, and indeed other comparatively high volume/low value freight, does still of course traverse the world but, in general, the size and value of the freight that is transported today is very different to that of times past. In the case of agriculture, many food producers, rather than transporting bulky foodstuffs, now tend to try and 'add value' to the product near to the point of production: for example, rather than ship live chickens, the international poultry trade generally comprises processed, ready-to-cook chicken. The same is true for many other trades, not just in agriculture but across a range of industries, whereby manufacturers try and increase the value : volume ratio of products being shipped. We will see in later chapters that there is also an increasing trend towards having the final value-adding stages in the production of various products as close as possible to the final customer.

Higher value freight is better able to 'absorb' transport costs than is low value freight, with the 'transport cost penalty' imposed by having to move freight over greater distances often being somewhat offset by the fact that the freight is of higher value. Hence, we refer to a generally reducing **transport cost sensitivity** of freight.

Indeed for some products it is now not even necessary to ship physical product at all. Just think, for example, of the way much software is now transmitted around the world via the internet. This replacement of physical product by virtual product is referred to as **material substitution**.

> For many individual shipments:
> increased value/decreased volume
> = lower transport cost penalty.

Falling product prices

In many markets, increased competition and falling marketplace prices have forced many companies to reduce costs. Just think of the falling prices of many electronics products in recent years, such as DVD players, or the fact that the prices of many motor cars have stayed flat in real terms at best, despite the fact that product specifications, performance and quality have improved dramatically. This has forced companies to focus on other areas where savings can be made, and the storage and movement of inventory is a key area in this regard. Thus companies will seek to ensure that any products (especially those with flat or declining value) being transported are configured (in terms of product design, packaging, etc.) so as to reduce as much as possible their transport cost sensitivity.

Deregulation of transport

The important role played by transport in logistics will be discussed later in the book, in Chapters 4 and 8 in particular. There are five principal modes of transport namely air, road, water, rail and pipeline. In recent decades transport markets in many countries have been **deregulated** by various governments. The essence of effective deregulation is that by removing unnecessary barriers to competition, markets become more contestable and (in theory at least) prices should fall and service should improve. We say 'in theory' because the reality in some deregulated markets has been somewhat different (with private monopolies sometimes replacing public ones) but, in general and over the long run, deregulation has had a positive impact on many transport markets, leading to the provision of both more and cheaper services. This of course in turn makes it easier and more efficient to move freight around the world.

A good example is that of *Fed Ex*, a company which today has one of the world's largest air freight fleets. Constrained by burdensome government regulations in the USA in the 1970s, it was not until the late 1970s with the deregulation of the US air freight market (which relaxed the rules governing who could operate in the market and how they could operate) that the company was able to expand and grow.

Productivity improvements

Up to the mid 1950s most maritime freight was carried on bulk vessels. This began to change, however, when some ship owners began to carry freight containers. In 1956 an iconoclastic entrepreneur Malcom McLean put 58 aluminium truck bodies aboard an ageing tanker ship (called the Ideal-X), which set sail from Newark to Houston in the USA. This marked the start of containerised transport as we know it today.[1] Containers can be stacked on top of each other on board the ship, thus allowing very efficient space utilisation and cargo handling. Furthermore, freight can now move from origin to destination across many modes and services with greater ease of handling. The introduction and growth of containerisation led to huge change in ports, which previously were dominated by large workforces responsible for manual handling of bulk cargo. Containerisation also reduced the costs of transporting freight by maritime transport and significantly improved its efficiency. Containerisation spread to other modes and various alliances were formed between combinations of transport companies.

There were of course many other improvements in transport, for example in propulsion technologies (faster transport) and the application of various information and communications technologies. Companies like DHL, Fed Ex and UPS have pioneered the use of barcoding and online tracking and tracing of freight, developments that also increase the efficiencies of logistics systems. Another technology, radio frequency identification (RFID), is now emerging and will in time also drive more efficiency into logistics systems. Technology is a very important component and enabler of logistics and SCM, and Chapter 9, in particular, will look in detail at information flows and technology applications.

Emphasis on inventory reduction

The final trend worth noting has been a shift of management and financial attention into analysing where an organisation's funds are tied up. Inventory management will be covered in detail in Chapter 6, but suffice to say for now that many organisations have become increasingly aware of the fact that often significant funds are lying tied up in unnecessary inventory. Furthermore, it became obvious in the latter years of the twentieth century that often inventory was not well managed. During the decades that followed World War II the responsibility for, and management of, inventory in many firms was very fragmented. The various functions in which inventory played a key role, for example transport, warehousing, purchasing and marketing, were usually considered by managers to be separate and distinct. However, firms began to realise that cost savings and significant efficiency gains could be harnessed from more integrated and focused management of inventory. As far back as 1962, the late Peter Drucker, one of the foremost management thinkers of the twentieth century, wrote a celebrated *Fortune* magazine article entitled 'The economy's dark continent'.[2] In this article he suggested that distribution represented the last frontier for significant cost reduction potential in the firm.

Increased market competition and customer requirements also led to the necessity to see improvements in the management of inventory as an essential competitive weapon. In the increasingly competitive, global marketplace firms began to realise that they could leverage marketplace advantage through superior logistics performance. Cost savings were identified through eliminating unnecessary inventory and just-in-time (JIT) deliveries became normal operating practice in many industries. Outsourcing became more common, with suppliers playing a more central role for many manufacturers (subsequent chapters in the book will consider in detail strategies and practices such as JIT, outsourcing, etc.). In more recent years, in particular, competition based on *time*, for example order to delivery time, became a key success factor (KSF) in many markets.

All of the above five trends, while they emerged independently, have both placed an increased emphasis on the role of transport and inventory, and have led to improvements in the way freight is handled and moved around the world. They have resulted in what is often termed the *supply chain revolution*.

Before proceeding further it is important to highlight one small, but important, distinction. People often use the terms 'freight' and 'cargo' interchangeably, however they are in fact distinct, at least in terms of their use within the logistics sector. In essence: *cargo = freight + mail*. Mail, also known as post, is of course still a very important component of trade and commerce, despite the many technological advances that shape today's world. It is an important and regular source of revenue for many transport companies, especially airlines. Sometimes people also use the term 'goods', usually to refer to freight (not cargo), but we will try to avoid use of this term. Another term worth defining at this juncture is 'consignment', which the *Collins English Dictionary* defines as 'a shipment of goods consigned'; we could thus regard a consignment as a shipment of freight which is passed on usually to some type of logistics service provider from a manufacturer or other source.

THE ROLE OF LOGISTICS IN NATIONAL ECONOMIES

The size of the logistics sector varies from country to country. In the UK, for example, it is estimated to be worth £55 billion to the economy, employing approximatety 1.7 million people and spanning some 65,000 companies.[3]

Economists note that a variety of factors determine the wealth and rate of growth of national economies. These factors are many and varied, and range from available energy sources to institutional factors such as a good banking system. In the late 1990s the US economy experienced a rapid rise in productivity. Closer examination of the economic data by researchers at the McKinsey Global Institute revealed the impact on national productivity of developments in the retail sector, and most notably the impact of the giant retailer Wal-Mart.

According to Beinhocker (2006)[4] 'Wal-Mart's innovations in large-store formats and highly efficient logistical systems in the late 1980s and early 1990s enabled the company to be 40 percent more productive than its competitors'. Wal-Mart has been a global leader in best practice retail logistics, with many other retailers imitating some of its strategies. In the case of the US economy, the increases in Wal-Mart's productivity led to an 'innovation race' with suppliers and other retailers also seeking to enhance their productivity, leading in turn to a rise in whole sector productivity. Wal-Mart is one of the world's largest companies and in the context of the discussion in this chapter it is interesting to observe the considerable impact and importance of how it organises its logistical systems.

WHAT IS LOGISTICS?

Now that the key developments which have shaped the evolution of logistics and SCM have been outlined, it is appropriate to attempt to describe and define these terms. While at one level defining logistics and SCM might seem an elementary task, it is in fact critically important to define, and differentiate, these terms correctly at this juncture as this will shape your understanding and interpretation of the remainder of this book. First to logistics. The *New Oxford Dictionary of English* defines logistics as:

> the detailed coordination of a complex operation involving many people, facilities, or supplies. Origin late 19th century in the sense 'movement and supplying of troops and equipment', from French *logistique*, from *loger* lodge

There are various views with regard to the linguistic origins of the word, with some pointing to the Greek adjective *logistikos,* which means 'skilled in calculating' (and which most likely gave us the mathematical term *logistic*). In Roman and Byzantine times there was a military official who was called *Logista*. In more recent times we have seen, as in the above definition, the French words *logistique* and *loger*. Most agree that the word entered the English language in the nineteenth century, with its application generally seen in military terms and concerned with the organisation of moving, lodging and supplying troops and equipment.

These origins suggest then that logistics has something to do with applications of mathematics and is primarily a military concern. Indeed, the field of military logistics has evolved quite considerably and is now quite sophisticated.[5] Similarly there are many useful applications of mathematics to logistics. Today, however, logistics spans beyond the military and mathematical domains. It was in fact only in the latter decades of the twentieth century that the term logistics entered into common non-military use. The US-based Council of Supply Chain Management Professionals (www.cscmp.org) has adopted the following as part of its definition of logistics management:

> Logistics management is that part of supply chain management that plans, implements, and controls the efficient, effective, forward and reverse flow and storage of goods, services, and related information between the point of origin and the point of consumption in order to meet customers' requirements …

The Chartered Institute of Logistics and Transport (CILT) in the UK (www.ciltuk.org. uk) describes logistics as involving:

> Getting the right product to the right place in the right quantity at the right time, in the best condition and at an acceptable cost.

Indeed, two other 'rights' could be added to this. Firstly, the right customer, because in many industrial locations today multiple different companies will typically be co-located. Even on the one production line there may be various subcontractors collaborating with the factory owner and there will be clear demarcation lines with regard to who has ownership of what, where and when. Therefore, getting the product to the right place may be only half the journey, the challenge would be to get it to the right customer at this right place. Secondly, there is now a substantial and growing interest in environmental and related issues, and Chapter 14 deals in detail with sustainability. Added to the definition of logistics could thus be the necessity to get the product to the customer in the 'right way', meaning in such a way as to cause as little as possible damage to the environment. Thus, in this book we adopt what we call the '8 Rs' definition of logistics.

Logistics was once described as 'just trucks and sheds'. As the discussion and definition illustrate, and notwithstanding the fact that trucks and sheds (warehouses) are indeed important components of logistics systems, it is obvious that logistics encapsulates much more than this.

> **Logistics** involves getting, in the right way, the right product, in the right quantity and right quality, in the right place at the right time, for the right customer at the right cost.

Getting some of these 'Rs' right may be easy for many, but getting all correct can be quite a challenge. For example, in both retail distribution and in high-value manufacturing it is now quite common to offer suppliers quite specific and narrow time windows within which to deliver freight. Not only will the suppliers be expected to execute deliveries within these strict time limits, but also they may be expected to deliver directly onto a specific retail outlet shelf or factory production cell.

WHAT IS SUPPLY CHAIN MANAGEMENT?

The various functions that now comprise the discipline of logistics were regarded as separate and distinct, and managed accordingly, up to the 1960s and 1970s. This began to change radically, however, in the 1980s and beyond with firms realising the benefits of integration and, more recently, collaboration.

The term supply chain management (SCM) was originally introduced by consultants in the early 1980s and, since then, has received considerable attention. The supply chain is a much wider, intercompany, boundary-spanning concept, than is the case with logistics. Figure 1.1 illustrates the evolution and structure of the integrated supply chain.

Martin Christopher, Professor of Marketing and Logistics at Cranfield School of Management, suggests that the *supply chain* is the network of organisations that are involved, through **upstream** (supplier end of the supply chain) and **downstream** (customer end of the supply chain) linkages, in the different processes and activities that produce value in the form of products and services in the hands of the ultimate consumer.[6] He distinguishes SCM from *vertical integration* – the latter concept implies ownership or at least control of upstream suppliers and downstream entities, whereas SCM does not necessarily imply any such ownership or control of supply chain partners. In this book we appropriate Professor Christopher's definition of the supply chain.

> The **supply chain** is the network of organisations that are involved, through upstream and downstream linkages, in the different processes and activities that produce value in the form of products and services in the hands of the ultimate consumer.

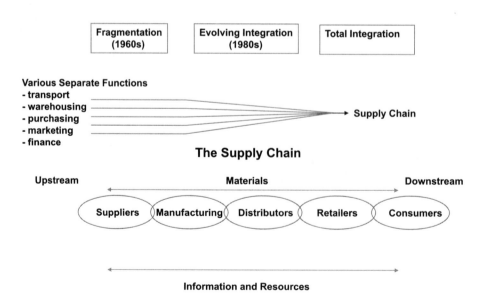

Figure 1.1   The evolution of the integrated supply chain

It is our view that supply chains encompass a number of key flows:

- physical flows of materials
- flows of information that inform the supply chain
- resources (especially finance, but also others such as people and equipment) which help the supply chain to operate effectively. Furthermore, not all resources in the supply chain are tangible, for example good quality inter-company relationships are often cited as a highly important ingredient of effective supply chains.

> **Supply chain management (SCM)** is the management across a network of upstream and downstream organisations of material, information and resource flows that lead to the creation of value in the form of products and/or services.

An important feature to note with regard to SCM is that it involves taking an 'end-to-end' perspective from upstream in the supply chain to the downstream end of the supply chain. Depending on the sector one is looking at, terminology such as the following can be used to describe the end-to-end supply chain:

- Farm to fork
- Cradle to grave
- Dust to rust

A final important point to note at this juncture is that increasingly it is the case that supply chains compete more so than individual firms and products. This represents something of a paradigm shift in terms of how people usually view the global business environment; this important issue is discussed further in Chapter 3.

DISTINGUISHING LOGISTICS AND SUPPLY CHAIN MANAGEMENT

Now that logistics and SCM have been defined, the issue of how both terms differ needs to be considered. This is in fact a question that has led

> Note the use of the word *network* in the definition of the supply chain. While the supply chain is usually depicted as a linear chain (as in Figure 1.1), it is perhaps better to envisage it as a *multidimensional network of collaborating entities*.
>
> Furthermore, such networks can be more fully understood as *systems*; taking a systems view highlights the impact of the interaction that occurs between the various entities. In logistics and SCM these various entities are sometimes referred to as *links* (for example transport services) and *nodes* (for example warehouses). The various links and nodes can of course contemporaneously play different roles across multiple supply chains.
>
> The term 'echelon' is sometimes also used to refer to different parts of the supply chain.

to much debate with people often coming up with their own distinctions. It has also been studied by a number of academics.[7] Larson and Halldorsson, for example, surveyed international logistics/SCM experts and identified four different perspectives which are illustrated in Figure 1.2.[8]

SCM in many respects evolved from logistics and the **traditionalist** view thus regards SCM as a subset of logistics, as if it were an add-on to logistics. In the **re-labelling** view it is contended that logistics has been re-labelled by the more recent term SCM. Indeed it is worth noting here also that sometimes transport gets re-labelled as logistics, for example the authors have observed heavy goods vehicles where the word 'logistics' is painted over the word 'transport' on the side of the vehicle! Becoming a professional logistics company, however, requires more than just a name change. In the **unionist** view logistics is seen as part of a wider entity, SCM. Finally the **intersectionist** view suggests that there is overlap between parts of both logistics and SCM, but also that each has parts that are separate and distinct.

In this book our approach is to adopt the *unionist view*; that is, that logistics is part of the wider entity which is SCM.[9] To reiterate what was stated earlier, the supply chain is a much wider, inter-company, boundary-spanning concept, than is the case with logistics. We believe that if you now look again at the definitions of logistics and SCM which are outlined above and the surrounding discussion in this chapter, this will be quite evident.

> Logistics is part of SCM; SCM is a wider, intercompany, boundary-spanning concept, than is the case with logistics.

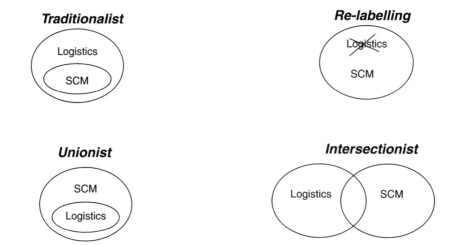

Figure 1.2   Four perspectives on logistics versus supply chain management. (Source: Larson, P. & Halldorsson, A. (2004)).[7]

APPLICATIONS TO MANUFACTURING *AND* SERVICES

The previous sections have given an insight into the origins and forces shaping the evolution of logistics and SCM. Much of the early application of both logistics and supply chain thinking has been in a manufacturing context and this will be considered in more detail in Chapter 3. It is now generally agreed that for those who take a supply chain view, two dimensions of value often arise, namely cost savings and also service enhancements. This is evident in the *Dell* case at the end of Part One of the book where the PC maker uses robust logistics strategies and competes using their entire supply chain. Not only do they sell relatively cheap PCs, but they also compete on the basis of certain service attributes (for example the ability for customers to purchase their products online and the fast delivery of purchased products to customers).

More and more manufacturers are using service criteria (for example, after sales service and delivery add-ons) in order to compete. Such has been their success that now many service companies are waking up to the advantages that can be gained from adopting best-in-class logistics practices and taking an end-to-end supply chain view. This is evident across a diverse range of service sectors such as retail, financial services, healthcare and tourism.

> Logistics and SCM can be used to generate both cost savings and service enhancements.

In the healthcare sector, for example, expensive advances in medical technology and increasing life expectancy are leading to greater demands on healthcare services with hospitals striving to offer better services at less cost. The average length of stay of patients within hospitals is declining, partly due to technological advances in healthcare, but partly also because increasingly hospitals both take a more holistic supply chain perspective on all aspects of patient care and also increasingly apply core logistics principles to their everyday activities. By eliminating unnecessary blockages and delays (for example by ensuring that required expertise in terms of medical skills and equipment is available when needed), patients get faster access to a range of services, allowing them to get better more quickly and leave hospital earlier, thus leading to improvements in whole system efficiency.

IKEA (WWW.IKEA.COM)

The Scandinavian home furnishings retailer IKEA is a good example of a company that uses best practice logistics and SCM in the manufacturing and services aspects of its business. Many products are manufactured for self-assembly by the customer. They are 'flat packed', making them easier to ship and store. Self-assembly is generally straightforward, with many products comprising components that easily assemble together. Even the instruction leaflets often have no words, only pictures, cutting down on the need for multiple language translations. Their network of worldwide stores are usually quite easily accessible and have similar layouts, making the shopping experience as easy and user friendly as possible for customers.

TRIAGE[10]

The concept of triage, originally devised by the French military, is now widely applied in medical emergency situations. Triage involves rapid assessment of patient needs and thus allows those most in need of care to be attended to first. The concept has evolved considerably and has moved beyond merely deciding between those who are critically ill and those who are not, into an activity that tries to match patients with the right care stream. This may involve various downstream activities from trauma care to bypassing hospital emergency departments completely and going straight to an appropriate community care facility. Importantly, more recent applications of triage involve not just assessment once the patient reaches the hospital, but also triage at other upstream points of contact (for example, via telephone or when an ambulance first arrives at an accident scene). Medical triage is an example of the application of logistics practices in a services context and is especially relevant given the pressures on many modern healthcare systems.

BOOK FRAMEWORK

A number of perspectives were adopted by the authors when writing this book; these are reflected in its content and summarised below.

Global perspective

Logistics and SCM are truly global disciplines that underpin international trade and span across international borders. Consequently, this book seeks to reflect this global nature of the subject matter and draws on diverse examples from multiple geographies. It is not our intention to present a particular 'Western' perspective on the subject matter, but instead to present a global worldview of what is happening in logistics and SCM today.

The terms 'international' and 'global' are often used interchangeably in a logistics context, but this is not in fact accurate. 'International' is defined by the *Collins English Dictionary* as 'of, concerning, or involving two or more nations or nationalities', while the same dictionary defines 'global' as 'covering, influencing, or relating to the whole world'. This book, then, aims to go beyond a focus on international logistics and to take a broader, whole world, global perspective on logistics and SCM issues.

Both practical and strategic perspectives

The book aims to comprise both a *practical element,* that is to help the reader to 'do' logistics (for example, select carriers, determine how much inventory to carry, select appropriate performance metrics, etc.) and a *strategic element* (understand the role of logistics and SCM in the wider business context and how it fits with the various functional areas).

In Chapter 15 the desired 'T shaped' profile of the effective logistics manager is discussed; suffice to note for now that logistics managers, as well as needing to know how to 'do' logistics, also require good interpersonal skills and in addition need to be able to work effectively with various functions such as marketing, finance, etc. As well as this they need to be good strategic thinkers. In this book, the aim is to present a balanced insight across all of these areas. We contend that while it is important to understand how global supply chain strategies are developed, it is also equally important to know how, for example, to calculate the cost of inventory in a warehouse or what information to put on an airwaybill. For a student at any level to have knowledge of supply chain strategy is vacuous, in our view, without concomitant knowledge of how to 'do' logistics.

Logistics is a part of SCM

As discussed already, the book adopts the unionist view of logistics, that is that logistics is part of the wider entity which is SCM.

Focus on material, information and resource flows

The three flows across supply chains, which were detailed above (material, information and resource), are each considered. None are regarded as more important; rather the book recognises the interdependency of each.

Neutral and nonpolitical perspective adopted

Despite the economic successes pointed to in Chapter 2, the world is not a perfect place; there are too many conflicts, injustices and poverty pervading in many regions. In this book we have adopted a neutral and nonpolitical perspective; any reference to individuals, situations or countries is only done to illustrate logistics/ SCM issues. Our hope is that best practice logistics and SCM, which this book hopes to advance, can help *all* regions to prosper.

The book is divided into three parts and these are now detailed.

Part One – Logistics and supply chain context

This first section sets the context for the book. The growth of logistics and SCM correlates directly with both increasing globalisation and international trade and this is the focus of Chapter 2. Pertinent issues such as trends in foreign direct investment flows (FDI), outsourcing and offshoring are also developed in Chapter 2. Application to both manufacturing and service contexts is highlighted in Part One, as is the relationship of logistics and SCM to other areas of business. Chapter 1 has already given an historical perspective vis-à-vis the origins of logistics and SCM, and in Chapter 3 we will see how in recent decades various strategies (such as leanness and agility) and trends have emerged and shaped the discipline, especially moving it from a producer-push paradigm to one of consumer-pull.

The aim of Part One of the book will be to bring the reader to a position whereby they accept the now generally held maxim that it is increasingly supply chains that compete and not individual products and/or companies. By the end of Part One, the reader will be sufficiently informed to progress to Part Two of the book, which focuses on logistics and supply chain operations.

Part Two – Logistics and supply chain operations

The second section of the book focuses on logistics and supply chain operations: how to 'do' logistics. The eight chapters in Part Two focus on different aspects of 'doing' logistics: how to identify sources for inputs both at home and overseas; how to purchase (trade regulations, terms of trade, supplier partnerships, etc.); how to arrange transportation and cognate value adding logistics activities; how to manage inventory; how to handle material (people requirements, warehouse design, etc.); and how to manage associated flows of resource (people, equipment, logistics providers, etc.), information (including requisite systems requirements) and, perhaps most importantly, money (currency exposures, asset ownership, available working capital, as well as cognate areas such as tax issues and incentives). Technology developments such as RFID (radio frequency identification) have a considerable bearing on logistics and these are given detailed treatment. The area of performance management (usually via various metrics), internally and externally, is of considerable importance in a logistics and SCM context and is also considered in Part Two. The sequence of chapters in Part Two is not accidental and follows the typical 'cradle to grave/farm to fork/dust to rust' sequence of many logistics activities.

Part Three – Supply chain designs

Having learned how to 'do' logistics, the focus of the third and final section of the book will move towards more strategic issues. Given recent significant and world altering events (such as for example 9/11 and the Asian tsunami), a lot of focus in SCM has turned to business continuity management and ensuring supply chains can cope with both uncertainty and the equally strong challenges that arise as a result of growing marketplace competition. This is the focus of Chapter 12, which deals with supply chain vulnerability, risk, robustness and resilience. Chapter 13 considers integration and collaboration in supply chains, while Chapter 14 covers the increasingly important issue of sustainability in the context of logistics and SCM. The concluding chapter in the book (Chapter 15) brings together the key issues covered throughout the book and considers logistics system and supply chain design for the future.

Part One of the book aimed to take you to the point whereby you understand that increasingly it is now supply chains that compete. The end point of the book will be to take you to the position whereby you understand that not only is it true that supply chains compete, but that, more and more, these supply chains are not simple, linear chains, but are instead complex, global, multidimensional, multipartner, networks.

LEARNING REVIEW

The chapter sought to explain the origins of logistics and SCM and both define and differentiate both terms. The importance of these areas to both manufacturing *and* services has been highlighted and the chapter showed how best practice logistics and SCM can yield both cost reductions *and* value addition. A framework for the book has also been outlined and the particular perspectives embraced in the book were elucidated.

Now that the origins and meaning of both logistics and SCM have been described, other developments which have been closely associated with the growth of logistics and SCM can be discussed. Chapter 2 looks at both increasing globalisation and international trade. Growth in both of these areas correlates closely with the growth in logistics and SCM, and indeed there is a significant level of interdependence between all of these areas.

QUESTIONS

- Are logistics and SCM only of interest to manufacturers?
- Explain the key developments behind the evolution of logistics and SCM.
- How do logistics and supply chain management differ?
- How can best practice logistics and SCM lead to both cost reduction and service enhancement?
- What are the benefits of deregulation of transport markets? Why does such deregulation sometimes not work out quite as planned?

APPLICATIONS OF LOGISTICS AND SCM IN A SERVICES CONTEXT

In this chapter we outlined key principles and concepts of logistics and SCM and how both can be applied in manufacturing and services contexts. Many application examples will be developed in the following chapters of this book. At this juncture, however, it is worth pausing to consider the application of logistics and SCM in a services context, as many students regard the subjects as only of relevance in a manufacturing context. Think of examples of sectors and organisations where logistics and SCM principles and concepts can be, or are already, applied. In the text above, for example, we developed the application of logistics and SCM principles and concepts to the medical context. Are there other services contexts where similar application is evident?

NOTES

1. For a fascinating insight into the life of McLean and the growth of containerisation see: Levinson, P. (2006) *The Box,* Princeton University Press, Princeton, NJ.

2. Drucker, P (1962) The economy's dark continent, *Fortune,* April, 103–104.

3. www.skillsforlogistics.org

4. Beinhocker, E. (2006) *The Origin of Wealth,* Random House Business Books, London, p. 262.

5. The Canadian military (www.forces.gc.ca), for example, define logistics as: 'Logistics is the provision of resources to support the strategy and tactics of combat forces'.

6. Christopher, M. (1998) *Logistics and Supply Chain Management (2nd Edition),* Financial Times/Pitman Publishing, London, p. 15.

7. See for example: Cooper, M.C., Lambert, D.M. & Pagh, J.D. (1997) Supply chain management: more than a new name for logistics, *International Journal of Logistics Management,* 8(1), 1–14; Lambert *et al.* (1998) Supply chain management: implementation issues and research opportunities, *International Journal of Logistics Management,* 9(2), 1–19; and Larson, P. & Halldorsson, A. (2004) Logistics versus supply chain management: an international survey, *International Journal of Logistics: Research and Applications,* 7(1), 17–31.

8. Larson, P. & Halldorsson, A. (2004) *op. cit.*

9. Recent empirical studies support this view, see for example: Larson, P., Poist, R. & Halldorsson, A. (2007) Perspectives on logistics vs SCM: a survey of SCM professionals, *Journal of Business Logistics,* 28(1), 1–25.

10. For more on medical triage see, for example: Robertson-Steel, I. (2006) Evolution of triage systems, *Emergency Medicine Journal,* 23, 154–155.

Globalisation and International Trade

INTRODUCTION

Chapter 1 both introduced and differentiated logistics and SCM, and their application in manufacturing and services contexts. It was also noted in Chapter 1 that best practice logistics and SCM can lead to both cost reduction and value addition. This chapter now turns to areas which over the past few decades have been closely associated with the evolution and growth of logistics and SCM, namely the growth of international trade and the emergence of the phenomenon known as globalisation.

Given the increased volumes in recent years of international trade and its related activities, many companies now have overseas facilities and supply chain partners. This chapter will chart the growth that has occurred in international trade and the emergence of globalisation. Issues which arise in this more international context will be examined, such as decisions to outsource (who, where, what) and decisions to locate certain activities outside of the company's home country ('offshoring'). Imbalances in freight volumes in opposite directions are a characteristic of many freight markets; how this arises and its consequences will also be discussed.

Chapter 2 comprises five core sections:

- Growth in international trade
- Globalisation
- Outsourcing
- Offshoring
- Directional imbalances

LEARNING OBJECTIVES

- Highlight the growth that has occurred in recent decades in international trade. Regional and country differences and relative shares will also be illustrated.
- Explain what is meant by globalisation, identify the most globalised countries in the world and explain the drivers for globalisation.
- Identify the (unequal) distribution of economic wealth among the world's countries.
- Explore the role of multinational companies in global trade, together with the impact of overseas investment by companies.
- Examine the role of both outsourcing and offshoring in global trade and logistics.
- Finally, look at what happens when unequal volumes or types of freight flow in opposite directions in freight markets.

GROWTH IN INTERNATIONAL TRADE

There has been considerable growth in recent decades in world trade; world exports grew from $62 billion in 1950 to $9,000 billion by 2004.

Global trade has grown considerably in recent decades and has fuelled the evolution of logistics and SCM, which was outlined in Chapter 1. Much of this growth has been facilitated by the reduction of trade barriers between countries and regions, thus making it easier for countries to trade with each other. **Regional trade agreements**, such as for example the EU (European Union) and ASEAN (Association of South East Asian Nations) have been, and continue to be, developed and allow more open trading within regions.[1] In 1950 the value of total merchandise exports from all countries in the world was just under $62 billion.[2] By 2004 this had risen to almost $9,000 billion (Figure 2.1). In 1960 the share of world merchandise exports in world gross domestic product was 10%. By 2000 it had climbed to 20%. So today, more than ever, more freight is moving all around the world, with logistics systems thus having to play an increasingly important role in the global economy.

The value of total exports of world services is much less than that of merchandise exports, but it is still quite significant. In 2002 the value of total exports of services was $1,611 billion. Almost three-quarters of these were from developed countries. The share of services in world output was 3% in 1960 and this grew to almost 5% by 2000.

Approximately two-thirds of the merchandise exports in 2004 were from developed counties. After a slow start, the participation in world trade by developing countries is growing. According to the United Nations Conference on Trade and Development (UNCTAD) developing countries' merchandise exports grew on average 12% a year in the period 1960–2002, while the corresponding figure for developed countries was 11%. Figure 2.2 ranks the world's largest exporting countries.[3]

There are of course regional variations with regard to the performance of individual developing economies with some countries demonstrating outstanding growth. China, for example, has been a very strong performer with regard to growth in its merchandise exports: in 1980 its annual merchandise exports were valued

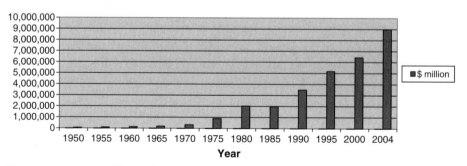

Figure 2.1 Total world merchandise exports 1950–2004

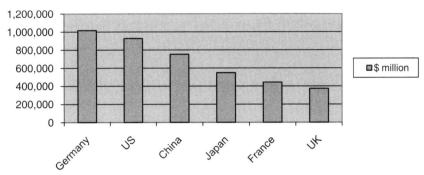

Figure 2.2   Exports by country (2005 estimates)[4]

at $18 billion but by 2004 this had grown to $574 billion. According to the World Trade Organisation (WTO), China's trade grew three times faster than that of the global economy in the 1990s, and while world trade stagnated between 2000 and 2002, China's imports and exports rose by 30 per cent.[5] In fact, China is sometimes described as 'the factory to the world'. In contrast to all of this, Liberia's merchandise exports for example, dropped from $600 million in 1980 to $220 million in 2004 as a result of political and other difficulties in that country.

There are considerable differences in terms of economic wealth among many countries across the world today. One way[6] to measure and compare the wealth of economies is to compare them in terms of their GNI (gross national income) per capita; Table 2.1 illustrates comparative data for a number of countries and highlights the considerable inter-country differences in economic wealth that exist in the world today. It is usually the case that more wealthy countries will have good quality transport systems, sometimes a measure known as *transport mobility* (an aggregate measure that comprises an assessment of the available services, quality of the transport infrastructure, ease with which people and freight can move into, around and out of a country, etc.) is used in this regard and is correlated quite closely with measures of a country's GDP. The section on planning transport infrastructure in Chapter 8 will consider these issues.

A more recent measure is the *global logistics performance index* (LPI) (www.gfptt. org/lpi) which ranks 150 different countries in terms of their logistics performance; seven key dimensions are used in the index:

- Customs
- Infrastructure
- International shipments
- Logistics competence
- Tracking and tracing
- Domestic logistics costs
- Timeliness.

Table 2.1 Ranking of gross national income (GNI) per capita in 2005[7] (measured in US dollars)

1. Luxembourg	65 630
2. Norway	59 590
3. Switzerland	54 930
4. Bermuda	Data not available, ranking is approximate
5. Denmark	47 390
6. Iceland	46 320
7. United States of America	43 740
8. Liechtenstein	Data not available, ranking is approximate
9. Sweden	41 060
10. Ireland	40 150
World Average	6 987
Lowest listed of 208 countries: Burundi	100

The aim of the index is to benchmark countries' overall performance on these dimensions and to assess the quality of a country's connections to the global market. Table 2.2 lists the top 10 countries in the index as reported in 2007.

One of the goals of logistics is to facilitate the process of trade, and this in turn can facilitate the economic well-being of all countries. Ensuring good logistics systems are in place is thus a key component in efforts to help developing countries in particular.

Table 2.2 Top 10 countries in the global logistics performance index (LPI)[8]

1.	Singapore
2.	Netherlands
3.	Germany
4.	Sweden
5.	Austria
6.	Japan
7.	Switzerland
8.	Hong Kong, China
9.	United Kingdom
10.	Canada

GLOBALISATION

The term '**globalisation**' has been in use now for a number of decades and is generally regarded as an umbrella term for a complex series of economic, social, technological, cultural and political changes that continue to take place throughout the world. Some argue that it is a force for good, allowing people and companies throughout the world to be interconnected. Others oppose it, some vehemently, and see it largely as a proxy for global capital flows exploiting especially the poor. You can make up your own mind; perhaps, in truth, globalisation is a mix of both extreme views. Regardless, it looks as if globalisation is here to stay.

BARBIE: THE ALL-AMERICAN GIRL[9]

Conceived in 1959 as the all-American toy doll, Barbie today is a true global citizen! Originally made in Japan (and not the USA), today different parts of Barbie are made in various different countries: for example her hair is still made in Japan, the plastic in her body comes from Taiwan, her cotton clothing from China, and the moulds and pigments used in production come from America.

One writer credited with bringing the term globalisation into mainstream use is the American academic Theodore Levitt. In a now famous 1983 article in the *Harvard Business Review*,[10] Levitt suggested that companies must learn to operate as if the world were one large market – ignoring superficial regional and national differences.

'GLOCALISATION' – THINK GLOBAL, ACT LOCAL

Much of what Levitt asserted in his famous 1983 *Harvard Business Review* article has stood the test of time and no doubt one can think of many global companies with global products. Conscious though of subtle, yet often important regional and local differences, many companies now adopt a policy which some refer to as '**glocalisation**' – thinking on a *global,* world market scale, but adapting to *local* wants as appropriate. Just think, for example, of how McDonald's has both globally recognised and desired products (burgers, Coca-Cola, etc.) side by side with locally desired products in its many different restaurants across the world. We will also see in later chapters how companies can employ modern manufacturing and distribution strategies that allow them to tailor, often at little extra cost, global products to satisfy local wants.

Individual countries vary considerably in terms of how globalised they actually are. This is measured each year in the annual 'A.T. Kearney/FOREIGN POLICY Globalization Index'.[11] In the index, the level of globalisation is assessed by measuring 12 variables which are divided into four 'baskets': economic integration, personal contact, technological connectivity, and political engagement. Often when one thinks of globalisation, areas such as finance and trade come to mind, but globalisation as measured in the index is in fact much broader than this, and the four baskets capture other factors such as, for example, internet connectivity and participation in international political affairs. Table 2.3 illustrates the top 20 countries in terms of globalisation in 2006.

Table 2.3 The top 20 most globalised countries in the world in 2006[13]

1.	Singapore
2.	Switzerland
3.	United States of America
4.	Ireland
5.	Denmark
6.	Canada
7.	Netherlands
8.	Australia
9.	Austria
10.	Sweden
11.	New Zealand
12.	United Kingdom
13.	Finland
14.	Norway
15.	Israel
16.	Czech Republic
17.	Slovenia
18.	Germany
19.	Malaysia
20.	Hungary

Figure 2.1 illustrated the growth in the value of total merchandise exports from all countries in the world and thus highlighted the growth in international trade. Using this and other data, the extent of increased globalisation in the world economy can be illustrated; this could be done by adding, for each year in a time series, world exports and world imports, and dividing the total by annual world GDP.

All of this is not to deny that cultural and other differences exist between countries. Such differences do exist and can impact on how effectively logistics systems work in practice. We will return to some of these issues in Chapter 5 which deals with sourcing and procurement, areas where understanding cultural differences is a matter of considerable importance as companies negotiate and manage across cultures.[12]

In terms of trading relationships, a number of different stages can be identified in the path towards globalisation. First countries begin to trade with each other, importing and exporting goods. As trade develops, sometimes companies will establish a presence in an overseas market. Such companies are usually referred to as **'multinational companies' (MNCs)** when they have operations in areas beyond their home country. In turn, entities sometimes referred to as **'transnational corporations' (TNCs)** emerge: these are companies that trade across many borders, with operations in multiple countries. Often it can be difficult to identify the 'home' country of a TNC, as they will

SINGAPORE – THE MOST GLOBALISED COUNTRY IN THE WORLD IN 2006

Singapore was ranked the world's most globalised country in 2006. Formed in 1965, Singapore is a parliamentary republic and is a small country by international standards with a total land area of just 683 square kilometres, which is fairly densely populated by some 4.5 million people. Its highly developed and successful free market economy is open to the world in trade and investment. Exports in 2006 were valued at over $200 billion dollars. It is also one of the world's most competitive economies, being ranked the third most competitive economy in the world in 2006 in the World Competitiveness Yearbook published by IMD in Switzerland (www.imd.ch). The government's aim is to establish Singapore as Southeast Asia's financial and high-tech hub.

typically portray a truly global identity. Three other terms are also worth noting and these relate to how companies think and behave as they internationalise:

- '**Ethnocentricity**': where the company, when doing business abroad, thinks only in terms of the home country environment (thinks and acts as if they were still operating in for example the USA, where the company may be headquartered, notwithstanding the fact that many business environments outside of the USA can be quite dissimilar to the USA).

- '**Polycentricity**': where the company adopts the host country perspective (to coin the old phrase: 'when in Rome, do as the Romans do').

- '**Geocentricity**': where the company acts completely independently of geography and adopts a global perspective, and will tailor to the local environment as appropriate (see the box on 'glocalisation' above).

As companies internationalise they set up operations in overseas locations. This can range from relatively simple activities, such as having a sales presence in an overseas market, to setting up production facilities, and even (in the case of TNCs) having core company functions located in countries other than where the company was originally established. Behind such developments lie what are referred to as **'FDI' (foreign direct investment)** flows. FDI flows are financial flows from a company in one country to invest (for example in a factory) in another country. Such flows are very significant in the overall global economy and in some cases can be key to dictating a country's success. Indeed many countries, and regions, compete quite strongly to attract external FDI, and some will put in place certain conditions (for example, low rates of corporate taxation) in order to attract more FDI.[14]

Table 2.4 outlines some of the many factors that have to be considered when deciding on an optimum location for an overseas facility. Indeed many of the factors listed for consideration arise regardless of the type or location of facility being considered,

Table 2.4   Site selection factors

Labour costs	Political stability
Employment regulations	Environmental regulations
Available skills	Taxation rates
Land costs and availability of suitable sites	Government supports
Energy costs	Currency stability
Availability of suitable suppliers	Benefits of being part of a cluster of
Transport and logistics costs	similar companies
Transport linkages	Preferred locations of competitors
Communications infrastructure and costs	Access to markets
	Community issues and quality of life

Table 2.5   FDI inflows and outflows in 2005 (US$ billion)[15]

Region	FDI inflow	FDI outflow
EU	422	555
USA	99	−13
Other developed economies	21	104
Africa	31	1
Latin America and the Caribbean	104	33
Asia	200	84
Oceania	0.4	0
South East Europe and the CIS	40	15
World Total	917	779

and in addition to their relevance in the context of the discussion here on FDI, they are also relevant in the context of issues considered in subsequent chapters of this book (for example, those dealing with outsourcing and with warehousing).

Table 2.5 illustrates the main sources and recipients of FDI in 2005. It is important to note that not all FDI is represented by companies themselves physically expanding overseas; a significant share is also represented by, for example, investment funds in one country purchasing companies in another country. Trends evident in FDI in recent years include growth spurred by cross-border mergers and acquisitions and also new emerging sources of FDI among developing and transition economies. In fact, a growing number of TNCs from these economies are emerging as major regional players, and in some cases as global players. Where FDI flows to is very important from a logistics perspective because freight flows will often arise as a result of the investment.

Table 2.6 lists the world's top 20 non-financial TNCs in 2004 ranked by foreign assets. This is not a listing of the world's 'biggest' companies, which could be assembled based on, for example, total revenue or market capitalisation. Our interest here is in companies with extensive global activities, as they are the companies

Table 2.6   World's top 20 non-financial TNCs in 2004 ranked by foreign assets[16]

Rank	Name	Home	Sector
1.	General Electric	USA	Electrical and electronic
2.	Vodafone	UK	Telecomms
3.	Ford Motor	USA	Motor vehicles
4.	General Motors	USA	Motor vehicles
5.	British Petroleum	UK	Petroleum
6.	Exxonmobil	USA	Petroleum
7.	Royal Dutch Shell	UK/NL	Petroleum
8.	Toyota Motor	Japan	Motor vehicles
9.	Total	France	Petroleum
10.	France Telecom	France	Telecomms
11.	Volkswagen	Germany	Motor vehicles
12.	Sanofi-Aventis	France	Pharmaceuticals
13.	Deutsche Telekom	Germany	Telecomms
14.	RWE Group	Germany	Electricity, gas and water
15.	Suez	France	Electricity, gas and water
16.	E.ON	Germany	Electricity, gas and water
17.	Hutchison Whampoa	Hong Kong	Diversified
18.	Siemens	Germany	Electrical and electronic
19.	Nestlé	Switzerland	Food and beverages
20.	Electric de France	France	Electricity, gas and water

generating large global logistics flows. Regardless of measure of company size, it is also important to note that many individual large companies (whether measured by foreign assets, revenue or market capitalisation) play a very significant role in the global economy and their power should not be underestimated. In fact, it is estimated that some of the largest companies have annual turnover greater than the annual GDP of some smaller European countries.[17] How such large companies arrange their logistics activities is thus highly relevant for various stakeholders.

Financial TNCs have been excluded from Table 2.6 as their global capital flows are very significant and thus would distort the list away from other types of companies; from a logistics perspective our interest is in those TNCs who move physical product around the world. Obviously this would exclude many of the activities of the utilities companies in the list (telecommunications, water, etc.), although they too often move product internationally, albeit virtually over telecommunications networks or via proprietary gas pipelines for example.

Some 85 of the world's top 100 TNCs in 2004 were from either the USA, Europe or Japan, with 53 from the EU alone (with France, Germany and the UK dominating). Firms from other countries are however advancing internationally, and in 2004 there were five companies from developing economies in the list of top 100 TNCs (all five were headquartered in Asia). Developments in the personal computer manufacturing sector are a good example of what is happening in terms of the evolution of TNCs and global brands. The Chinese company Lenovo recently purchased the PC manufacturing division of IBM, while in mid 2007 Acer of Taiwan purchased Gateway of the USA. As a result Acer and Lenovo are now two of the world's largest PC manufacturers.

OUTSOURCING

Sometimes companies, for various reasons, decide to outsource certain activities to other companies, commonly referred to as 'third parties'. Some companies outsource for *cost* reasons, as the outsource partner may be able to provide the service more cheaply than the outsourcing company can itself provide it for. Increased *flexibility* is another reason to outsource as the outsource partner may be more readily able to provide more or less of the service as required by the outsourcing company, and thus save them having to commit their own resources. A third reason often cited for outsourcing is more of a strategic one whereby a company decides to focus on its *core competences* – that is, areas which it is good at or has advantages in – and outsource all other activities. Finally, given the rapid advances everywhere in *technology*, companies may no longer always necessarily have the most up-to-date technology available to them and thus will outsource to partners who do have such technology. These and other factors will be explored in more detail in Chapter 5, which covers this topic in more detail.

> **Outsourcing** can be defined as the transfer to a third party of the management and delivery of a process previously performed by the company itself.

Obviously each of these four reasons is not mutually exclusive and a company may decide to outsource for any combination of the four reasons.

There are a number of issues to be considered in outsourcing: firstly how to go about selecting an outsource partner, and then how to effectively manage the chosen partner. In order to effectively manage the outsource arrangement, companies generally put in place a service level agreement and performance metrics. Later chapters will return to these issues: Chapter 4 will look in particular at the selection of logistics service providers, Chapter 5 will look at procurement and outsourcing, and Chapter 11 will look at performance management.

Another important issue for any organisation to consider is exactly which activities to outsource and which activities to do itself, the classic ' do versus buy decision'. In fact some organisations, especially many in the e-business sector, outsource almost everything. These organisations are sometimes referred to as **virtual organisations.** In contrast other organisations, more so in the past than today, outsource little or nothing. For example, the motor company Ford was reputed in the first half of the twentieth century to even own farm animals in order to guarantee a source of supply of fabric for its cars! (It was noted in Chapter 1 that the technical term for this is vertical integration; that is, how much of the upstream and downstream activities does the company actually own or control itself.)

Since the mid 1990s there has also been a shift in the way suppliers are arranged. Previously, many companies, especially in the manufacturing sector, had multiple suppliers. Indeed it was not unknown for some large multinational companies to have thousands of suppliers, and this is still the case today for some companies. Managing so many suppliers can of course bring its own problems; similarly with large numbers of suppliers it can be difficult to leverage other advantages from them such as, for example, sharing research and development and new product development (generally speaking better done with few, rather than many, suppliers). The response to much of this has been the organisation of suppliers into tiers, and this will be examined further in Chapter 5.

Finally, it is important to note that just because outsourcing can at times be the right thing to do, it does not always follow that all outsourcing arrangements always run smoothly. In fact the opposite can often be the case. For example some research has shown that four out of five business process outsourcing (BPO) contracts signed today will need to be renegotiated within two years and that 20% of such contracts will collapse.[18]

OFFSHORING

With increased competition in many markets, combined with in some instances falling prices, many companies are looking at ways in which to reduce their costs. It was noted in Chapter 1 that effective management of logistics can lead to cost savings and value advantages for companies. *Offshoring* is another, and increasingly popular, approach that many companies are using to reduce costs.

Offshoring and outsourcing are often confused, so first the term offshoring will be defined and then both terms will be differentiated.

Offshoring is not the same as outsourcing because outsourcing involves handing process ownership over to a third party, whereas with offshoring the company may still own and control the process itself in the lower cost location. Of course one can both outsource and offshore a process at the same time in that the outsource partner can also decide to offshore and transfer the newly acquired outsourced process to a lower cost location in another country.

> **Offshoring** can be defined as the transfer of specific processes to lower cost locations in other countries.

Some leading authors have noted that the lure of cost savings, largely due to fewer regulatory controls and significantly lower wages, has prompted the mass migration of manufacturing from the developed world to emergent economies in other regions.[19] They note that geopolitical events moving in step with technological developments and the deregulation of trade have made global sourcing and supply a reality. It is important to note that it is not just manufacturing processes that

Table 2.7 Some of the reasons why companies offshore

Lower costs in offshore regions
Less stringent regulatory controls in offshore regions
Deregulation of trade facilitates offshoring
Lower communication and IT costs
Improving capabilities in many offshore regions
Clusters of specific activities (for example call centres) emerging in certain regions

are offshored, but that many service based processes are often also offshored. Examples include call centres, transaction processing (for example, typical accounts functions such as invoicing) and even aspects of human resource management. Table 2.7 outlines some of the reasons behind companies' decisions to offshore.

One of the questions which sometimes emerges with regard to offshoring is: can the cost savings enjoyed by offshoring be offset by other unforeseen costs? Examples of such costs include extra monitoring costs incurred as a result of the location of the offshore activities. The other main set of costs is extra transaction costs as a result of, for example, moving materials over greater distances. Ultimately the challenge is to ensure that these extra monitoring and transaction costs are less than the savings enjoyed as a result of offshoring. Chapter 5 will discuss further certain aspects of both outsourcing and offshoring.

DIRECTIONAL IMBALANCES

As Figure 2.1 above illustrated, world trade has grown considerably over the past 50 years. This has been driven by various developments discussed above such as the growth of globalisation, and more recent trends such as the growth of offshoring. One particular characteristic of freight transport markets that distinguishes them from passenger transport markets is what are commonly referred to as **directional imbalances**. A simple analogy explains. Most people who make a journey today aim to make a return trip at some point. This, however, is not the case with freight, which usually moves to either be consumed at the destination point or have further value added to it before making another journey. In other words most freight makes one-way, and not return, journeys. Figure 2.3 illustrates the traffic volumes on the main global trade corridors.

Directional imbalances arise in freight markets when there are mismatches in the volumes or types of freight moving in opposite directions in a freight market.

This of course would be fine if the same volume and type of freight (certain types of freight have particular handling and equipment characteristics, e.g. refrigerated containers for perishable freight) went in both directions on all routes. But of course it doesn't, and in some cases the differences can be quite pronounced. This in turn raises interesting challenges for the

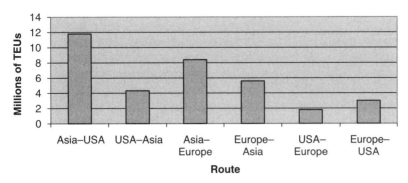

Figure 2.3   Major trade corridors[20]

transport companies who are faced with variable directional utilisation of their equipment.

DIRECTIONAL IMBALANCES: THE CHINA–EU ROUTE

- It can cost the same amount to transport a container unit by road between Munich and Hamburg in Germany as it does to ship the same container by sea from Shanghai in China to Hamburg in Germany.
- It can cost twice as much to ship a typical 20 foot container between Hong Kong and the EU when compared with the opposite direction (EU–Hong Kong). This is because of the huge volume of exports from China into European markets.

Sometimes directional imbalances can exist in opposite directions on the same route for different commodities. This can arise with, for example, perishable products such as foodstuffs and flowers which usually require refrigerated containers. There could be a surplus of empty containers in one direction, thus allowing low rates to be charged for freight in that direction. Perishable products, however, might not be able to use this available equipment and special refrigerated containers would have to be imported to carry the refrigerated products.

The challenge for carriers is obviously to match, as much as possible, inbound freight capacity with outbound freight capacity.[21] When, however, there are gross imbalances in import and export volumes and cargo types this is not always possible. As a result empty containers may need to be repositioned to where they are required. Furthermore, this can lead to problems for ports who sometimes have to store such empty containers. Shipping companies have also endeavoured to come up with solutions such as developing new routing patterns that minimise empty container movements and seek to maximise operations on routes with higher traffic densities (Figure 2.4). New container designs are also emerging (such as collapsible and foldable containers) making the movement of empty containers less expensive.

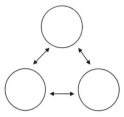

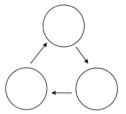

In the **traditional** system vessels move in both directions on each route. If imbalances exist on any of the routes then these will not be avoided.

In the **circular** system vessels move in one direction only, preferably in the direction of greatest traffic volume. Of course in reality different combinations and mixes of frequencies will be used (for example where an imbalance exists one in four vessels may ply in the opposite direction where there are lower traffic volumes).

Sometimes circular routings are referred to as liner routings as this is a pattern that was in the past, and to an extent still is, adopted by many passenger liner vessels.

Figure 2.4   Traditional versus circular routings

LEARNING REVIEW

The chapter sought to introduce the concept of globalisation and the nature of international trade in the global economy, and in turn the interrelationship of both with logistics systems. The role played by multinational companies, the trends towards outsourcing and offshoring, and the impact of directional imbalances in freight markets, were also explored. The global economy today is increasingly interconnected with logistics playing an essential *lubricating* role – just as oil lubricates a car engine (without oil the engine would quickly seize up), so too the global economy relies on efficient and effective logistics systems in order to function (just look for example at what happens when transport services are delayed or there is industrial action at a port or airport). As the data and trends outlined in this chapter have attempted to illustrate, the global economy has evolved and grown quite considerably, especially in the latter decades of the twentieth century and into the current century. To facilitate this, the logistics sector has also had to evolve and grow.

Chapters 1 and 2 have sought to give an understanding of both the drivers for the evolution of logistics and SCM, and the global context within which both operate. The next chapter will turn to identifying the various strategies that companies employ in order to survive and compete within this complex and dynamic environment.

QUESTIONS

- Is your country among the world's most globalised countries? If not, what could it do to improve its position?
- Identify examples of companies/products who attempt to think global and act local ('glocalisation').
- Differentiate ethnocentricity, polycentricity and geocentricity, and give examples of companies from your own country who you believe fit into each category.
- Taking your own country as an example, identify freight routes where you believe directional imbalances exist.

LARGE COMPANIES AND THEIR LOGISTICS ACTIVITIES

It was noted above that some very large companies can be bigger than some small countries (for example, in terms of company revenue when compared with country GDP). How such large companies arrange their logistics activities is thus highly relevant for various stakeholders.

Take a large company with which you are familiar and attempt to evaluate its logistics activities. Examination of company annual reports, company websites, and other information sources should generate information of interest. Detailed investigation may highlight specific issues of interest from a logistics perspective: for example, it is not uncommon for some sea ports to be highly dependent on individual large manufacturers in their hinterland. Try and identify linkages such as these and their implications. For example, what would happen to such a port if the manufacturer decided to relocate production to another factory in its global network?

NOTES

1. Many of these have of course evolved from being just trading agreements into wider social, political and economic entities (a good example being the EU, which started life originally as an agreement for trading coal and steel between a small number of countries).

2. Merchandise exports are goods leaving the statistical territory of a country. Data are in current US dollars. A lot of detailed statistics on world trade can be accessed via the website of the United Nations Conference on Trade and Development (www.unctad.org) and this is the source of many of the statistics quoted in this chapter.

3. Sometimes people are surprised to see Germany ranked ahead of the USA as the world's largest exporter. Two points are worth noting in this regard: (1) some of Germany's exports are to other (nearby) EU countries and (2) the USA consumes, rather than exports, a lot of what it produces, thus reducing its export

performance (it also imports a lot of freight and runs a trade deficit). In any event Germany (East and West reunited in 1990) is a powerful economy and home to some of the world's leading companies.

4. Country export data sourced from the CIA World Factbook, available at www.cia.gov.

5. Quoted in Christopher, M., Peck, H. & Towill, D. (2006) A taxonomy for selecting global supply chain strategies, *International Journal of Logistics Management*, 17(2), 276.

6. GNI per capita is one of a number of ways to measure and compare economies; a variation of the technique (PPP GNI: purchasing power parity gross national income) is often used and takes into account differences in the relative prices of goods and services among economies, particularly nontradables, and therefore is often regarded as providing a better comparative measure. The data source we used for GNI per capita data was the World Development Indicators database, World Bank, 1 July 2005 (web.worldbank.org).

7. *Ibid.*

8. Results presented at the GFP Semi-Annual Meeting hosted by the World Customs Organization in Brussels, Belgium; presentation available on www.gfptt.org/lpi, accessed August 2007.

9. Adapted from Levinson, P. (2006) *The Box*, Princeton University Press, Princeton, NJ, p. 265.

10. Levitt, T. (1983) The globalization of markets, *Harvard Business Review*, May–June, 92–102.

11. Anonymous (2006) The Global Top 20, Foreign Policy, Nov–Dec.

12. For further reading on the issue of cultural differences we recommend you look at some of the many writings of the Dutch academic Geert Hofstede who has pioneered research in this area.

13. *Ibid.*

14. For more on this topic see, for example, Ferdows, K. (1997) Making the most of foreign factories, *Harvard Business Review*, March–April, 73–88; Mangan, J., Hannigan, K. & Cullen, J. (2006) Behind the cost-savings advantage, *Sloan Management Review*, 47(2), 8.

15. UNCTAD World Investment Report 2006.

16. UNCTAD/Erasmus University in UNCTAD World Investment Report 2006.

17. Wal-Mart, for example, is apparently the world's largest retailer and was one of the world's largest corporations when measured in revenue terms in 2007 with revenues of some $351 billion. Recall the discussion in Chapter 1 on the role of logistics in national economies and in particular the role of Wal-Mart in the US economy.

18. SAP INFO Solutions quoted in *Sloan Management Review*, Winter, 2006.

19. Christopher *et al.* (2006) *op. cit.*

20. Rodrigue, J. & Hesse, M. (2007) Globalized trade and logistics: North American perspectives. In Leinbach, T. & Capineri, C. (eds), *Globalized Freight Transport*, Edward Elgar, Chichester.

21. Olivo, A., Zuddas, P., Di Francesco, M. & Manca, A. (2005) An operational model for empty container management, *Maritime Economics and Logistics*, 7, 199–222.

Supply Chain Strategies

INTRODUCTION

Chapters 1 and 2 gave us an understanding of both the drivers for the evolution of logistics and SCM, and the global context within which both operate. This chapter now turns to introducing the various logistics and supply chain strategies that companies employ in order to survive and compete within this complex and dynamic environment. Logistics and supply chain strategy is not, however, divorced from a firm's strategy, and so we first have to look at firm strategy and examine its relationship to logistics and supply chain strategy. We will also see in this chapter that not only is logistics and supply chain strategy part of firm strategy, but that in many instances logistics and supply chain strategy can be the key component within, and driver of, firm strategy.

Chapter 3 comprises six core sections:

- Strategy
- The evolution of manufacturing
- Lean production
- Agile supply chains and mass customisation
- Combined logistics strategies
- Critical factors to consider in supply chain planning

LEARNING OBJECTIVES

- Highlight the role of logistics and supply chain strategy in the context of firm strategy, and see how logistics and supply chain strategy can actually sometimes drive firm strategy.
- Outline the evolution of manufacturing, from which various logistics and supply chain strategies have emerged.
- Look at both lean and agile logistics strategies, and the role of mass customisation in the latter.
- Develop a taxonomy of supply chain strategies.

STRATEGY

The field of business strategy is wide, fascinating and varied. It is also of crucial importance as an organisation without a strategy is, in our view, like a ship without a compass. Strategy can be generally described as being concerned with planning and configuring the organisation for the future in accordance with certain stakeholder expectations. More simply, the *Collins English Dictionary* defines strategy as 'a particular long term plan for success'. Our specific purpose in this chapter is not however to explore the whole field of strategy, but instead to examine the link between strategy and both logistics and SCM, and also to consider specific logistics and supply chain strategies. In fact we will view logistics strategy and supply chain strategy together – as we already noted in Chapter 1, in this book we adopt the *unionist view*; that is, that logistics is part of the wider entity which is SCM. It follows then that logistics strategy and supply chain strategy will be closely connected and for the purposes of this book we consider both conjointly.

A usual starting point when considering a firm's strategy is to work from 'the top down'. Thus people will often first consider the wider whole organisation or *corporate strategy* and its objectives. For example, what are the overall financial and growth targets for the organisation. Similarly, they need to decide what technologies and markets they want to focus on. Increasingly of late, organisations are also turning to consider the impact of their operations on the environment. We will return to this issue of sustainability, and its link to global logistics, in Chapter 14.

Below the whole organisation level is what is often referred to as the *business unit* level. Many large organisations are divided into such business units, which focus on specific products and markets. For example, some large logistics service providers may have separate warehousing, transport and other business units, and may develop separate strategies for each of these areas.

The final level is often referred to as *functional strategy* and refers to the development of strategies for specific areas of activity within a business unit (for example, marketing, IT and logistics). Figure 3.1 depicts this top–down structure.

Not everyone agrees, however, that this is the best way to formulate strategy. Two questions that arise are: (1) it doesn't allow for a 'bottom–up' perspective and (2) in

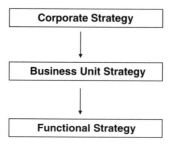

Figure 3.1   Top–down perspective on strategy

the case of logistics and to a lesser extent SCM, it assumes that these are functions just like other functions within the organisation. Furthermore, there is an increasingly held view that much of what constitutes strategy is *emergent*; that is, that companies need to evolve their strategies to meet the challenges of the dynamic, ever changing business environment. More and more then the view that a strategy can be dictated from the 'top' of an organisation and not revised for a number of years is becoming redundant.

Taking a 'bottom–up' perspective of strategy allows us to see how logistics can contribute to the wider business unit and firm strategies. Some argue that logistics can in fact be the foundation for overall strategic action.[1] In this context it would not seem to be appropriate to reduce the formulation of logistics and supply chain strategy to the same level as that which pertains to most other functions. Furthermore, SCM is an activity that is truly cross-functional and not limited to one functional area. Many firms are organised into what are sometimes referred to as functional silos, for example marketing and production, and often the various functions do not integrate sufficiently with each other. Such a structure, however, is often not sufficiently responsive to meeting customer demands, which typically do not (and should not) respect internal organisational barriers.

SCM in contrast seeks to take a cross-functional, process perspective. To quote Fabbe-Costes and Colin[2], there is a mature perception of logistics as a cross-functional and deliberately open-ended management domain in the firm, and as a proactive interface with external partners in the supply chain. Figure 3.2 attempts to capture a more holistic view then of strategy formulation as it applies to logistics and SCM.

> The term 'integration' was already used in Chapter 1 when illustrating our model of the integrated supply chain; integration is a key feature of effective SCM and is an important term, which you will see arises many more times in this book.

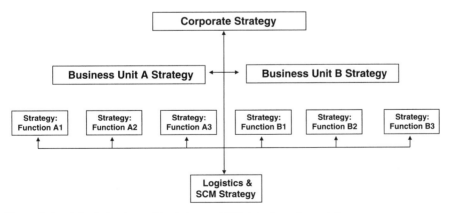

Figure 3.2   A holistic view of logistics and SCM strategy formulation

> Formulating a strategy for logistics and SCM should not be restricted to the logistics function: instead it should involve taking a cross-functional, process based perspective.

We started out this section by highlighting the importance of strategy, and it is indeed important. We must not lose sight, however, of the fact that what is also very important is that organisations effectively implement their strategies (some call this strategy execution), as many elaborate strategy planning exercises no doubt just remain sitting on office shelves. To quote the famous management thinker Henry Mintzberg, 90% of strategy is implementation. What is important then is that the organisation monitors the implementation of its strategy, and makes whatever changes are necessary and appropriate in the following weeks, months and indeed years, without being bound to a plan that may not be working out in practice.

Two principal logistics and supply chain strategies (although there are others, and indeed combinations of strategies are also used; more on this later) have emerged in recent decades, namely *lean* and *agile*. We will review these in turn in subsequent sections. We will then progress on to an understanding that a 'one size fits all' approach to logistics strategy increasingly makes less sense, and thus we will consider combined logistics strategies.

Before we start to look specifically at lean and agile logistics and supply chain strategies, however, it is useful first to look briefly at how different models of manufacturing have evolved over the past one hundred years or so. In the evolution of manufacturing two key output criteria, namely output volume and output variety, have been goals which firms have aspired to. It is only in recent years, however, that the goal of simultaneously achieving both has really been achieved.

THE EVOLUTION OF MANUFACTURING

Other things being equal, most production units will endeavour to produce goods and services that satisfy high levels of customer demand (via a high level of output variety), while at the same time producing large volumes so as to enjoy economies of scale in production. However, it was not always like this. Prior to the industrial revolution, and indeed for many years during and after it in some industries, skilled artisans produced goods customised for individual customers' needs. This was called *craft production*. Just think of the history of shoe production, for example. While this undoubtedly satisfied customer needs, it was a costly form of production. Craft production still, of course, exists in certain specialist, high value industries.

If we fast forward to the early twentieth century, one of the most exciting developments was the widespread development of *mass production* (see Figure 3.3). One of the most notable examples was that of car manufacturing by Henry Ford. His company certainly exploited economies of scale in manufacturing and earned the company tremendous success for many years. The choice of products was,

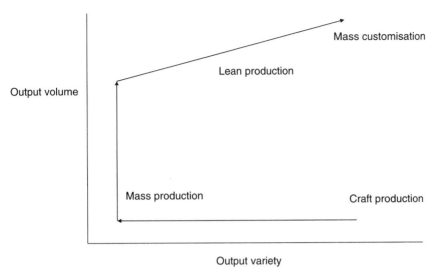

Figure 3.3   Production strategies[3]

however, quite limited; just think of his famous maxim concerning the Model T motor car that customers could have any colour as long as it was black! (In other words, no variety, just one colour would be available.) We had yet to arrive at a situation where both volume and variety of output could be maximised. We will consider the remainder of Figure 3.3, the emergence of lean production and mass customisation, via the sections that follow.

LEAN PRODUCTION

The origins of **lean** production and logistics can be traced back in particular to the car company Toyota and their ingenious Toyota Production System, pioneered by people such as Kiichiro Toyoda (son of the company's founder), Taiichi Ohno and others during the 1930s and especially after World War II. In developing the Toyota Production System they drew heavily on the work of Ford and identified areas in the Ford model which could be improved. They also drew on the work of the American quality guru, W. Edwards Deming. In fact much of Deming's early work received a richer response in Japan than it did in the USA, and the Japanese were to enjoy significant competitive advantage as a result by their embracing what came to be called *total quality management* (TQM).

Toyota sought to develop a production system where the emphasis was not on the efficiency of individual machines, but on total flows through a system. Significant emphasis was placed on quick machine turnovers, elimination of waste (known in Japanese as *muda*), even production flows, low levels of inventory, faster total process time and achieving total quality. Where many production systems are '**push**' based, Toyota sought to develop a system where inventory is '**pulled**' downstream through the system. This prevents stockpiling and inefficiency and is known as **just-in-time (JIT)** inventory replenishment (discussed further in Chapter 6, p. 106), where inventory is kept to a minimum and replenished only as it is used. The **Toyota Production System (TPS)** was born and in particular it sought to eliminate waste (in the form of unnecessary inventory and inefficient processes) in seven key areas (discussing these areas gives us insights into much of the thinking behind lean):

- Overproduction – basically producing too much. In this instance some inventory ends up being held in a warehouse or other holding area. This is referred to as **make-to-stock (MTS)**, as opposed to the more efficient **make-to-order (MTO)**.

- Waiting – poor process design and/or poor planning may result in work-in-progress inventory waiting until a machine or operator becomes available so that it can go through the next stage of production. Many aspects of the TPS philosophy also find application outside of manufacturing contexts. In the case of 'waiting' think, for example, of the inefficiencies that arise in some healthcare systems where patients have to wait in hospital, sometimes for days, for the appropriate doctor to examine them or read their test results (in many hospitals senior clinicians only work weekday office hours).

- Transportation – except in the case of products such as software, invariably most products have to be physically transported to the marketplace. In a sense this is nonvalue adding time with the freight just sitting on the truck. Again, adopting the TPS philosophy, one might try and think of ways in which value could be added to the product during this idle time. Just think, for example, of bananas ripening in transit. Another example concerns certain medial devices that have to be sterilised after production but before use. Some manufacturers have developed special packaging that allows chemicals to dissipate from the post-production sterilised product within the package over a fixed period of time. During this fixed period the devices can of course still be transported to the market, the only caveat is that the product is not opened until the due date. Beyond such value-adding examples, transportation can be wasteful when it is managed inefficiently (for example, under-utilised transport equipment).

- Inappropriate processing – in some production systems sometimes all products may enjoy the same level of processing, even though this might only be required for some of the products. An example might be using a certain advanced type of packaging on all products, even though this might only be required in certain markets.

- Unnecessary inventory – inventory has various costs associated with it which we will study in detail in Chapter 6. Suffice to note for now that holding unnecessary inventory *just-in-case* it may be required is costly and may also actually hide problems.

- Unnecessary motion – in a poorly designed production system it may be the case that work-in-progress inventory moves in an erratic route between stages around the factory. In a retail distribution example in Chapter 8 a similar scenario (albeit on a larger scale) is illustrated whereby a supplier delivers a product from region X to a consolidation centre in region Y, only for the product to then be moved back to a regional distribution centre operated by the retailer near region X.

- Defects – a product that is defective invariably causes production delays as it may be necessary to see what caused the defect. Furthermore, if the defect is only observed at the end stage of production, it may take time to discover where exactly the problem arose. This is all wasteful downtime, which total quality systems, by their emphasis on zero defects, seek to minimise.

A key aspect of lean is ensuring that value is added at each stage of the process ('the value stream') and steps in the process that do not add value are eliminated.

In recent years an eighth area, underutilisation of resources, has been added to the list. Toyota became one of the world's most successful manufacturers and while companies in the West were initially sceptical of Toyota's ideas, they quickly began to embrace them. A key study of the worldwide auto industry, the International Motor Vehicle Programme, by Womack, Roos and Jones in 1990 brought the world of lean to a wide audience. The study by Womack *et al.* was published in a highly influential book called *The Machine that Changed the World*[4] and resulted from a five-year, $5 million, 14-country study conducted by MIT, apparently the largest and most thorough study ever undertaken in any industry.

Traditionally, many production systems worked on a *push* mentality, that is materials are produced according to a planned forecast (which may or may not be accurate) and moved to the next stage of the supply chain; in *pull* based systems inventory is only produced and moved when it is required, and thus is more closely aligned with actual demand. (In essence, push systems relate to MTS, while pull systems relate to MTO – see the first bullet point above).

Such has been the success of lean production and logistics that in recent years many of the ideas in lean have been translated to the services sector. Two of the authors of the book *The Machine that Changed the World*, Womack and Jones, wrote that 'lean production transformed manufacturing. Now it's time to apply lean thinking to the processes of consumption. By minimising customers' time and effort and delivering exactly what they want when and where they want it, companies can reap huge benefits'.[5] Womack and Jones developed their principles of lean consumption:[6]

- Solve the customer's problem completely
- Don't waste the customer's time
- Provide exactly what the customer wants
- Provide what's wanted exactly where it's wanted
- Provide what's wanted where it's wanted exactly when it's wanted
- Continually aggregate solutions to reduce the customer's time and hassle.

AGILE SUPPLY CHAINS AND MASS CUSTOMISATION

Lean production and logistics is concerned with eliminating waste in a pull based value stream of activities with level production (i.e. even production runs with neither idle time nor surges in demand) and just-in-time inventory management.

Managing supply chains effectively is a complex and challenging task, due to the current business trends of expanding product variety, short product life cycles, increased outsourcing, globalisation of businesses, and continuous advances in information technology.[7] Indeed we can add more factors to this list such as hyper competition in markets and increasing demands from customers. In recent years, the area of risk in supply chains, whether from natural sources (for example disease in the food supply chain) or man-made sources (for example terrorism), is adding to the challenges in SCM (we will return to this growing and important area in Chapter 12). All of these disparate factors have led to a high level of volatility in demand for products.

To meet such volatility a new supply chain model has emerged, the **agile** supply chain. Pioneered by Professor Martin Christopher and colleagues at Cranfield University, and others, the agile supply chain is designed to cope with such volatility. According to Professor Christopher, 'to a truly agile business volatility of demand is not a problem; its processes and organisational structure as well as its supply chain relationships enable it to cope with whatever demands are placed upon it'.[8] A particular characteristic of the agile supply chain is that in effect it seeks to act as a 'demand chain' with all movement upstream in the supply chain as a result of customer demand.

One of the key enablers of agile supply chains is use of a technique known as **mass customisation**. This involves *customisation* into various different finished products of what are often largely *mass* produced products. Even when different product configurations contain a majority of shared components and features, the customer will usually concentrate on the dissimilar features among the similar products.

Mass customisation makes use of a production philosophy known as the *principle of postponement* (Figure 3.4). Production processes with many different parallel production lines can be very inefficient (left-hand side of Figure 3.4), especially if demand reduces for the output of one line and increases for that of another. However, by reconfiguring processes and standardising certain inputs and steps, the impact of variability in demand for finished products can be reduced. We can see on the right-hand side of Figure 3.4 that if it is discovered during the production process that demand for certain finished products reduces, semi-processed product can more easily be 'diverted' into the production of other finished products.

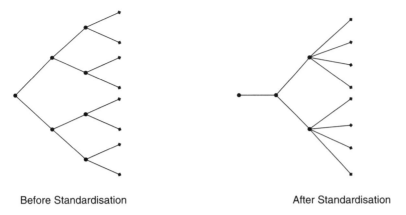

Before Standardisation   After Standardisation

Figure 3.4 The principle of postponement

Many manufacturers are realising the benefits of producing products on what have now come to be known as common or shared platforms. Various labels have been given to these shared platforms in different industries, such as for example the base product, the core product, the vanilla product (using the ice cream analogy of undyed plain ice cream), the generic product, and the grey product (a term used in garment manufacturing to refer to undyed fabric). In a postponed production system, ideally the final value-adding activities in the supply chain are delayed until customer orders are received.

The point at which we move from the base product to customised products is called the **decoupling point**. If you look at the case study on Dell at the end of Part one of the book, the decoupling point is the point in the production process where the core PC platforms are configured into final products demanded by customers.

The automobile manufacturing industry has been a keen user of mass customisation (see the diagram Small Car Manufacturing: Cooperation between Toyota, Peugeot and Citroën). Indeed Toyota, Peugeot and Citroën were not the first to

Mass customisation is enabled by a production philosophy known as **postponement** which involves the reconfiguration of product and process design so as to allow postponement of final product customisation as far downstream as possible. Other names for this approach are simply 'delayed product configuration', 'delayed product differentiation', and 'late stage customisation'.

The postponement approach doesn't just apply to manufacturing. *Packaging postponement* for example is merely delaying final packaging of products until customer orders are received (different packaging may be required for different customers, and rather than make different packaged product lines to stock, product could be quickly packaged as required once specific orders are received).

Toyota, Citroën and Peugeot decided to adopt a different approach for the manufacture of a new range of cars.

All three are produced in the new, purpose-built joint TPCA factory in the Czech Republic.

All three share 92% of the same components.

Peugeot/Citroën are responsible for sourcing & procurement and Toyota for production.

Small Car Manufacturing: Cooperation between Toyota, Peugeot and Citroën

do so. Other advocates of the approach include the Volkswagen Group, which comprises among others the brands: Volkswagen, Audi, Skoda and Seat. Many of the product offerings in the different car models across these brands share similar platforms and components. Apart from making sense from production and financial perspectives, consolidation in the automobile manufacturing sector where once many companies that were keen competitors but are now working together, and sometimes even merging, is now driving increased application of mass customisation in the industry.

Now back to agility. Professor Christopher describes agility as 'the ability to respond rapidly to unpredictable changes in demand'.[9] In his view 'agility is not a single company concept, it extends from one end of the supply chain to the other.' Christopher points out that 'agility is concerned primarily with responsiveness. It is about the ability to match supply and demand in turbulent and unpredictable markets.'[10]

> The agile supply chain is a demand-pull chain designed to cope with volatile demand. It is structured so as to allow maximum flexibility and will often incorporate postponed production.

The questions that now arise are: which approach is better, lean or agile? And are the lean and agile supply chain approaches mutually exclusive; that is, can we have both together? These are questions of much debate in the academic literature and which we attempt to answer in the next section.

BUYING PAINT

It's not just the automobile manufacturing industry that employs mass customisation, many other industries have also adopted the technique. Just think of the way in which the purchase of paint has changed. Because of developments in both production technology and the marketing of paint, the range of different paint colours it is now possible to purchase has increased dramatically. In addition, it is usually possible to buy paint in various different can sizes (e.g. 1 litre, 5 litres, etc.). The range of potential stock keeping units (SKUs) in paint distribution is thus huge.

Rather than keeping all possible SKUs in each store, mass customisation has become very popular in paint distribution. Each store holds the primary colours of paint and a machine then mixes these to a specific formula to produce the exact required colour of paint from a range of possible colours. All that is otherwise required are paint cans in the different sizes and a simple printing machine which can produce labels with the name of the paint.

Note: A **stock keeping unit (SKU)** is a unique version in terms of size, packaging, etc. of a particular product type; for example, 2 litre cans of white paint would be one unique SKU, 2 litre cans of harvest yellow paint would be another unique SKU, while 1 litre cartons of harvest yellow paint would be yet another unique SKU, and so forth.

COMBINED LOGISTICS STRATEGIES

So which is better, a lean or agile supply chain strategy? And can we have both together? Certainly it is now becoming apparent that there is no one generic supply chain typology which works in all situations. A simple scenario is to use lean strategies to manage base demand (a forecast driven approach) and to use agile strategies to manage surge demand (a demand driven approach). We can build further on this as we consider the variable nature of product lead times, life cycles, marketplace demand, etc.

In an often quoted paper from the *Harvard Business Review* in 1997, Professor Marshall Fisher from the University of Pennsylvania put forward a framework for supply chain selection based on the nature of product demand.[11] He distinguished functional products, which have predictable demand, long product life cycles, low variety and long lead times, from innovative products, which have unpredictable demand, short product life cycles, high variety and short lead times. Fisher suggested that two different types of supply chains are required for these two different types of products, which he termed efficient supply chains for functional products and responsive supply chains for innovative products.

Christopher *et al.*, building on the work of Fisher and others, have put forward a taxonomy (Figure 3.5) for selecting global supply chain strategies, which uses both predictability of demand for products and replenishment lead times. It also incorporates lean and agile philosophies as appropriate. They again argue that a 'one size fits all' approach will not work and that companies need to continually

	Predictable demand	Unpredictable demand
Long lead time	**Lean** Plan and Execute	**Leagile** Postponement
Short lead time	**Lean** Continuous replenishment	**Agile** Quick response

Supply demand characteristics	Resulting pipelines
Short lead time + predictable demand	Lean, continuous replenishment
Short lead time + unpredictable demand	Agile, quick response
Long lead time + predictable demand	Lean, planning and execution
Long lead time + unpredictable demand	Leagile production/logistics postponement

Figure 3.5   A taxonomy for selecting global supply chain strategies[12]

assess their product range and market characteristics so that changing scenarios may be identified and appropriate supply chain designs configured. This is the approach also taken by other authors, such as Professor John Gattorna whom we will discuss in the next section. He argues for a dynamic capability in supply chain designs so that they can respond to any changes and he argues against designing supply chains for specific products because, as he argues, different types of demand can in fact exist for the same product, even among the same customer depending on when and why they want to buy the product.

Lean, continuous replenishment: this applies in situations where demand is predictable and replenishment lead times are relatively short. This would apply for example in the case of a supplier making regular deliveries to a retailer. Over time a steady demand pattern will likely be apparent, allowing the supplier to 'lean' the supply chain with a high level of certainty. In such situations it is often the case that the supplier will take total responsibility for stock replenishment (we refer to this as vendor managed inventory – it will be discussed further in Chapter 9), sometimes even directly onto retailers' shelves. Predictability in the supply chain can be enhanced by retailers facilitating full visibility in the supply chain and allowing suppliers direct access to **electronic point of sale (EPOS)** data.

Agile, quick response: this applies in situations where replenishment lead times are still short but where demand is now unpredictable. In such situations suppliers need to respond rapidly to changes in demand. An excellent example is that of the Spanish clothing manufacturer and retailer Zara (see the case study below) which has designed a highly responsive supply chain that can translate the latest fashion trends into new products and deliver them to stores within a very short space of time. Because of the unpredictability in demand, manufacturers such as Zara can make use of postponed production/delayed configuration so that they can quickly configure the base product (referred to by clothing manufacturers as the *grey* garment) into the required final product.

Lean, planning and execution: this applies in situations where demand is predictable and replenishment lead times are long. It is a similar scenario to 'lean, continuous replenishment' described above, except here lead times are longer so more planning is required at a point well ahead of when demand will actually be realised. Lean principles can be applied in such supply chains once any uncertainty caused by long lead times can be managed. A classic example cited by Christopher *et al.* is that of artificial Christmas trees sourced into Europe each year from Asia.

Leagile: this applies in situations where replenishment lead times are still long, but now, to add to the complexity, demand is unpredictable. In this scenario we can combine both lean and agile logistics philosophies to create what is termed the '**leagile supply chain**'. Using postponed production/delayed configuration as described above, the base product can be manufactured at a remote location and shipped to locations nearer the final market (with both manufacturing and

ZARA

Based in La Coruna in North Western Spain, Zara is one of the fastest growing apparel companies in the world. Its supply chain is key to its success, in particular in terms of speed and lower inventory levels than its peers. As a result it is not hindered by product obsolescence, a key difficulty for many apparel manufacturers who are often stuck with fashion lines that the market does not want and which they cannot get rid of.

Zara's designers stay close to the latest fashion trends and design and manufacture new products within a short timeframe. All of this is done within the same facility to minimise delays and ensure maximum interaction among colleagues. Industry observers describe the Zara model as 'fast fashion' where buyers don't have to wait months for the latest fashions. After manufacture, product is shipped to Zara's various stores according to a fixed distribution schedule. Most store managers use handheld electronic devices to post real time orders from the distribution centre that organises twice weekly deliveries according to a fixed schedule. Products contain multi-country labels so if a line is not selling, the store manager simply puts it back on the truck and it is redistributed via Zara's hub and spoke network to another store where it may fare better.

From the store managers with their handheld ordering devices all the way back upstream to the single design and manufacturing site, Zara has full visibility of its supply chain. Another key feature of Zara's supply chain is that it has spare capacity on hand (in terms of trucks, warehousing and production not always being full) and it can facilitate fast response when needed. Professor Kasra Ferdows of Georgetown University and cowriters labelled this 'rapid fire fulfilment'.[13] Many other companies in the retail sector have closely examined Zara to see where they themselves can apply some of its key success factors.

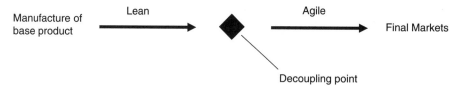

Figure 3.6   The leagile supply chain

distribution using lean principles), where it is then configured into the required final product (using agile principles). The final postponement could range from something as simple as using different types of packaging for different markets to manufacturing postponement where different components are added to the base product downstream as required.

If we now consider the concept of the decoupling point, which was described in the previous section, in the leagile supply chain lean principles can apply up to the decoupling point, and agile principles can apply downstream beyond the decoupling point (Figure 3.6).

CRITICAL FACTORS TO CONSIDER IN SUPPLY CHAIN PLANNING

Now that we have looked in detail at various aspects of different supply chain strategies, it is useful to look at some overarching principles that help managers develop their supply chain strategies and facilitate best fit with overall firm strategy.

Living supply chains

Hopefully the preceding section has shown that a 'one size fits all' approach to supply chain design just will not work. There is just too much variability in terms of lead times, product life cycles, marketplace demand, etc., to allow this to be the case.

Professor John Gattorna from the University of Wollongong describes the supply chains that are required in today's complex and competitive world as 'living supply chains', with companies using a process of 'dynamic alignment' to match changing customer needs and desires with different supply chain strategies.[14] He suggests that to succeed companies need different supply chain configurations in place to 'align' with the dominant buying behaviours of their customers, and that the best companies are achieving this multiple supply chain alignment.

Focus on processes and flows

Many companies get stuck in what we call a functional or silo mentality where they focus individually on separate areas, instead of configuring according to customer needs (a demand driven supply chain approach). This is one of the advantages of taking a supply chain approach in that it allows a full end-to-end perspective to be taken.

Some authors argue that the functional (or silo) nature of many organisations at an operational level acts as a barrier to aligning supply chains effectively with the markets they serve, thus obviating against a customer responsive supply chain strategy being pursued.[15]

Another way to understand supply chain strategy is to observe some of the many strategic activities that take place along typical supply chains. Tang,[16] for example, identified nine areas that facilitate more robust supply chain strategies: postponement, strategic stock, flexible supply base, make-and-buy, economic supply incentives, flexible transportation, revenue management, assortment planning, and silent product rollover. While Tang's focus was on robust strategies to mitigate supply chain disruptions (we will return to this topic in Chapter 12), the list of nine areas is useful because it gives an insight into the many strategies and activities that can be pursued along supply chains. Indeed, there are a number of other strategies that can also be pursued along supply chains such as, for example, factory gate pricing and cross docking. We will look at many of these in various parts of the book. It is also important to note that companies can adopt different roles in different supply chains, for example be the leader of one supply chain and be a participating member of another.

Focus on high-level objectives

Some writers argue that supply chains need to meet certain high-level objectives. Professor Hau Lee from Stanford, for example, argued that the best supply chains are *agile*, *adaptable* and have *aligned* interests among the firms in the supply chain.[17] He calls this the 'Triple A Supply Chain'. It is also important to note of course that the supply chain cannot, and is not, the solution to all ills. Professor Christopher and colleagues highlight this when they state that 'responsive supply chains … cannot overcome poor design and buying decisions which fail to introduce attractive products in the first place'.[18]

The importance of people

It is obvious that SCM has grown in significance in recent years. As we will also see in Chapter 9 in particular, SCM is benefiting from the application of some powerful technologies. Often overlooked, however, is the role played by people in the supply chain. Professor John Gattorna notes that 'it's people who drive the supply chain, both inside and outside your business, not hard assets or technology'.[19] Similarly James Quinn notes that to achieve any measure of supply chain success, three critical elements (people, process and technology) need to be kept in balance.[20] He adds that there is no single answer as to which of these three is the most important to supply chain success, although he does add that 'you can't do *anything* without the right people'.

It's supply chains that compete

> Increasingly it is supply chains that compete more so than individual firms and products.

You will see in the Dell case study at the end of Part One of the book that the PC maker uses robust logistics strategies and competes using its entire supply chain. The idea of supply chains competing was put forward by Professor Martin Christopher in his seminal book *Logistics and Supply Chain Management*, the first edition of which appeared in 1992. It is a powerful concept, and one that is becoming more and more relevant as we see the way that companies structure their supply chains often being a key determinant of success. A company can have the best and most sophisticated product in the world, but if it doesn't have a good supply chain behind it, then it will likely not be able to compete, especially in terms of cost and speed, and indeed many other attributes also.

LEARNING REVIEW

The chapter sought to identify the various different logistics and supply chain strategies, and their origins and evolution. This culminates in particular in strategies based around lean and agile principles, and varying combinations of both. We saw a useful taxonomy which helps choose strategies appropriate to various demand and lead time characteristics. The importance of logistics and supply chain strategy in the context of overall firm strategy was also highlighted. To again quote Fabbe-Costes and Colin, 'at the least logistics offers new ways of thinking about strategy'.[21] In their view, because it motivates and supports organisational change, it also offers new frames for piloting managerial action in a strategic way. And in their view this is why logistics and SCM are now of such strategic importance.

We are now ready to move into the second part of the book. We have laid the foundations for logistics and SCM, explained where they have come from and defined key terms. The link with globalisation and international trade has been discussed in detail and we have worked through various logistics strategies. Part Two of the book now moves into supply chain operations, how supply chains actually work in operational detail.

QUESTIONS

- What are the three typical levels of firm strategy?
- Outline the various stages in the evolution of manufacturing.
- Explain how mass customisation works.
- Outline the various scenarios in which we can use combined logistics strategies.
- Outline how some of the principles outlined in the Toyota Production System could be applied in a services context.

LOGISTICS AND THE WIDER STRATEGY OF THE FIRM

In this chapter we illustrated examples of companies such as Zara where a good logistics and supply strategy is at the core of the company's wider strategy. Can you think of other examples of companies where their logistics and supply chain strategies are central both to the company's wider strategy and in turn to their success?

NOTES

1. See, for example, Fabbe-Costes, N. & Colin, J. (2001) Formulating logistics strategy, in Waters, D. (ed.), *Global Logistics: New Directions in Supply Chain Management*, Kogan Page, London.

2. *Ibid.*, p.37.

3. The ideas in this diagram are based on a diagram originally contained in Womack, J., Roos, D. & Jones, D. (1991) *The Machine that Changed the World: The Story of Lean Production*, Harper Perennial, New York.

4. *Ibid.*

5. Womack, J. & Jones, D. (2005) Lean consumption, *Harvard Business Review*, March, 58–68.

6. *Ibid.*

7. Lee, H. (2002) Aligning supply chain strategies with product uncertainties, *California Management Review*, 44(3), 105–119.

8. Christopher, M., *Creating the Agile Supply Chain*, available at www.martin-christopher.info; for a wider elucidation of Professor Christopher's work see his seminal textbook, now in its third edition, *Logistics and Supply Chain Management* (2005), London, Financial Times/Prentice Hall.

9. Christopher, M. (2006) Keynote address to the Humber International Logistics Convention, Hull, June.

10. Christopher, M., Peck, H. & Towill, D. (2006) A taxonomy for selecting global supply chain strategies, *International Journal of Logistics Management*, 17(2), 277–287.

11. Fisher, M. (1997) What is the right supply chain for your product? *Harvard Business Review*, March/April, 105–116.

12. Christopher *et al.*, *op. cit.*

13. Ferdows, K., Lewis, M. & Machuna, J. (2004) Rapid fire fulfilment, *Harvard Business Review*, November, 104–110.

14. Gattorna, J. (2006) *Living Supply Chains*, London, Financial Times/Prentice Hall.

15. Godsell, J., Harrison, A., Emberson, C. & Storey, J. (2006) Customer responsive supply chain strategy: an unnatural act?, *International Journal of Logistics: Research and Applications*, 9(1), 47–56.

16. Tang, C. (2006) Robust strategies for mitigating supply chain disruptions, *International Journal of Logistics: Research and Applications*, 9(1), 33–45.

17. Lee, H. (2004) The triple-A supply chain, *Harvard Business Review*, October, 102–112.

18. Christopher *et al.*, *op. cit.*

19. Gattorna, *op. cit.*, p. xiii.

20. Quinn, J. (2004) People, process, technology, *Supply Chain Management Review*, January/February, 3.

21. Fabbe-Costes & Colin, *op. cit.*, p.53.

Dell: High Velocity, Focused Supply Chain Management

Dell (www.dell.com) has grown phenomenally since its establishment in 1983 by Michael Dell, then a medical student, now a multi-millionaire. The company's mission is simply 'to be the most successful computer company in the world at delivering the best customer experience in the markets we serve'.

By 2005 Dell was one the world's leading technology companies with a market capitalisation of $82 billion and a pre-tax return on invested capital of 240%. In the midst of stagnant global economic conditions, Dell recorded its best ever financial quarter in early 2003. Company revenue for the past four quarters totalled $36.9 billion and Dell had its sights set high with an aggressive growth target to double in size by 2007. Dell ascribes much of its success to its expertise in supply chain management and the velocity with which it is able to process and deliver orders – where competitors take weeks to build and ship product, Dell's metrics are hours and days.

DIRECT TO CUSTOMER

Central to Dell's phenomenal success is its distribution strategy: since it started to build its own machines in 1985 (prior to this the company had focused on upgrading old IBM machines) it has sold direct to the customer, disintermediating any middlemen and getting product faster to the customer. The computers themselves were viewed by some as not particularly remarkable from a technological perspective, so much so that in 1996 *The Economist* magazine described Dell as 'selling PCs like bananas'. The business market segment is highly important to Dell and the company has invested in Customer Relationship Management (CRM) systems in order to stay close to key customers, while similarly evaluating the cost-to-serve different customer segments and designing product offerings accordingly. Finished products are delivered by third-party logistics partners direct from the manufacturing plants to customers, often merging-in-transit with peripherals.

FULL VISIBILITY AND PARTNERSHIPS WITH SUPPLIERS

The internet is key to Dell's strategy, allowing direct communication with customers and real time visibility of purchasing patterns. Indeed, a key attribute of the Dell supply chain is full visibility along the chain with sales and production systems linked to suppliers who supply components just-in-time, usually direct to the production line and often with very short lead times (sometimes just one hour!). Consequently, Dell needs limited warehouse space for in-bound raw materials. These preferred suppliers play a key role in Dell's success according to their senior VP for worldwide procurement: 'our suppliers play an essential role in helping us provide customers with the quality and value they come to expect from Dell'. Each year Dell conducts an awards programme to acknowledge the eight suppliers who stand out in terms of quality, technology, service, continuity of supply and cost.

FOCUSED MANUFACTURING AND BUILDING TO ORDER

Dell pioneered the adoption of standardisation and postponed manufacturing (also known as mass customisation) in the electronics industry (Figure C1.1). This involves producing a small number of common platforms which are then customised according to customer demands (the customer generally recognises more so what is different among products, not what is the same). Before standardisation (left side of Figure C1.1) there are multiple product lines at both the upstream and downstream ends, whereas after standardisation (right side of Figure C1.1) the number of different product lines upstream reduces drastically and products are only customised (i.e. configured into different products) at the downstream end (once customer orders are visible).

The benefits of this strategy are many and include sharing of common components across product lines, thus reducing the number of stock keeping units (SKUs) that have to be carried. This strategy is also adopted in a number of other sectors where

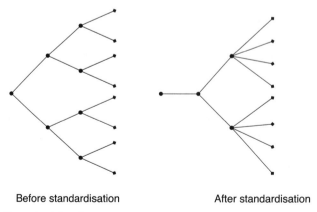

Before standardisation   After standardisation

Figure C1.1   The principle of postponement

demand is volatile and margins are tight, such as the automobile industry (Volkswagen, Audi, Seat and Skoda) and the fashion industry (Benetton and Zara).

Dell's 'manufacturing associates' can assemble desktops at a rate of 16–17 per day using 'single person build' rather than traditional assembly line techniques. This leads to both increased job satisfaction and product quality. In early 2000 the company introduced business process improvement in order to change and improve work practices right across the business and eliminate non-value-adding work. Modular manufacturing using standardised components is employed to build the 'vanilla products', which are then customised for market.

PROBLEMS OF LATE?

Increasingly, Dell is moving into higher value offerings and markets. In their view, they sell solutions, not products. Of late, however, the company has suffered some turbulence. Faulty laptop batteries led to the recall of 4 million laptop batteries in 2006.[1] Following on from the company's loss of first position to rival HP, Dell replaced its CEO with chairman and founder Michael Dell stepping back into the position.

The company then appointed Michael Cannon as president, global operations, effective 26 February 2007.[2] Most recently president and CEO of contract manufacturer Solectron Corp., Cannon will report directly to Michael Dell, the company's chairman and CEO. 'As we continue to grow worldwide, it is important that we increase our ability, via the Direct Model, to manufacture close to our customer and fully integrate our supply chain into one global organization. This will allow us to drive for even greater excellence in quality, cycle time and delivered cost', said Dell. 'We will innovate and adapt our supply chain model to help drive differentiated product design, manufacturing and distribution models.' Cannon will lead a new global organisation that will combine all of Dell's manufacturing, procurement and supply chain activities. All operations for the Americas, Europe/Middle East/Africa region and Asia Pacific/Japan will report to Cannon. Dell now has nine manufacturing plants in five countries, including the United States of America and will soon add new factories in Poland, India and Brazil.

QUESTIONS

- What are the fundamental reasons for Dell's success?
- What should Dell do next to maintain its competitive advantage? Is its business model still viable?
- Will the Dell formula work elsewhere? If not, why not?

---

[1]BBC News, January 2007.
[2]'Dell refocuses on supply chain', *Logistics Today*, 20 February 2007.

The Medical Devices Company

MDC is a successful and innovative multinational company which manufactures and distributes a range of sophisticated medical devices used by surgeons in the operating room. Individual unit value for MDC's product range is high and begins at €2,000 for some standard, widely used devices. Products for the European market are manufactured at two plants, one in Ireland and one in Poland. Other products and peripherals are also sold under the MDC brand and these are shipped in the first instance to both of the European manufacturing plants, before being moved downstream in the MDC supply chain. From both manufacturing plants the entire product range is then shipped to some 15 warehouses located across Europe. These 15 warehouses act as hubs and feed a further 40 warehouses, located mostly near the large urban centres across Europe. It is from these latter 40 warehouses that MDC's sales representatives and distribution agents draw their inventory.

MDC faces a range of challenges. Advances in medical technology and an expanded product range are driving business growth. Many customers (i.e. hospitals) want improved service solutions centred around increased product availability combined (paradoxically) with lower levels of stock holding. Indeed, many users are demanding a solution whereby a number of different variants of a particular device are readily available for immediate use, but whereby payment is only made for the particular variant actually used during the operation. Competition in the marketplace is increasing with some competitors beginning to offer such solutions. Inventory turnover is however problematic for MDC's European operation and has steadily fallen to five turns per year (the industry norm is about 10) resulting in increased inventory in the system, while issues with product obsolescence have also arisen on a number of occasions. Stock-outs at various stages along the chain are also becoming common (especially in the case of patients ready for surgery and requiring a specific device immediately in order for the surgery to go ahead) with the resulting need to expedite inventory direct to users from either manufacturing plant.

QUESTIONS

- Could you recommend a logistics strategy that could enable MDC in Europe to improve service to its customers and simultaneously reduce the total inventory in its European network?

LOGISTICS AND SUPPLY CHAIN OPERATIONS

Logistics Service Providers

INTRODUCTION

The first part of the book set out the context of logistics and SCM in today's global, highly competitive world. Building on our understanding of what logistics and SCM are, how they evolved, and their role in today's complex world, the next step is to learn how to actually 'do' logistics and SCM, and this is the focus of Part Two of the book.

'Doing' logistics involves various activities such as sourcing and purchasing inputs, managing inventory, maintaining warehouses, and arranging transportation and delivery. In fact within supply chains we can generally identify three key flows:

- Flows of materials
- Flows of information
- Flows involving resources such as people, equipment, logistics partners and financial flows – the latter are the basis of trade. Logisticians need to be as competent in following the money trail as they are in following the product trail. We will return to this important topic in Chapter 10.

Each of these interrelated flows is very important and is treated in depth across the following chapters. In this section of the book we will follow a sequence similar to that taken by many products as they move along supply chains: procurement and outsourcing (Chapter 5), managing inventory (Chapter 6), handling materials and warehousing (Chapter 7), transportation (Chapter 8), information flows and related technologies (Chapter 9), and financial flows (Chapter 10), and finally the whole area of measuring and managing logistics performance is covered in Chapter 11. We can then proceed in Part Three of the book to consider how all of these aspects can be aggregated together into supply chain designs that are effective and perform well in today's volatile and competitive business environment.

In recent years providers of logistics services have grown both in scale and in terms of the services that they provide. Increasingly many companies no longer perform many of their own logistics activities. We thus start Part Two of the book by looking at the range of such logistics providers, and the various services that they provide, and in particular how organisations go about selecting such companies. Traditionally the only services provided were transport, warehousing and customs clearance. This, however, has expanded to encompass a raft of other activities, which we will explore later in the chapter.

At the outset it is important to clarify two important terms: the **'consignor'** is the company or individual who sends the consignment, and the **'consignee'** is the company or individual who actually receives the consignment.

Chapter 4 comprises four core sections:
- Classifying logistics companies
- Fourth party logistics
- Carrier responsibilities
- Selecting logistics service providers and services

LEARNING OBJECTIVES

- Describe, and differentiate, the various types of companies that provide logistics services.
- Discuss the role of fourth party logistics.
- Illustrate the use of incoterms and bills of lading to show how responsibility along the supply chain is clarified and managed.
- Examine the range of issues in, and the process employed for, selecting logistics service providers.
- Also illustrate a number of other pertinent concepts and terms often used in logistics systems.

CLASSIFYING LOGISTICS COMPANIES

Chapter 8, which deals with transportation, will describe the various modes of transportation in detail. Suffice to note for now that there are essentially five such modes:

- Air
- Road
- Water
- Rail
- Pipeline

A sixth mode of transport is sometimes also referred to and labelled the 'information superhighway' to refer to the movement of information (where previously materials may have moved instead – software is a good example) over the internet.

Traditionally, companies evolved to provide services within individual modes (for example trucking companies, airlines, and so forth). Generally speaking this worked quite well for people who wanted to have their freight moved. In fact one of the world's largest and most successful logistics companies (UPS) is reputed to have started life delivering parcels by bicycle in North America (indeed this mode of transport is now popular again for distributing very light parcels in congested urban areas). As we saw in Chapter 1, in recent decades the fields of logistics and SCM grew both in popularity and complexity, spurred on by developments such as the proliferation of containerisation and advances in tracking technologies. For freight transport companies there was both a need and an opportunity to do more than just simply move freight using a single mode of transport from A to B.

We also saw in Chapter 2 the increasing tendency, for a variety of reasons, of companies to outsource various activities, many of which they may regard as noncore, and focus on their core competencies. In recent years many companies have sought in particular to move away from '**own account**' to third-party transportation, and this has provided many opportunities for transport and logistics companies.

> Own account transportation is when a company provides its own transport services.

A dynamic and profitable new sector of activity has emerged in recent decades, and we can use the generic label of **logistics service providers (LSPs)** to describe companies that operate in this sector. In fact a myriad of different types of companies operate in this sector, which we can broadly categorise as follows:

- *Hauliers or trucking companies* do just that: carry freight on trucks. Similarly, operators in the other modes also carry freight – train companies, airlines (with the exception in particular of many of the 'low cost airlines' who do not generally carry freight), and shipping companies.

- *Freight forwarders* are just like high street travel agents, except that they arrange transportation for freight, not people. Different types of freight forwarders have evolved in recent years.

  A big area of activity for many freight forwarders is in arranging customs clearance for freight that moves internationally (this is sometimes referred to as brokerage and encompasses not just dealing with customs agencies, but also managing all documentation that should accompany freight). With the development of regional trade agreements (which we discussed in Chapter 2), increasingly freight can move freely within regions, thus obviating the need for customs clearance for that freight (customs clearance will of course still be required for freight moving *into* the region).

  Freight forwarders have thus broadened out their product portfolio to encompass many other activities. For example, some act as ships' agents for vessels that arrive into a port. Some freight forwarders have evolved to a stage where they now operate their own vehicles and warehouses. Sometimes freight forwarders are called *freight agents* or *brokers*, again there are minor distinctions between all of these terms, which there is no need to go into here.

- The term **NVOCC** (non-vessel-owning common carrier) has come into use in logistics and refers to companies who consolidate smaller shipments from various consignees into full container loads which the NVOCC then takes responsibility for. The terms **'groupage'** and **'consolidated shipment'** (a shipment that comprises a number of unique, individual shipments all placed together in the one loading unit) are also used in the logistics sector to refer to aspects of this activity. Many freight forwarders offer such groupage services, some quite extensively. In this case, then, the freight forwarder acts not just as an *agent* but also as a *principal*.

- *Couriers* grew significantly, especially in the 1980s and 1990s, in response to a growing demand for immediate delivery of products. Many operate within and between large urban areas and service organisations such as banks who wish to move valuable documents quickly. In fact some people predicted that the proliferation of fax machines would eliminate the need for couriers. However, this has not been the case with consignees still demanding in many cases 'hard copies' of documents.

- A final group of companies are those that have become known as *integrators*. Examples of integrators include Fed Ex, United Parcels Service (UPS), and DHL. These companies' unique sales proposition is that they offer a seamless (i.e. integrated) end-to-end service from consignor to consignee (i.e. responsibility for the consignment doesn't move from, for example, a haulier to a freight forwarder to an airline, and so forth). They have evolved into becoming very substantial companies who provide a range of logistics services (see the case below). One of the difficulties which often arises in supply chains is that when freight gets lost or damaged it is usually at what are known as the 'touch points' (these are where freight is handled or transferred from one carrier to another). Integrators argue that the service they provide often circumvents these problems as they retain sole responsibility for freight from origin to destination, and they will usually 'track and trace' freight as it moves along their transport chains and thus have enhanced visibility of the product and any problems which may arise.

A final organisation type, which doesn't fit easily into any of the above categories although is close to the NVOCC concept, is where individual companies come together to form an agency to arrange their freight movements and use their combined buying power to get capacity at reduced rates from carriers.

There is considerable overlap between these categories. For example, a company that operates ships can also have its own freight forwarding operations. The classification above is given then purely to illustrate the various activities and types of companies that operate across the sector. As freight companies provide a broader and more integrated range of services, many have come to be known as **third-party logistics companies (3PLs)**. The evolution of 3PLs is evident in the 'Fed Ex and the Hub and Spoke System' case below. DHL (which can be described as an integrator and as a 3PL; in fact they also provide 4PL® services, an area discussed in the next section) started life as an air courier company, while Kuehne and Nagel's origins, for example, were more so as a traditional freight forwarder, but it is now a full service 3PL.

> It may sound trite but the term 'shipping' has in fact two common meanings in logistics: firstly to refer to the act of sending freight from a consignor to a consignee (for example to *ship* something by air), and secondly (the more common meaning) to move freight using the maritime mode.

> Distinguishing LSPs and 3PLs: as has already been noted, there is considerable overlap between the pertinent terminology used to describe the various companies that provide logistics services. We regard all such companies as *logistics service providers (LSPs)*. Those LSPs that provide multiple logistics services, often in an integrated fashion, we refer to as *third-party logistics companies (3PLs)*.

Some of the many different services provided by 3PLs are given below. As the list illustrates, transportation/delivery is just one of the many services that 3PLs provide. The 3PL sector has now become quite sophisticated. It is also quite common for some consignors to forge quite close links with their 3PLs who often will have people working within the consignors' logistics department.

- Transportation – often using multiple modes.
- Warehousing – including providing capacity for seasonal and other fluctuations.
- Pick and pack – for example picking multiple different SKUs and packing these into single units.
- Light manufacturing – we will see later in the section 'Sourcing, purchasing and procurement' in Chapter 5 that 3PLs often act as contract manufacturers for OEMs, this is quite prevalent in for example the electronics sector.

- Vendor managed inventory – see Chapters 9 and 13.
- Customs clearance – and associated regulatory requirements, such as, for example, hazardous goods clearances and food safety certificates.
- Trade financing – for example mitigating currency exposure.
- Managing reverse logistics – in some instances 3PLs manage the entire reverse logistics process for a client and manage all repairs and returns.
- Critical parts distribution – with their extensive networks of warehouses, it is sometimes more economical and effective for 3PLs to take over the management of critical spare parts inventories. This is quite prevalent in sectors such as electronics, automotive spares and medical technologies.
- Inventory management – management of inventory has considerable financial implications and we will explore these issues in detail in Chapter 6.

Professor Robert Lieb from Northeastern University in the USA conducts annual surveys[1] of the US 3PL industry and he has noted that since the mid 1990s the industry has undergone significant changes in areas such as industry size and make-up (growth and consolidation are evident), services offered, geographical reach, and IT support. He also notes that during that time the customers for 3PL services have grown bigger and have given a greater share of their logistics operating budget to 3PLs through larger contracts. He notes that the percentage of *Fortune* 500 manufacturers using 3PL services has increased from 38% to more than 80%.

FED EX AND THE HUB AND SPOKE SYSTEM

Fed Ex (www.fedex.com) started life in the early 1970s and was founded by Frederick Smith. As a student at Yale, Smith had pondered the economics of the route systems then dominant in US air freight markets. His deliberations were to lead to the pioneering introduction by Fed Ex of hub and spoke networks into air freight markets.

Rather than offer point-to-point services between all city pairs, hub and spoke networks operate on the simple, but highly effective, principle whereby freight is shipped from all origin points to a central hub, re-sorted, and then shipped out to destination. Customers were initially sceptical of this concept in that if they were sending a parcel from for example Boston to Chicago, they got confused as to why its routing would take it to Memphis (the location of Fed Ex's central hub, and a place some distance away from both Boston and Chicago). The logic and economics of Smith's hub and spoke model, however, quickly won out and today all of the integrators have large hubs and associated networks across most continents.

Fed Ex itself has also grown considerably. Today it has one of the world's largest air freight fleets and employs some 275 000 people. The company also operates a diverse range of logistics-related Fed Ex branded companies under the core Fed Ex brand.

EXAMPLES OF LEADING LOGISTICS SERVICE PROVIDERS

DHL (www.dhl.com)

DHL (the letters stand for the first letters of the last names of the three company founders) started life in 1969. In fact it was one of the first air courier companies in that its original product was the delivery by air of ships' papers from San Francisco to Honolulu (allowing customs clearance of a ship in Honolulu before the ship actually arrived, thus dramatically reducing time spent waiting in the harbour). Today the company is 100% owned by Deutsche Post World Net, a global organisation with a workforce of over 500 000 employees present in more than 220 countries and territories. Along the way it has acquired a number of logistics companies including Danzas and Exel, making DHL today one of the world's largest logistics companies.

Kuehne and Nagel (www.kn-portal.com)

Kuehne and Nagel is one of the world's oldest logistics companies. It was founded in 1890 in Bremen, Germany and today has more than 830 offices in over 100 countries with 45 000 employees. It has evolved to become a full service 3PL, active across all modes of transport. Today it is estimated to be the number one global sea freight forwarder and in the top five global air cargo forwarders. It also moves freight by road and rail and is engaged in contract logistics with a variety of companies, being now ranked as one of the top three global contract logistics providers.

A.P. Moller – Maersk Group (www.maersk.com)

The company is probably best known today for its deep-sea container vessels that traverse the world. It is, however, much more than a shipping company. Established in Denmark in 1904, today the group employs over 110 000 people in over 125 countries. In the shipping sector, the group's subsidiaries operate more than 550 container vessels (including some of the world's largest container vessels) and more than 45 terminals. As well as being involved in unitised (i.e. containerised) shipping, the group is also active in other shipping areas, such as crude oil transportation and supporting offshore oil and gas activities. It has also diversified extensively into other transport and non-transport areas such as shipyards, air freight, and even the retail supermarket sector.

FOURTH PARTY LOGISTICS

In the preceding section we noted the shift from own account transportation towards increased use of LSPs, with more companies outsourcing more logistics activity to 3PLs. Some companies of course still undertake some or all of their own logistics activities, although the share of companies doing this is declining. The topic of outsourcing was discussed in Chapter 2, and we will return to it in more detail in Chapter 5. In Chapter 5 we will go into further detail in terms of when it is most appropriate to outsource versus keep a function in-house. When companies do outsource, in many cases they will use more than one 3PL, either to ensure competitive rates are secured or because different 3PLs will have strengths in different markets or trades. In addition, the outsourcing company will still have to have a logistics department (even though all freight handling may be done by the 3PLs) in order to manage the 3PLs which it retains.

In recent years a new concept known as **fourth party logistics (4PL®)** has emerged. It sought to offer a radical solution that would offer companies total outsource supply chain solutions. It was invented and trademarked by Accenture in 1996 who originally defined it 'as a supply chain integrator that assembles and manages the resources, capabilities and technology of its own organisation, with those of complementary service providers, to deliver a comprehensive supply chain solution'.[2]

The concept has evolved since then with the Australian author John Gattorna in his insightful book *Living Supply Chains* noting that 'some of the essential elements that differentiate 3PL and 4PL® business models have been lost'.[3] While a number of genuine 4PL® solutions have emerged, in practice it is now more common for some 3PLs to offer 4PL® type solutions. This involves 3PLs in turn outsourcing, where it makes most sense for the final customer, certain activities to other 3PLs. We can thus envisage a 4PL® type concept today where individual 3PLs offer an overarching solution for an individual customer and which encompasses offerings from different (competitor) 3PLs.

CARRIER RESPONSIBILITIES

Once freight leaves a consignor, it is up to responsible LSPs to ensure that it reaches the consignee in the right condition, at the right time, etc. (recall the '8 Rs' definition of logistics in Chapter 1). Unlike passengers, freight cannot, of course, speak for itself (although we will see in Chapter 9, which deals with technology in the supply chain, that advances are being made in intelligent tracking systems at the individual item level). Documentation (either in physical or soft format) will need to accompany the freight so as to ensure that anyone who comes into contact with the freight will know where it comes from, what it comprises, where it is going, and how it is going to get there. Customs and security agencies, who do not have time to physically check each consignment, will also want to know the various details about individual consignments that are moving over international borders.

The document that typically contains all of this requisite information is known as a **bill of lading**, or in air freight the more common term is an airwaybill, or AWB for short. In the case of consolidated shipments, the entire shipment will be covered by a master airwaybill, with the individual shipments covered by documents known as house airwaybills.

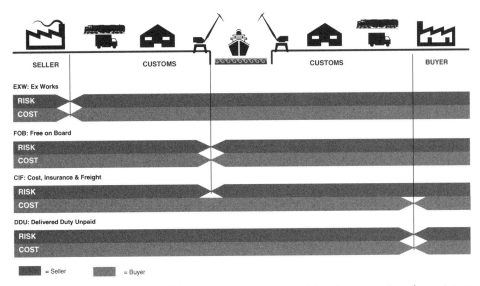

Figure 4.1 Incoterms 2000. The most commonly used incoterms, noting the point at which responsibility for goods is transferred between buyer and seller
Source and copyright: Royal & Sun Alliance Insurance plc (2007). All rights reserved[4]

When freight moves from consignors to consignees, it is important to understand who has responsibility for it at various stages. If something happens to the freight, for example it becomes damaged, who will be held responsible? Similarly, if charges for customs clearance are to be paid before the freight can be collected, then who should pay such charges, the consignor or the consignee?

Issues such as these are resolved by using what are called '**incoterms**', an abbreviation for international commercial terms, which were first published in 1936 by the International Chamber of Commerce (www.iccwbo.org) and are now commonly accepted standards in global trade. While incoterms are very useful with regard to various cost and risk issues, they are not intended to replace legal agreements such as contracts of sale. There are, in fact, 13 incoterms, divided into four groups. Figure 4.1 illustrates the four that are most commonly used.

The four groups, and the thirteen incoterms, are:

- Group E: Departure
  - **EXW   ex-works**
- Group F: Main carriage not paid by seller
  - **FCA   free carrier**
  - **FAS   free alongside ship**
  - **FOB   free on board**

- Group C: Main carriage paid by the seller
  - **CFR**   **cost and freight**
  - **CIF**   **cost, insurance and freight**
  - **CPT**   **carriage paid to**
  - **CIP**   **carriage and insurance paid**
- Group D: Arrival
  - **DAF**   **delivered at frontier**
  - **DES**   **delivered ex ship**
  - **DEQ**   **delivered ex quay**
  - **DDU**   **delivered duty unpaid**
  - **DDP**   **delivered duty paid**

SELECTING LOGISTICS SERVICE PROVIDERS AND SERVICES

Decision making is an ongoing and important part of many logistics managers' jobs: for example, trying to decide which routing to use for a particular shipment, which carriers to use, and how much inventory to hold. Different people, depending on their role in the supply chain, will have varying views on what the optimum decision is, and it is the job of the logistics manager to reconcile these conflicting views.

With regard to using LSPs, a strategy that is often used by logistics managers is to give a large share of their business to one carrier, and the remaining smaller share to a competitor carrier. This has two advantages: firstly if there are any problems (such as for example delays) with the preferred carrier, then they can, if necessary, switch traffic to the alternative carrier; secondly this dual approach has the advantage of keeping both carriers 'on their toes', because they know there is an alternative available if their performance starts to weaken.

More generally, companies also need to decide which 3PL(s) to use. The list below gives some of the many factors that have to be considered when selecting LSPs.[5] Contracts with LSPs can often be worth large amounts of money and obviously cover an important area of a company's activities, therefore it is essential to choose the right partner(s).

- Services to be provided (geographical areas, volumes including fluctuations, time frame, etc.)
- Costs and costing approach (open book, gain share, penalties, inflation/cost increases, etc.)
- Insurance (responsibility for damage and shrinkage)
- Speed/transit time
- Performance metrics and service levels, reliability
- Information systems (especially with regard to systems integration), other technology issues (e.g. capability to 'track and trace' freight

and requirement to use advanced technologies such as RFID), and documentation requirements

- Core vs value-adding services required
- Staffing issues (e.g. transfer of undertakings with respect to previous employees, legal responsibilities, image and responsibility, union recognition, disruptions)
- Reverse logistics issues (packaging, returns – damaged and faulty goods, failed deliveries, etc.)
- Implementation/termination/ability to alter conditions
- Details on the logistics service provider's history, client references, etc.

In the section on 'Sourcing, purchasing and procurement' in Chapter 5 we will look more generally at the various stages in procuring products and services; the various steps applied there can be and are applied in the procurement of logistics services also.

Chapter 11, which deals with performance management, will discuss the role of service level agreements in the ongoing management of LSPs. Obviously once the appropriate providers are selected the next and important stage is to manage them effectively.

As well as deciding which LSP(s) to use, logistics managers also often need to decide which transport mode(s) to use. We say *often,* not *always,* because sometimes consignors do not know exactly which transport mode their freight travels on, they leave this decision to the 3PL. Furthermore, it is often not a simple matter of trading off one mode against another. Sometimes multiple transport modes are used in combination – in air transport, for example, the concept of **air trucking** is quite prevalent whereby freight is transported by road (sometimes over a relatively long distance) to a hub airport from where it travels onwards by air. Direct cost comparisons between alternative modes and services can be complex – this is the concept of **generalised costs** discussed in the box.

Much work has been done by academics and others into investigating the various criteria involved in logistics decision making and how such decisions are actually made in practice.[6] We do not have time to investigate the actual mechanics of logistics decision making here. Suffice to note for now that as well as identifying the relevant variables (such as those considered in the list above), it is important to understand how these variables interrelate in logistics decision making. In a paper in 1983, academics Davies and Gunton put forward a hierarchy of needs for freight purchasing, which is illustrated in Figure 4.2. They based it on Maslow's hierarchy of human needs and it gives a good insight into the relevant positioning of the criteria that transport and logistics decision makers regard as being important. Although we would like to think that logistics decision makers always engage in objective analysis and decision making, the reality is often different. In fact many logistics decision makers often engage in what is known as *satisficing* (as opposed to *maximising*) decision-making behaviour; that is, they select routes and services which they know are not optimum, but with which they will nonetheless be largely content.

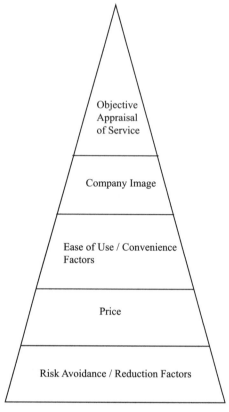

Figure 4.2   Hierarchy of needs for freight purchasing[7]

THE CONCEPT OF GENERALISED COSTS

At this juncture it is opportune to introduce a common concept in transport economics, namely the concept of generalised costs. Button[8] noted that consignors are concerned not simply with the financial costs of carriage, but also the speed, reliability and time-tabling of the service. According to Button, the demand for transport is not, therefore, simply dependent on financial costs but rather on the overall opportunity costs involved. The generalised cost of a trip can thus be expressed as a single, usually monetary, measure combining, generally in linear form, most of the important but disparate costs that form the overall opportunity costs of the trip:

$$G = g\left(C_1,\ C_2,\ C_3,\ ...C_n\right)$$

where G is generalised cost and C_1, C_2, C_3, ... are the various time, money and other costs of travel.

Lalwani et al.[9] noted that the three main components of the generalised cost of freight transport are the money costs, the time taken, and the effects of loss, damage and delay because, in their view, it is the total effect of these, in any particular set of circumstances, which determines the choice of transport mode.

The concept of generalised transport costs is important in logistics because it helps us to understand the importance of trade-offs in decision making and how optimum decisions can be made. People engaged in marketing logistics services, for example, make use of the concept of generalised transport costs. Rates to ship freight by air are usually higher than by alternative surface modes. If, however, we factor in other costs/savings, such as the fact that because the freight is in transit for a shorter period when transported by air and as a result the opportunity cost of capital is lower, then the overall cost of air freight compared with surface freight may for some shipments actually be lower. Even though air freight rates are usually higher, air freight benefits then by usually having lower other costs associated with it over other modes such as, for example, insurance and the aforementioned opportunity cost of capital.

LEARNING REVIEW

This chapter described the important role played in supply chains by logistics service providers (LSPs). We discussed the various, and overlapping, types of LSPs and noted in particular the growth of a category of LSPs called 3PLs; the latter we described as LSPs who generally offer multiple logistics services, often in an integrated fashion. We then considered the raft of different services which such 3PLs actually provide, with transportation/delivery being just one of the many services offered. The concept of fourth party logistics was then explored and we noted the reality that in many instances it is actually 3PLs that offer 4PL® type solutions.

The issue of LSP responsibilities was next explored and we looked at the important role played by the bill of lading in international transportation. The issue of who has responsibility for what at different stages in the supply chain is an important one and we considered the role that incoterms can play in clarifying this.

How consignors go about selecting LSPs and services was explored, and we saw the application of the concept of generalised costs, which helps explain trade-offs between different sets of costs in supply chains. We noted that many variables need to be considered when selecting LSPs and that a hierarchy of decision makers' needs can be identified in logistics purchasing.

The next chapter will continue the journey along the supply chain and will deal with procurement of raw materials and also the topic of outsourcing, already discussed briefly in Chapter 2.

QUESTIONS

- What is 'own account' transportation?
- Describe the different types of logistics service providers.
- Describe the various factors that have to be considered when selecting logistics service providers. How in practice do you think consignors make decisions concerning choosing logistics services?
- What is fourth party logistics (4PL®) and how has the concept evolved in recent years?
- How might we distinguish 3PLs from other LSPs?

'ASSET UNENCUMBERED' 3PLS

In recent years many 3PLs have grown in scale and become quite sophisticated. In this chapter we also saw how some 3PLs are in practice offering 4PL® type solutions. In fact some 3PLs have advanced to the point where they believe that their knowledge and systems, and not the physical capital which they own and operate (warehouses, transport, etc.), are what gives them critical, competitive advantage. Some commentators refer to such 3PLs as 'asset unencumbered' in that they increasingly divest themselves of physical assets, yet concomitantly grow their business via more effective use of people, knowledge and systems.

  Search the web for examples of 3PLs becoming 'asset unencumbered'. Is such a strategy sustainable in the long term, in your view?

NOTES

1. Lieb, R. (2005) The 3PL industry: where it's been, where it's going, *Supply Chain Management Review,* 9(6), 20–27.

2. Quoted in Gattorna, J. (2006) *Living Supply Chains,* Harlow, Pearson Education, p.204.

3. *Ibid.,* p.208.

4. Source: John Perera, Royal and Sun Alliance, England.

5. Adapted from: Mangan, J., Lalwani, C. & Gardner, B. (2001) Identifying relevant variables and modelling the choice process in freight transportation, *International Journal of Maritime Economics,* 3, 278–297.

6. See for example Mangan *et al., op. cit.,* which includes a summary of the literature on relevant variables and transport choice decision making.

7. Davies, G.J. & Gunton, C.E. (1983) The buying of freight services: the implications for marketers, *The Quarterly Review of Marketing,* Spring, 1–10.

8. Button, K. (1993) *Transport Economics* (2nd edition), Aldershot, Edward Elgar Publishing.

9. Lalwani, C., Goss, R., Gardner, B. & Beresford, A. (1991) Modelling freight traffic, in J. Rickard & J. Larkinson (eds), *Longer Term Issues in Transport*, Aldershot, Avebury.

Procurement and Outsourcing

INTRODUCTION

Chapter 2 on 'Globalisation and International Trade' looked at the growth in recent decades of international trade and the emergence of the phenomenon known as globalisation. This has given rise to global outsourcing in both the manufacturing and service sectors. In this chapter the impact of outsourcing on international SCM is analysed. We build on the discussion in Chapter 2 and consider the increasing tendency in particular of companies in Europe and North America to outsource their noncore processes to Asia and South America. A large number of outsourcing arrangements fail in the first year. We look at the factors that cause this failure. Building effective outsourcer–outsourcee relationships is one of the most important factors leading to success in outsourcing. We consider different scenarios in which the relationships can change from the lowest level of 'master–servant' through to higher, mutually beneficial levels. Before we discuss all of these issues, however, the chapter begins with a review of the basic issues involved in sourcing, purchasing and procurement.

Chapter 5 comprises five core sections:
- Sourcing, purchasing and procurement
- Growth in international trade, outsourcing and offshoring
- Failures in outsourcing
- Evaluating and selecting outsourcees
- Outsourcer and outsourcee relationship development.

LEARNING OBJECTIVES

- Explain the procurement process.
- Consider factors affecting outsourcing and procurement decisions.
- Highlight the need for outsourcing in view of both globalisation and the growth of international trade.
- Identify the problems faced by outsourcing companies which can result in failure.
- Outline how outsourcees are selected and distinguish order winning and order qualifying criteria.
- Examine how outsourcer–outsourcee relationships develop.

SOURCING, PURCHASING AND PROCUREMENT

Sourcing raw materials, other inputs and support services are important areas in all companies and involve considerable expenditure of both time and money.

The term 'sourcing' is often used interchangeably with the terms 'purchasing' and 'procurement' but to be more specific **sourcing** relates to identifying and working with appropriate suppliers, while **purchasing** relates to the specific functions associated with the actual buying of goods and services from such suppliers. **Procurement** includes sourcing and purchasing and covers all of the activities involved in the product/service sourcing, purchasing and delivery from supplier to the customer. For example, the procurement department of a typical manufacturing company may have engineers working internationally with their industry peers and identifying appropriate suppliers; this we regard as *sourcing*. When it comes to actually buying materials from these suppliers, agreeing delivery schedules and so forth, the function that handles this we refer to as *purchasing*.

Regardless of the terminology used, it is a very important activity in manufacturing supply chains as purchased parts and materials account for over 60% of the cost of finished goods. For retail companies within the supply chain this percentage can be as high as 90%.[1] The quality of purchased material, costs of goods bought, delivery of goods or services on time, supplier management, and supplier relationships are some of the factors that have a significant impact on SCM and place particular demands on procurement managers.

> Procurement includes sourcing and purchasing and covers all of the activities from identifying potential suppliers through to delivery from supplier to the customer.

We saw in Chapter 1 that in some instances practitioners simply re-label traditional transport activities as 'logistics', although we know, of course, that logistics involves more than just operating some trucks. In much the same way, sometimes purchasing merely gets re-labelled as procurement, but by the end of this chapter you should be of the view that procurement involves more than merely managing purchase order transactions.

The procurement process involves a number of stages:

- *Preparing the specification,* including the quality, quantity and dates required, etc. There are various approaches that can be followed here. Typically the outsourcer will issue an **RFQ/RFT/RFI/RFP** (request for quote/tender/information/proposal). Sometimes they will adopt a tiered approach– for example, first issue an RFI and then select from the responses to the RFI a shortlist of companies from whom RFQs will subsequently be sourced. The RFQ/RFT/RFI/RFP should typically contain information about the product or service being requested. An advantage of the process is that it can allow standardised information to come back from the interested providers, thus allowing benchmarking among the prospective outsourcees. Furthermore various scenarios can also be tested (e.g. what would be the range of costs and add-on services across the range of prospective providers for a particular product). In Chapter 4 we looked at the selection of LSPs and the services that they provide. Within the logistics sector it is quite common to also follow the process outlined above of issuing RFQs, and indeed also at times adopting a tiered approach of first issuing an RFI.

- *Supplier selection,* which is based on various criteria such as assessment of the supplier's capability, previous performance, price, service and relationship with the purchasing company. The flexibility of a supplier to respond to changes in specification, delivery, or quantity is another factor often considered, as often the purchasing company may not be sure of exactly what it wants to purchase and when. Various mechanisms are used for supplier selection, including direct negotiations, competitive bids, and in recent years internet based auctions have become popular. Sometimes these are *'reverse auctions'* whereby potential suppliers compete on the basis of lowest price or other parameters. Many purchasers are aware though that this can easily become a 'race to the bottom' with quality or other parameters being compromised and thus they manage such reverse auctions very carefully.

  It is usual that potential suppliers have to first qualify by meeting certain criteria and/or performance expectations before they are given proper consideration. We refer to these minimum requirements as **order qualifiers**, while the criteria that allow the supplier to actually be selected we refer to as **order winners**. We discuss both of these terms in more detail later in this chapter.

  We will look in more detail at supplier evaluation and selection in the section 'Evaluating and selecting outsourcees' later in this chapter.

- *Placing the purchase order,* including entry into the purchaser's system for handling the orders for costing and visibility.
- *Order management,* including monitoring, tracking, and modifying as appropriate.
- *Receiving the purchases* and making sure that they comply with set specification in terms of quality, quantity, and cost.

Procurement managers are also involved in ongoing monitoring of suppliers and managing the buyer–supplier relationship. Service level agreements, discussed in more detail in Chapter 11, will typically be used in this context. Sometimes the relationship can extend to **supplier development** where, in both parties' interests, improvement efforts are made leading to, for example, new and better products and solutions being provided by suppliers. Japanese companies such as Toyota, for example, were some of the first to realise the benefits that could be enjoyed by close collaboration with suppliers. Such an approach 'inverts' the traditional approach that sought to squeeze suppliers as much as possible on price. Of course price is still regarded as an important, but now not the only, criterion to be considered. We will return to these issues in Chapter 13, which deals with integration and collaboration in supply chains, and the roles therein of suppliers.

Many studies have shown that good supplier relationship management leads to better results and added benefits, especially when it is over an extended period of time sharing risks and benefits.[2] Partnership helps by improving quality, product development, and logistics efficiency as both parties are able to share information on forecasts, sales, supply requirements, production schedules, and problem alerts in advance. Additional benefits such as higher quality, lower inventories, and better planning can also be achieved.

Another important consideration in procurement is whether to opt for *single sourcing* or *multiple sourcing*. Multiple sourcing has the advantage that it brings in competition and back-up in case of problems of delivery associated with using a single source. But it is of course easier to engage in supplier development with one or few suppliers than it is to do so with many suppliers.

ORIGINAL EQUIPMENT MANUFACTURERS (OEMs) AND TIERED SUPPLIER STRUCTURES

A tiered supplier structure has emerged in recent years in many industries. Companies have evolved, which have come to be known as OEMs **(original equipment manufacturers)**, and these are the producers of the final product that carries their brand. OEMs purchase their components from first-tier suppliers, which are sometimes called **contract manufacturers**. These first-tier suppliers buy their components from second-tier suppliers, and so forth.

For example a PC manufacturer (OEM) is likely to have first-tier suppliers for the computer screens, motherboards, disk drives, hard disks, etc. The first-tier suppliers for computer screens are likely to have their own suppliers for components such as the metal casing required for the production of the screens. These suppliers are second-tier suppliers for the OEMs, and there can also be third-tier suppliers and so on. In order to guarantee efficient supply, OEMs have to work closely not only with the first-tier suppliers, but also support them in having efficient and effective supply chain relationships with their second and other tier suppliers.

GROWTH IN INTERNATIONAL TRADE, OUTSOURCING AND OFFSHORING

Now that we understand the procurement process, it is appropriate to recap and remind ourselves what is meant by both outsourcing and offshoring. We saw in Chapter 2 that outsourcing involves the transfer to a third party of the management and delivery of a process previously performed by the company itself, and that offshoring is the transfer of specific processes to lower cost locations in other countries.

We also saw that offshoring is not the same as outsourcing because outsourcing involves handing process ownership over to a third party, whereas with offshoring the company may still own and control the process itself in the lower cost location. Of course you can also both outsource and offshore a particular process in that the newly acquired outsource partner can also decide to offshore and transfer the newly acquired process to a lower cost location in another country.

In the manufacturing and service sectors new sourcing patterns have emerged due to the growth in international trade and global competition. In the manufacturing sector international networks of production are being established. Within this scenario the development of supply networks is a critical issue for multinational enterprises in order to achieve efficiency and quality of the final product. Multinational enterprises have the tendency to implement their own supply chain operations and management practices across countries within their global networks of subsidiaries and operational units.

In Asia, China and India have become global centres for a large number of sectors such as manufacturing, software development, retailing and financial services, and in recent years there has been an unprecedented increase in companies outsourcing and/or offshoring processes from Europe to Asia. Rates of pay, when compared to those in Europe and North America, are much lower, although we will see later in the chapter in the context of the *total cost of outsourcing*, that these are not the only factors to be considered.[3] In a recent count it was found that 400 companies out of the Fortune 500 have research bases in China, while 125 have bases in India.[4] This approach, however, of transferring operations and activities from Europe/North America to Asia has caused a number of difficulties leading to failure for some, as many firms are unable to contextualise to factors such as infrastructure (energy, materials, transport and communication), education, training, local and national regulations, culture and organisational networks.

VOLVO TRUCK (INDIA)

Volvo Trucks India is a wholly owned subsidiary of a Swedish firm, which is the world's second largest producer of heavy trucks. Volvo has approximately 72 000 employees and production in 25 countries. It has completed six years of operations in India and is based near Bangalore. The vendor development department at Volvo India plays a major role in the selection and development of Indian vendors for global supplies. Their responsibility ranges from verification of parts against specification to training of suppliers on Volvo specifications and methodology. The exports from Indian suppliers amount to €26 million from a total of 10 suppliers. Of these 2–3 suppliers are strategic suppliers; that is, they are 100% suppliers to Volvo.

In the manufacturing sector there have been a number of changes in recent years. Manufacturing organisations now give greater importance to the relationship/collaboration with partners in their supply chains. There has been an increase in outsourcing in non-core competency areas (15% in 1998; 40% in 2004). It was estimated that in 2004 the outsourcing industry including all sectors was worth over US$5 trillion.[5]

We saw in Chapter 2 that companies outsource for a number of reasons including cost, flexibility, focus on core competence, and for technological reasons. Research on a number of manufacturing companies in the UK and India, for example, has shown that companies are outsourcing and/or offshoring mostly due to the following reasons:[6]

- Reduce direct and indirect costs
- Reduce capital costs
- Reduce taxes
- Reduce logistics costs
- Overcome tariff barriers
- Provide better customer service
- Spread foreign exchange risks
- Share risk
- Build alternative supply sources
- Pre-empt potential competitors
- Learn from local suppliers, foreign customers or competitors
- Gain access to world-class capabilities or attract talent globally.

Furthermore, globalisation in the manufacturing sector has resulted in the following trends:

- Global markets
- Global competition
- Competitors, partners and customers from around the world
- Global sourcing
- Global presence
- Global value chains resulting in increasing complexity and competition
- Global access to knowledge and new technologies
- High level of customer awareness and expectations
- Rapid pace of technological change
- Fast rate of product commoditisation
- SCM expertise and innovation are preconditions for business success.

FAILURES IN OUTSOURCING

We saw in Chapter 2 that research[7] has shown that four out of five business process outsourcing (BPO) contracts signed today will need to be renegotiated within two years and that 20% of such contracts will collapse. Similarly, in a recent survey it was found that 50% of outsourcing relationships worldwide fail within five years; the most reported reasons for failure are summarised in Figure 5.1. Some of the various problems illustrated in Figure 5.1 are now discussed.

Late delivery is one of the most common causes of failure in outsourcing relationships and this in turn leads to outsourcers not being able to meet their own customer expectations. 'Delivery on time' in the evaluation of potential outsourcees is usually considered as an order winning factor and failure to provide this service can cause serious problems in relationships. In the manufacturing sector this can also lead to outsourcees incurring additional costs using for example more expensive, faster modes of transport in order to compensate for late delivery. In an article on the importance of time in the supply chain, it was noted that high speed transportation can be used to compensate for manufacturing delays where the penalty for failure might cost as much as £1 million an hour.[8] Because of the risk of late delivery, outsourcers sometimes insist that the supplier holds safety stock (we will discuss this in more detail in the next chapter) nearby so as to mitigate against the problems that late delivery can cause.

Consistency of quality of products or service delivered by the outsourcee is one of the problems frequently faced by outsourcers. This relates to the outsourcee delivering high quality at the start of the operation but not maintaining it over time. This leads to rejects and returns by outsourcers and additional costs for

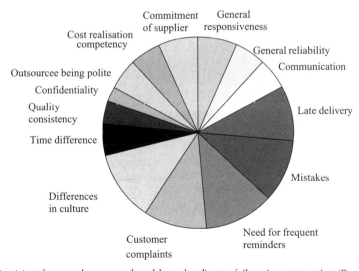

Figure 5.1   Most frequently reported problems leading to failure in outsourcing (Pandit, 2005)[9]

outsourcees. This also leads to poor customer service levels for both outsourcer and outsourcee.

General reliability problems can lead to the necessity for excessive checks by outsourcers and this could raise mistrust between outsourcer and outsourcee. Reliability on quality, delivery, cost and service are the expectations that have to be met by the outsourcee.

General responsiveness problems could mean that the outsourcee is not being flexible in making changes to specifications, outsourcees not responding to queries made by the outsourcer, and also relates to being in regular contact to adapt to the changing circumstances beyond the control of both parties.

Cost realisation relates to the outsourcee not working out the costs properly when quoting to the outsourcer at the evaluation/negotiating stage. This could lead to the outsourcee asking for a subsequent increase in the quoted price.

Confidentiality is a serious issue relating to intellectual property (IP) rights and confidential information being passed over to competitors.

One of the reported problems shown in Figure 5.1 is the outsourcee being overly polite in negotiations. This relates to the problem that could develop due to an outsourcee agreeing to everything the outsourcer asks for but then failing to deliver. This could be due to the culture of the country where saying 'no' to a request is considered rude and saying 'yes' is being polite.

In view of the issues that commonly lead to the failure of outsourcing, it is important to evaluate potential outsourcees before selection and agreement. In addition, a good outsourcer–outsourcee relationship development strategy can help to overcome a number of factors causing failure in outsourcing and we consider these later in the chapter.

EVALUATING AND SELECTING OUTSOURCEES

Once the outsourcing decision has been made, the first step is to evaluate potential outsourcees for possible agreement to outsource. As shown in Figure 5.2, the first step of the evaluation comprises ascertaining if the outsourcee meets the qualifier parameters determined for the process under consideration. These parameters will vary depending on the product or service to be outsourced.

As already noted, order qualifiers are those criteria and/or performance expectations that a company must meet for a customer to even consider it as a possible supplier. In Asia, for example, vendors in the manufacturing sector often get certification under the ISO 9000 series as in most cases it allows them to bid or be considered for an order as a potential supplier.

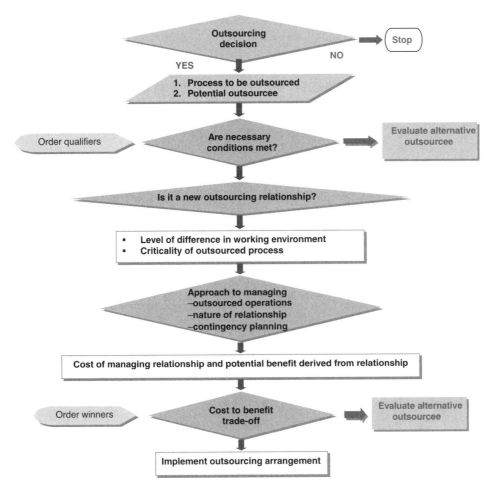

Figure 5.2   A framework for evaluating potential outsourcees[6]

Some criteria which could be included as order qualifiers include:

- Reliability of delivery on time
- Quality certifications
- Conformance to agreed specifications
- Delivery lead time
- Financial capability
- Performance track record
- Price or cost reduction
- Senior management attitude
- Responsiveness to demand uncertainty
- Record of corporate social responsibility.

The issue of **corporate social responsibility (CSR)** is growing in importance in business. CSR covers a multitude of activities and issues, and in essence concerns how 'ethical' a company's activities are. In this regard, the external image of a company is critical. In recent years many companies have become embarrassed by revelations that they outsource upstream activities to suppliers with poor labour and safety records for example. More recently, CSR issues have arisen downstream in the marketplace with concerns among consumers that some toys, largely produced by suppliers in low cost locations, might comprise harmful components. This in turn raises the issue of how closely outsourcers need to monitor outsourcees.

It is usual that some order qualifiers will be more critical than other order qualifiers in terms of the outsourcer's requirements and these are distinguished by labelling them as **order losing sensitive qualifiers**. For example it may be the case that if a supplier does not perform to a delivery reliability of at least 95%, then they would cease to be an outsourcee for that particular line of business. In this case the delivery reliability forms an order losing sensitive qualifier.

If the qualifier parameters are not met, then the outsourcer starts looking at alternative outsourcees. If the qualifier conditions are satisfied, but the outsourcer has no prior working experience with the outsourcee, then it is important to look at the level of difference between the working environments (the **environmental separation index**) of the outsourcer and outsourcee companies (or perhaps between the two countries). In addition, the outsourcer should consider how critical the outsourced product/process or service is to their core business. This will determine the management approach the outsourcer should use for supplier development, monitoring and supervision.

THE ENVIRONMENTAL SEPARATION INDEX (ESI)[5]

The environmental separation index (ESI) is used to assess the level of difference between the working environments of the outsourcer and outsourcee companies. A higher value of ESI indicates large differences in work practices, culture, and perceptions. Once the outsourcee gains experience in working closely with the outsourcer and performs as per the expectation of each other, the ESI could reduce to a lower value.

In addition to qualifying for orders, some criteria may also act as order winners for a particular outsourced process. Depending on the situation, one or more of the qualifying criteria may give an advantage on the cost benefit to become order-winning criteria for the supplier. The cost–benefit trade-off for implementing and managing an outsourcing arrangement has to be positive to constitute an order winner for the outsourcee.

We noted above that in a supplier development context, price is not the only criterion to be considered.

The outsourcer should consider the *total cost of outsourcing* and this should include, as well as the basic cost of the product or service, the cost incurred by the outsourcer to manage the outsourcing arrangement. This is the cost of monitoring the outsourcee and the cost of setting up the relationship right from initiation through to operations and to termination. This cost should also reflect the risks involved in terms of transfer of technologies and intellectual property for example. In addition to the cost of coordination, there is also the cost of contingency planning to ensure delivery on time, for example by keeping higher inventory levels in the outsourcer country, or the need at times to deliver by air at premium costs due to not being able to meet the agreed schedule when using cheaper forms of transport. Related to the total cost of outsourcing is the concept of 'landed costs', which we will discuss further in Chapter 11.

OUTSOURCER AND OUTSOURCEE RELATIONSHIP DEVELOPMENT

The relationship between the outsourcer and the outsourcee evolves over time. It is possible that the initial outsourcing arrangement could change as the outsourcer starts to have more confidence in the capability of the outsourcee. This could also mean that the level of monitoring carried out by the outsourcer with respect to the outsourcee's operations is likely to reduce. It may be that the outsourcer was involved in day-to-day operations management of the outsourced activity in the initial phases of the arrangement; however, as the relationship evolves the outsourcer would gradually reduce involvement in the outsourced activity. In fact research has shown that outsourcer–outsourcee relationships can move across four stages:[10]

- *Master–Servant Stage*: in this conventional relationship the outsourcer sets the expectations and the rules and the outsourcee delivers as per the stipulated norms. Low cost is the main driver of the outsourcing arrangement.
- *Consultative Stage*: This stage is a type of a 'consultant–client' relationship. The outsourcer consults with the outsourcee on regular basis. In addition to the cost, other factors such as quality, reliability and responsiveness are also important for sustaining the outsourcing arrangement.
- *Peer-to-Peer Relationship Stage:* This is considered to be the ideal stage where the outsourcer and the outsourcee share a peer-to-peer relationship. This stage of collaboration results in a more synergistic long-term relationship creating 'win-win' situations for both parties.
- *Competitive Stage:* In this stage the original outsourcee company takes the lead role and starts to compete with the outsourcing company in global markets.

We noted already that sometimes the relationship between both parties can involve supplier development, a topic we will return to again later in the book in Chapter 13.

LEARNING REVIEW

In this chapter we have explored, and differentiated, the areas of sourcing, purchasing, procurement, outsourcing and offshoring. We discussed the need for outsourcing and explained the most frequently reported problems leading to failure in outsourcing arrangements. We identified and differentiated order qualifying and order winning criteria in terms of what outsourcers look at when deciding who to outsource to, and we detailed the process typically followed for evaluating and selecting suppliers. Outsourcer–outsourcee relationship development is generally regarded to evolve through phases of development and we also examined these phases.

It is apparent that for outsourcing companies, a range of possibilities exists with regard to how they interact with their outsourcees. In our discussion around CSR we noted that for some outsourcing companies, the outsourcee can end up being a source of embarrassment. At the other end of the spectrum some leading companies engage in supplier development programmes with their outsource partners, leading to mutual benefit for both parties.

In order to gain further insights into procurement and outsourcing, the reader is referred to two case studies. The first is a short end-of-chapter case study on outsourcing to India of shoe production by an Italian company. The second case is the 'Managing Supply Chain Information at HBOS' case, which is at the end of Part Two of the book and which considers among other issues procurement and information sharing with suppliers.

Continuing on our journey along the supply chain from source to market, and now that we have identified how we are going to procure our inputs, the next chapter looks at what is involved in managing the inventory that we have procured. In subsequent chapters we will then look at how we warehouse and transport such inventory.

QUESTIONS

- Explain the distinction between outsourcing and offshoring.
- Using examples, describe the various stages in the purchasing process.
- What are the most frequently reported problems in outsourcing?
- Explain what factors would typically be considered in contingency planning in outsourcing arrangements.

NORTH EUROPEAN SHOE COMPANY (OUTSOURCER)– BX SHOES (OUTSOURCEE)[5]

BX Shoes is a subsidiary of one of the leading brands in India. It has a completely export oriented partnership with an Italian shoe company. The supplier selection parameters for the Italian firm as outsourcer were that the outsourcee should be financially strong – since it is a cash intensive, high working capital business. BX Shoes was a good fit to the outsourcer's requirements. There are inherent problems in procurement of leather such as long lead times, it is a very cash intensive activity and the quality can only be judged at the final product stage. Due to these risks, a supplier-partnership approach was preferred by the outsourcer to reduce the uncertainties. The entire manufacturing activity is outsourced, including the procurement of raw material, with a lot of ongoing close cooperation between the management of the outsourcer and the management of the outsourcee.

Let us look at the partnership evolution of BX Shoes with its Italian outsourcer:

- In 1997 the Italian partner was looking at extending its manufacturing operations to India and BX was looking at getting into a new business. The two companies signed a memorandum of understanding specifying broadly the roles and responsibilities of both parties. BX was looking for somebody who knew the business and the Italian partner was looking for someone who was an established group in India.

- The arrangement was not exclusive initially. The Italian outsourcer was working with multiple outsourcees in India. The arrangement started on a small scale initially. The business model essentially at the beginning was pure finished goods outsourcing. However, down the line BX decided that procurement of some key raw material would be done by them – essentially material contributing 70–80% of material costs.

- Revenues in year 2 went up by 50%, but fell by 20% in year 3. This was a period of trial. It was establishing the business but not making headway. Then in 1999–2000 an 'exclusive marriage' between the Italian partner and BX took place and growth began again.

- The partnership effectively works like a joint venture – it is a collaboration. Their involvement does not stop at the design stage. Other players feel that the collaboration is an innovative way of doing things. The normal practice is to have a model with less involvement and operate through agents. In the BX case the participation by both the partners is complete. For example, if improper material is procured both partners will work together to resolve the issue there and then. The material either needs to be sent back or repaired. The trust between BX and the Italian partner has been built up over time – at the top management level. At the trade fairs both the names, BX and the Italian partner, are displayed.

NOTES

1. Stevensson, W.J. (2007) *Operations Management*, New York, McGraw-Hill International Edition.

2. Van Weele, A.J. (2005) *Purchasing Supply Chain Management: Analysis, Strategy, Planning and Practice*, London, Thomson Learning.

3. Rates of pay in, for example, China and India, are much lower than in Europe and North America. This varies significantly both by sector and also by geographical region (in effect basic laws of supply and demand are at work with workers in more industrialised regions commanding higher pay). In 2005 we estimate that some workers were earning as little as one-tenth the comparable 'Western' salary; however, it is important to note that this gap is narrowing quite quickly.

4. *India Today*, 21 August 2006, India in Numbers, The India Today Group, New Delhi.

5. USER-MIND (2006) Understanding Potential Synergies in Manufacturing Supply Chains between Europe and India, EU Asia IT & C project, www.usermind.org (investigators: C.S. Lalwani, K.S. Pawar, J. Shah and K.-D. Thoben).

6. Lalwani, C.S., Pawar, K.S. and Shah, J. (2007) Contextualisation framework for the manufacturing supply chain, published by Centre for Concurrent Enterprise, University of Nottingham Business School, Nottingham, UK. ISBN 978-0-85358-242-7.

7. SAP INFO Solutions quoted *in Sloan Management Review*, Winter, 2006.

8. Whittle, G. (2007) Critical limits, *Logistics and Transport Focus*, 9(2), March.

9. Pandit, P. (2005) Quality of customer service in outsourcing, unpublished dissertation, Nottingham University Business School: Operations Management Division, Nottingham, UK.

10. Pawar, K.S., Gupta, A., Lalwani, C.S., Shah, J., Ghosh, D. & Eschenbacher, J. (2005) Outsourcing to India: exploring the management implications for the outsourcer and outsourcee, Proceedings of the 37th Annual Convention of OR Society of India, Ahmedabad, India, IIM.

Inventory Management

Chuda Basnet and Paul Childerhouse

University of Waikato

INTRODUCTION

In this chapter we discuss the place of inventory in logistics and supply chain management. Both theoretical and practical aspects of inventory management are considered.

Chapter 6 comprises six core sections:
- The importance of inventory management
- The economic order quantity model
- Inventory control systems
- Supply chain inventory management
- Matching inventory policy with inventory type
- Inventory reduction principles

LEARNING OBJECTIVES

- Explain the significance of inventory in logistics and SCM.
- Introduce the costs involved in inventory management.
- Introduce common inventory control systems designed to reduce costs.
- Identify inventory reduction strategies including 'just-in-time' inventory management.

THE IMPORTANCE OF INVENTORY MANAGEMENT

The central focus in this book is on flows through supply chains. One of the flows we have been discussing throughout this book is the physical flow of materials. '**Inventory**' is another name for *materials* and is any materials that a firm holds in order to satisfy customer demand (and these customers may be internal and/or external to the firm). Figure 6.1 shows inventory locations throughout a supply chain. This illustration should give a sense of the ubiquitous nature of inventory, and the various forms in which it is held. Supply chains hold raw materials in order to convert these inputs into finished products. When the raw materials are processed, but are not yet completely finished, they are called *work-in-progress*. Once the product is ready for shipment, they are *finished goods*. Notice also the *in transit* inventory in Figure 6.1. This is inventory being moved from one location to another.

Inventory costs money. Supply chain partners invest significant amounts of money in holding inventory in various forms. This is money that could be invested elsewhere, earning a return. Inventory ties up working capital and affects cash flow, sometimes even threatening the survival of a firm. Inventory also takes up space, and firms need to hire people to take care of inventory. Thus firms are always on the look-out for ways to reduce their inventory holding. However, inventory cannot be reduced to zero, because firms need to have raw materials, work-in-progress and finished goods in order for the firm to function. Without these in place, customer orders will take unduly long to fulfil. Therefore, the goal in inventory management is to *minimise* inventory holding while maintaining a desired customer service level.

Inventory turnover is a concept used to measure a firm's performance in inventory management. This measure compares the annual sales a firm achieves with the

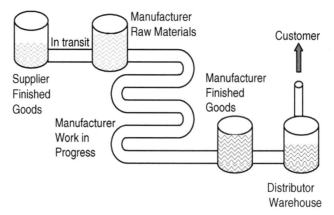

Figure 6.1   Supply chain pipeline

amount of average inventory held throughout the year: the higher the turnover, the better a firm is doing in keeping its inventory costs down.

$$\text{Inventory turnover} = \frac{\text{Cost of all goods sold in a year}}{\text{Value of average inventory held throughout the year}}$$

Most firms achieve an inventory turnover of about 10, while well-performing firms can achieve a turnover of 50 or more.

PROBLEM 6.1

The YouRace Company builds racing cars. In 2006, the total cost of cars they sold was $3 million. Their total inventory holding changed throughout the year, but the average holding was worth $250 000. At the end of 2006, they implemented just-in-time principles to improve their inventory performance. In 2007, their sales increased and the cost of cars was $4.5 million, while the average inventory holding was $300 000. Has the performance improved?

Answer
Inventory turnover in 2006 = 3 000 000 / 250 000 = 12
Inventory turnover in 2007 = 4 500 000 / 300 000 = 15

Thus the performance has improved, but only slightly.

Inventory can be viewed as a necessary evil. Without inventory one minor problem in the supply chain would result in a stoppage of the entire chain. Hence inventory is used as a buffer between processes along a supply chain. Table 6.1 expands on this point and highlights a range of reasons why this buffer is required. Despite managers' best efforts, supply chains never quite work to plan, hence buffers are required to absorb the variability in demand, supply and internal processes.

An alternative view of holding inventory is based around the central theme of trade-offs. Inventory holding costs are traded-off with other economical advantages; these are also outlined in Table 6.1. It is often more economical to produce in reasonable batch sizes to minimise the downtime resulting from production line change-overs, hence inventory is built up to cover for a number of days then stored until required. This principle can also be applied to transportation where full loads are more economical than delivering single items, hence this saving is traded-off with the additional cost of holding the extra inventory. This secondary reason for holding inventory has been challenged over the past decade as just-in-time (JIT, see below) and modern information and communication have drastically reduced batch sizes and processing costs. A well-known example of an economic trade-off is explained in depth in the following section where the cost of placing an order is balanced against the cost of holding inventory.

Table 6.1   Reasons for holding inventory

Buffer against uncertainty	Economic trade-offs
Maintain customer service levels for volatile demand	Production batch size
Hedges against price and exchange rate fluctuations	Transportation batch size
Protects against delivery lead-time variability	Transportation mode
Buffer against unreliable supply sources	Order quantity size
Buffer against seasonal demand and supply	Order frequency duration
Maintain supply of scarce supply	Bulk purchase savings
Provide cover for emergencies	Supply price fluctuations

THE ECONOMIC ORDER QUANTITY MODEL

The costs associated with inventory can be classified into two broad categories: one associated with procuring the inventory and the other associated with actually holding the inventory. The procurement costs can be broken into two parts: money spent to process a procurement order, and the money spent to actually buy the inventory. We present some symbols before considering minimisation of the total inventory costs.

Notation:

D: Annual use of a particular item, in number of items per year

S: Order-processing cost, in \$/order

P: Price per item, in \$/unit

H: Holding cost per unit per year, in \$/unit/year

Q: Number of items ordered in one purchase order, in units

T: Time periods between purchase orders in fraction of a year

SS: Safety stock, in units

L: Lead time, in fraction of a year

I: Current inventory on hand, units

TAC: Total annual cost.

Figure 6.2 is an idealised depiction of inventory levels of an item over time. The figure shows initially the inventory level of an item dropping steadily because of usage of this item. When the inventory level is at a certain level, called the '**reorder point**', a purchase order is issued for this item. After the passage of a certain length of time, called the '**lead time**', this order is filled and the inventory level increases by the amount of the order, Q. This cycle of inventory depletion and order fulfilment repeats itself. Note also that in the diagram the inventory level is kept above a certain amount, called the '**safety stock**'. Various questions arise, such as what level of safety stock should be held, what should be the reorder point, and what should the order quantity be. Let us look at the cost considerations of order quantity first.

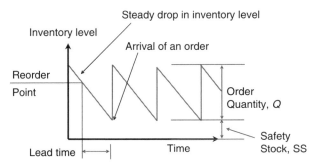

Figure 6.2   Inventory build-up and depletion

Calculating the annual costs to buy this item is straightforward, since the usage per year is D units and the price per unit is p ($).

Purchase cost $= p \times D$

Annual holding cost is the amount of money spent in renting the space to hold the inventory, in looking after it and in paying for insurance. This also includes the **opportunity cost** of investing the money currently tied up in the inventory: this is the amount of money the firm would have earned if the money was invested elsewhere other than in inventory. Calculation of the annual holding cost is based on the average inventory held. From Figure 6.2, the maximum inventory held is $SS + Q$, decreasing gradually to minimum inventory level, SS. Thus the average inventory held is:

Average inventory level $= (SS + Q + SS)/2 = SS + Q/2$

And the annual holding cost $= (SS + Q/2)\,H$

Since D is the annual usage of the item, and each time an order is placed for this item the number of items purchased per order is Q, the number of orders placed over the whole year is D/Q. The annual order processing cost includes the cost of identifying the supplier, preparing a purchase order, chasing it, and receiving the item. If S is the order processing cost per order, we can calculate the annual order processing cost:

Annual order processing cost $= (D/Q)\,S$

Adding these three costs the total annual inventory costs associated with this item are calculated below.

$$\text{Total annual cost (TAC)} = \text{Purchase} + \text{Holding} + \text{Order-processing cost}$$
$$= p \times D + (SS + Q/2)H + (D/Q)S$$

How does the order quantity Q influence the total annual cost? The effect of changing the order quantity from small to large is illustrated in Figure 6.3. With

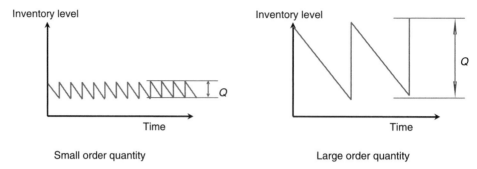

Figure 6.3   Small vs large order quantities

small order quantity, there is a large number of orders, but smaller average inventory holdings. When order quantity increases, fewer orders are placed, with consequent rise in average inventory holding.

The variation of total annual cost with order quantity is shown in Figure 6.4. To minimise the total annual cost, there is a best order quantity, known as the 'economic order quantity', as depicted in the diagram. This represents a balance between order processing costs and inventory holding costs. With lower order quantities there are too many orders, the order-processing costs are high and dominate the total costs. With higher order quantities, the average inventory holding cost is high and dominates the total costs.

The order quantity with the least total annual cost is known as the **economic order quantity (EOQ)** and is given by (see the box for an explanation as to how the EOQ is derived):

$$EOQ = \sqrt{\frac{2DS}{H}}$$

By ordering in lots of economic order quantity, the total annual cost is the lowest it can be.

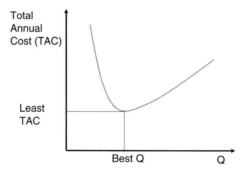

Figure 6.4   Order quantity vs total annual cost

It is straightforward to derive the EOQ formula. Differentiating the expression for TAC and setting to zero for minimisation (at a point of inflection the slope – the derivative – of the curve is zero),

$$\frac{d(TAC)}{dQ} = 0,$$

$$\Rightarrow \frac{d\left(p \times D + \left(SS + \frac{Q}{2}\right)H + \frac{D}{Q}S\right)}{dQ} = 0$$

$$\Rightarrow \frac{H}{2} - \frac{D \times S}{Q^2} = 0$$

(Assuming that the purchasing cost is constant (no bulk discounts). We also assume that the safety stock remains fixed as order quantity is changed.)

$$\Rightarrow Q = \sqrt{\frac{D \times S}{H}}$$

To confirm that this is indeed a minimal-cost order quantity (i.e. a point of inflection at the lowest point in the curve), and not the maximal-cost one (i.e. a point of inflection at the highest point in the curve), we need to check that the double derivative is positive at this quantity (it is always positive for a point of inflection at the lowest point in the curve).

Thus, differentiating again,

$$\frac{d^2(TAC)}{dQ^2} = \frac{d\left(\frac{H}{2} - \frac{D \times S}{Q^2}\right)}{dQ} = -(-2)\frac{D \times S}{Q^3} = 2\frac{D \times S}{Q^3}$$

This quantity is always positive for $Q > 0$, and confirms that the EOQ is the order quantity with the least total annual cost.

PROBLEM 6.2

The Fine Garments Company sells fashion clothing. The forecasted annual demand for their premium leather jacket is 1200. The order-processing cost per order is $25, and inventory holding cost is $50/item/year. How many leather jackets should they order in one shipment?

Answer

$$EOQ = \sqrt{\frac{2DS}{H}}$$

$$= \sqrt{\frac{2 \times 1200 \times 25}{50}}$$

$$= 34.64$$

$$\approx 35$$

Fine Garments should order 35 leather jackets each time they place an order on their supplier in order to minimise their annual inventory costs.

INVENTORY CONTROL SYSTEMS

Inventory control systems help an inventory manager decide when to order inventory and in what quantity. Inventory control systems may be set up on the basis of the economic order quantity, discussed above. There are two basic systems used in practice. These are explained below.

The reorder point inventory control system

In this system, inventory levels are continuously monitored, and orders are issued when the inventory is depleted to a predetermined level, called the *reorder point* (*ROP*), as shown in Figure 6.2. The order quantity is calculated on the basis of the EOQ formula, as given above.

The reorder point is set as follows. When an order is issued at the reorder point, it is gradually depleted to the safety stock (*SS*) level over the lead time L (see Figure 6.2). The use of inventory over the lead time L is $D \times L$, since the annual demand is D Thus the reorder point is given by

$$ROP = D \times L + SS$$

PROBLEM 6.3

The Fine Garments Company (in Problem 6.2) wants to use a reorder point system. It has the order quantity set at 35, calculated as above. To allow for uncertainties in delivery and in customer demand, it wishes to hold four weeks of demand as safety stock. What should its reorder point be if the delivery lead time is two weeks?

Answer
Safety stock to cover four weeks of demand = 1200 × (4/52) = 92, since 1200 is the annual demand.

$ROP = D \times L + SS = 1200 \times (2/52) + 92 = 138$

Fine Garments should reorder whenever its inventory drops below 138.

The periodic inventory control system

In this system, orders are reviewed periodically (not continuously as in the reorder point system), after the passage of a fixed time period (T) (see Figure 6.5). At each review time, the current inventory level (I) is determined, and enough inventory is ordered to bring the inventory level to a target maximum level (M).

Often firms may decide on a weekly or a fortnightly ordering cycle, but in the absence of such a policy, the time period T may be calculated on the basis of the *EOQ*. If orders are made in quantities of *EOQ*, each order will cover a period of *EOQ* / *D*. This time period may be used as the fixed time period.

$$T = EOQ / D$$

In Figure 6.5, current inventory level at the time of review is I; the inventory ordered now will arrive after lead time L, and the next order after that will arrive after a further lapse of the review period T. There is no inventory arrival for an elapsed period of $T + L$; thus the order at the time of review needs to cover inventory demand over the lead time (L) and over the next time period (T). The inventory should also allow for the safety stock *SS*. Thus the target maximum level is given by the following expression.

$$M = D (L + T) + SS$$

However, some of this requirement will be met by the current inventory level (I). Thus the order quantity is given by:

$$Q = M - I$$

In the above formula for M, demand D is annual demand, so L and T should also be measured in time units of years.

The reorder point system allows closer control of inventory than the periodic system, the latter only reviewing inventory at specific periodic intervals. The reorder point

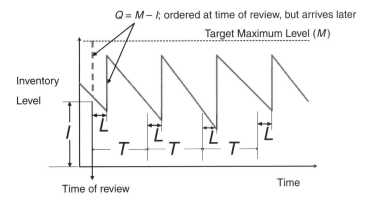

Figure 6.5 Periodic system

system is thus preferred for high-value inventory items in particular. The periodic system may be used for other inventory items because of its convenience.

PROBLEM 6.4

Design a periodic inventory control system for The Fine Garments Company (Problems 6.2 and 6.3) if it wishes to hold five weeks of demand as safety stock. If on a day of review, the inventory of the premium leather jacket is 102, how many leather jackets should be ordered?

Answer

Fixed time period, T is given by

$T = EOQ / D = 35 / 1200 = 0.029167$ year $= 0.029167 \times 365$ days $= 11$ days

The target maximum level, $M = D (L + T) + SS$

$= 1200 \times (2/52 + 11/ 365) + 1200 \times (5/52)$

$= 198$

A periodic review system for The Fine Garments Company should have a review period of 11 days, ordering enough inventor at the time of review to bring inventory to a maximum level of 198 leather jackets.

The order quantity for the given inventory level is $Q = M - I = 198 - 102 = 96$. Ninety six leather jackets should be ordered if there are 102 on hand.

Safety stock

In the discussion above, the inventory control systems allow for a safety stock, SS. This is the amount of inventory stocked by the system to allow for unforeseen events. There are many events that could occur and disrupt the careful inventory planning. For example, consider late deliveries. Without safety stock, if the delivery takes longer than the average lead time L, some inventory demand may not be met, possibly causing serious disruptions. Consider again what happens if the inventory use is higher than that forecast. Without safety stock, customer service will suffer. Other reasons for maintaining safety stock include providing a safeguard against issues such as poor quality, production problems, and transportation problems. Safety stock is thus sometimes referred to as **buffer stock**.

The root reason for safety stock could be described as variation – variation of demand, variation of lead time, variation of production, etc. If there was no variation, firms would not need safety stock. Safety stock needs to be held in proportion to such variations.

Safety stock is not free. Note in the discussion above that the cost of holding safety stock is included in the total annual cost. This part of the cost is: $SS * H$.

SUPPLY CHAIN INVENTORY MANAGEMENT

Figure 6.1 showed inventory locations across a supply chain. In a nonintegrated supply chain, inventory managers in each firm along the supply chain manage their own inventory. Each location will hold its own safety stock. Consider first the inventory of the finished product from manufacturer down to the retailer (the distribution side of the supply chain).

Inventory centralisation

Manufacturers, distributors, and retailers have all their own demand variations to consider. This means holding safety stock, in proportion to the variations, at each location. What if all the inventory could be centralised, say at the manufacturer's location? The manufacturer will need to consider the total demand, but the variation of the total demand will be less than the total variation of the demand considered separately. Thus less safety stock will be needed.

The first three graphs in Figure 6.6 show demand fluctuations at three distribution centres (DCs). Safety stock is maintained in each DC, in proportion to the amount of variation of demand. The bottom graph in Figure 6.6 presents an alternative scenario, where all the demand is supplied from one central location. The demand at the central location is a combination of the demand at the three DCs, however the variation of the total demand is less than the sum of variations at the three DCs. Hence, the safety stock needed is less than the safety stock needed for multiple locations.

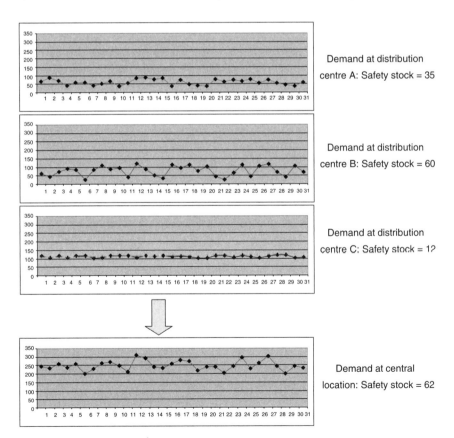

Figure 6.6 Inventory centralisation

With integrated supply chains, the central location could be anywhere, inventory may even be distributed at different centres (and still inventory would be saved), so long as all locations have access to inventory information and the transfers between locations can be quick. This concept is called *replacing inventory by information*.

The concept of inventory reduction by centralisation is sometimes stated as the **square root rule**; this is an approximation and states that inventory buffer needed is proportional to the square root of the number of locations. Thus, in the above instance, the inventory buffer at the central location would be in the ratio $\left(\sqrt{1} : \sqrt{3} = 0.58\right)$ of the combined buffer at the three locations, a saving of *approximately* 42%.

Delayed product differentiation

(This inventory reduction strategy makes use of the principle of postponement discussed in Chapter 3, p. 42.) Another instance of reducing variation by combining demand at different points is the case of a manufacturer making multiple products. The manufacturer will need to manage inventories of each of these products, with safety stocks for each product. Now consider that each of these products has a precursor: some intermediate product from which all the (different) final products are made. If the processing steps from the intermediate product to the final products are not that significant, the manufacturer could stock the intermediate product in place of the final product, thus combining the safety stock required and gaining a similar advantage as above. This gives the manufacturer the flexibility of meeting the demand for the final products, using the intermediate product, as the demand occurs. Many manufacturers are redesigning their products so that earlier stages of the products are the same across their product portfolio, and differentiating the product into distinct products as late as possible in the production process. This delayed product differentiation has the potential to not only save on inventory holding, but also gives greater flexibility and simplicity to manufacturing.

Part commonality

The concept of part commonality is similar to that of delayed product differentiation discussed above. Delayed product differentiation would use the same parts and processes in all earlier stages of manufacture, differentiating products as late as possible. However, the concept of part commonality attempts simply to reduce the number of different parts wherever possible. Figure 6.7 shows product A as built up from components B and C, while product X as made from components Y and Z. If components B and Y are quite similar, and the designers could substitute both B and Y by a third component D, then the manufacturer needs to hold a combined inventory of D in place of separate inventories for B and Y. This is often possible to do in manufacturing since engineered products often use similar components, such as simple nuts and bolts, or even complex components such as fuel injectors.

Transit inventory

When inventory moves across a supply chain, it is in transit. Regardless of whether the upstream or the downstream stage of the supply chain owns this inventory,

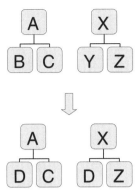

Figure 6.7 Using common parts across products

holding costs are incurred and this cost is a cost to the supply chain. What is the magnitude of this cost? Using the same symbols as above, Q is the order quantity or the quantity that is transferred in one consignment, and L is the delivery lead time or the duration when the order is in transit, and H is the inventory holding cost per item per year.

Holding cost for one order $= Q \times L \times H$, since it is held only for period L

Number of orders in a year $= D / Q$

Annual transit inventory cost $= Q \times L \times H \times (D / Q) = D \times L \times H$

The above relationship clearly demonstrates a reason to reduce lead time wherever possible, since it directly affects cost. Often in making transport mode choice decisions, a cheaper mode of transport may be chosen to lower the cost of transportation, but the cheaper mode is slower, resulting in higher transit time and thus higher transit inventory costs. Transit inventory exists in each part of the supply chain pipeline where inventory is in transit, such as from the supplier to the manufacturer and from the manufacturer to the distributor, as shown in Figure 6.1.

IN-TRANSIT INVENTORY

A key strategy of most organisations is to reduce the amount of inventory that they hold. In many instances warehouses are eliminated altogether. One consequence of this is that sometimes companies use transport as a 'mobile warehouse'. The mode of transport that they use may depend on how fast they want to get product to market. One industry professional describes this as the 'gearbox' approach to inventory management: speeding up and slowing down the flow of inventory through the supply chain by using alternative transport modes. In-transit inventory is thus an important category of inventory, and one which can sometimes account for large volumes of inventory.

PROBLEM 6.5

The Fine Garments Company (Problems 6.2, 6.3 and 6.4) has opted for the reorder point system, and it has two options for transportation: by truck and by rail. Truck transportation takes one week, while rail transportation takes two weeks of lead time. Truck transportation costs $2 per leather jacket, while by rail the transportation cost is $1 per leather jacket. It is the policy of Fine Garments to hold enough inventory to cover demand for twice the lead time. Which transportation option costs less? What is the reorder point for each option?

Answer

This decision is impacted only by the safety stock needed, transportation cost, and the transit inventory cost, all other costs remaining equal.

Truck option:

Safety stock = SS = 1200 × (2 × 1 / 52) = 46 leather jackets

Annual cost of holding the safety stock = $SS \times H$ = 46 × 50 = $2300.00

Annual cost of transportation = 1200 × 2 = $2400.00 (all the annual demand is transported)

Annual transit inventory cost = $D \times L \times H$ = 1200 × (1/52) × 50 = $1153.84

Total of the above costs = $5853.84

The reorder point, $ROP = D \times L + SS$ = 1200 × (1/52) + 46 = 69

Rail option:

Safety stock = SS = 1200 × (2 × 2 / 52) = 92 leather jackets

Annual cost of holding the safety stock = $SS \times H$ = 92 × 50 = $4600.00

Annual cost of transportation = 1200 × 1 = $1200.00

Annual transit inventory cost = $D \times L \times H$ = 1200 × (2/52) × 50 = $2307.69

Total of the above costs = $8107.69

The reorder point, $ROP = D \times L + SS$ = 1200 × (2/52) + 92 = 138

The truck option is cheaper by quite a margin, even though its transportation cost alone is double that of the rail transportation.

Note that in this problem we only considered costs associated with inventory and transport, all other costs remaining equal. Introducing other costs (for example, cost implications of the reliability and security of alternative transport modes) leads us into the concept of generalised costs of transport considered in Chapter 4.

MATCHING INVENTORY POLICY WITH INVENTORY TYPE

ABC analysis

Most firms have far too many inventory items (i.e. stock-keeping units or SKUs) to manage. They often use a tool called ABC analysis to separate out the most important items so that more attention can be focused on those items (this is derived from the 'Pareto' or '80/20' rule first elaborated by the Italian economist Vilfredo Pareto in 1897). ABC analysis is based on the principle that out of the myriad items an inventory manager needs to handle, there are only a few that account for most of the inventory expenses. To carry out this analysis, the expenses incurred annually for each individual item are collected and the items are listed in order from the highest expense to the lowest expense. An example is presented in Table 6.2.

Table 6.2   Expenditure on inventory items

Item#	Annual Expenses	Percentage of Total	Classification
373	46 335	45.77%	A
539	19 611	19.37%	A
455	8 007	7.91%	B
769	6 181	6.11%	B
441	5 526	5.46%	B
65	5 503	5.44%	B
205	3 278	3.24%	C
401	3 063	3.03%	C
352	2 845	2.81%	C
543	603	0.60%	C
454	179	0.18%	C
432	111	0.11%	C
Totals	101 242	100.00%	

This is only an illustrative example. An actual table is likely to have thousands of items in practice. It can be seen that the top two items (373 and 539) account for approximately 65% of the expense. So from an inventory management perspective it is sensible to lavish more attention on these items. The items in the table may thus be divided into three classes (see Figure 6.8): the count of items in the 'A' class constituting only 20% of the count, but accounting for 65% of the expense, 'B' class has the next 30% of the count, and 'C' class includes the rest of the items. There is no suggestion that these percentage figures must be exactly followed – the idea is to use a classification scheme so that a few important items are given more attention than the more numerous but less important items.

ABC analysis is a focusing tool, permitting attention to be focused on the most important inventory items. For instance, different inventory control

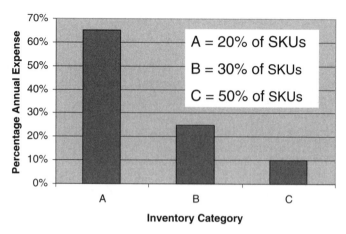

Figure 6.8   ABC classification

systems may be used for the different classifications: 'A' items may be controlled closely, using the reorder point system, the less demanding periodic system may be used for 'B' items, and 'C' items may be blanket purchased once or twice in a year.

The ABC analysis illustrated above uses the criterion of item expense, the amount of money spent on an item (or SKUs) per year; but an ABC analysis can be done with a different criterion as the need dictates. Thus a retailer may use the criterion of total sales per year. Other criteria used for ABC analysis include frequency of order picking (examining which items are picked more often than others) and frequency of customer complaints received on product items.

Inventory flow types

Gattorna and Walters[1] argue that inventory can be categorised into three flow types as illustrated in Figure 6.9. The core business products are stable and constitute the base flow inventory. The wave flow inventory is more unstable and is typified by seasonal or fashion type products. The fad products have extremely variable demand and therefore the inventory is very spiky as illustrated in the diagram (surge flow inventory).

The management approach for each of these inventory types needs to be tailored to the product and market characteristics. Gattorna and Walters go on to explain the most appropriate match between inventory policy and flow type as summarised in Table 6.3. Given the stability of the base flow, minimal inventory is required to maintain high service levels. Conversely, the wave flow inventory is perishable and slower moving, therefore a more responsive approach is suggested

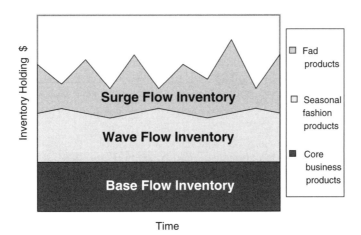

Figure 6.9   Inventory flow types (Gattorna & Walters, 1996)

where inventory is built during times of high demand. The surge flow has been further divided into two subcategories in Table 6.3. Type 1 has long replenishment lead times and is highly critical (e.g. maintenance parts), hence high inventory levels are required to make sure there are minimal stock-outs. The type 2 surge flow inventory is not so critical but costs more to purchase and hold. As a result it is better to minimise inventory levels and ideally to persuade suppliers to deliver directly when required.

Table 6.3   Stockholding policies for alternative inventory flow types (Gattorna & Walters, 1996)

Type	Characteristics	Stockholding policy
Base flow	Predictable high flow rates	Minimum stocks. Direct deliveries from suppliers
Wave flow	Slow moving flow rates. High criticality. Perishable. Peaks are relatively predictable	Minimise stockholding, building them during peak demand period. Direct delivery from supplier where possible
Surge flow (1)	High criticality. Low value. Long lead time. Small physical size	Hold high level of stock thereby allowing safety stock delivery lead time and demand fluctuations
Surge flow (2)	Low criticality. High value. Bulky physical characteristics. Peaks are relatively predictable	Minimise stockholding, building them only during peak demand period. Direct delivery from supplier where possible

INVENTORY REDUCTION PRINCIPLES

It has been mentioned before that reduction of inventory holding is a primary goal in SCM. This reduction, however, needs to be consistent with the strategic goals of customer service. Drawing from the above discussions, the following principles are outlined for inventory reduction:

Pool inventory

Wherever demand for inventory can be combined, the safety stock can be lowered, still providing the same service level. This is the case in inventory centralisation where demand from different locations is combined, or in delayed product differentiation where demand for different products is combined, or by using common components where demands for different components are combined. Inventory pooling has the added bonus of reduced inventory management.

Reduce variation

Recall that the reason for holding safety stock is variation. Variation of lead time, variation of demand, variation of supply, variation of quality, all contribute to safety stock. Wherever variation can be reduced, safety stock can be reduced too. Ironing out the wrinkles in a supply chain so that it delivers reliably the right quantity at the right time will cause safety-stock holding to be reduced. A similar effect can be had if quality is improved. With variable quality, more inventory is needed in case the inventory turns out to be defective.

Reduce lead time

Lead time directly affects inventory held. For example, the reorder point formula shows that the ROP can be reduced if the lead time can be reduced. Likewise transit inventory costs can be reduced by reducing the lead time. Consider the accuracy of the forecast of demand. It is well known that the further into the future we forecast, the less accurate our forecast is. When the lead time is long, we need to forecast more into the future, thus the accuracy of the forecast suffers, increasing the variability of demand and consequently requiring higher safety stock.

Just-in-time inventory system

Just-in-time inventory system (JIT) is as much a philosophy as it is a technique;[2] popularised by the automobile industry and largely credited with propelling Toyota[3] to the top of the automotive industry in the world. JIT has many components and principles, but at the core of JIT is the idea of making do with the minimum possible level of inventory holding. The core concepts of inventory reduction in JIT are:

- *Inventory hides problems.* Inventory holding is needed because of variation of all kinds, as pointed out above. Equipment failures, production of bad quality, etc., all of these problems cause variations in manufacturing, and inventory is needed to cover (i.e. to *hide*!) them. JIT tackles these problems directly and goes to the root of why inventory needs to be held; by purposely removing inventory holdings, the problems the inventory was covering are surfaced, and the problems are then proactively fixed.

- *Small lot production.* The advantage of ordering in small quantities, which in turn keeps the average inventory level small, was seen above. What is the difficulty in achieving this? The difficulty is that there are too many orders, with associated order processing costs. JIT seeks to reduce order processing costs so that the ideal of small quantity ordering can be accomplished. For example, suppliers are located close by and the ordering protocol is simplified. In manufacturing, order processing involves setting up or reconfiguring manufacturing tools and machines. As each order arrives the machines have to be set up (or changed over) for the order. The time and effort spent in setups are the manufacturing equivalent of order processing costs. Thus manufacturing in small quantities is hindered by an excessive number of setups and the time spent in setups. JIT seeks to facilitate small lot production by actively improving the setup process so that the time and effort involved in setups are reduced drastically.

LEARNING REVIEW

In this chapter we discussed the important topic of inventory management in the supply chain. Inventory is one of the most important flows in the supply chain, and how it is managed can significantly impact on firm success. It was noted that inventory can be found at multiple points in the supply chain, and that by measuring inventory turnover one can ascertain a measure of how effectively an organisation manages its inventory. In many instances inventory is used to buffer against uncertainty, and furthermore it can hide problems. Later in the chapter we reviewed the just-in-time inventory management approach, one of the objectives of which is to minimise inventory holding, thus highlighting any problems which need to be solved.

Trade-offs are often a feature of logistics systems, especially in the case of inventory management. We looked in detail at the EOQ model, which seeks to balance two important sets of costs associated with inventory: the costs associated with ordering and receiving freight, and the costs associated with actually holding the freight. Organisations also need to know when to reorder, and we looked at the two principal approaches in this regard: reordering when inventory drops to a certain level and reordering at fixed time intervals. We also looked at strategies to manage and reduce where possible inventory volumes in the supply chain such as centralisation, delayed product differentiation, part commonality, and reduction of in-transit inventory.

Matching inventory policy with inventory type is another key concern of inventory management, and we looked at two principal approaches here, namely ABC analysis and analysis of inventory flow types. The chapter concluded by identifying four key principles that organisations can pursue to effectively manage and reduce inventory holding: pooling, reduction of variation, reduction of lead time, and following JIT principles. No matter how essential inventory is, costs are accrued by inventory holding, and supply chains and firms need to reduce such costs while keeping customer service at a satisfactory level.

QUESTIONS

- Explain how a reduction in lead time can help a supply chain reduce its inventory buffer without hurting customer service.
- Why is Amazon.com able to provide a large variety of books and music with less safety inventory than a similar bookstore chain selling through retail stores?
- Discuss the concept of replacing inventory by information.
- Why should a customer be concerned about transit inventory cost, if they pay for the inventory only when the merchandise arrives in their premises?

PROBLEM

Daily demand for a product is 100 units. Design a reorder point inventory system for this product if the cost of holding the inventory is $2 per item per year, and the setup costs to manufacture this product are estimated to be $20 per setup. The replenishment lead time averages six days. It is desired to hold a safety stock covering twice the lead time.

Answer

$D = 100 \times 365$ (per year)
$L = 6 / 365$ (year)
$H = 2\$/item/year$
$S = 20\$/setup$

$$EOQ = \sqrt{\frac{2DS}{H}}$$

$$= \sqrt{\frac{2 \times 100 \times 365 \times 20}{2}}$$

$$= 854.04$$

$$\approx 854$$

$SS = (100 \times 365) \times (6 / 365) \times 2 = 1200$
$ROP = D \times L + SS = (100 \times 365) \times (6 / 365) + 1200$
$\quad = 1800$

The reorder point system should have 1800 as the reorder point, and 854 units as order quantity.

Problem

The annual demand for a product in a periodic inventory system is 50 000 units; the replenishment lead time is nine days. The review period has been established as 16 days. The inventory manager wants to hold enough safety stock to cover 15 days of demand. During a particular review, the on-hand inventory was 1 000 units. How many units should be ordered?

Answer

$D = 50\ 000$
$L = 9 / 365$
$T = 16 / 365$
$I = 1\ 000$
$SS = 50\ 000 \times (15 / 365) = 2\ 054.79 \approx 2\ 055$. This is 15 days' worth of demand.
$M = D(L+T) + SS$

$\quad = 50\ 000 \times (9 / 365 + 16 / 365) + 2055$

$\quad = 5479.66 \approx 5480$

$Q = M - I = 5480 - 1000 = 4480$

The inventory manager should order 4480 units now.

NOTES

1. Gattorna, J.L. & Walters, D.W. (1996) *Managing the Supply Chain*, Chapter 8, London, Macmillan Press.
2. Christopher, M. (2005) *Logistics and Supply Chain Management* (3rd edn), London, FT Prentice Hall.
3. Petersen, P.B. (2002) The misplaced origin of just-in-time production methods, *Management Decision*, 40(1/2), 82–88.

FURTHER READING

Fisher, M.L., Raman, A. & McClelland, A.S. (2000) Rocket science retailing is almost here: are you ready? *Harvard Business Review*, 78(4), 115–124.

Lee, H.L. & Billington, C. (1992) Managing supply chain inventory: pitfalls and opportunities, *Sloan Management Review*, 33(3), 65–73.

Suzuki, Y. (2004) Structure of the Japanese production system: elusiveness and reality, *Asian Business & Management*, 3, 201–219.

Water, D. (2003) *Logistics – An Introduction to Supply Chain Management*, Chapter 10, New York, Palgrave Macmillan.

Warehousing and Materials Management

INTRODUCTION

Chapter 6 introduced the theory and practice of inventory management. This chapter now focuses on the logistics operations that store those inventories. As well as needing to know how much inventory we have in our global supply chains, we also need to know how and where to store it. In this chapter, we will also discuss the processes, technologies and people employed in warehousing and materials management.

Chapter 7 comprises seven core sections:
- Warehousing in global supply chains
- Warehouse layout and design
- Capacity management
- The 'bullwhip effect'
- Materials planning and control
- Warehouse management systems and automation
- Work organisation and job design

LEARNING OBJECTIVES

- Define the role of warehousing in contemporary global supply chains.
- Explain materials handling processes within warehouses and distribution centres.
- Explain how materials movements are planned and controlled, including computer-based information and automated materials handling functions.
- Offer insights into how warehouses are managed and how work is organised.

WAREHOUSING IN GLOBAL SUPPLY CHAINS

Global supply chains commonly require multiple echelons, spread across various international locations (Figure 7.1). As well as extended in-transit inventory travelling between disparate locations, supply chains also have inventory stored at multiple stages in various states of manufacture or assembly. Hence warehousing and materials management systems have become highly sophisticated to maintain the flow of products to the end customer. At each echelon, different types of warehouse perform different functions.

As discussed in Chapter 6, inventory holding is a cost we would rather not have. A supply chain not only incurs the cost of the inventory itself, but also the fixed asset costs of warehouses and plant such as racks and forklifts, and the associated costs of labour and administration. Hence, the conventional view of warehousing is of it being a costly necessity of an inefficient supply chain. While it is true that we must seek to minimise inventory holding and handling, the paradox is that contemporary supply chains require more inventory staging posts than ever before. Material storage and handling systems therefore have two key objectives: to minimise cost and to add value. That is to say that if warehouses and distribution centres are essential to global supply chains, they should complement other supply chain activities to ensure effective and efficient delivery of products to the end customer.

Value-adding activities are those supply chain activities that enhance products to increase the customer's perceptions of those products' benefits.[1] Customer value can be added to a product by improving its quality (e.g. whiskey, wine, cheese, or cured meats); by improving the service associated with it (e.g. delivery information availability or specialist packaging); by reducing its costs (e.g. reduced packaging or reduced administration costs); and/or by reducing its lead time (e.g. cross docking – this will be explained later). Warehousing operations can achieve each of these objectives in various ways, such as:

- Creating bulk consignments
- Breaking bulk consignments
- Combining components
- Smoothing supply to meet demand.

These material related value-adding activities are illustrated in Figure 7.2. Furthermore, warehousing plays an increasingly important role in manufacturing and logistics postponement (as discussed in Chapter 3, p. 42). With the recognised benefits of postponing final assembly, combining of components and/or packaging, downstream distribution centres today offer much more than just storage and handling. Hence, some such facilities include assembly and packaging processes to ensure that order fulfilment can occur as close to the end customer as possible, postponing stock handling until the order is confirmed.

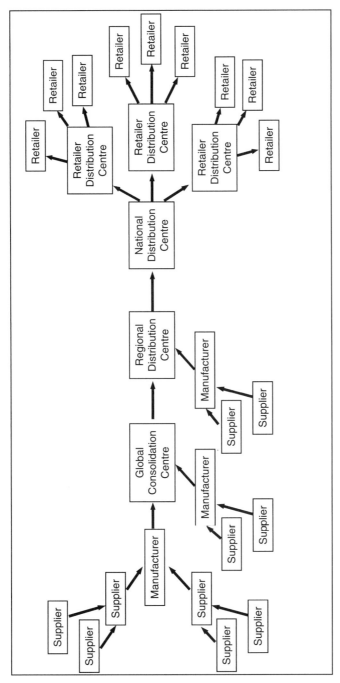

Figure 7.1   A typical map of warehousing operations in a global supply chain

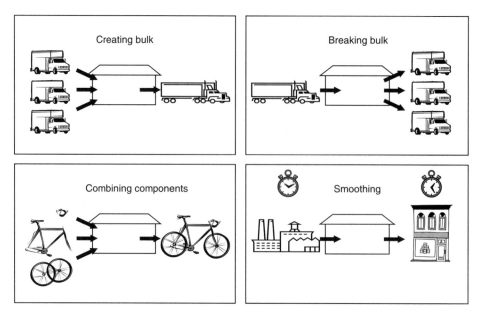

Figure 7.2   Using warehouses to add value (after Jessop & Morrison, 1994)[2]

> Warehouses should aim to provide value-adding services as well as minimising operating costs.

Increasingly, global supply chains are as concerned with information flows as they are with material flows. Hence, information related value-adding activities such as product tracking and cycle counting are also essential warehousing functions that improve supply chain performance.

This chapter will continue by explaining how modern warehouse operations are designed to not only maintain the flow of freight, but also enhance its perceived value.

WAREHOUSE LAYOUT AND DESIGN

All activities within a warehouse can be associated with one of the four functions illustrated in Figure 7.3.

Warehouse layouts should be primarily designed to optimise the flow of materials through these four functions. However, warehouse designers should also aim to achieve optimal output, reduced costs, excellent customer service and sound working conditions.[3] At the inbound receiving area, core activities include unloading, unpacking, quality control inspection and recording the receipt of materials. From here materials will follow one of two possible routes, either to 'put away' or directly to dispatch. This second option is referred to as 'cross docking',

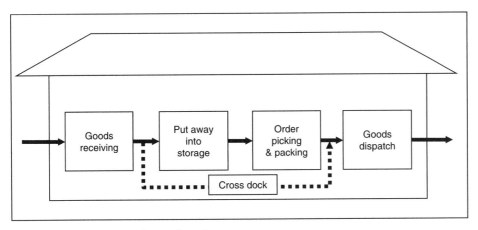

Figure 7.3   Generic warehouse functions

which is discussed below. At 'put away', freight is moved to and stored at a predetermined location, either manually or via automated materials handling systems (also discussed later).

Another auxiliary function associated with put away is replenishment. In some warehouses there will be a series of line-side storage locations to pick from. These locations are replenished as required from a central storage location. When orders are received, a 'pick list' is created and items are 'picked' from storage and 'packed' ready for 'dispatch'. During these two processes freight will be either broken down from a bulk consignment, grouped into a bulk consignment, combined with other freight, or simply held until required; thereby meeting one of the four objectives in Figure 7.2. At dispatch, the materials and associated information are inspected against the original order and moved to the shipping area.

No matter what the scale is of a warehouse or its role in the supply chain, the four core functions in Figure 7.3 will be necessary. This may involve a number of processes. These processes must be designed to suit the materials being handled and stored, and to minimise movements and handling. This can be achieved by minimising the distance materials travel through the warehouse and/or through automated handling systems such as cranes, conveyors, forklift trucks or **AGVs (automated guided vehicles)**. In doing so, processes are standardised to reduce human error and therefore maintain the quality of the product. Figure 7.4 illustrates three common warehouse layouts designed to reduce movement and handling.

Cross docking bypasses the storage areas in warehouses and distribution centres. Storage should be avoided unless materials require one of the four value-adding activities in Figure 7.2, otherwise storage is costly and nonvalue adding. Cross docking reduces cost and improves customer service by accelerating the processing of materials requiring reshipment. In bypassing put away, storage, picking and packing, the associated costs and nonvalue-adding functions are eliminated to enhance customer service. Cross docking is typically employed for fast-moving products with constant demand that spends less than 24 hours on-site.[4] This function is therefore a key enabler of lean logistics as it will maintain the flow of freight and reduce lead time.

Note that boxes in Figure 7.4 labelled A, B or C refer to the classifications discussed in Chapter 6, p. 102, where materials classified A are frequently ordered, B less so, and C rarely ordered.

Besides the primary focus on freight flowing downstream in the supply chain, contemporary logistics operations must also manage the upstream movement of freight in the form of defects and customer returns. The impact on warehousing is the requirement for additional processes to inspect, redirect and/or re-store such freight. Furthermore, concerns about environmental impact are driving legislation such as the European Union's Waste Electrical and Electronic Equipment (WEEE) Directive to require producers to reduce, reuse and recycle. Such developments lead to increased interest in reverse logistics. Clearly, in global supply networks, warehouses and distribution centres play an important role in managing the upstream movement of products that have reached the end of their usable life. While distribution centres located downstream will store or redirect end-of-life products, upstream warehouses may employ processes to disassemble products, and reuse or recycle their components.

CAPACITY MANAGEMENT

In designing a warehouse or distribution centre, we must first have knowledge of demand for the materials it will handle. We should then aim to match supply to demand, so as to design an operation that neither greatly exceeds nor fails to meet demand. Consequently, costs will be minimised. Nevertheless, there is an exception to this rule, discussed later.

Supply consists of inventory and the capacity to handle that inventory. While Chapter 6 offers an appreciation of how to determine required inventory levels, this section explains how to calculate capacity requirements. This is the purpose of capacity management. However, before we discuss capacity, let us first discuss the nature of demand.

To match capacity with demand, we require accurate knowledge of demand. Conventionally, demand knowledge is gained from forecasts, but increasingly real-time demand knowledge is acquired via electronic transmission of point-of-sale data. Real-time data transmission is explained in Chapter 9, but the important consideration here is that forecasts are based on historical information such as sales trends and not actual demand. In markets where demand patterns are constant from year to year or month to month, forecasts will be useful. However, where demand is difficult to predict, historical data is less relevant.

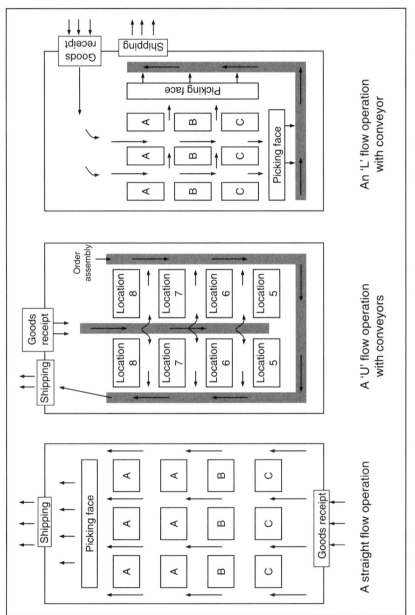

Figure 7.4   Three warehouse layout examples. From Warman, J. (1971) *Warehouse Management*, London, Heinemann, p.57.

A G BARR

Based in Cumbernauld, Scotland, A G Barr is a market-leading soft drinks producer and distributor. In Scotland, A G Barr's *Irn Bru* drinks outsell both *Coca Cola* and *Pepsi*. To some extent, this can be attributed to Barr's traditional distribution network in which delivery drivers 'hawk' their wares to small retailers along well-established routes. This traditional approach to sales offers the flexibility required by small retailers, due to unpredictable demand fluctuations. For example, an unseasonably hot day in March may cause an unexpected stockout of a particular soft drink at the retailer. Drivers build up extensive knowledge of their customers and stock their trucks accordingly. However, this unpredictability does cause drivers to return to the distribution centre with approximately 26% of the products they went out with each day. Meanwhile, A G Barr also services larger customers including wholesalers and major supermarkets. A G Barr has therefore designed its distribution centre to manage the large volume orders from large retailers, high variety orders from small retailers, and returned products.

The Cumbernauld distribution centre holds 350 product lines, of which there are 6 500 stock keeping units (SKUs). Inventory is transported from the adjacent production plant on pallets via automated conveyors direct to an 11-storey automated high bay storage system coordinated by a warehouse management system (WMS). A total of 32 million cases of soft drinks are shipped per year. Orders are input into the WMS and SKUs are automatically picked from the storage system and conveyed to truck loading bays. While some retailers require palletised products, others prefer wheeled totes. Totes enable retailers to wheel large batches of products direct to the aisles in their stores. However, this creates an additional task at the distribution centre, where batches are removed from pallets, onto totes and repackaged before being loaded onto trucks. Meanwhile, products returned after a day's trading must be restocked. These items do not return to the automated storage system. Instead they are manually sorted and stored on conventional racks ready for manual repicking at a later date. Soft drinks have a shelf life, this therefore creates a further complication in terms of stock rotation.

Hence, A G Barr not only benefits from the effectiveness and efficiency of automated handling of its high volume products, but also gains from the flexibility offered by its more conventional storage and handling methods. An important consideration in warehouse and distribution centre design is to be *fit for purpose*. The high-tech solutions are not always the most suitable solutions.

Demand fluctuations can be classified based on their behaviour. Seasonality is a demand fluctuation that many supply chains have to cope with. This is a pattern of demand that is determined by the time of year. For example, ice-cream sales peak during the summer months but are much lower at other times of year. Seasonality can also be a characteristic of supply. This is most common in the supply of fresh seasonal fruit and vegetables. On a more regular basis, retailers encounter weekly or daily demand fluctuations. High street electronic retailers will have more customers at weekends than during the week, while newsagents will typically sell more newspapers in the morning than in the afternoon.

The causes of demand fluctuations are many and varied. The ice cream example is influenced by climate, while the retailer examples are a combination of behavioural, social and financial influences. Increasingly, supply chains are learning to manage demand fluctuations by changing the pattern of supply or via sophisticated marketing campaigns. In today's supermarkets a wide array of fruit and vegetables is available, not all of which will be 'in season' in the country where they are being sold. For example, summer fruits such as strawberries can be bought in winter. This is due either to temperature control technologies being employed, or sourcing from different countries. Elsewhere in the supermarket, marketing is employed to sell particular products, examples of this include 'three for the price of two' offers and offers on a particular product when we buy another. Such efforts to influence consumer behaviour extend beyond the retailer's shelves to our television screens and via our loyalty cards.

Despite so many influences on customer demand, supply chains must gain a measure of aggregate demand in order to determine their operational capacity. Capacity is defined as the maximum level of value-adding activity over a period of time.[5] To clarify, capacity is the rate of doing work, not the quantity of work done.[6] Capacity measurement is also complex. Measures of capacity must also take account of fluctuations in supply, product variety and volume.

In any process in a warehouse, distribution centre or other supply chain operation, we can measure performance in terms of capacity. A measure of **capacity utilisation at a process** enables us to determine performance based on the maximum capacity that process was designed for. Capacity utilisation can be calculated as:

$$\text{Capacity utilisation} = \frac{\text{actual output}}{\text{design capacity}}$$

It is rare that a particular process will run at full (i.e. design) capacity, hence this is an important measure that can inform process improvement and cost reduction. For example, a 56% utilisation of a packing process should lead to investigation of the reason why this is the case, and subsequent improvement. Causes in this case may include processing delays or errors, which are unplanned or avoidable. However, it should be expected that processing time will be lost to unavoidable occurrences such as process setup, changeover and planned maintenance. Consequently, it is also important to allow for such losses. This is achieved by calculating the **effective capacity** of a process. Using this measure in the place of design capacity will produce a measure of **capacity efficiency**:

$$\text{Capacity efficiency} = \frac{\text{actual output}}{\text{effective capacity}}$$

A worked example is provided.

CAPACITY MEASUREMENT EXAMPLE

An automated packing machine designed to fold and seal the tops of cardboard boxes is employed at the end of a picking line, before the boxes are transferred to the dispatch area in a national distribution centre. The packing machine can fold and seal a variety of box sizes, one at a time at an average time of 6 seconds per box (i.e. 10 boxes per minute, or 600 boxes an hour). The distribution centre operates 24 hours a day, seven days a week (i.e. 168 hours per week). Hence, the design capacity of the process is 600 x 168 = 100 800 boxes per week.

Referring to last week's production records, it can be seen that time was lost to the following stoppages:

Planned occurrences	Non-productive time (hrs)
Machine setups	21
Preventive maintenance	7
Quality control	9
Shift changes	7
Unplanned occurrences	
Machine breakdowns	15
Quality noncompliance analysis	8
Conveyor delays	14

The total hours of unavoidable occurrences is 44, and the total hours of avoidable occurrences is 37. We can therefore calculate the following:

$$\text{Design capacity} = 168 \text{ hrs}$$

$$\text{Effective capacity} = 168 - 44 = 124 \text{ hrs}$$

$$\text{Actual output} = 168 - (44 + 37) = 87 \text{ hrs}$$

$$\text{Capacity utilisation} = \text{actual output} / \text{design capacity} = 87 / 168 = 0.518 = \textbf{52\%}$$

$$\text{Capacity efficiency} = \text{actual output} / \text{effective capacity} = 87 / 124 = 0.702 = \textbf{70\%}$$

With demand and capacity measured, we can identify and implement a capacity plan to meet demand during a selected period. There are three distinct types of capacity plan (Figure 7.5):

- Level capacity – maintain a constant level of throughput, irrespective of demand fluctuations
- Chase demand – adjust capacity to match demand
- Manage demand – attempt to influence demand to fit capacity.

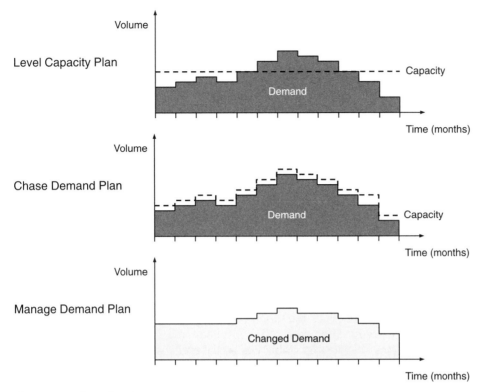

Figure 7.5   Capacity plans

In practice, most supply chains will adopt a combination of these plans to meet demand. Furthermore, extensions of these plans are increasingly employed. One example is deliberately sizing warehouses to meet average demand, supported by outsourcing arrangements with other local storage providers to meet peaks in demand. Another tactic is the shared storage of products with opposite seasonality (for example, ice cream and frozen vegetables) in the same warehouse but at opposite times of the year.

Finally, a caveat with regard to defining capacity requirements. To reduce costs, warehouses should aim not to have excess capacity. However, in increasingly turbulent markets, warehouses will require excess capacity to remain responsive to evermore demand fluctuations. Thus, a trade-off must be sought between

Capacity management plans should consider a trade-off between minimising capacity to reduce cost and providing additional capacity to maintain responsiveness to unexpected demand fluctuations.

management's need to reduce costs and the market requirement for supply chain agility. A responsive supply chain should *'forecast for capacity, but execute for demand'*.[7]

THE 'BULLWHIP EFFECT'

Following our discussion of supply and demand, another important consideration is the **'bullwhip effect'**. This is the distortion of orders along the supply chain, where small fluctuations in end customer demand result in amplification of demand upstream (**demand amplification**). Hence the term 'bullwhip', where just a small flick of the wrist at the handle will create a large crack of the whip at its tip.

Bullwhip is a serious problem for any supply chain. Demand amplification creates excess inventory, which in turn consumes warehouse capacity, has serious cost implications, and may indeed never be used. Bullwhip has one or more of five causes: non-zero lead times and demand signal processing, order batching, price variations, and rationing and gaming.[8] Each is now discussed in turn.

Non-zero lead times and *demand signal processing* are each causes of the *Forrester effect*. By developing the DYNAMO simulation, Jay Forrester demonstrated that the time lag between orders along the supply chain and a lack of downstream visibility of orders causes inaccurate decisions about upstream orders.[9] If decision makers at upstream operations have limited visibility of actual end customer demand and/or the order processing lead time is greater than zero, they will have to make assumptions about how many to manufacture and/or deliver. Such assumptions will commonly be based on knowledge of previous order quantities and frequencies or forecasts of demand. This is reasonable if demand trends are constant, but this is rarely the case.

Order batching, or the *Burbidge effect*, refers to the impact of ordering in batches.[10] Conventional materials management employs a calculation of economic order quantities (EOQ) (discussed in the previous chapter). This benefits supply, but not demand. That is to say that, by manufacturing and delivering in batches of a certain quantity the cost effective use of supply-side resources will be ensured, but this will not necessarily fit demand. Hence, order batching is not conducive to supply chains with end-customer demand fluctuations. The just-in-time (JIT) principle of 'a batch size of one', for example, overcomes order batching, but must be implemented as part of a complete JIT philosophy to guarantee success.

Price variation, such as three items for the price of two promotions, is increasingly common to stimulate demand.[11] Consequently, customers will buy more than they need at that point in time and 'stock up' for the future. While this generates sales, it causes ever-greater peaks and troughs in demand, which are in turn amplified upstream. Such sales and marketing campaigns should therefore be entered into with due consideration of their operational consequences.

Rationing and gaming, such as customers over-ordering due to stock shortages causes the *Houlihan effect*. That is to say that customers who experience missed orders from their suppliers or stock-outs will typically over-order in future to prevent those situations reoccurring. Consequently demand is distorted upstream, with suppliers reacting by over-producing to compensate.[12]

Thus materials management decisions should consider their consequences across the supply chain. Management of actual end-customer demand will minimise demand fluctuations and thereby enable supply to better meet demand. This is difficult to achieve, however, particularly in consumer markets. Hence, stratagems must be employed to cope with demand amplification and limit the bullwhip effects discussed.

MATERIALS PLANNING AND CONTROL

Different products can be defined as having either **independent demand** or **dependent demand**. Products with independent demand are those that are ordered independently of any other products; whereas products with dependent demand are part of an order for multiple interrelated items. This concept can be explained using the example of a European distribution centre (EDC) that specialises in the storage and distribution of bicycles and bicycle components. Bicycles are delivered and stored as sub-assemblies, rather than as complete bicycles so as to enable customisation to particular market requirements. The EDC receives orders from wholesalers and retailers for either complete bicycles or for bicycle spares (i.e. components). When customers order bicycle tyres as spares to be sold separately, this demand is 'independent' of demand for any other items. However, when complete bicycles are ordered, tyres are required to be picked from storage and fitted to the bicycles before shipping. Demand for these tyres is therefore 'dependent' on demand for the complete bicycles.

Throughout a supply chain, any number and combination of various materials with either independent or dependent demand will be ordered. This creates myriad complexities for the various production plants, warehouses and distribution centres across the supply chain. The tool for planning and controlling the manufacture and assembly of orders with dependent demand is **materials requirements planning (MRP)**. This is a software package consisting of the modules illustrated in Figure 7.6. (You will recall that in Chapter 3 we distinguished *push* and *pull* systems – MRP is more associated with *push systems* and items with *dependent* demand.)

A combination of demand forecasts and customer orders is input into the *master production schedule* (MPS), which informs the shopfloor of what should be manufactured and/or assembled and when. However, production cannot begin without the required materials, components and/or sub-assemblies. The MRP system therefore interrogates the *bill of materials* (i.e. list of materials and quantities required for each product) and the inventory database to generate orders for those materials as and when required. While some materials will be stored in-house others will be sourced from suppliers. Up to this point no physical work has been done. The final stage is for the MRP system

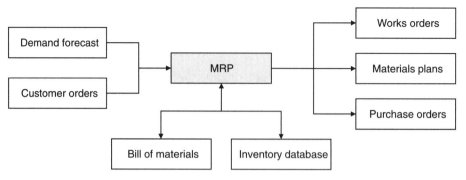

Figure 7.6   An MRP system

to generate works orders to trigger production and/or assembly, materials plans to call materials from in-house storage, and purchase orders to be sent to suppliers.

MRP forms the basis for wider business planning and control information systems, namely **MRPII (manufacturing resource planning)** and latterly **ERP (enterprise resource planning)** to integrate information from beyond the shopfloor. A common misconception is that MRPII is simply an update of MRP. This is not the case. MRPII utilises the core functionality of MRP but integrates business functions beyond manufacturing and logistics to include finance, procurement, marketing, sales, etc. ERP is discussed in Chapter 9, and the Scala system in the Gate Gourmet case at the end of Part Two represents a bespoke example of such a system.

WAREHOUSE MANAGEMENT SYSTEMS AND AUTOMATION

MRP and ERP systems define the material requirements that are transmitted to the warehouse or distribution centre, but they do not manage the information processes within the warehouse. This is the role of a **warehouse management system (WMS)**, which can be designed to interface with an MRP or ERP system. As alluded to previously, product proliferation in the supply chain creates complexity in the warehouse. A warehouse system manages this complexity to trigger the right work at the right time across the operation, as illustrated in Figure 7.7.

Information may be manually or automatically uploaded and downloaded to and from a WMS. Yet, increasingly, electronic data capture is proving to be more effective and efficient than conventional paper-based systems, particularly at the shopfloor. Warehouse operatives undertaking selected information tasks in Figure 7.7 are today most likely to use handheld RF (radio frequency) or barcode readers, PCs, label printers, and pick-to-voice technologies. Each of these technologies aims to minimise human effort and to reduce the time taken, errors and costs. Furthermore, processes are standardised to improve accuracy and repeatability. Meanwhile some information tasks may be fully automated within the WMS. Table 7.1 lists particular technologies for selected information tasks. Chapter 9 will discuss in more detail the role and application of information technology in the supply chain.

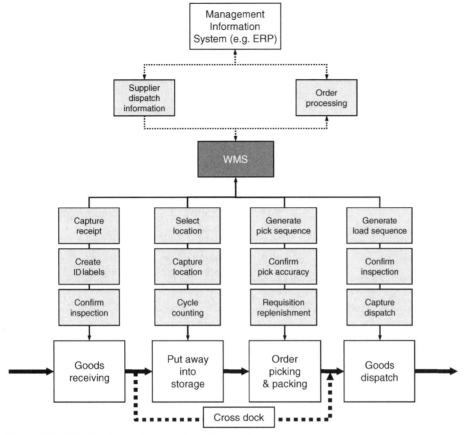

Figure 7.7   WMS information inputs and outputs

The automation of shopfloor information tasks is a relatively recent development in warehousing, but materials handling automation is well established. Cranes, fork-lifts, reach trucks, pallet trucks, AGVs and conveyors are widely used to minimise human effort and intervention (the term **MHE – materials handling equipment** – is sometimes used to describe the various types of equipment for handling inven-tory). As in automated information tasks, automated materials handling improves and standardises warehouse performance by minimising human intervention. A further consequence is the optimisation of warehouse space. By employing mechanical and automated handling technologies, floor space between storage locations can be minimised and the locations themselves are able to occupy multi-ple levels, as in the A G Barr case. A G Barr's 11-storey automated high bay storage system is serviced via automated conveyors and requires no manual intervention other than for maintenance.

Despite the obvious benefits of automation, technologies must be fit-for-purpose. That is to say that different warehouses and distribution centres serve different

Table 7.1   WMS data capture and transmission technologies

WMS information task	Technology used
Capture receipt	Read barcode or RFID tag (via handheld or fully-automated)
Create identification labels	Print barcode label or RFID tag (via PC/handheld or fully-automated) (if required)
Confirm inspection	Read barcode or RFID tag (via PC/handheld)
Select location	Fully-automated
Capture location	Read barcode or RFID tag (via handheld or fully-automated)
Cycle counting	Fully-automated
Generate pick sequence	Fully-automated
Confirm pick accuracy	Read barcode, RFID tag or verbal confirm (via handheld, pick-to-voice or fully-automated)
Requisition replenishment	Fully-automated
Generate load sequence	Fully-automated
Confirm inspection	Read barcode, RFID tag or verbal confirm (via handheld, pick-to-voice or fully-automated)
Capture dispatch	Read barcode, RFID tag or verbal confirm (via handheld, pick-to-voice or fully-automated)

purposes. A warehouse storing 20-metre steel girders will require very different handling and information technologies to a supermarket NDC (national distribution centre).

WORK ORGANISATION AND JOB DESIGN

Another important consideration in implementing warehousing technologies is the impact of those technologies on the workforce. This is the focus of **socio-technical systems (STS)** *theory* (Figure 7.8). The fundamental principles of STS theory are:

- Joint optimisation of the technical and social system
- Quality of work life
- Employee participation in system design
- Semi-autonomous work groups.

Despite attempts during the 1980s to promote the vision of the 'lights-off factory', automated factories and warehouses remain dependent on people. Labour remains the greatest cost in warehousing as operators provide the dexterity, flexibility and adaptability to maintain high levels of performance. For example, it may be perceived to be more cost efficient to replace a human picker with

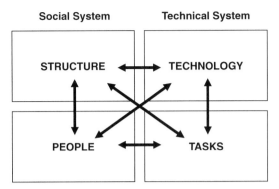

Figure 7.8   Socio-technical systems theory. From Bostrom, R. & Heinen, J. (1977) MIS problems and failures: a socio-technical perspective, *MIS Quarterly*, September, 17–31.

a robot, but it is not cost effective because the robot does not have the same dexterity or the ability to think laterally and multi-task.

Addressing the four principles of STS theory, the capabilities of a social system (i.e. people) and a technical system should be balanced. There is no point in implementing high-tech solutions that operators cannot use. This also has a knock-on effect on workers' quality of work life. This will include human factors such as ergonomics. Unhappy workers are not effective workers. Indeed, this is a key concern regarding the implementation of RFID devices in warehousing. As will be discussed later in Chapter 9, RFID has the potential to greatly reduce human input in shopfloor data collection and retrieval.[13] If STS principles are not adhered to, RFID implementation could result in reduced scope of work, reduced job satisfaction, demotivation and consequently reduced operational performance. This is where employee participation in system design is important. The people who know how best to improve a process are often the people who work in it every day. Involvement encourages ownership and therefore improves motivation. Finally, ownership and motivation can also be promoted via semi-autonomous teams. Given sufficient autonomy, teams can self-manage and coordinate their work. Consequently, there is less of a burden on management through less referral of decisions.

Work organisation and structure are important considerations in contemporary warehousing. Market pressures drive down operational costs, but at the same time demand greater responsiveness, reliability and resilience. Supply chains cannot afford the time engaged in, or the cost of, the complex hierarchical management structures of the past. Flat hierarchies and devolved decision making via semi-autonomous teams goes partway to addressing this issue. Other considerations will include effective and efficient information and communication systems to facilitate improved management reporting and supply chain integration.

At the warehouse shopfloor, the number and scope of individual job roles will be dependent on the warehouse layout and design, types of products, processes and technologies employed. Nevertheless, typical job roles are focused around the four functions outlined in Figure 7.3 and include receipt, quality control, put away and replenishment, picking, packing and loading. Usually there are dedicated teams in each section. However, work in warehousing is generally regarded as standardised and unskilled, requiring minimal education and training. It is therefore realistic to expect operators in selected operations to rotate around different processes or even multi-task (e.g. undertake put away and do picking and packing) to maintain motivation. In the A G Barr case, shopfloor job roles encompass all tasks throughout the operation. On any given day an operative could be working on any given task, or a number of different tasks. This promotes job enlargement (i.e. multi-tasking) and enrichment to maintain motivation and therefore employee retention.

Nevertheless, as previously discussed, increased automation is reducing the amount of manual handling and increasing the amount of information processing in warehousing. Job roles are changing. Warehouse operatives today interact more with information than they do with physical materials. This evolution has socio-technical implications. Conventionally, there has not been a requirement for unskilled warehouse operatives to read and write, or indeed to be fluent in a particular language. Within the European Union for example, workers are able to migrate across national borders for work. Hence, in UK-based warehouses, it is common to find employees from a number of countries, with differing levels of education. Thus written communication of information is not always the most effective mode of communication. Technologies such as pick-to-voice therefore play an important role in communicating instructions. Operatives receive verbal picking instructions via a headset in one of many preloaded languages. Operatives respond verbally in the same language or by reading a barcode at the pick location to indicate that the correct item has been picked. The design of technologies appropriate to the capabilities of the workforce is therefore increasingly important.

Finally, the reduction in physical handling tasks and increase in information tasks offers an opportunity for supply chains to engage their workforces in new and different tasks. With increased information, there is scope to use that information in new and innovative ways to further improve supply chain performance. Within warehouse semi-autonomous teams, opportunities will emerge for people to shift their focus from 'doing' tasks to 'thinking' tasks. Critical thinking, problem-solving and decision-making skills will therefore become important at the shopfloor.

> Automation and computerisation is reducing human intervention in the physical handling of freight, and increasing information interaction. This has implications for job design.

LEARNING REVIEW

This chapter described the important role played in supply chains by warehouse operations. We discussed the need to minimise the costs of warehousing and inventory holding, while maximising the value added in these essential operations. At different points in a supply chain, warehouses and distribution centres will perform different functions, as detailed. Equally, different internal processes will be employed for different types of products, as highlighted by the A G Barr case.

We next discussed customer demand and its influence on storage capacity decisions. End-customer demand fluctuations create a bullwhip effect through the supply chain, causing inaccurate inventory and capacity decisions to be made. We discussed the causes of bullwhip and how it can be minimised. If bullwhip can be controlled, warehousing operations can be run more effectively and efficiently.

Materials management was then discussed, explaining the roles of information systems such as MRP and WMS. The provision of such integrated information systems enables the management of freight through warehouses and distribution centres. Nevertheless, the role of people should not be ignored. Hence the chapter closes with a discussion of the need to achieve equilibrium between people, processes and technology. As warehouses become more high-tech, the important roles that people play must not be neglected.

The next chapter will shift our focus to the movement of freight between the various nodes in a supply chain and discuss the role of transport operations.

QUESTIONS

- In the context of postponement, how might downstream distribution centres be viewed as value-adding?
- Referring to the capacity measurement example, recommend how capacity efficiency and utilisation of the box-packing machine can be improved.
- Consider the Forrester effect. How might capacity plans in upstream warehouses be different to those downstream as a result of demand volatility?
- List the various information sources from across the supply chain that will improve order delivery and discuss how not having each would impact delivery.

SERVING DIFFERENT MARKET SEGMENTS AT A G BARR

Review the A G Barr case. They operate a fully automated storage system to service low variety–high volume, large-scale retailers, and a human-centred storage system to service high variety–low volume, small-scale retailers.

List the benefits of each and discuss how each system meets the demands of the two market segments they serve.

NOTES

1. Christopher, M. (2005) *Logistics and Supply Chain Management: Strategies for Reducing Cost and Improving Service*, 3rd edn, London, Financial Times/Pitman, p.45.
2. Jessop, D. & Morrison, A. (1994) *Storage and Supply of Materials*, 6th edn, London, Pitman Publishing, p.5.
3. Grant, D., Lambert, D., Stock, J. & Ellram, L. (2005) *Fundamentals of Logistics Management*, European edn, London, McGraw Hill, p.247.
4. Gümüs, M. & Bookbinder, J. (2004) Cross-docking and its implications in location-distribution systems, *Journal of Business Logistics*, 25(2), 199–227.
5. Slack, N., Chambers, S. & Johnston, R. (2007) *Operations Management*, 5th edn, London, FT/Prentice Hall, p.320.
6. Arnold, J. & Chapman, S. (2004) *Introduction to Materials Management*, 5th edn, New Jersey, Pearson Prentice Hall, p.118.
7. Christopher, M. (2006) 'The agile supply chain', guest lecture at the University of Hull Logistics Institute, 29th November.
8. Lee, H., Padmanaghan, P. & Whang, S. (1997) The bullwhip effect in supply chains, *Sloan Management Review*, Spring, 93–102.
9. Forrester, J. (1958) Industrial dynamics: a major breakthrough for decision makers, *Harvard Business Review*, July–August, 37–66.
10. Disney, S. & Towill, D. (2003) Vendor-managed inventory and bullwhip reduction in a two level supply chain, *International Journal of Operations and Production Management*, 23(6), 625–651.
11. *Ibid.*
12. *Ibid.*
13. Butcher, T. (2006) The socio-technical impact of RFID technologies in supply chain management, Research Memorandum 57, Hull University Business School, ISBN: 1-90203-454-6.

Transport in Supply Chains

INTRODUCTION

In Chapter 4 we looked at the role of logistics service providers, and in particular third (and fourth) party logistics, in supply chains. As we saw in Chapter 4, provision of transport services is one of the key but not only activities of LSPs. In this chapter we will focus specifically on physical flows using transport in supply chains. Freight transport is an integral part of SCM, but traditionally has been treated as a service that is easily available when required by suppliers and distributors. Also, transport is typically regarded as a nonvalue-adding activity in the supply chain, although we challenge this assumption on the basis that it plays an essential role in the supply chain, and when managed properly can allow supply chains to work more efficiently and effectively.

As we already noted in Chapter 4 there are essentially five modes of transport:

- Air
- Road
- Water
- Rail
- Pipeline.

We also mentioned the 'information superhighway' in Chapter 4 as a possible sixth mode of transport.

Chapter 8 comprises five core sections:

- Characteristics of the different transport modes
- Planning transport infrastructure
- Transport operations, distribution centres and the role of factory gate pricing
- The transportation model
- Efficiency of transport services

LEARNING OBJECTIVES

- Understand the cost structures and operating characteristics of the different transport modes, and the relationships between freight rates and consignment weight, dimensions and distance to be travelled.
- Highlight key terms used in transport.
- Identify the range of issues to be considered in planning transport infrastructure.
- Discuss the roles of distribution centres and highlight the concept of factory gate pricing.
- Explain the application of a technique known as the *transportation model*.
- Identify some of the many issues (including the effect of supply chain strategies) that can impact the efficiency of transport services.

CHARACTERISTICS OF THE DIFFERENT TRANSPORT MODES

Choosing which mode(s) to use for freight transportation will usually be a function of the volume, weight and value of the freight, the distance to be travelled, the availability of different services, freight rates to be charged and so forth. We have already viewed some of the issues involved in selecting LSPs and services, and the concept of generalised costs, in Chapter 4.

Once the appropriate mode of transport has been chosen, it is usually the case that there is not a simple linear relationship between the freight rate charged and both the weight of the freight and the distance to be travelled (Figures 8.1 and 8.2). Regardless of how short the distance to be travelled, the LSP will still have to recover certain fixed costs for transporting a consignment (Figure 8.1). For heavier shipments, the rate per kilo will typically decrease as the fixed costs can be spread over a larger weight (Figure 8.2). For bulky or difficult to handle shipments, LSPs will typically apply what is known as **volumetric charging** based on the dimensions of the consignment. This is to compensate for lost capacity as a result of carrying the bulky shipment where applying a rate per kilo would not sufficiently cover the costs incurred for carrying the shipment. Think, for example, of a roll of carpet in an aircraft hold: by weight this shipment may be quite light, but because of its

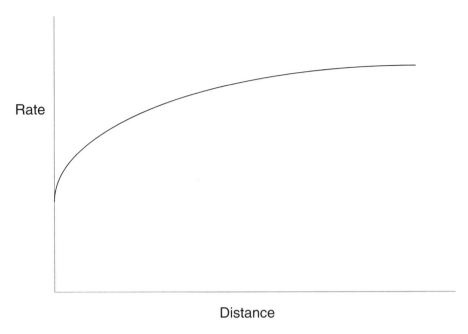

Figure 8.1   Relationship between rate and distance

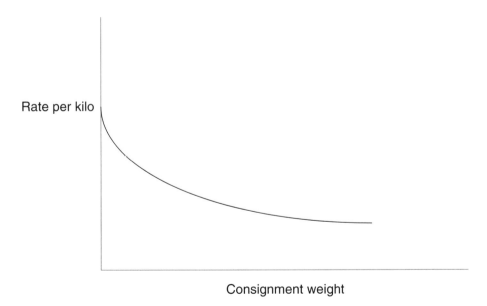

Figure 8.2   Relationship between rate per kilo and consignment weight

dimensions there may be a lot of lost space in the aircraft hold which cannot now be utilised.

Indeed, we also noted in Chapter 4 that sometimes consignors do not know exactly which transport mode their freight travels on, they leave this decision to the 3PL. We also noted that it is not a simple matter of trading off one mode against another, sometimes multiple transport modes are used in combination. Table 8.1 illustrates the cost structures and operating characteristics of the different transport modes.

Table 8.1   A summary of costs and relative operating characteristics of the different transport modes

Mode	Relative costs and operating characteristics by mode
Air	Fixed cost is on the lower side but variable cost, including fuel, maintenance, security requirements, etc., is high. The main advantage of air is speed; it is however limited in uplift capacity, similarly other modes of transport are required to take freight to and from airports, thus air cannot directly link individual consignors and consignees.
Road	Fixed cost is low as the physical transport infrastructure, such as motorways, is in place through public funding; variable cost is medium in terms of rising fuel costs, maintenance and increasing use of road and congestion charges. In terms of operating characteristics, road as a mode of transport scores favourably on speed, availability, dependability, and frequency, but not so good on capability due to limited capacity on weight and volume. Uniquely among transport modes, it can allow direct access to consignor and consignee sites.
Water	Fixed cost is on the medium side, including vessels, handling equipment and terminals. Variable cost is low due to the economies of scale that can be enjoyed from carrying large volumes of freight, this is the main advantage of the water mode, together with its capability to uplift large volumes of freight. Like air, it cannot offer direct consignor to consignee connectivity, and vessels are sometimes limited in terms of what ports they can use. It is also quite a slow mode.
Rail	Fixed cost is high and the variable cost is relatively low. Fixed cost is high due to expensive equipment requirements, such as locomotives, wagons, tracks and facilities, such as freight terminals. On relative operating characteristics, rail is considered good on speed, dependability, and especially capability to move larger quantities of freight.
Pipeline	Fixed cost is high due to rights-of-way, construction and installation, but the variable cost is relatively low and generally just encompasses routine maintenance and ongoing inspection/security. On operational characteristics, the dependability is excellent but this mode can only be used in very limited situations.

**Goods transport by mode in the EU –
2005 (% of tonne kilometres)**

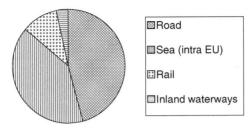

Road

Sea (intra EU)

Rail

Inland waterways

Figure 8.3   Modal split for freight transport in the EU 25 in 2005 (% tonne kilometres)[1]

The split of freight among different modes varies by region and type of freight; Figure 8.3, for example, shows the modal split within the European Union.

Maritime transport is the dominant mode of transport for international transport movements. Some six billion tonnes of freight moves by maritime transport each year and is estimated to comprise 45% liquid bulks, 23% dry bulks and 32% general cargo.

Road transport is the dominant mode of transport for inland transport. Due mainly to the flexibility, directness and speed that the movement of freight by road offers, when compared with rail, inland waterway or sea transport, it has become the principal freight transport mode, carrying the majority of inland freight.[2] It is also the most environmentally damaging mode of transport, however; an issue we will return to in Chapter 14, which deals with sustainability. Policy makers are thus endeavouring to shift freight from road to more environmentally friendly transport modes, in particular to rail and inland waterway. This is not an easy task as many transport systems are predicated on extensive use of road transport.

The term **intermodal transport** is often used in transport. This is where freight moves within a loading unit (known as an ITU – intermodal transport unit), this unit may move on a number of different transport modes, but the freight remains within the unit at all times. There are various types of ITUs, the most common being the standard sized containers (typically 20 and 40 feet in length) one sees on ships, trains and trucks. These containers are typically measured in numbers of TEUs (twenty foot equivalent units). Other types of ITUs include the 'igloo' containers used in air freight.

Macro volumes of freight are usually measured in **freight tonne kilometres** (FTKs), that is volume of freight measured in tonnes multiplied by the distance the freight travels measured in kilometres. Macro volumes of passengers are usually measured in revenue passenger kilometres (RPKs), the *revenue* denotes that the passengers are fare paying (as opposed to positioning crew, staff travelling on concession, etc.).

PLANNING TRANSPORT INFRASTRUCTURE

Planning what transport infrastructure to provide, and where, is a complex task for policy makers. A key feature of transport is that it is a **derived demand**; that is, people or freight do not travel for the sake of making a journey, they travel for some other reason (for example, in the case of people to go on holidays or to go on a business trip; in the case of freight to go to a market or another factory for further processing). The case below illustrates the range of issues to be considered in planning transport infrastructure.

PLANNING TRANSPORT INFRASTRUCTURE

by Tom Ferris

Transport Economist and former President of the Chartered Institute of Transport, Ireland

Transport demand

Economists like to point out that transport is a derived demand. Transport infrastructure and facilities have to be planned to accommodate economic requirements and social needs. They don't just happen. Transport is needed to get freight from A to B, either as raw materials or as finished products. Equally, transport is needed to get people from Y to Z, either for work or for social activities. Getting the balance right, throughout an economy, means avoiding over-investment, while not suffering under-investment. This case looks at the example of transport infrastructure planning in Ireland. Initially the country had relatively poor transport infrastructure when compared with other developed economies, but in recent years there has been considerable investment in transport infrastructure spurred on by strong economic growth.

The 'Celtic Tiger' and its infrastructure deficit

Ireland is an open globalised economy[3] hosting a large number of multinational companies, whose activities contribute significantly to economic growth. The performance of Ireland's economy had been very sluggish during most of the 1980s and the early 1990s. Budgetary stability was then introduced, which underpinned remarkable economic growth during the 1990s and 2000s, earning Ireland the title of 'Celtic Tiger'. However, because of insufficient transport investment in the past, and the demands of an emerging 'Celtic Tiger', Ireland's transport infrastructure came under serious pressure.

At the beginning of the 1990s, Ireland had underdeveloped transport infrastructure, which constrained economic growth. The EU provided considerable funding to assist transport investment between 1989 and 2005, but there was still a backlog in investment. In November 2005, the Irish

Government decided on a massive transport investment programme – called *Transport 21* – to tackle this transport infrastructure deficit. This 10-year programme provides a capital investment framework through which the transport system in Ireland will be developed over the period up to 2016. It places the transport sector in the unique position of having a 10-year capital envelope agreed with the Ministry of Finance. *Transport 21* aims to develop Ireland's transport system by significantly *expanding capacity, increasing integration* (i.e. ensuring all passengers and freight can transfer seamlessly between modes), *enhancing quality, increasing accessibility* and *ensuring sustainability.* These are all key elements in the design of modern transport systems.

The programme plans for investment in transport infrastructure of €34 billion over the period up to 2016. The scale of this investment can be gauged from the fact that Ireland's annual gross domestic product is currently €175 billion, catering for a population of 4.2 million people.

Achieving balanced investment?

While planning transport systems is important, executing the delivery of such systems is equally important. Key issues in executing the delivery of such systems include *cost-benefit appraisal, project evaluation and approval* and *management of large-scale capital expenditure.*

In the case of transport planning in Ireland, the question might well be asked – is there too much investment being planned for transport, at the one time? An economic think-tank, the Dublin based Economic and Social Research Institute, has, in fact, sounded a note of caution about the capacity of the Irish economy to deliver all of the projects included in *Transport 21.*[4] It has also pointed out that, even if all of the projects envisaged in *Transport 21* pass the required cost–benefit hurdle, some of them should be postponed until after 2013, to avoid over-heating in the economy. The Irish Government rejected this advice, however, and is eager to progress all of the projects as quickly as possible so as to redress infrastructure deficits. The pace of roll-out of projects, however, needs to be kept continually under review to ensure the Irish economy is not over-stretched.[5]

TRANSPORT OPERATIONS, DISTRIBUTION CENTRES AND THE ROLE OF FACTORY GATE PRICING

We saw in Chapter 7 that inventory is stored at multiple points in supply chains. In this section we will consider the role of distribution centres and in particular a concept known as 'factory gate pricing'. Since the mid 1970s, supply chain configurations have been changing to achieve higher levels of logistics performance and customer service. In the 1970s and 1980s, **distribution centres (DCs)** were introduced in the retail sector, with retailers taking over responsibility for deliveries to their stores (sometimes DCs are referred to as **RDCs – regional distribution**

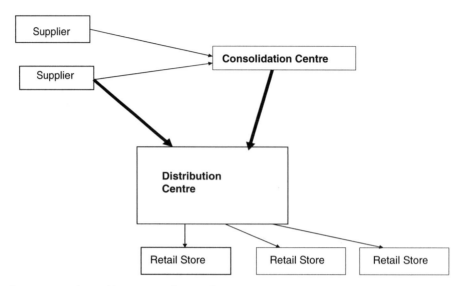

Figure 8.4 Inbound logistics in the retail sector

centres, and NDCs – national distribution centres). A distribution centre is a type of warehouse where a large number of products are delivered by different suppliers preferably in full truck loads. Each distribution centre services a number of retail stores in the regional area. In the 1990s, *consolidation centres* (CCs) were added and served to consolidate deliveries from multiple suppliers into full loads that could be delivered onwards to the DCs (see Figure 8.4). A recent development has been for the retailers to take control of the delivery of goods into their DCs and this is known as **factory gate pricing (FGP)**. An advantage of FGP is that it gives a single point of control for the inbound logistics network.

Factory Gate Pricing (FGP) is the use of an ex-works price for a product plus the organisation and optimisation of transport by the purchaser to the point of delivery.[6]

The case below on FGP highlights the savings for a retailer due to increased supply chain visibility and better management of transport leading to reduction in delays in their inbound logistics.

Figure 8.5 illustrates the evolution of grocery distribution over the past number of decades.

In addition to the control of their inbound logistics using FGP, retailers are also looking at further improving their efficiency by increasing the backloading of store delivery vehicles and the consolidation of smaller loads into full loads at the consolidation centres. In the grocery sector in the UK, Tesco was the first to move towards FGP in 2001, and subsequently other retailers applied the concept. In addition to the retail sector, FGP has also been used in a number of other industry sectors.

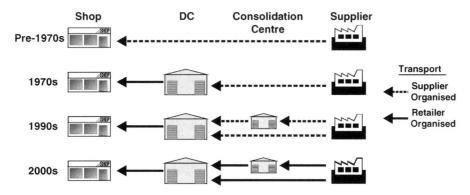

Figure 8.5   The evolution of grocery distribution[7]

The application of FGP within the grocery sector has complexities due to the large number of suppliers, large number of products and the scale of distribution. With regard to the impact of FGP on transport, LSPs could feel that the retailers can use it as a lever to reduce haulage rates and reduce their profit margins. Research by the ITeLS research team at Cardiff University suggests that there are a number of operational benefits that arise for the retailer from implementing FGP.[8] These include increased supply chain visibility provided to the retailer giving them greater insight into the behaviour of their replenishment processes in response to changes in demand; in addition, the research showed that the retailer benefits from higher delivery service levels. For the suppliers, FGP enables them to focus on their core competencies. In the grocery sector, this is pertinent as the retailers do not add value to the product through manufacturing, but do so through the efficient delivery of products. Therefore, distribution is one of their key strengths. Conversely, many suppliers outsource their distribution in order to focus on the core competency of manufacturing.[9]

For FGP implementation a single point of control is required in the supply chain. With no overall single point of control, there will be additional costs such as in achieving collaboration between all parties for transport movements. In the grocery sector, the power of the retailers makes FGP suitable for managing the single point of control. However, this may not apply in all cases. The implementation of FGP heavily depends on the use of ICT, particularly for transport planning but also for communication with the LSPs.

The next section turns to the issue of minimising total transport cost within a transport network. Minimum total transport cost solutions could be arrived at by balancing the distribution centre demands with suppliers' capacities in an existing transport network. In addition, where there is a possibility of redesigning the network, the total transport cost could be further minimised by optimising the location of consolidation centres and/or distribution centres in relation to the supplier network. One of the methods of doing this is using what is known as the *transportation model*.

AN EXAMPLE OF THE APPLICATION OF FACTORY GATE PRICING (FGP)[10]

This example illustrates that implementation of FGP could generate savings to justify the investment for its adoption in the retail sector. The case company is a leading UK grocery retailer with over 1 750 stores in the UK and nearly 2 000 own-brand primary suppliers in 98 countries. The example discussed here is based on the UK suppliers, UK distribution centres, and UK consolidation centres only.

The suppliers to the case company retailer could deliver products in full or less than full truckloads. Less than truckload suppliers are defined by the retailer as those supplying fewer than 18 pallets per day to a DC (a full vehicle can hold 24–26 pallets). With less than full truckload suppliers, the decision was taken by the retailer to consolidate these shipments through a new network of consolidation centres (CCs) so as to make deliveries to the DC in full vehicle loads.

In analysing the data collected from the retailer on flows of existing consolidated products, it was found in some cases that a supplier was transporting products across the UK to a CC, only for them to then be moved back along almost the same route for delivery to a DC. This obviously increased transport costs. Under FGP, products are routed more rationally, going from suppliers to the local CC for onward movement to the DCs. Where the supplier is close to the DC, direct deliveries to the DC continue to be the most cost-effective approach. With full truckload suppliers, the ability of the retailer to have visibility of their whole inbound distribution network also created opportunities for transport cost reduction.

While the application of FGP delivers reductions in transport miles and costs, the implementation has required the use of the latest developments in ICT. If the technology was not available, the efficiency of the process would be significantly reduced due to the number of people required to plan and manage the inbound distribution process. Through the acquisition of an effective transport management system, the retailer can control the whole inbound distribution network with a limited number of people working at any one time.

In 2004, the ITeLS research team at Cardiff University carried out a mini-project with the case company and made an attempt to quantify the transport benefits. In the context of the retailer's business, less than full truckload deliveries accounted for 18% of the total ambient volume, 57% of composite volume and 35% of total grocery volume. Composite distribution networks are the centres used for distributing multi-temperature controlled products (fresh, chilled and frozen). The data from the retailer was modelled in a network planning software package to determine the transport distance and cost benefits.[11] The results for both ambient and composite networks are detailed in Table 8.2. There are a number of assumptions that should be kept in mind in interpreting the results. It is assumed that the demand is spread evenly over time, with 100% availability at the supplier. The decision on less than truckload suppliers was made strategically at the retailer, rather than incorporating all suppliers into the model. Costs were based on current charges incurred by the retailer and levied on a per mile basis for transport and per pallet basis for handling charges at the CCs. Finally, the figures only represent the movement of products from the supplier to the DC and do not take into account any costs in positioning the vehicle at the supplier. Because the retailer uses third party logistics providers for the majority of their requirements, it has been assumed that any cost associated with this is included in the haulage cost.

Table 8.2   The impact of the primary consolidation network with FGP[11]

Product type	Scenario	Weekly transport miles (normalised)	Total weekly cost (normalised)	Volume Direct	Consolidated
Ambient	As is	100	100	88.7%	11.3%
	FGP design	74.7	86.1	16.7%	83.3%
Composite	As is	100	100	39.0%	61.0%
	FGP design	77.0	82.8	12.8%	87.2%

By controlling the consolidation network from a single point through FGP, it is possible to reduce the total distance products travel between suppliers and stores by 23–25% (see Table 8.2). This results from reducing the number of suppliers that deliver directly to the DC, particularly for ambient products. The relative reduction in transport costs is less, being 13.9% and 17.2% for ambient and composite products respectively. This is because there is cost associated with handling the pallets at the consolidation centre. The researchers estimate that, given the volume of products these savings are achieved on, it can be extrapolated that FGP will reduce the retailer's total distribution cost by approximately 5.7%. However, this value does not consider any gains from implementing the strategies for full vehicle loads or the potential for the retailer, as a large user of transport, to realise economies of scale for freight rates.

In this example, the benefits of FGP in the retail sector have been highlighted, but it is important to comment on potential issues that arise through its implementation. First of all it is likely that there will be additional costs for achieving collaboration between all parties for the transport movements if it is implemented using the consolidation centres. Second, there is the question of who manages the point of control. In the grocery sector, the power of the retailers makes FGP suitable. However, this may not apply in all instances. Finally, the implementation of FGP has been heavily dependent on ICT, particularly for transport planning but also for communication with hauliers.

THE TRANSPORTATION MODEL

One of the most commonly used models that seeks to work out a minimum total transport cost solution for the number of units of a single commodity that should be transported from given suppliers to a number of destinations is the **transportation model**. The input data required for this model include the number of units of the product required by the destination store/warehouse/distribution centre (destination) and the number of units available with each supplier (origin). In addition, the unit transport cost of the product from each origin to each destination is also required for finding the solution using the transportation model. When it is not possible to have the data on unit transport costs, it is common practice to use the actual travelling distance between each origin and each destination. The model application aims to determine the number of units that should be transported from each supplier to each destination such that total transport cost or total units-transport distance is minimised.

There are a number of assumptions made in the application of the model.[12] The main assumption is that there is a linear relationship between the transport cost and the number of units being transported. It is important that the units of supply and the demand (requirement) from destinations are consistent.

Let us assume that the amount of supply at origin i is s_i and demand at destination j is d_j and the unit cost between i and j is c_{ij}. Let x_{ij} be the amount or the number of units transported from origin i to destination j. The transportation problem using linear programming can be defined as follows:

Minimise total transport cost $\quad C = \sum_{i=1}^{m} \sum_{j=1}^{n} c_{ij} x_{ij}$

$$(1)$$

subject to

$$\sum_{j=1}^{n} x_{ij} \leq s_i \qquad \text{for } i = 1, 2, \ldots, m \qquad (2)$$

$$\sum_{i=1}^{m} x_{ij} \leq d_i \qquad \text{for } j = 1, 2, \ldots, n \qquad (3)$$

$$x_{ij} \geq 0 \qquad \text{for all } i \text{ and } j \qquad (4)$$

Equation (2) suggests that the total of supply shipments from a supplier should be less than or equal to the available supply. Equation (3) means that the sum of shipments to a destination should be less than or equal to the demand or the requirement by that destination. These constraints have to be satisfied with the objective of minimising total transport cost C given in equation (1). In addition to these constraints the transport problem formulation must also satisfy equation (4) implying that the goods are only shipped from origins to the destinations, which means from warehouses (origins) to shops (destinations) but not in the reverse direction. There is a special requirement of the transportation allocation problem that *the total plant capacity (origins) must be equal to the total warehouse (destinations) demand*. This helps in finding the solution of the problem.

Chapter 8   Transport in Supply Chains   143

STANDARD TRANSPORTATION MODEL: A SIMPLE EXERCISE

The Alpha Limited manufactures washing machines with factories in Birmingham, Manchester and Glasgow. Its main distribution centres are located in Doncaster and Newcastle. The capacities of the three factories in the next month are respectively 300, 200 and 150 washing machines. The monthly demand for the washing machines from distribution centres are respectively 400 and 250 washing machines. The transport cost per washing machine from factories to distribution centres is shown in the following cost table:

	Doncaster (1)	Newcastle (2)
Birmingham (1)	25	35
Manchester (2)	15	20
Glasgow (3)	40	30

Calculate the least total transport cost solution for delivery of the required washing machines by the two distribution centres. Operations research software normally includes the transportation problem solution algorithm.[12]

The solution is worked out using the equations (1) to (4) as follows:

Minimise transport cost $C = 25x_{11} + 35x_{12} + 15x_{21} + 20x_{22} + 40x_{31} + 30x_{32}$

subject to

$$x_{11} + x_{12} = 300$$
$$x_{21} + x_{22} = 200$$
$$x_{31} + x_{32} = 150$$

and

$$x_{11} + x_{21} + x_{31} = 400$$
$$x_{12} + x_{22} + x_{32} = 250$$

The final solution for this simple exercise is worked out solving the above equations for x_{ij} for $i = 1, 2$ and 3 and for $j = 1$ and 2. The exact solution is given below:

	Doncaster (1)	Newcastle (2)	Plant capacity
Birmingham (1)	300		300
Manchester (2)	100	100	200
Glasgow (3)		150	150
Distribution centre demand	400	250	

Total cost for this solution is = 300x25 + 100x15 + 100x20 + 150x30

= 15 500

The above solution allocates the number of washing machines that should be transported from a specific factory to a specific warehouse to achieve minimum total transport cost which is 15,500. Any variation in the allocation given in the above solution will increase the total transport cost.

Note: It should be noted in the above example that the total of plant capacity is exactly the same as the total of the distribution centre demand, which is 650 as shown below:

$$300 + 200 + 150 = 400 + 250$$

This is required for solving the transportation problem for allocation using the transportation model algorithm. In most practical applications this will not be the case and this would require setting up a dummy plant or a dummy distribution centre as needed to make the two totals exactly match.

EFFICIENCY OF TRANSPORT SERVICES

A variety of issues impact the efficiency and effectiveness of transport services. These include congestion problems, waste including empty running of vehicles, carbon emissions, regulatory directives on maximum permitted working time, road user charges and skill shortages. These problems cause inefficiencies and waste such as excessive waiting time, poor turnaround time, low vehicle fill rates, poor asset utilisation, unnecessary administration and excessive inventory holding.

Poor asset utilisation is illustrated in Figure 8.6, which uses real life data from the steel sector. It can be seen that the demand placed by corporate customers

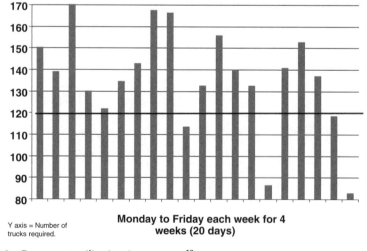

Y axis = Number of trucks required.

Monday to Friday each week for 4 weeks (20 days)

Figure 8.6   Poor asset utilisation in transport[13]

on the transport operator per day during a week can vary from 83 vehicles to 170 vehicles.

The strategies pursued in a supply chain impact the efficiency of the transport services demanded. Pursuing a JIT strategy, for example, has many advantages, but one of its downsides is that it can lead to inefficient transport utilisation with frequent small loads. In fact from the LSP's perspective JIT can lead to: inconsistent fleet utilisation, reduced payload optimisation, reduced ability to effectively plan fleet operations, lead to an image of expendable and infinitely flexible resource in the eyes of customers, etc.[14]

In Chapter 14 we will return to this issue of the efficiency and effectiveness of transport and look in particular at the various solutions that LSPs can pursue.

> The term '**FCL**' is used in transport to refer to **full container load** while the term '**LCL**' is used to refer to **less than full container load**. When carriers have a consignment that will not fill an entire loading unit they will usually try and build a consolidated shipment to make up a FCL.

LEARNING REVIEW

This chapter focused on physical flows using transport in supply chains. The characteristics of the five principal transport modes were described and issues in planning transport infrastructure and determining freight rates were reviewed. The role of distribution centres and in particular the concept of factory gate pricing were described, while the transportation model was introduced as a way of minimising total transport costs in a network. This led us to a discussion around the efficiency and effectiveness of transport services, an issue we will return to later in the book in Chapter 14, which deals with sustainability and logistics.

We noted at the outset to this chapter that transport is typically regarded as a nonvalue-adding activity in the supply chain. In conjunction with our understanding from Chapter 4 of the key roles played by LSPs, and the contributions we will see in Chapter 14 that transport can make around issues concerning sustainability, it is evident that transport plays a vital role in ensuring that supply chains operate both efficiently and effectively.

The next chapter will continue the journey along the supply chain and will focus on another key enabler of SCM, namely information technology.

QUESTIONS

- In your view, does transport add value in the supply chain?
- What is volumetric charging?
- What are the key characteristics of the five principal modes of transport?
- Why do we say that transport is a derived demand?
- What is factory gate pricing?

MODAL SPLIT BY COUNTRY

Try and determine what the modal split is for freight in your country. You will usually be able to find this in government transport statistics. What are the reasons for this modal split and how does it compare with other countries and regions?

In view of increased awareness of environmental and related issues, is this modal split sustainable going forward? If it is not, what future changes in transport industry structure in your country do you envisage?

NOTES

1. Source: European Commission European Road Statistics, 2007.
2. Davies, I., Mason, R.J. & Lalwani, C.S. (2006) Assessing the impact of ICT on UK general haulage companies, *International Journal of Production Economics*, 106, 1, 12–27.
3. The EU version of the term 'globalisation' is used here – see EUROPEAN ECONOMY, The EU Economy: 2005 Review, No.6, 2005, Brussels.
4. Economic and Social Research Institute (2006) Ex-ante evaluation of the investment priorities for the National Development Plan, 2007–2013, *Policy Research Series*, 59, Dublin, October.
5. Ferris, T. (2007) *A New Road for Transport Policy?*, LINKLINE, Chartered Institute of Logistics and Transport, Dublin, July 2007.
6. Potter, A.T., Lalwani, C.S., Disney, S.M. & Velho, H. (2003) Modelling the impact of factory gate pricing on transport and logistics, *Proceedings of the 7th International Symposium on Logistics,* seville, 6–8 July, University of Nottingham, Nottingham, pp.625–630.
7. Potter, A.T., Mason, R.J. & Lalwani, C.S. (2007) Analysis of factory gate pricing in the UK grocery supply chain, *International Journal of Retail & Distribution Management*, 35, 10, 821–834.
8. Lalwani, C.S, Mason, R.J., Potter, A.T. & Yang, B. (eds) *Transport in Supply Chains*, Cardiff, Cardiff Business School.

9. Rushton, A., Oxley, J. & Croucher, P. (2000) *Handbook of Logistics and Distribution Management*, 2nd edn, London, Kogan Page.

10. Potter *et al.*, *op. cit.*

11. Potter, A.T., Lalwani, C.S., Disney, S.M. & Velho, H. (2003) Modelling the impact of factory gate pricing on transport and logistics, in Lalwani, C.S., Mason, R.J., Potter, A.T. & Yang, B. (eds), *Transport in Supply Chains*, Cardiff, Cardiff Business School, pp.103–108.

12. Taha, H.A. (2002) *Operations Research: An Introduction*, 7th edn, New Jersey, Prentice Hall.

13. Lalwani *et al.*, *op. cit.*

14. Mason, R.J., Lalwani, C.S. & Boughton, R. (2006) Alternative models for collaboration in transport optimisation management, *Supply Chain Management: An International Journal*, 12, 3, 187–199.

Information Flows and Technology

INTRODUCTION

Chapter 8 discussed physical flows in the supply chain; that is, the movement of freight. This chapter now focuses on the information flows that trigger and support those physical flows. Today's market-driven global supply chains are information intensive and require adaptive information systems to manage logistics complexities. In this chapter we will learn about the information systems and technologies employed in SCM.

Chapter 9 comprises five core sections:

- The role of information in global supply chains
- Information visibility and transparency
- Information technology applications
- Radio frequency identification (RFID)
- Supply chain knowledge management

LEARNING OBJECTIVES

- Define the role of information in contemporary global supply chains.
- Explain the need for information visibility and transparency across the supply network, and outline the barriers to achieving it.
- Define various information technologies employed in logistics and SCM.
- Discuss the use of RFID in SCM to provide real time information visibility.
- Discuss the emerging importance of knowledge management in supply networks.

THE ROLE OF INFORMATION IN GLOBAL SUPPLY CHAINS

As previously discussed in Chapter 1, there are three key flows in any supply chain; namely material, resource and information flows. Material flows enable delivery of freight and resource flows, such as finance, ensure supply partners get paid. Information flows are more complex and multi-faceted. Information is the key that unlocks supply chain responsiveness to demand.

As previously discussed, matching supply with demand is essential to delivering products at the right time, in the right quantity and to the customer's specification. But how do suppliers know when their products are required, in what quantities or, indeed, what the customer's exact specification is? This is the role that demand-side information plays. Furthermore, how do downstream supply chain partners and customers know when product will be delivered by suppliers, what quantities they will arrive in or to what specification? Supply-side information therefore plays a second essential role.

With today's global supply networks distributed across multiple, widely dispersed echelons, comes information complexity and proliferation on the supply-side. On the demand-side, ever more-fickle consumers expect the availability of high varieties and volumes of specific consignments in shortening time frames. This creates the need for accurate, high-velocity market information. So, contemporary supply chains are information intensive. *Information complexity, proliferation, diffusion, velocity* and *accuracy* are thus key drivers of developing increasingly sophisticated supply chain information technologies, as illustrated in the Gate Gourmet case at the end of Part Two. In fact, as discussed in Chapter 7, managers and workers in logistics and SCM are today less connected with the physical handling of freight, but more in contact with the associated information.

> Information complexity, proliferation, diffusion, velocity and accuracy are key drivers of developing increasingly sophisticated supply chain information technologies.

Hence, it is not just the information itself that is important, but also how we store, retrieve and use it.

Access to timely and accurate information is fundamental to effective SCM. Information must also be useful and useable. Hence, networked desktop and mobile devices such as laptops, personal digital assistants (PDAs) and mobile phones are now not only the toolkit of management, but are also used at the 'shop floor' to access real time information from upstream and downstream in the supply chain. This information accessibility not only supports the ability to plan and control supply chain activities, but also, and arguably more importantly, provides 24/7 visibility of when things don't go to plan. For example, the availability of demand information from a range of high street stores at a national distribution centre (NDC) will enable particular products to be rerouted to the stores where there is demand for them.

Clearly the more timely and accurate that information is, the greater the chances of meeting demand, thereby reducing the probability of overstocking some stores while understocking others. Imagine the benefits of having such information visibility across an entire supply network.

INFORMATION VISIBILITY AND TRANSPARENCY

The above discussion introduces the benefits of information in the supply chain, and also refers to the issue of complexity. **Information visibility** is the ability to see information at the various points across the supply chain as and when required, which can help to manage that complexity. Visibility of information is highly desirable, but is difficult to achieve. The number of supply partners alone is a major contributing factor, but is also compounded by barriers to sharing information. Effective information visibility is not only facilitated by information technologies, but also by integrated and collaborative relationships between supply chain partners. Without integrated information systems and collaborative, as opposed to competitive, relationships, information will not be shared effectively and efficiently. This is discussed further in Chapter 13, which deals with integration and collaboration in the supply chain, but it is noteworthy that disparity between trading partners' capabilities and information security are commonly significant barriers to an IT-enabled supply chain.[1] *Cultural barriers* between supply chain partners should therefore be addressed before embarking on the implementation of supply chain wide information technology.

There are further barriers to gaining total visibility of information across a supply chain. The costs of implementing and maintaining supply chain spanning information technologies can be immense. These cost implications become *financial barriers* if the aforementioned disparities between trading partners exist. For example, it would be unreasonable for a major multinational supermarket to expect their small-scale third or fourth tier suppliers (such as market gardeners and small dairies) to implement cutting edge information systems. In such supply chains, the further upstream a supplier is, the tighter the profit margins; hence, fewer resources are available to invest in new technologies. For example, competitiveness between supermarkets drives down store prices, which in turn drives down the prices they are willing to pay their suppliers. In May 2007, one UK market gardener's cost of producing a single cauliflower was 38 pence. However, one customer, a major supermarket, would only pay 15 pence per cauliflower head![2]

Furthermore, the various information systems at each supply chain partner should either be the same, or at least have the ability to 'talk' to each other. This issue does not end with the hardware and software. Supply chain partners must also agree on what data is required to be transmitted, when and to whom. Hence, there are myriad complex *technical barriers* to overcome before implementing information visibility solutions.[3]

FLORAHOLLAND

FloraHolland is the global market leader in cut flower and ornamental plant supply based in five locations in the Netherlands. It acts as an intermediary between growers (i.e. suppliers) and wholesale or retail buyers with 26 auctions operating simultaneously at its five sites (70% of sales), plus a direct sales (i.e. mediation) operation (30% of sales). The business is a cooperative formed by Dutch growers to offer timely supply across the globe and to act as a conduit for market demand information.

Cut flowers and ornamental plants are highly seasonal and have short shelf lives. Demand fluctuations and time to market are therefore key considerations in the FloraHolland supply chain. Individual growers operate on a small scale, focusing on product variety rather than volume to remain responsive to demand. With 3 000 customers who are large-scale wholesalers and major retailers demanding high volume and variety, growers operating independently would not be able to meet demand. The 5 000 growers with a stake in FloraHolland therefore operate cooperatively, distributing through the auction houses and the FloraHolland direct sales system, to gain the economies of scale necessary to survive in this fast-moving market. With 3 000 employees, FloraHolland not only provides auctions but also works closely with growers to develop the products and processes necessary to remain competitive, and works with buyers to improve supply chain integration.

Although buyers are not a part of the cooperative, the benefits of information integration are recognised by all supply chain partners. The traditional supply chain model was based on a series of purely transactional relationships between the auction house and the buyers. Yet with increasing market pressures such as new market entrants, FloraHolland today works closely with buyers to better meet demand and retain their business. Indeed, through integrated solutions, buyers can inform growers about consumer preferences such as a preference for four buds per stem rather than three. Of the 3 000 buyers, the top 100 buyers account for 80% of turnover. Hence FloraHolland operates an account management system to maintain a sound working relationship with them. Furthermore, the top 50 buyers have FloraHolland personal account managers.

e-Business is essential to this high velocity supply network. It is in everyone's interest for buyers' information systems to be integrated with those of the auction house, direct sales, and growers. As buyers each have their own IT packages, FloraHolland needs to be able to offer compatible and tailored integration solutions. Hence a dedicated IT team is employed to develop, implement and maintain supply chain integration software. The top 50 buyers' IT requirements are managed individually by a 'supply chain automation consultant'. The cost and resource implications are immense, but are offset by the business benefit gained.

Finally, *organisational barriers* to implementing supply chain spanning technologies can inevitably exist. Divergent processes can exist within single organisations, and are commonly realigned via large-scale, resource intensive socio-technical systems (STS) or **business process reengineering (BPR)** projects. Thus to align the numerous disparate processes across multiple supply chain echelons, a highly complex programme of activities is required.

We can therefore classify the barriers to gaining information visibility and transparency as: cultural, financial, technical or organisational. Each of these four types of barrier should be addressed to gain business benefit from supply chain spanning information technologies.[4] Nevertheless, such substantial effort is worthwhile, as the benefits are substantial, and can include:[5]

- Customer oriented operations
- Time compression
- Reduced schedule variability
- Shorter planning periods
- Consistent partnerships
- Supply chain synchronisation and coordination
- A single point of control
- Integrated information systems.

> Barriers to gaining information visibility and transparency can be classified as: cultural, financial, technical or organisational. Each of these should be addressed to gain business benefit from supply chain spanning information technologies.

Ultimately, a supply chain with information sharing, visibility and transparency can become customer-focused and responsive to demand, thereby remaining competitive.

INFORMATION TECHNOLOGY APPLICATIONS

As supply chains have evolved and grown, so have information flows and technologies. Information technologies (IT) such as materials requirements planning (MRP, discussed in Chapter 7) were developed in the 1970s to meet the planning and execution needs of individual operations. As business functions have become more integrated, so have IT applications. For example, enterprise resource planning (ERP), the modern derivative of MRP, spans across organisations. Collaborative planning, forecasting and replenishment (CPFR) extends further still by spanning supply chains. CPFR is discussed below and further in Chapter 13.

This section defines a selection of common core IT applications used in global logistics and supply chain management. Their application and reach are summarised in Figure 9.1.

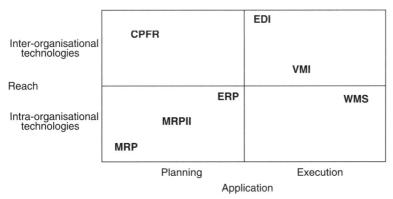

Figure 9.1   Information technologies in global logistics and supply chain management (adapted from Sherer, 2005)[6]

e-Business

Before discussing particular applications, it is important to appreciate their context. e-Business is now integral to trade and commerce in the world today. Many of us purchase products and services on-line. This is also true of trade between businesses across supply chains. Yet the term e-business encompasses more than just trading via the internet, to include all electronically mediated information exchanges across a supply chain that support the various business processes.[7] As already implied above, e-business is essential to both maintaining and improving supply chain performance.

Electronic data interchange

Electronic data interchange (EDI) is a technology for the electronic interchange of data between two or more companies. The predominant forms of data transfer via EDI are purchase orders from customers to suppliers, invoices for payment from suppliers to customers, delivery schedule data, and payment instructions. EDI can be linked to an electronic funds transfer (EFT) application that enables payment.

Data transmitted via EDI is typically automated; that is, it doesn't require human intervention. For example, when the delivery date of a particular order is reached, the supplier computer automatically sends an invoice to the appropriate customer's computer. When integrated with other IT applications across the supply chain, EDI becomes a more powerful tool. In this last example, the data is sent when the delivery date is reached, but not necessarily when the order is dispatched. When linked to an **automatic identification and data capture (AIDC)** technology such as radio frequency identification (RFID), the invoice can be sent precisely at the time the order leaves the factory gates. For example, delivery trucks pass through an RFID reader located at the factory gates. The reader automatically sends the product location data to the EDI application, which in turn transmits the invoice to the customer (see Figure 9.2). RFID is discussed at length below.

Enterprise resource planning

You will recall we briefly introduced ERP in the context of the discussion on MRP and MRPII in Chapter 7. This application spans an enterprise to integrate the various business functions across multiple locations. First developed in the late 1980s, ERP is today a core application in multinational manufacturing and logistics companies, offering visibility and integration of the many complex interactions around the globe. Nevertheless, such integration cannot be achieved by just the ERP application. Before implementing an ERP application, an enterprise must shift from a functional to a product and process organisational structure to enable more effective and efficient communication channels. Best practice is then for the ERP system to be tailored to fit that new organisational structure and communication channels. This is normally achieved via business process reengineering (BPR) to jointly optimise the organisation and the technology, thereby aligning previously divergent business processes, as discussed above. Without appropriately aligned business processes, ERP implementation is more likely to fail. All too often, enterprises view ERP as the solution to their integration problems, implementing the technology without consideration of the organisational structure, and then wonder why it doesn't achieve the benefits they had expected.

ERP requires a substantial financial, resource and time investment at implementation and for maintenance and development. Hence, it is uncommon for small and medium size enterprises (SMEs) to operate ERP systems. Instead MRPII is the application of choice. Nevertheless, scaled down versions of ERP are now available from the major software vendors, increasing its reach and applicability. Yet ERP has one major flaw. It does not extend across the complete supply chain and therefore constrains collaborative planning and control between supply chain partners. Nevertheless, the Scala system in the Gate Gourmet case at the end of Part Two represents a bespoke example of a planning and control system that is integrated with their suppliers.

Collaborative planning, forecasting and replenishment

Collaborative planning, forecasting and replenishment (CPFR) was developed in the late 1990s to fill the inter-organisational gap that ERP could not fill. First developed at Wal-Mart to enable collaborative scheduling with their first tier suppliers, CPFR is more than just a software application. It is fundamentally a new collaborative method of scheduling logistics between suppliers and customers. It is dependent, however, on timely and accurate information sharing, visibility and transparency. Hence, IT-enabled CPFR is essential in high velocity supply chains such as those of the major supermarkets. With CPFR still in its infancy, a number of software vendors offer various solutions. However, as with any business IT, software integration is paramount. Hence, the major ERP software vendors are now offering CPFR 'bolt-ons' to their ERP solutions. However, the fundamental concept of CPFR has far-reaching supply chain benefits, and should therefore be considered a core application. As ERP superseded MRPII, a standard CPFR solution should soon supplant ERP.

Warehouse management systems

Warehouse management systems (WMS) functionality was discussed in Chapter 7. WMS applications have become essential to the management and control of warehouses and distribution centres. As with the other applications discussed, their integration with other software applications is desirable in order to integrate warehouse operations with the rest of the supply chain. For example, a customer order transmitted via EDI will trigger the ERP system to call for materials from production and/or from stock (refer back to Figure 7.6). This will then trigger the WMS to pick from stock and dispatch (refer back to Figure 7.7).

Vendor managed inventory

As with CPFR, **vendor managed inventory (VMI)** is more than just a software application. VMI is again self-explanatory. Simply put, customers, such as high street retailers, outsource their inventory management to their suppliers. In some cases, although suppliers are accountable for the VMI system, they may elect to outsource it to a specialist 3PL. Such collaborative arrangements are common in the fast moving consumer goods (FMCG) sector. Dedicated VMI software solutions are available to manage the intricacies of such systems. VMI is explained further in Chapter 13.

RADIO FREQUENCY IDENTIFICATION

When applied in logistics and SCM, **radio frequency identification (RFID)** technologies automatically identify and locate physical assets (freight and handling equipment). Individual items, batches of materials or the containers in which they are held can carry an RFID transponder or 'tag' that transmits a radio frequency signal. This signal can be remotely detected by an RFID 'reader'. When connected to a materials management system, the data downloaded from the reader is used to monitor and control the movement of the assets.[8] A basic RFID application is illustrated in Figure 9.2. With RFID, line of sight is not required as is the case with traditional barcode reading systems.

The remote communication capability of RFID is what differentiates it from existing traceability technologies. Existing technologies, such as printed batch cards and bar coding, require operatives to read or scan the item or batch specific data at the location of the asset. This can be time consuming, laborious and prone to inaccuracies, due to the scale and complexity of typical warehousing and distribution operations. Hence design and layout of logistics operations across the supply chain have, until now, needed to accommodate this constraint. For example, the delivery of a consignment via truck to the receiving area of a warehouse would conventionally be manually scanned using a handheld barcode reader or recorded in writing. In an RFID enabled receiving area, the truck will typically pass through a reader 'gate' to automatically record the time of delivery and quantity delivered.

The advent of RFID as a supply chain traceability technology results from the drive for agility, to respond to increasing product proliferation and demand volatility. An agile, or 'quick response' supply chain is reliant on the timeliness and quality of shared information. The ability to access real time product information anywhere along the supply chain is thus a key component of becoming truly agile. Yet existing traceability technologies cannot offer real time information. Indeed, until the introduction of RFID, the 'Achilles heel' of supply chains has been data acquisition.[9]

> Access to real time product information anywhere along the supply chain is a key enabler of agility.

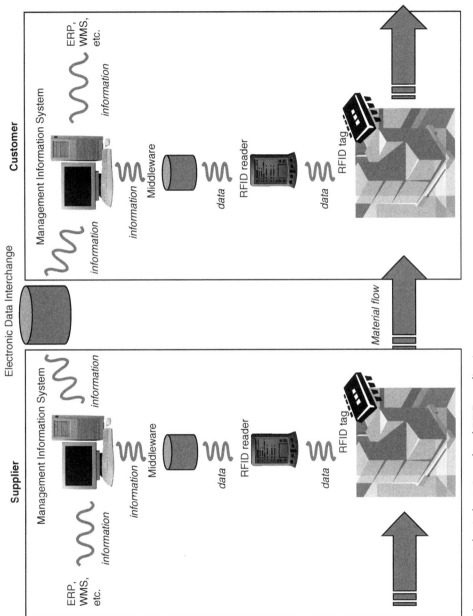

Figure 9.2   A basic logistics-related RFID application

RFID provides real time visibility of point of sale data across the supply chain to trigger production and/or movement of products for automatic replenishment. Consequently, inventory holding will be minimised across the supply chain, which will lead to reduced capacity and resource requirements and in turn dramatically reduce logistics costs. This is, however, just one of the potential benefits of RFID. This new technology is multifunctional. The RFID primary applications up to point of sale can be classified under the following four headings:[10]

- Asset tracking and management
- Increased security of assets
- Improved stock management and availability
- Reduced errors in product data handling.

In fact, RFID tags can be made to: resist extreme temperatures, harmful chemicals and fluids; provide the ability to scan multiple items; and be reusable. Barcodes and other existing technologies cannot. RFID can therefore achieve greater efficiencies than any other existing technology. For example, in the UK, Marks & Spencer uses disposable RFID tags on high value products such as suits for in-store stock control. A typical retail store will contain hundreds of suits in various styles, colours and sizes. Conventionally, the weekly stock check was conducted manually by reading the barcode of each individual item. This was a time consuming and laborious task. The implementation of RFID has enabled reading of multiple items simultaneously using a handheld reader (as illustrated in Figure 9.2). In doing so, the time taken is greatly reduced. Meanwhile read accuracy has also improved. Thus, the suit supply network benefits by gaining more regular and accurate information to enable production of only those items in demand and delivery in smaller more frequent batches, preventing both overproduction and stock-outs.

More generically, the operational improvements from RFID include:[11]

- Shipping consolidation
- Conveyance loading
- Conveyance tracking
- Shipment and item tracking
- Verification
- Storage
- Item tracking within a manufacturing plant
- Warehouse efficiency, reach, productivity and accuracy
- Reduced retail out-of-stock, labour requirements, pilferage, and phantom stock problems.

There is also potential for consumers to benefit directly from RFID through transaction support, increased customer interaction, improved customer monitoring and increased integration of retail partners. For example, with item level tagging, a 'smart fridge'[12] could interact directly with the supermarket to automatically reorder products to restock the fridge. Despite predicted consumer applications such as this, the omnipresent nature of RFID has led to some concern amongst consumers. RFID is a ubiquitous computing technology. As in the smart fridge example, ubiquitous computing aims to seamlessly connect the physical world with a representation of it in information systems. Hence, early RFID adopters such as Wal-Mart, Tesco, Metro and Marks & Spencer have employed strategies to 'switch off' RFID technology at point of sale to prevent consumer distrust issues. So it is likely to be several years before practical consumer benefits are seen.

With RFID still in its infancy, supply chain and logistics applications are limited. RFID is nevertheless set to transform people and processes within supply chains. As discussed, conventional traceability processes have been designed around the need for operators to be in the same physical location as the asset; more specifically, the asset must be in the operator's line of sight. With the elimination of the line of sight requirement, the automation offered by RFID will enable management to reconsider the design of shipping, transportation, manufacturing, warehousing and retail operations. Current predictions of future operational innovations include:[13]

- The 'store of the future': including continuous shelf inventory checking and more frequent replenishment, currently being trialled by Procter & Gamble, Phillip Morris and Metro
- 'Future warehousing': reducing floor space requirements in warehouses, enabling them to be located closer to urban areas
- Increased customisation in manufacturing and increased visibility of end customer requirements.

Such innovations will change the work structures and job content for workers and create new job roles across the supply chain. As discussed in Chapter 7, the reduction in manual handling and the increase in information in logistics is creating new tasks and job roles at the shopfloor. In fact, the extent to which RFID will replace barcoding remains unclear. Traditionally, the diffusion of significant innovations, such as the car, the refrigerator and the personal computer, has led to human impacts unforeseen by the original inventors. While it is recognised that RFID can significantly transform the way humans interact with products and services, its long-term impact has not yet been fully envisaged.[14]

Meanwhile, in the short term, early adopters must bear the burden of high RFID tag costs. Typically RFID tagging can add 20–67% to the cost of distribution when implemented at pallet or case (i.e. batch) level.[15] It is anticipated, however, that widespread implementation will bring with it sufficient economies of scale. Consequently, early adopters are typically very large organisations such as Wal-Mart and Tesco. More significantly, upstream manufacturers and suppliers are concerned that the information transparency that RFID can offer will hand greater power and control to such retailers. Indeed, the success of an IT-enabled supply chain is highly dependent on all parties gaining mutual benefit. As discussed above, resistance to change, disparity between trading partners' capabilities, and information security are commonly viewed by practitioners as significant barriers to an IT-enabled supply chain.[16] Hence, there are several infrastructural issues to overcome before tangible wholesale benefit can be gained from RFID.

In summary, RFID has the potential to deliver real time supply chain agility. This relatively new technology can offer accurate and precise product traceability at any point in the supply chain at any time, thereby enabling even the most complex supply networks to respond immediately to fluctuations in demand. Yet, while tag manufacturers and leading retailers continue research and development into cost-efficient technological solutions, substantial barriers to effective implementation remain.

FLORAHOLLAND

As noted earlier in the chapter, FloraHolland takes supply chain information very seriously. In 2001, FloraHolland implemented RFID to manage the movement of carts across its short supply chain (growers' greenhouses are located near to each of FloraHolland's five sites) (Figure 9.3). An RFID tag on each cart and readers at strategic points in the short supply chain enable them to locate and transfer these valuable assets to other locations where they are required. FloraHolland currently manages 150 000 carts across the short supply chain. The technology also reduces processing errors. Prior to 2001, track and trace was a manual operation requiring workers to input data manually into the central information system. Furthermore, labour requirements at the auction house are greatly reduced and simplified. Before RFID implementation, two operators were required for each cart: one to transport the cart and one to enter the associated data in Dutch. Now only one operator is required, and the language requirement is no longer necessary because data input is automated. FloraHolland employs approximately 42 different nationalities.

FloraHolland views RFID as a key enabler of further supply chain improvement. To date RFID has enabled asset management across the supply chain, internal process data accuracy and precision, and labour reduction. Its next key challenge is to track and trace product batches after passing the auction clock. Up to the auction clock, each batch is associated with a cart, but afterwards the batches are split and transferred to other carts for distribution to particular wholesalers. The ability to track and trace product batches as well as assets will enable improvement of processes downstream of the auction clock to enable lead time reduction, process rationalisation and service quality improvement. Solutions are currently being piloted, but FloraHolland has adopted an evolutionary approach to RFID technology roll-out. The corporate vision is to evolve from asset management, through track and trace, to capturing consumer market data in approximately the next 10 years.

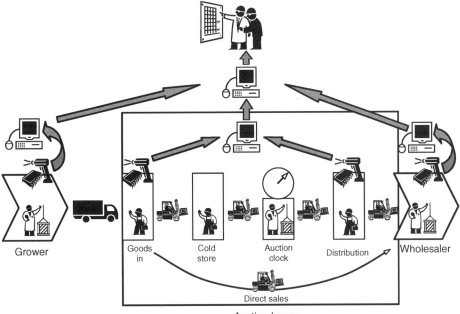

Figure 9.3   The RFID-enabled FloraHolland short supply chain[17]

SUPPLY CHAIN KNOWLEDGE MANAGEMENT

This chapter has discussed the multitude of data and information in contemporary global supply chains and how they can be managed and used. Through the synthesis and analysis of data, we gain information. For example, from the interaction between an RFID reader and RFID tags, time and location data can be acquired. By transmitting this to a middleware for synthesis and analysis, information about the movement of freight and delivery lead time can be generated and transmitted to a central management information system to be interrogated by other software applications such as ERP and accessed by users. Using this information and synthesising it with other business information can create knowledge. That is to say, through internalisation and understanding of information, knowledge is gained. Hence global supply chains are also filled with knowledge, some of which is *tacit* (i.e. held in the heads of employees) and some of which is made *explicit* (available to all) via knowledge repositories and information systems. Knowledge management is the term used to describe the capture, storage, use and sharing of knowledge within an organisation. The term '**supply chain knowledge management**' is therefore introduced here to describe those knowledge management processes that span a supply chain.

In new product development, knowledge creation has long been recognised as being fundamental to developing new and innovative products, which in turn delivers competitive advantage. This is also true of knowledge creation in other areas of a business.[18] In logistics and SCM, supply-side and demand-side knowledge is critical to managing supply chain performance. Conventionally logistics and supply chain knowledge has been largely tacit, with individual managers and workers holding the knowledge necessary to 'work around' inherent inefficiencies in logistics processes. This means that such individuals are critical to maintaining and improving supply chain performance.[19] However, this is an undesirable situation. If a particular '**knowledge worker**' leaves the company, their knowledge leaves with them. Hence, the ability to create knowledge, capture it and make it explicit is essential for long-term supply chain improvement.

Supply chain knowledge management is an emerging area of research. As with information, knowledge created at one point in a supply network should be accessible across that network. For example, demand-side information is essential for understanding market demand. However, knowing what to do with that information enables an effective and efficient response to demand. Furthermore, building up that knowledge over a period of time enables a supply chain to begin to *sense and respond* to actual demand. Hence, the knowledge creating supply chain is able to be first to market, gaining competitive advantage.

LEARNING REVIEW

This chapter focused on the information systems employed in contemporary supply chains. We began by discussing the role of information in the supply chain. The provision of timely and accurate information is essential for the management of both supply- and demand-side functions. Nevertheless, supply chains are typically diverse and dispersed across disparate locations. Hence, this causes issues with information visibility and transparency. Our discussion therefore addressed the barriers and solutions to achieving information visibility and transparency.

We continued by discussing common information technology applications in contemporary supply chains and their roles. These technologies are designed to manage the increasing information complexity, proliferation, diffusion, velocity and accuracy we are confronted with. One particular technology, RFID, is a key enabler of managing each of these issues, via the provision of real time supply and demand data. This was therefore discussed at length.

Finally, it was also noted that the synthesis of the multitude of supply chain information creates knowledge. This in turn enables learning, which can be used to continually improve supply chain performance.

The next chapter will continue the journey along the supply chain and will focus on finance flows through the supply chain.

QUESTIONS

- As discussed above, *information complexity*, *proliferation*, *diffusion*, *velocity* and *accuracy* are key concerns in contemporary SCM. Information technologies are evolving to manage these issues, but what of the users?

- As discussed in Chapter 7, logistics tasks are increasingly more information intensive. Hence, how can we ensure that logistics managers and workers are able to cope with their increasingly complex information tasks?

- Discuss the four barriers to information visibility and transparency. If you were designing a new supply chain, how would you prevent each of these barriers occurring?

- A major issue for information technology adoption in SCM is the financial and resource investments required by all supply chain partners to implement state-of-the-art applications. For small-scale suppliers with low profit margins, this is difficult, if not an impossibility. How might their larger supplier partners support them?

- ERP links the operations and logistics functions with other business functions. CPFR links supply chain partner organisations. The next logical step is to link consumers with the supply chain. Are there any examples of this already (e.g. supermarket loyalty cards)? What would such an application look like?

MAPPING INFORMATION FLOWS IN THE FLORAHOLLAND SUPPLY CHAIN

Review the FloraHolland case above. In particular, Figure 9.3 illustrates the application of RFID across their short supply chain. Real time demand information flows electronically from the auctions and from direct sales. FloraHolland responds to this information, delivering the right products to the right customers within the tight time parameters set. This generates more information, which is in turn passed up the supply chain to the growers, who use it to understand actual demand and tailor their products to changing market needs.

Map the information flows across this supply chain. How many information interactions are there?

NOTES

1. Jharkharia, S. & Shankar, R. (2005) IT-enablement of supply chains: understanding the barriers, *Journal of Enterprise Information*, 18(1), 11–27.

2. BBC News 24 (2007) Cauliflower growers' pricing plea, http://news.bbc. co.uk/1/hi/england/6679557.stm, accessed 26/6/07.

3. Childerhouse, P., Hermiz, R., Mason-Jones, R., Popp, A. & Towill, D. (2003) Information flow in automotive supply chains – identifying and learning to overcome barriers to change, *Industrial Management & Data Systems*, 103(7), 491–502.

4. *Ibid.*

5. Adapted from Childerhouse *et al.*, *op. cit.*

6. Adapted from Sherer, S. (2005) From supply-chain management to value network advocacy: implications for e-supply chains, *Supply Chain Management: An International Journal*, 10(2), 77–83.

7. Adapted from Chaffey, D. (2004) *e-Business and e-Commerce Management*, 2nd edn, Harlow, FT/Prentice Hall, p.10.

8. Wilding, R. & Delgado, T. (2004) RFID demystified: supply-chain applications, *Logistics and Transport Focus*, 6(4), 42–48.

9. McFarlane, D. & Sheffi, Y. (2003) The impact of automatic identification on supply chain operations, *International Journal of Logistics Management*, 14(1), 1–17.

10. Wilding & Delgado, *op. cit.*

11. McFarlane & Sheffi, *op. cit.*

12. http://www.lexicle.com/smartfridge/ accessed 11/6/07.

13. McFarlane & Sheffi, *op. cit.*

14. Sheffi, Y. (2004) RFID and the innovation cycle, *International Journal of Logistics Management*, 15(1), 1–10.

15. Twist, D. (2005) The impact of radio frequency identification on supply chain facilities, *Journal of Facilities Management*, 3(3), 226–240.

16. Jharkharia & Shankar, *op. cit.*

17. Butcher, T. (2007) RFID: an enabler of agile supply chain decision-making, *International Journal of Agile Systems and Management*, 2(3), 305–320.

18. Nonaka I. & Takeuchi, H. (1995) *The Knowledge Creating Company: How Japanese Companies Create the Dynamics of Innovation*, New York, Oxford University Press, p.6.

19. Butcher, T. (2007) Supply chain knowledge work: restructuring the workforce for improved agility, *International Journal of Agile Systems and Management*, 2(4), 376–392.

Logistics and Financial Management

Mike Tayles

The University of Hull

INTRODUCTION

This chapter is concerned with the flow of financial resources through the supply chain. As we noted earlier, financial flows are the basis of trade, and logisticians need to be as competent in following the money trail as they are in following the product trail.

In this chapter we will discuss financial management and place particular emphasis on areas to which a logistics application applies. Within companies the term 'finance department' is probably the contemporary title for the department that carries out all matters concerned with accounting and financial management of the enterprise. Accounting and financial information is analysed and interpreted in different ways to meet the needs of various parties. An understanding of this is important for all managers because their fortunes, and that of their companies, are inevitably connected to financial performance in some way. Finance is the use of financial or accounting information by management at all levels to assist in planning, making decisions and controlling the activities of an enterprise. In the widest sense, this includes drawing financial information from, and communicating it to, interested parties both inside and outside the organisation.

Information traditionally presented to outsiders is usually in summary form, for the whole organisation. To insiders, the focus of information is on the part of the organisation for which they take responsibility. A consequence of this is that the finance function tends to see the organisation as consisting of vertical structures, silos, in line with the traditional organisational hierarchy. This does not fit with the process or flow mentality of providing logistics and supply chain solutions. Here management must place greater emphasis on the horizontal process; that is, the flow of product along a value chain and the support of this with appropriate finance information. If an appropriate or optimum solution to a supply chain problem requires cooperation between businesses, then this would involve creating accounting arrangements that deal with this and which perhaps share the benefits provided by the solution. Managers and accountants have to be open therefore to developments such as 'open book costing' where the parties are prepared to show each other their internal costing and profitability information, or increasing 'trust' between parties; that is, not relying on formal rules and regulations but acknowledging that all parties can, in the long term, benefit from a genuine cooperation between related parties.

As businesses develop more innovative solutions to supply chain problems it is possible that a tension may exist between accounting and supply chain managers. This offers both opportunities and problems. Opportunities to do things differently, which will contribute to the development and success of a business, and problems of complying with accepted accounting principles of recording and reporting accounting information.

Accounting and financial management can be defined as the process of defining, measuring and communicating economic information about an organisation to permit informed judgements and decisions by users of the information. This definition is very broad; for example, users may be shareholders or bankers outside the organisation, and directors or managers inside it. They will receive different forms of information depending on their position and relationship with the company and they may make different use of that information. In fact accounting and financial management consists of a few different types of activities: financial accounting, management accounting, and financial management. These activities are not discrete, they are interrelated as we shall see in the remainder of this chapter.

Chapter 10 comprises three core sections:

- Financial accounting
- Financial management
- Management accounting

In addition, in order to illustrate further application of material in the chapter, a case study (Deutsche Post/DHL) at the end of Part Two reviews financial data pertaining to that company.

LEARNING OBJECTIVES

- Describe and differentiate the accounting and financial information generated within logistics companies.
- Explain the key accounting statements, their purpose and implications.
- Demonstrate the importance of cash flow to a logistics company.
- Discuss business risk for a logistics company and currency risk in the context of international logistics activities.
- Outline the taxation implications of international transfers within a logistics company.
- Understand the role played by cost and management accounting information in a logistics company.
- Identify typical components of a balanced scorecard of a logistics company.

FINANCIAL ACCOUNTING

Financial accounting is ultimately concerned with reporting to and meeting the requirements of parties outside the organisation. These include:

- *Investors*; that is, those who have subscribed to an issue of shares by the company and who are therefore part owners of the company; or *prospective investors*, people or institutions who might be thinking of buying shares in the company. Both of these parties are informed by *financial analysts* who provide investment advice or offer general commentary in the press.
- The *Government*, in the form of the Registrar of Companies, or similar entity who performs a regulatory role on companies; and the *Revenue and Customs*, or similar entity, who are concerned with the taxation assessment made on companies and any duties incurred on imports, etc.
- *Business contacts*, for example *bankers* who may be approached to lend money to the company or *trade contacts*, such as *suppliers* and *customers*, who need information about the company to assess its reliability regarding a regular trading relationship. This is obviously important where a logistics solution may be provided by an external party or where external provision (outsourcing) is being considered in comparison to in-house (i.e. own account) provision of logistics.

Many other parties may also have an interest in the accounts of an organisation, for example competitors, pressure groups, employees and trades unions.

In public limited companies there is often a separation between the management of the company (including the directors), those entrusted to run it, and the owners (shareholders). The shareholders employ the directors to run the business for them. Directors may be shareholders but in most public limited companies they are not majority shareholders. Financial accounts are prepared for these public limited companies (and must be placed before the shareholders in an Annual General Meeting) and also for sole traders, partnerships and private limited companies. We, however, will focus mostly here on public limited companies.

Companies, while having a legal entity, are not human: they can't make decisions, the directors of companies do that. In recent years there has been considerable interest in *corporate governance*; that is, the way companies are directed and controlled. This involves issues such as *disclosure* – what is disclosed and when; *accountability* – the roles and duties of directors; and *fairness* – that directors do not benefit from 'inside' information. There have been various efforts by the accounting profession in the UK, for example, to address this involving the development of a Combined Code of Best Practice issued in 1998, revised in 2003. Corporate governance is an evolving phenomenon, for example there have been dramatic and world-wide repercussions because of a small number of scandals involving large companies, for example Enron who were accused of manipulation of accounting rules and their auditors Arthur Anderson, and WorldCom, a long-distance phone company, who used fraudulent accounting methods to mask a declining accounting condition. In the USA, in response to these events, legislation was enacted to improve the oversight of accounting and reporting practices, called the **Sarbanes–Oxley Act** or **SOX** after the US Senators who sponsored the act. It established a Public Company Accounting Oversight Board to deal with overseeing, regulating, inspecting and disciplining firms.

Selected information from the financial accounts of a company is required by law to be made available to the public and deposited with the appropriate government agency. The resulting documents are referred to as the published accounts, the annual accounts or the corporate report. The law and the recommendations of financial reporting practice dictate what minimum information should be disclosed. The accounting profession recommends the style and content of the published accounts. In the UK, for example, these are known as financial reporting standards (FRS). These are not legally binding, but accountants are expected to follow them and can be disciplined if they do not do so. The Stock Exchange also has requirements which must be met by companies wishing to be quoted on it. As companies become increasingly global and in line with European and international integration, there is an increasing move to develop international reporting standards (IRS).

Financial statements in general, and published accounts in particular, perform the role of stewardship; that is, demonstrating that the directors of the company have managed the funds entrusted to them by shareholders in an appropriate manner. In other words, they have not spent unnecessarily on assets or made inappropriate decisions on the buying or selling of goods and services and making contracts with third parties. The main documents that are used as evidence in this context are the **balance sheet**, the **profit and loss account** and the **cash flow statement**. In the published accounts these are supplemented by extensive notes, a Directors' Report and a Chairman's Statement. The fact that the accounts represent a 'true and fair view' of the state of the affairs of the company has to be established by independent professional accountants in practice (known as auditors).

The accounting documents in the published accounts are important summaries of the current financial position of the organisation, the results of the transactions of a trading or accounting period and a statement to help people to judge the current *liquid position* of the company. That is, whether the company has sufficient funds in cash or near cash to be able to pay its bills when they fall due. These documents will be examined in more detail below, but it is important to appreciate initially that:

- All the information is historical, the documents report actual past transactions. To fulfil the stewardship role only past events can be audited and reported on with any accuracy and objectivity.

- The information contains only those matters relating to the organisation that can be expressed in monetary terms.

- Only matters that can be established with objectivity are included. Values that are subjective, or a matter of opinion and which cannot be verified or audited would not be included. The company or the auditors would be expected to comment if any items of a subjective or doubtful nature existed in the accounts in order to draw attention to them.

- The published accounts are prepared annually, though interim statements are often made half yearly.

Financial accounts

The *balance sheet* aims to convey the financial position of an organisation at a particular point in time. It is always dated and the information contained in it is a snapshot of the financial position of the organisation at that date, usually the end of the accounting period, typically the accounting year. It consists of a list of assets and liabilities. Assets are resources owned by the company – buildings, plant and equipment (fixed assets), stock, debtors and cash (current assets). Liabilities are obligations owed by the company to other people who may have provided funds, goods or services (for example shareholders), banks who have made loans to the company and creditors for goods or services who have not yet been paid.

Fixed assets are shown at their cost price or at some value below that which is an adjustment to reflect their age or wearing out, called depreciation. Depreciation in accounting is how the original cost of an asset is shared out over each accounting period in which it is used. Assets may be further reduced in value if it is estimated that their market value is even lower (a concept called conservatism). Assets may be revalued upwards if they are felt to have experienced appreciation of a reasonably reliable permanent nature, though they must have been formally revalued by a professional valuer. Depreciation is an important concept in logistics due to the heavy capital-intensive nature of the sector (warehouses, vehicles, etc.).

Some companies, not least those in logistics, may lease rather than buy some of their assets. Traditionally it was believed to be important to 'own' assets but the business imperative has moved towards simply the 'right to use' assets rather than own them. This has tended to be so popular recently that owners of valuable assets (a warehouse, for example) have been encouraged to sell the asset to a finance house and lease it back (**sale and lease back**). This can have valuable tax benefits on which the finance house is better positioned to capitalise and can make the company look more efficient, earning high revenues from an apparent lower investment in assets. Accounting rules have some approaches to deal with these situations of the difference between the 'substance over form' of a transaction in the accounts, but the readers of accounts should bear in mind that where any variations occur from very traditional ways of doing business, then what is reflected in the accounts should be read carefully.

Additionally companies in logistics may also own sophisticated systems and processes based on IT systems such as SAP and while the hardware may be owned as assets, the software may not have been 'capitalised', rather it may have been written into the books as an expense of the profit and loss account. The skill and ability of employees to operate these systems will also be recorded as expenses. These *intangible* assets are rarely recorded in the balance sheet, in fact, current regulation discourages it. This fact could, in this event, distort the apparent state of affairs of the business and its performance as shown in various accounting measures or in its appearance to investors. Only if these intangible assets were acquired from a third party by a 'market-based' transaction would they be recorded in the accounts.

It is important to note that the balance sheet relates to the business (a legal entity), not to the shareholders. Any share capital is therefore a liability of the business because it is owed to the shareholders. Any net profit earned is also the property of the shareholders. This is paid to them either as a dividend or reinvested in the business on their behalf in which it is called a 'reserve'. A balance sheet should always balance, that is to say, assets should equal liabilities because these two aspects are looking at the same thing but from two different perspectives – what the company owns and what it owes.

The *profit and loss account* or *income statement* aims to convey to the reader the result of the trading activity of the business for a defined period of time. Profit or loss is determined by comparing revenue from sales made with expenses consumed in making and selling the products and services sold. Expenses are often subdivided into the costs of different functions of the organisation, typically manufacturing, administration, selling, research and development.

Various rules and conventions dictate how revenues and costs should be compared (called matching). It is important to appreciate that some costs incurred in one accounting period can be carried into the next accounting period, for example if they are attached to some stock which is unsold. Naturally this applies only to manufacturing costs. Nonmanufacturing costs are often dealt with as an expense of the accounting period in which they are incurred, often called period costs.

From the information contained in the profit and loss account a gross profit can be determined (sales less cost of sales). The operating profit is determined by deducting other expenses, administration and selling costs, etc. from the gross profit. An item that falls within normal trading activities but is individually significant is called an exceptional item and disclosed separately. An example of a nonrecurring exceptional item could be the retirement of an old fleet of aeroplanes before they were fully depreciated or the replacement of an obsolete company-wide IT system with a newer, more efficient version. Profit after deduction of tax is available to be paid to shareholders as a dividend or to be retained in the company for reinvestment, for example in new plant and machinery. An adjustment may be made to the profit after tax for any item that is derived from events outside the ordinary activities of the business, called an extraordinary item. This is sometimes referred to as an adjustment below the line.

Cash flow is sometimes called the lifeblood of the business. It is important for all businesses to trade at a profit, that is to sell their goods or services at a price that exceeds their cost. It is equally important, however, to ensure that an organisation manages the way in which cash is generated and used. That is not the same thing as ensuring profitability. A business can be profitable but short of cash and the converse can also apply. It is useful for both management inside the company and outsiders who are appraising the company to examine how cash has been controlled in the past accounting period. The cash flow statement provides such a basis by showing *where funds have come from*, such as outside the organisation (share capital and loans), and inside the organisation (from the manufacturing trading cycle), and *where the funds go to* outside the organisation (dividends, taxation, loan interest), and inside the organisation (in the investment in fixed assets or the manufacturing trading cycle). See Figure 10.1 for the flow of funds round a traditional business.

For funds to be tied up in the business for a long time (in working capital) is wasteful and inefficient for the business, it means asking shareholders to subscribe more money than is realistically needed, and it is therefore to be discouraged. Making the amount of cash tied up as small as possible is a way to enhance performance and profit. Just-in-time manufacturers realised this a long time ago, and attempts to minimise stock and work in progress are a way to use capital and cash efficiently, providing production flow and supply can be guaranteed. Time has emerged as an important dimension of performance and logistics companies should be trying to deliver a product or service in a minimum required time, with resources committed for only a short time, thus minimising the amount of cash involved, the shortest possible cash-to-cash cycle. This is likely to result in a higher accounting performance all other things being equal.

Dell Computer Corporation, which we studied at the end of Part One, has this off to a fine art; they have a reputation for starting to assemble a computer for a customer only once the order is placed. In other words, they receive an order and within a relatively short period of time are likely to receive payment from the customer. They simultaneously source the components and transport requirements from various suppliers, paying for them on normal credit terms (most likely anywhere between 30 and 90 days). It is quite likely that Dell has a very short cash-to-cash cycle and therefore needs to have only a very small level of working capital in its balance sheet.

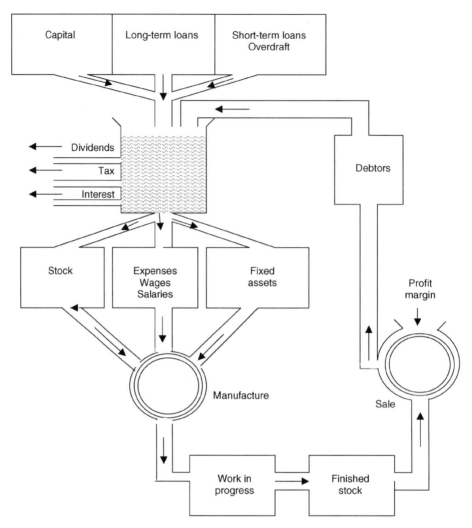

Figure 10.1   Flow of funds in a typical manufacturing business

FINANCIAL MANAGEMENT

Financial management is concerned with how the company manages its funds over the longer term. This involves, for example, decisions on the extent of its financing – how many shares it issues and at what price, whether it borrows money from the bank or not to supplement its financing, whether it pays a dividend from its profit to shareholders or retains this in the company. It extends to decisions as to how the company spends its finances in the acquisition of new buildings, plant and equipment and the management of its working capital – stock, debtors and cash.

Ordinary shares are the basic form of business finance. Shareholders may be a private individual, an insurance company, a unit trust, a bank, a trades union and so on. Shares are issued with a nominal value (25p for example, or in the case of Deutsche Post 1 euro, see the case below), which is shown on the face of the share certificate. They may be issued by the company at any price if it is believed the investor will be willing to pay something different (a premium). This will depend on the company's prospects. Once shares are in the market they will change hands between shareholders at various prices, depending again on the company's prospects. The market price is of concern to the company but it is not incorporated into the accounts of the company in any way, other than when the shares are first issued to the public.

Ordinary shareholders carry the main investment risk of the business. They get the rewards in the form of dividend or increased share price if the company does well, but they lose some or all of their investment if it does badly. The most they can lose is the value of their shares: the principle of *limited liability* states that shareholders' liability is limited to the sum they have paid or agreed to pay for their shares.

Risk is a fundamental aspect of doing business and has taken on increasing importance recently (see Chapter 12). In any stock market, or indeed any market economy, the greater the risk incurred the greater the reward that is expected. No one wants to take on more risk than they need to for a given level of return, likewise in competitive situations companies and investors will always select a higher rather than lower level of return for the same risk.

International business

A logistics company doing business internationally faces greater risks than one operating only nationally. It faces the higher business risk and uncertainty (market demand, delivery reliability, etc.) that may exist in the international environment and the different countries in which it does business. There may be different levels of political risk in the countries and the company may have only limited information on which to make judgements about this; naturally more information can be obtained but this is only at a cost and its validity may be suspect. A company also has to face currency risk; those trading in various international currencies must make decisions on the currency in which they will buy and sell their services. If they do not wish to operate as currency speculators, and most will not because they do not have the expertise, they will have to anticipate their currency needs and 'hedge' their risk in some way so that a trading profit is revealed rather than a currency fluctuation. It also means incorporating into the accounts of companies the 'home country' equivalent value of international transactions so they can all be accumulated in one currency for the appropriate financial reports.

Doing business, either buying or selling, in another currency, means that a company is exposed to fluctuations in that currency, called currency exposure. If the proportion of that business is considerable, it is wise for the company to obtain or develop expertise in dealing with the exposure. The accounting impacts can be various and affect both the profit and loss and balance sheet. **Transaction exposure** is related to the profit reported from a foreign transaction. For example, if a UK company is selling something in China and the contract is signed for payment to be made in the foreign currency (RMB), and between the date of the contract and the cash flow payment actually being received the currency falls in value by 4% relative to the UK currency (GBP), this will be a real loss to the company. **Translation exposure** is more of an accounting recording issue; that is, it is related to the value of assets held in China by a UK registered company which prepares consolidated accounts in the UK. The assets would be translated into the current UK balance sheet at a value relevant at the balance sheet date. This will affect the apparent value of the company on the balance sheet, but not the profitability of its trading. The same implication applies to borrowings undertaken in a foreign currency.

An international company must therefore consider its economic exposure. It may buy and sell goods and services in many parts of the world and hence the value of the stream of foreign cash flows when denominated in the 'home' currency (e.g. GBP for a UK based company) will alter over time; this will affect the sterling value of the whole operation. It may move to favour the company or to its detriment, depending on the currency movement. Obviously it is good for say a UK based company to sell to companies whose currency is likely to rise in value against GBP and to buy from those whose currency value is likely to fall, but this is clearly not always possible. One way to avoid this uncertainty is to establish all contracts in the home currency of the company and shift all risk to the trading partner. This would leave the foreign company to convert any purchase and sales to its own currency and make decisions as to the relative levels of business to undertake. Often these relative levels of economic exposure are affected by long term and political factors affecting economic growth, taxation, etc.

Where an international company has operations in different parts of the world, *taxation* can have a significant impact on the reported financial results. This is not the same as undertaking transactions internationally, but involves operating and earning profits from activities and owning assets in different parts of the world. A fundamental point here is that the profits earned in different countries throughout the world should be taxed based on the rules existing in the country in which they were earned. This may be even though the accounts may be subsequently consolidated into a currency of the country of the holding company. It can have implications for international transactions and the transfer, say, of components between companies within the same group in different countries.

When goods or services are transferred between divisions of the same company a value is attributed to them called a **transfer price**. This is an internal price and is recorded in the books of account in order to compute the profit arising on the transaction accumulating to the profit of the two entities involved. The two parties inevitably will seek a price that makes the results in their respective accounts look best for them, that is the highest possible selling price or the lowest possible buying price. The company as a whole may take a slightly different view when this occurs internationally. Setting a transfer price at a level to reduce the overall company tax bill may be to the financial benefit of the whole company, but this might not be what is desired by either of the businesses in their respective countries. The company would like the higher profit on the transaction to be reported in the country that has the most favourable (lowest) tax rates, or for example in the division which has accumulated losses (to act as offset), rather than a division operating in a high tax region or that already has a high level of profits. This must be acceptable to both the auditors and the taxation authorities, it must therefore reflect a reasonable price for the product or service and must not be used fraudulently. In other words, it must follow generally accepted accounting principles and appear to be a reasonable price in the circumstances, not out of line with other business by this or similar companies. Some multinational companies might move work-in-progress materials (which they would not necessarily have to move) between regions so as to use transfer pricing to minimise their overall tax charge in the accounts. An important distinction must be observed between tax avoidance, that is arranging affairs to minimise tax, and tax evasion, which is attempting to mislead and defraud the tax authorities, which is illegal.

Borrowing

An important source of finance is borrowing. Borrowing may be described variously as a loan, mortgage or debenture. Debt is often secured on the assets of the business and is basically a contract between the company and the bank for a loan of a particular term. An overdraft, which is agreed with the bank to apply over a relatively long period, may also fall into this category. Company law permits the interest paid for borrowed funds to be offset against any taxation liability and this is an important benefit for a company which engages in borrowing. In other words, the loan interest that is payable is an expense of the profit and loss account before the assessment of taxation. In contrast, dividends are paid out to shareholders out of profits after the interest and tax have been deducted. A company which has borrowed money to buy an asset, for example a warehouse, will benefit by the loan interest and the depreciation[1] being allowable against tax. This is in some contrast to sale and lease back mentioned earlier where the finance house effectively raises the loan, owns the warehouse and benefits from the tax allowance of depreciation.

The extent to which a company is financed by shares or debt is described as its *gearing*. Little or no debt is called low gearing. If a company has a large proportion of debt this is described as high gearing. In the case of high gearing much of the business risk is applied to the relatively smaller proportion of share capital and hence is a high-risk investment for any shareholder. However, if the company is successful the rewards can be proportionally greater. Naturally risk is different for different businesses and also depends on the products and markets in which the company does business.

The accounts of a company represent the results of the financial management and trading decisions made by its management. It is important for all logisticians to be able to undertake an interpretation of the accounts of a company and make judgements about the trading prospects and financial management of it. These judgements are often assisted by examining the relationship between pieces of information in the accounts called *ratios*.

To demonstrate with financial numbers from a real logistics company some of the issues discussed above, the reader is referred to the case (p. 205) on Deutsche Post/DHL, a leading 3PL we already mentioned briefly in Chapter 4.

MANAGEMENT ACCOUNTING

A large multi-product organisation is a complex entity and to ensure that the financial accounts and financial management of the company display a relatively stable picture is very important. That is, that it does not hold any surprises or shocks for the investors, because this will inevitably affect its share price. This requires detailed internal information with which to manage the development of the enterprise on a more short-term basis. This is often called **management accounting** and is undertaken to ensure that the long-term financial management of the enterprise is on track. The exact distinction between management accounting and financial management is not always clearly defined, it does not need to be, the content of this information overlaps. One thing it has in common is that information on this is internal to the company and its management, the detail and rationale does not have to be shared with the public in general, though the outcomes in the financial accounts are eventually apparent.

Inside the organisation the finance department produces information for management, which is not published because it contains details of the company's plans and its strategies for going forward. This is called *management accounting* or sometimes *cost accounting*. Management and cost accounting serves internal members of the organisation and often relates to segments of it (departments, machine groups, sales regions, individuals). It is future oriented, not governed by any legal regulation and entirely optional to the company. Its aim will be to produce the information that is most useful to management in the achievement of their organisational objectives.

Cost accounting involves accumulating cost information to value stock, help with judgements on pricing and profitability analysis, decide whether a product or a contract is worth proceeding with, etc. Management accounting has a wider role, which could involve special studies relating to decision making, for example whether to make or buy a product (in-house provision or outsourcing) or whether to take a special order. It also involves the generation of financial plans and regular reporting of actual results in order to monitor the performance of departments within a company (budgetary control). Another example of a major nonrecurring decision is the investment in large-scale capital projects with a time horizon of many years. Here a comparison of cost, revenue and profit is rarely sufficient and so special techniques are required. Finally, management accounting is not only inward-looking, it can also extend to the collection of valuable external information about competitors, their prices, market shares and meeting customer requirements.

Costing

Costing is concerned with the collection of costs and their relation to activities of the company, often called a cost object, which could be a product or service, a department, an operation, a machine or a sales territory. A useful and common framework within which to consider the provision of cost information is related to the major areas in which accounting information supports management. These are stock valuation and the calculation of profit, decision making and planning and control.

The calculation of a product cost requires the identification and measurement of all costs that are directly or indirectly associated with a product or any activity. Costs that can be easily and conveniently associated with a finished product are called *direct costs*. There is usually no ambiguity over the association of these costs with the item that is being 'costed', raw material or purchased components for example. All costs that are not direct are called *indirect costs*, although *overhead* tends to be a more usual term: costs of management and supervision are typical indirect labour costs. Indirect expenses are the costs incurred in providing the supporting and general facilities of the company. Rent, rates, heat and light are all examples of indirect expenses.

For a logistics company the costing may be undertaken in relation to a service, for example the delivery of the product of another company to a new location and perhaps in a different form, but the same principle applies. To an extent there may be greater complexity because costing of a service may be more difficult. Services are intangible, they are difficult to measure, for example in terms of quality, they cannot be stored (they are perishable), so if not undertaken when required they are lost forever. In services few of the costs are often direct and many are indirect and this makes the arbitrariness more of a problem. This may be compounded in that logistics arrangements may be undertaken by more than one company working in harmony so that the total cost of a logistics operation may be the sum of various subsidiary operations carried out by different suppliers.

Many service businesses carry out costing procedures but often, given the complexity mentioned above, they either choose to (1) prepare a simplistic costing that deals very arbitrarily with the ambiguity of overhead costs, or (2) alternatively incur the higher costs of installing a sophisticated costing system to track the detail of costs along all of the supply chain. Such an arrangement is optional and entirely in the hands of the company. Internal management accounting information is not a requirement for companies, they use it only if it is seen to be helpful.

The objective when dealing with indirect costs or overheads in product costing is to try and apportion them as equitably as possible to products. One principal reason for this is to arrive at a cost that will help in setting a selling price. It would be possible to add up all the overheads for a whole factory and apportion these at a single universal average rate applied in accordance with the number of each type of unit produced or relative to the number of production hours consumed by each product. However, such a single 'blanket rate' is only suited to very small operations or where only one product is manufactured; it is not very accurate. A more usual method of dealing with overheads starts with the calculation of an overhead rate for each department. Some costs can be directly identified with a department and others which are indirect can be shared between departments on an equitable basis. As a result the approximate cost of running each department is determined. A problem with this approach for modern businesses however is that it reinforces the department-centred or silo approach that has existed in businesses for such a long time. It runs counter to the (horizontal) cross-business culture which SCM and logistics encourage and one which managers envisage the products or services they provide actually follow.

Activity based costing

The approach mentioned above using departmental rates has been established for many years. Recently, with the increasing use of sophisticated techniques in both manufacturing and operations management, the accuracy and value of these costing exercises has been called into question. It is suggested that it might be fruitful for organisations to examine in more detail the activities they carry out in the production and delivery of a product. They may be able to identify a number of activities which may be used to apply overheads to products more appropriately, such as number of orders processed, number of quality inspections or machine setups, deliveries, etc. Some companies have experimented with this approach, called *activity based costing* (ABC, and not to be confused with the stock classification system discussed in Chapter 6, also called ABC), and have produced results that are interesting and different from the traditional method.

One useful feature of the ABC approach is that it identifies the processes and activities that a product or service incurs in a company. That is, the thinking behind it is close to the product flow or process envisaged by management and mapped out as part of a logistics operation in many companies. This was often not the case with traditional costing, which took the silo or department-centred approach mentioned earlier. The fact that it requires a more detailed analysis of activities and their costs means that the system is more expensive to operate, unless some of the data is available already, and thus often only larger companies have the resources to undertake this costing in any great detail. There is nothing to prevent smaller businesses also experimenting with the approach to determine whether it can support their decision making and control.

DHL chose to install a detailed ABC system in the 1990s because they felt that their administrative indirect (overhead) costs had grown considerably and more than some of their operations and customer service costs. The ABC system helped them explore the costs of some of the processes and activities they were undertaking and exactly what they were getting for these costs, did they add value, etc.[2] They felt they needed to get 'a handle' on the causes of these costs and it was not happening with the information they were currently producing. Additionally, as a customer-focused company they needed an analysis of the profitability of customers and customer groups, and this was not available in any meaningful way with their present system.

It should be pointed out that having the profitability information such as this is a first step in managing costs that are incurred. Observing that the cost of a particular process is high does not alter the situation, it is up to management to respond to this by taking decisions. It might be observed that some activities are very expensive, compared with the use of competitors or external suppliers, so is outsourcing these activities an option? Alternatively, how can the company become smarter at some of these activities or processes so as reduce their cost? Does the customer value the activity (say, delivery at an agreed time), does the customer pay for this service, does it add value?

Most of the above approach to costing is carried out for the accounting year in which the company is operating. This is in line with the annual reporting that a company undertakes to shareholders. This does not have to be so. One alternative that is sometimes used is called **lifecycle costing** or **whole life costing**. It can be applied to a product or to a resource of the company like an asset. It rejects the notion that performance can be broken down into an arbitrary annual time to suit financial reporting and instead explores costs and performance over the whole life from design to retirement or cradle to grave. It therefore gives an overview of cost performance without being distorted by showing periods of high cost at, say, introduction and relatively low cost at eventual steady state operation. This aligns with the product lifecycle concept which management are well aware of, but which accountants have given less emphasis to, perhaps because of imperatives of periodic financial reporting that drive many company accounting systems.

Management accounting information can help management with a wider range of decisions and provide an insight into the financial consequences of a particular course of action. Ad hoc tactical decisions can vary depending on the circumstances in which the decisions are made; for example, if a business is working to full capacity it is likely to seek to establish a selling price that will cover all of its costs (assuming it is a profit seeking company). It will want the highest price it can get allowing for any issues concerned with both the wider business strategy and business ethics. If, however, a company has spare capacity it may be prepared to accept (in some cases) a price that does not cover all of its costs. That is, it may be prepared to omit any costs that in total would remain virtually unaffected by the decision to do a deal (for example rent or management salaries). It would only consider the costs that will change because of the decision, said to be the *costs at the margin* or the *marginal costs*. A special cost analysis would be necessary to identify marginal costs. A tactic such as using marginal costs must not, however, be allowed to offend regular customers who pay the full price, so such deals may need to take place in segregated markets.

One factor that is often singled out for detailed attention is the volume of output of a business; this may be influenced by manipulating price, for example. A typical decision may be to identify how many units of a particular product to make and sell at a certain price. This decision requires the identification of likely revenue, cost and profit at different levels of output, called **cost, volume, profit (CVP) analysis**. This particularly relies on the identification of variable and fixed costs. Variable costs are those that change approximately in proportion to output; fixed costs are those that in total remain unchanged despite changes in activity. In addition there are a number of mixed costs that need to be analysed as to their fixed and variable components to be incorporated into such analysis. There are no hard and fast rules governing accounting for decision making. The example just described only introduces the issues; each decision making situation requires its own unique arrangement of costs and revenues.

Management accounting also supports managers with financial planning and control. Planning is a most important managerial function and associated with this is the need to implement plans and monitor them. Accounting can support this process using budgeting and variance analysis. The issue and use of departmental budgets is part of a system of responsibility accounting where actual results are compared with plans predicted for each department with the intention of taking action to correct any divergences. Only those costs and revenues over which a manager can exercise significant influence should be included in their responsibility report, this is a fundamental principle of controllability.

Using nonfinancial information

It should be noted also that control information should be in a form that is most useful and understandable to the appropriate manager. Following on from this, it is logical that some information may be of a nonfinancial nature. This may be provided sooner than any equivalent financial measure and would be in a form more suited to the manager's situation. Such nonfinancial information helps to put the financial measures into a more appropriate context and helps to ensure that wider objectives than the purely financial ones are addressed. In many companies the use of nonfinancial measures is not new; however they have often been

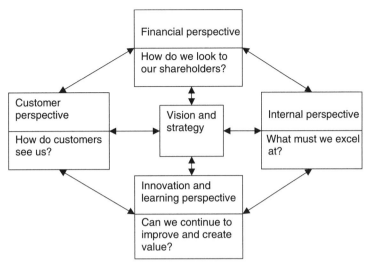

Figure 10.2   The balanced scorecard. Source: Kaplan, R. & Norton, D. (1992) The balanced scorecard – measures that drive performance, *Harvard Business Review,* January–February.

generated on a somewhat random basis without much structure as to which are the most important ones. There are various approaches or frameworks that have been put forward to help structure a meaningful set of nonfinancial and financial performance measures. One approach that has been used widely and quite successfully in this context is the **balanced scorecard (BSC)**,[3] which has received considerable promotion in the literature and through consultancies (see Figure 10.2). This seeks to set performance measures from the top of the organisation; that is, those that are most important to the achievement of an organisation's strategy.

The original version of the BSC had four sectors: customer, finance, operations, and innovation and learning. Management would then pose the question, 'in what ways do we need to excel in these areas in order to be successful?' This would give rise to a set of measures that would be the key to the performance and adding value in the company. They would be set by, and would help set the strategy of, the company. In setting these, the company would identify appropriate objectives, measures that reflect the objectives, targets it would be expected to achieve in each measure and any initiatives to help reach the targets. The key is in having a small number of measures that reflect the strategy, not a wide range of measures over which there is no clarity. An important component is the existence of a supposed cause-and-effect relationship between the various measures.

For example, a logistics company might perceive that for them customer satisfaction was critical, in terms of delivering on schedule within the prescribed time frame. In the customer segment a *soft* measure would involve a survey of customers' scoring of their performance, a *hard* measure would be the number of times a delivery was refused. In operations, schedule adherence would be an important measure, perhaps analysed by teams, this being achieved within a target or budgeted cost. In order to achieve good operational performance, employee training may be important, so number of days on training courses may be used to encourage employee development; employee morale may also be measured. Finally, the views of shareholders may be reflected in the achievement in typical financial measures such as return on capital employed or cash flow. The cause-and-effect argument goes that better trained and motivated employees will deliver a better operational service to customers, which will result in greater customer satisfaction, more business and recommendations, and ultimately higher profit. The measures can then be cascaded down the organisation hierarchy to ensure that managers in an organisation give attention to the measures they can influence, which reflect strategic issues related to customers, innovation and operations, in addition to financial performance.

We will return to discuss other nonfinancial performance measures in Chapter 11.

LEARNING REVIEW

In this chapter we have seen that logistics and financial management has both internal and external perspectives. The key financial accounting documents through which a company informs existing and potential investors, governments and other business contacts have been discussed. The structure, content and importance of the profit and loss account, balance sheet and cash flow statement have been outlined. We have pointed out how expertise in logistics and supply chain activity can have a beneficial effect on cash flow.

When dealing with finance issues we have drawn attention to the distinction between shares and loans, and to the use of sale and lease back in modern finance decisions. We have discussed the implications of risk on business performance and particularly currency risk in an international logistics company. We have pointed out typical forms of internal accounting information for managers that relate to product or service costs including ABC. A wider range of management accounting information was covered with reference to cost, volume, profit analysis. Planning and control have been mentioned including the emergence of the balanced scorecard.

The next chapter, Chapter 11, Measuring and Managing Logistics Peformance, further discusses some of the issues developed in this chapter, in particular the use of nonfinancial performance measures. As the concluding chapter in Part Two, the focus of which was 'doing' logistics, Chapter 11 endeavours to bring together all of the various logistics nodes, links and flows discussed in this part of the book and outlines how logistics and supply chain performance can be measured and managed.

QUESTIONS

- Briefly distinguish between financial accounting, financial management and management accounting.
- Who may be interested in the accounting information produced by a logistics company?
- In what ways might an international logistics company face currency risk?
- Differentiate between transaction and translation exposure.
- In what ways might a logistics company legally manipulate its tax bill?
- Outline typical direct and indirect costs of a logistics company known to you.
- Contrast activity based costing with traditional costing.
- Outline possible measures on a balanced scorecard of a logistics company.

NOTES

1. In taxation assessment this is called capital allowances and specific rules apply.
2. Holton, M. (1998) Implementing ABC in a service-driven business – DHL worldwide, in Innes, J. (ed.) *Handbook of Management Accounting*, London, Gee, 23A 1–12.
3. Kaplan, R. & Norton, D. (1992) The balanced scorecard – measures that drive performance, *Harvard Business* Review, January–February, 71–79.

FURTHER READING

Drury, C. (2005) *Management Accounting for Business*, 3rd edn, London, Thomson.

McLaney, E. & Atrill, P. (2005) *Accounting: An Introduction,* 3rd edn, London, FT Prentice Hall.

Pike, R. & Neale, B. (2003) *Corporate Finance and Investment*, 4th edn, London, FT Prentice Hall.

Tayles, M. & Drury, C. (2001) Moving from make/buy to strategic sourcing: case study insights, *Long Range Planning,* 34, 605–622.

Measuring and Managing Logistics Performance

Noel McGlynn

Microsoft

INTRODUCTION

The traditional practice in logistics service providers (LSPs) and related companies has been that managers in these companies do not spend substantial periods of time on measuring and managing performance. Instead, they tend to focus only on operational execution (i.e. getting the job done), and meeting only the most basic of measurable criteria. As a result they tend not to spend much time on performance measurement, except only where deemed absolutely necessary.

This is changing, however, driven by both competition and, especially, as a result of increasing demands from customers who want to be assured of effective management of their business. This chapter is thus concerned with the measurement and management of performance in the logistics context. As such it endeavours to bring together all of the various logistics nodes, links and flows discussed in Part Two and outline how logistics and supply chain performance can be measured and managed.

Chapter 11 comprises seven core sections:
- Basic measurement
- A contemporary viewpoint
- Driving forces for performance measurement
- Selecting the best measures
- Commonly used metrics
- Inventory/warehouse related metrics
- Logistics costs performance

LEARNING OBJECTIVES

- Understand basic forms of performance measurement used in a logistics context such as tachographs in road haulage and space utilisation in warehousing.
- Illustrate the trend towards measurement of a wider array of activities and the eight driving forces behind this trend.
- Explain why many LSPs now routinely share key performance data with customers.
- Understand the role of benchmarking in the context of logistics performance management.
- Identify how many and which key performance indicators (KPIs) to track, how they are embedded within the organisation, how they fit with wider company objectives, where the requisite data will come from, and who (at what levels within the organisation) should receive the information generated by these KPIs.
- Understand in particular warehouse/inventory metrics and total landed costs.

BASIC MEASUREMENT

The performance measures that logistics companies traditionally spent some time on are those measures that were either very basic from an operational viewpoint, or imposed on them by law.

As such, LSPs would have concerned themselves with ensuring that statutory requirements were met and that their financial obligations regarding preparation and filing of annual accounts and so forth were given some time and focus. For many small and larger companies alike, the main focus of this work may have been to ensure that tax affairs were in order and that the correct returns to the relevant government agencies were made. The overall profit margin of the company would also have been recorded and used as a key part of internal reviews, though little of this information would have been shared outside the company. The general exception to this would be the annual report, which would have to be filed and, depending on local legislation, be publicly available.

LSPs providing transportation have, for a number of years, been required to record their transport operations. A device known as a **tachograph** is fitted to a truck and is used to record the speed of the truck, distance travelled and any breaks taken by the driver. It is an instrument used by many police forces worldwide to ensure that laws relating to the maximum hours a truck driver can work are obeyed. Although there are variations among different countries, the rules are designed to limit continuous driving time and detail minimum breaks and rest periods. For vehicles over a certain payload, often defined as four tonnes or more, the tachograph is considered a legal requirement, and must be regularly tested to ensure that it is in good working order. In certain geographies the results from tachographs must be recorded and filed by the truck operator. The tachograph is still in use, though more recently instead of recording the relevant information onto a paper disk, the digital tachograph records the information onto a smart card or digital memory device.

Another area that traditionally has been a focus of measurement by LSPs has been around warehouse and other resource utilisation measures. These would typically include total number of pallet or carton spaces consumed versus total available, or simple measures of total space consumed within the warehouse. Some measure of throughput would generally also be looked at, for example the total number of shipments received. At the broader company level the key inventory measure, from a financial perspective, would be to measure inventory turnover (as already described in Chapter 6). For road transport companies, the basic operational measure could include total number of deliveries successfully completed versus '**dropped deliveries**' (a term sometimes used to refer to failed deliveries, i.e. the consignment that could not be delivered for whatever reason).

An important point to note is that such traditional measurements would generally not have been shared with or presented to the customer. These various measurements would have been analysed internally and customers in general would not be overly concerned with them as long as their basic needs had been served.

A CONTEMPORARY VIEWPOINT

Traditional LSPs are finding that since the 1990s, their business is either undergoing major change in order for them to hold their market position, or they are moving into niche markets. Most successful warehousing companies, for example, have had to invest significantly in IT, with warehouse management systems (WMS) used to record all movements within a warehouse, often controlled by a radio frequency (RF) handheld computer scanner, now seen in most modern warehouses. Traditional transport companies too have seen significant changes, with many of them moving into providing warehousing services in addition to their transportation offerings.

This physical flow of product through the supply chain is now joined by the flow of information, which records details of each transaction every time a pallet or box is touched or altered. Today's 3PLs not only have to display expertise in operational management, they must also keep track of each transaction and ensure that they and their customers and agents can have access to information relating to this flow as and when it is required. In fact, such is the importance of monitoring this information that many 3PLs now have dedicated staff whose job it is to record data that can be used in the development of **metrics**.

Metric reviews are thus now an important part of all business reviews, not just in logistics. In the past where the management of the company would not have reviewed any performance results, now such information in the form of metrics and **key performance indicators** (KPIs)[1] is shared with staff at all levels and in all functions, with partners and agents, and most importantly with customers. Indeed, most large customers now hold formal business reviews with their 3PLs where the presentation of such KPIs is a key part of the meeting's focus. Instead of providing performance data on a few select topics, logistics businesses now see measurement of the performance of all operational areas as a common requirement from their customers.

DRIVING FORCES FOR PERFORMANCE MEASUREMENT

At least eight driving forces behind the increased use of performance measurement in a logistics context can be identified:

1. Increased reliance on contract manufacturers
2. Strategic importance of LSPs to supply chain success
3. Adoption of manufacturing management principles
4. Impact on customer experience
5. Increased competition
6. Information technology improvements
7. Empowerment practices
8. Employee motivation

Increased reliance on contract manufacturers

Outsourcing by manufacturing companies keen to focus on their core competencies has seen them outsource more supply chain activities. Many of the large electronics companies, for example, have long since stopped manufacturing their own products and instead for a number of years have been outsourcing their manufacturing to contract manufacturers (we discussed the distinction between contract manufacturers and OEMs in Chapter 5). Companies such as Flextronics Inc and Foxconn are now responsible for manufacturing numerous electronics items from mobile phones and electronic organisers for Apple Inc, to computers and printers for OEM customers such as Hewlett Packard Inc and Dell Inc, and games consoles for companies such as Microsoft and Sony. By outsourcing manufacturing and logistics, these companies can spend more time focusing on their key competencies, such as research and development, sales and marketing, and indeed SCM. As these companies outsource more and more elements of their business including logistics, they tend to rely more on tools that can help measure the performance of their suppliers.

Strategic importance of LSPs to supply chain success

The strategic importance of LSPs cannot be underestimated as it is often these companies that have a direct impact on the end customer. In an era of online purchasing and marketing through the various media channels, certain businesses do not 'touch' their customers until the point of product delivery, and this latter activity is often subcontracted to a LSP. A late delivery or indeed a negative service encounter at point of delivery could affect the consumer's impression of the product or the retailer. And this could be the fault not of the seller, but of their LSP.

Adoption of manufacturing management principles

In the recent past, 3PLs are increasingly being asked by their customers to adopt more and more world-class manufacturing based principles such as just-in-time (JIT), total quality management (TQM), six sigma, and more recently lean principles, among others. Quality assurance management too is often a prerequisite, with most progressive 3PLs ensuring that they have been accredited with ISO certification. Motorola for example works very closely with its logistics providers to implement six sigma quality throughout the supply chain. This push for mainstream LSPs to become familiar with such practices has forced them too to ensure that they are better positioned to measure key areas of performance.

Impact on customer experience

Customer satisfaction is seen as an important business philosophy. Today's consumer is much better informed and often has much more available choice. To ensure that your customers (in both the B2B and B2C contexts) are satisfied is a key requirement for any business looking to be successful in the long term. As such, this requires companies to better understand performance through quality programmes, customer polls and customer service metrics.

Increased competition

A focus on commercial goals is never more important than in a market with high levels of competition. Today's LSPs compete not only against local competitors, but in more and more areas the presence of a multi national or global 3PL is almost always also seen. In recent years, the merger of a large number of LSPs into multinational players has started to change the face of the logistics industry. For example DHL's mergers and acquisitions have allowed it to grow not only into one of the largest logistics companies globally, but one of the largest employers in the world for any industry.

The larger 3PLs generally bring financial stability that may allow them to take certain risks in order to gain market share. Thus for all smaller competitors, it is important that they better understand and control their costs. Although the amount of work outsourced to 3PLs continues to increase, the profit margin of most companies operating in this industry is being eroded, and most now operate in a low margin business that requires significant capital investment. Measures need to be available to give management good visibility of resource utilisation, and importantly reports should be detailed to show those specific areas of the business where profits or losses are being recorded.

Information technology improvements

Improvements in the IT employed both in warehouses and to control and track shipments has led to a greater availability of data. This data can now importantly be accessed and presented as useful information without significant employee input as many reports can be run from systems electronically. As these systems become more and more advanced, data is often available in real time in the form of automatic emails, via EDI onto vendors' and customers' systems, or via web reporting tools. The information reported should also be less prone to error and so can be better used for important decision making.

Empowerment practices

Empowerment of lower level employees with tasks and responsibilities that were once reserved for managers has been a tool used by many successful companies to improve employee productivity. Within the logistics industry this has been used to good effect with employees allowed to make decisions quickly so as not to hold up receipt of freight or an important customer shipment. However, it is important that management is more conscious of the potential negative impact that an employee who is empowered with more tasks could make if they make mistakes in their job. As such management need to make better use of KPIs to monitor their employees' performance.

Employee motivation

Use of performance metrics as a motivation tool was initially seen in advanced manufacturing operations, but is now also common within logistics operations. In order to motivate employees to 'beat' the previous number of pallets received or orders executed, for example, some companies put more and more effort into communicating such metrics with all employees. Sometimes public recognition within the workplace for the best performing team is enough to drive the whole operation to higher levels of productivity; in other operations these metrics may need to be linked to employees' rewards to generate the same results. If metrics are used in this manner it is important to stress however that they must be designed to reflect employees' controllable actions.

SELECTING THE BEST MEASURES

In the area of performance measurement a useful maxim is to 'measure results, not activities'. This is valuable advice, as it is all too easy to focus on simply assimilating data without necessarily understanding how this data may be used. When first trying to design a set of indicators, the focus should not as such be directed towards what data may be easily available, but rather towards what benefit one hopes to gain as a result of having these measures in place. For example within a warehousing environment, one may measure the number of trucks that arrive to collect freight, rather than measuring the number of pallets loaded onto trucks, the latter being a more useful result rather than simply an indication of activity occurring. In practice many metrics are developed without much thought put into what the company can do with the information collected, so as part of the process to develop the right measures one should attempt to focus on how they may impact the operation.

The majority of measures should be focused on *quantitative* results; that is, measures which have their basis in numerical data. Although it is always good to add some *qualitative* measures to a set of KPIs, it is very important to stress that measures based on raw data can often be better for accurately comparing performance over time, and indeed for predicting future results. Also quantitative measures should in general be more reliable when comparing over time, as long as the data used to generate them can be replicated without error.

Benchmarking costs and other variables

When deciding on which measures to use, a company should always ensure that benchmarking against other competing companies is not made impossible by their choice of metrics. Companies should always look to emulate best in class, however without benchmarking it can be very difficult to do this. Some larger logistics companies use their marketing budgets to try to convince not only their potential customers that they are among the best within their industry, but also attempt to persuade their competitors that this is also the case!

The logistics industry is one that relies on referrals from not just customers, but also from competing firms, where the referring company may not have the required capability (in terms of warehouse space, transport capacity or other capabilities) but wants to fulfil their customer's requirement. For one firm to give business to another in this manner, it is very important that some benchmarking of performance can first take place, and that both parties can see through the marketing and sales pitch put forward.

In order to benchmark against the industry, the company needs to use a similar set of measures in order to map performance against the companies being benchmarked. Thus the time to first consider benchmarking is when a company is initially putting together a set of performance measures. Benchmarking should be seen as a continuous process, and not as a one-off project. Today's logistics industry is very dynamic and benchmark levels of performance can constantly change.

Benchmarking logistics costs from one supplier to another can be a complicated task as there are almost no standard cost templates used by different firms. It also can be quite difficult for the 3PL's customer to estimate their specific business requirement at the request for quotation (RFQ) stage. As such the 3PL might quote a price against a given scope of work, only to find that, once they start the business, the scope of work does not represent all of their customers' requirements.

Number of metrics to report

Evaluating the optimum number of measures is always a difficult task but is one that should be given some thought. Too many metrics will result in an unnecessarily large scorecard, with measures of lesser importance having the effect of adding just 'background noise' while simultaneously making it an arduous task to actually identify the critical ones. The optimum scorecard will highlight the vital indicators needed to monitor the health of the organisation's key organs.

With logistics companies being so process-focused, the measures used will need to ensure that they can capture the performance of these processes. As such it will be important to tailor measures to reflect the actual work performed in the operation. Prior to putting together a set of measures, the company must first ensure that its processes and procedures are documented, as often it is only after completing this exercise that management will fully understand all of the different processes employed. If a new process is introduced, for example to meet exacting customer requirements, then a new performance measure should be developed in tandem.

Designing key performance indicators

Once a company understands the need for performance indicators, and also has an understanding of what the right measures may encompass, the design of a set of KPIs is the next step. Before KPIs are introduced, the company itself must be clear about its own aspirations (i.e. what does it regard as 'success') and how performance can be measured against this.

As we already noted above, globalisation of the logistics industry has been seen in recent times with the acquisition and mergers market for LSPs being increasingly busy. As some of the largest 3PLs strive to have a footprint globally to support international customers, measurement of the performance of different entities takes on an additional dimension. 3PLs now have to compare sites in completely different geographies against each other as they may be serving the same or similar customers.

Geodis for example provide warehousing solutions to IBM across Europe using common metrics where possible. Such common sets of metrics between distant sites is most important, and might be required as part of contractual obligations. Indeed, as companies grow into differing markets, so too is there often an increase in the distance or boundary between senior management in headquarters and the local operations. In order to close this apparent gap, management at headquarters can use the timely flow of information and performance indicators to allow them to see what is happening.

Drafting of metrics is a task that needs to be approached with some degree of patience. Typically many measures will be reported and tracked before a key set will emerge. It is important to consider at first a large range of potential measures, and not to shortlist too many until an attempt is made to first trial them. Expectations of how a metric may perform often change quickly once results start to be seen. During this period of testing new metrics, it can be useful to see if a baseline, against which future performance may be measured, can be determined.

Imposing metrics on the shopfloor is often not a good idea. Resistance from warehouse and transport operations can often result in incomplete or incorrect data recorded. In the same way in which it is important to communicate the company's objectives with all employees, so too is it important to ensure that shopfloor employees are in agreement with any metrics introduced. Employees must understand the measures, take ownership of the data and also stand by the results. Instead of senior management dictating the format of metrics, employees should be asked for their own ideas of what areas need measurement. Very often the most knowledge about the operation lies with the shopfloor, and management, without realising it, can often be out of touch with the reality of problems faced daily within the operation.

Sources of data

As part of the activity to develop a set of metrics, a company should look at what resources it has available to contribute the data needed.

Information technology is an area of key investment for most logistics companies. It is also an area where companies need to first look for data that will allow them to generate metrics. A system controlling processes and managing the huge number of transactions seen is also a system that could potentially be able to generate automated reports. System generated data should help reduce the possibility of errors in data collection, increase reporting time by having the ability to operate day and night, and most importantly limit direct employee involvement and control the costs of metric development.

Operational employees can also make a valuable contribution towards providing certain data which is otherwise difficult to source. Logbooks for shipments and warehouse capacity reports, for example, are traditionally the type of reports that employees may measure manually, though advances in warehouse systems mean that the majority of measures no longer need to be manually derived.

COMMONLY USED METRICS

When designing a set of KPIs, the logistics company must take into account any requirements that its customers may have for specific reporting. This does not necessarily mean, however, that the metrics should simply be what the customer demands, as the customer may not understand the full business offering.

Companies should appreciate that there is a need to differentiate between the measures reported to different levels within the organisation. KPIs that may be very important to the warehouse manager, for example, may not prove useful for senior management. When creating a set of metrics it is sometimes useful to split the metrics into three different categories, catering for senior management, operational management, and functional operations. Figure 11.1 illustrates metrics for each of

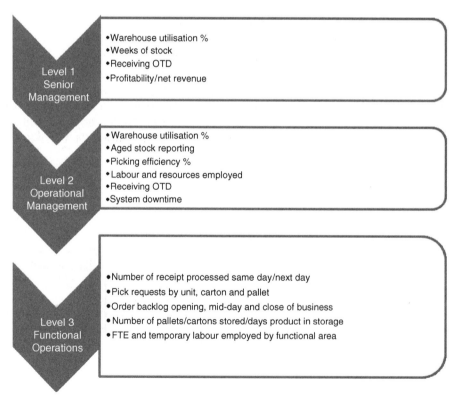

Figure 11.1   Category of metric reporting. (OTD is on-time delivery; FTE is full-time equivalent, i.e. the equivalent of one employee)

these three categories. Many of these metrics will be discussed in more detail in the next section.

In practice, most LSPs tend to have a generic set of metrics, and also additional customer specific metrics, which would include measures relevant only to that customer. If this approach is taken, then it can result in the customer thinking that they have been handed a complete set of customised metrics, while at the same time requiring the company only to add a small number of specific metrics for each customer, with the remainder being generic to the complete business (in effect this is a form of mass customisation).

In certain situations, for example where a 3PL is managing an on-site warehouse within the customer's manufacturing plant, one can find that almost all of the metrics are tailored to the operation. This, in many situations, is a result of the on-site operation often using the customer's IT systems, rather than the WMS system used in other sites operated by the 3PL.

The balanced scorecard, which was discussed in the previous chapter, is a very useful, and popular, performance measurement tool. Figure 11.2 illustrates goals and appropriate metrics for use in a typical balanced scorecard.[2]

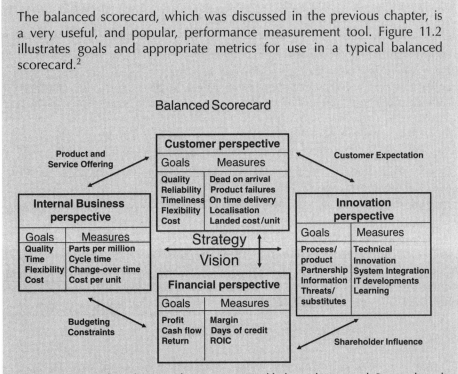

Figure 11.2 Goals and Metrics for use in a typical balanced scorecard. Source: based on Kaplan, R. & Norton, D. (1992) The balanced scorecard – measures that drive performance, *Harvard Business Review*, January–February.

INVENTORY/WAREHOUSE RELATED METRICS

External metrics for a warehousing based operation need to be specific to the activities carried out. The following list gives a taste of the type of measures that a typical warehouse operation may employ.

Receiving

Receiving metrics are generally the first to be recorded, because receiving of product into the warehouse is often the most important transaction. If the receiving process is well thought out and implemented, then one would find that stock accuracy and product integrity should also be managed well. Indeed if product is received into the correct location, and in the correct quantity, then the subsequent picking process too has a good chance of being problem free.

Receiving time acts as a key metric in this area. Most WMS systems can track the time between a shipment arriving into the warehouse through to it being formally received onto the WMS system. Depending on how well developed the WMS system is, advance notification of an inbound shipment from the freight system can automatically initiate the inbound process prior to the shipment arriving. This 'advanced shipment notification' (ASN) is used by the warehouse manager to determine workload and space requirements.

Once the shipment arrives, the receiving process will generally include a physical inspection before the formal system receipt can be completed. The specific metric can vary by facility but should always try to measure the effectiveness of receiving processes, which will include the following:

- Delivery paperwork detail is correct, ensuring exact delivery location, business unit and company delivering the product are mentioned.
- Part numbers, lot numbers and purchase order numbers match those on the paperwork and on the ASN.
- Product is physically inspected with unit/carton or pallet count completed, product inspected for any signs of in-transit damage, repackaging, etc.

Adherence to the processes listed above is a basic requirement before one would measure the core metric in receiving, namely 'receiving on-time delivery'. This metric refers to the ability to receive, both systematically and physically, product that has been shipped to the warehouse within a set time, generally same day or next day.

Put away

For ease of understanding we will assume that receiving and put away are distinct tasks, though it is common to find both combined into one process and completed by the same personnel.

Put away involves physically moving product that has just been received onto the IT system to a pallet or carton location where the product will be stored. Within some environments, product may at this stage be brought directly to the point of consumption such as a line-side kanban.

Metrics should include activity measures such as number of pallets, cartons or units put away, which in turn could be compared against the resource available to produce a productivity measure. Percentage of product put away within a stated time is another key metric. This is very important, as many warehouses might have good receiving metrics, but may end up having a lot of product sitting on the floor yet to be put away at the close of business.

Inventory accuracy

Cycle-counting of product is an activity that customers usually take a keen interest in because the material being counted generally sits on their balance sheet rather than the 3PL's balance sheet. Inventory metrics really act as a measure of operational performance, and reflect the adherence to processes, rather than the performance of the inventory team who conduct the cycle counts. For example, if the receiving team makes mistakes and put product into the incorrect aisle or stocking location, this may only be noticed during cycle counts.

System generated cycle counts, often completed by the inventory team using a handheld RF terminal or alternatively a printed stock report, are used as the starting point for compiling inventory metrics. More advanced WMS have the capability to generate cycle counts automatically, often taking into account any product classification (such as 'ABC' classification), which may exist to determine when products of a certain value should be counted. In order to ensure that accurate counting is maintained it is important that count sheets, or counts using the RF terminals, do not give visibility of the system quantity to the counter.

Cycle counts can be completed where a complete rack or segment of the warehouse is checked in sequential order. Random counts will require the cycle counter to count all inventory held in certain pallet locations across the warehouse. Part counts may exist to count all locations where a particular product is stored, and empty cycle counts should direct a counter to locations where the system does not show any stock as stored on the assumption that if the counter finds anything then it indicates an inventory accuracy problem.

Inventory accuracy may also need to be compared against that stated on the 3PL's WMS system and the customers' own systems. From a financial auditing perspective, there can only be one system of record, but in many environments dual systems without real time electronic data interchange (EDI) linkage are seen. In some warehouses, dual keying of stock transactions onto two systems can be seen, though every effort should be made to avoid such a system solution, and in these environments more stringent inventory control metrics need to be designed and monitored.

- 'Unadjusted inventory accuracy': inventory metrics should show 'first count results', i.e. the initial count results before the inventory team carries out any stock reconciliation.
- 'Adjusted inventory accuracy': once any required adjustments have been carried out, the inventory should be recounted and the results published.
- 'Net variance': the metric used to compare the total quantity of units for all part numbers on the system with that counted.
- 'Absolute variance': takes into account the complete variance, i.e. it is arrived at by adding any positive and negative stock discrepancies. If reported that absolute variance was high, but net variance was low, it would signal that stock was out of position.

It is important to remember that inventory metrics can often highlight a particular problem within warehouse processes. In order to improve inventory accuracy, improvements need to be made in either the design or execution of the warehouse transactions. Although most inventory metrics will be quantitative in nature, there should be some effort to also record some qualitative measures such as for example 'housekeeping' or 'completion of cycle counts'.

Measures may exist to measure the length of time that inventory is sitting in the warehouse. An aged stock report, detailing by part number the number of weeks product is in stock, is the easiest of these metrics to report. Alternatively, an overall view of stock movements within the warehouse can be given with a report outlining the number of inventory turns (as we saw in Chapter 6, this is the number of times on average the complete stock in the warehouse moves in and out).

LOGISTICS COSTS PERFORMANCE

Total landed costs

Financial measures are obviously key metrics for 3PLs, and indeed ones upon which their shareholders will place ultimate importance. The customers of 3PLs too are becoming more focused on analysing their overall logistics costs, and comparing them across different regions and product lines. They are demanding more and more information to allow them to better understand the cost of their logistics activities.

We discussed in both Chapters 2 and 5 the growth that has taken place in recent years in both outsourcing and offshoring. Once the various strategic issues concerning whether or not to outsource and so forth have been resolved, companies need a tool that will enable them to compare alternative sources while taking account of all of the various costs that will be incurred. This is the concept of **total landed costs** (Figure 11.3) and takes into account any inbound transportation, localisation and customs duty in addition to the basic product costs. It allows managers to

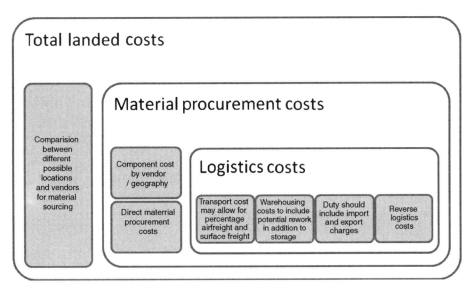

Figure 11.3   Total landed costs

make better decisions regarding raw material sourcing, and rather than just going with the lowest possible product cost, companies can compare the overall financial impact from using different potential suppliers in different markets.

Cost of materials on an 'ex works' basis is not adequate to make a purchasing decision and so it is important that all related costs are considered, and compared:

- *Freight.* The further from the intended destination that the raw materials are sourced, the greater the freight costs. Even if freight is planned to be moved via ocean, the greater distance will result in longer lead times, and the chance of moving at least some product via air (at up to 10 times the cost) will increase.

- *Carrying costs.* Longer transit time will often lead to higher inventory in the supply chain, which in turn will increase the working capital employed and the risk of obsolescence, damage and shrinkage.

- *Duty.* Local sourcing is often the only way to minimise potential import duty of raw materials. Although some countries offer certain duty avoidance measures for materials bought overseas, the risk of paying higher rates of duty and inbound taxes, along with charges for more complicated clearance processes, increases.

- *Packaging.* The longer a product is in transit, the better the packaging needs to be. Also the potential for using reusable packaging decreases.

- *Warehousing.* Longer lead time for products may increase buffer inventory storage locally.

- *Localisation.* Converting product for a local country may be cost prohibitive.

As freight costs can change dramatically over the short term, due to changing fuel and security surcharges and differing demand patterns for cargo along with changing air and ocean timetables, it is important that companies continually review their landed product costs by having metrics to measure these costs on an on-going basis.

Unit based costing, which often has its basis in management accounting principles such as 'activity based costing' (ABC), is another important measure. Manufacturing and distribution companies need to understand the entire logistics costs on a per SKU basis because small changes in product specification or packaging can have a dramatic effect on the overall logistics costs. Nokia has, for example, tried to standardise its mobile phone packaging, so that different models use packing that is the same size and differs only by print. This has given it an advantage over competitors who appear to have different packaging for each model.

3PL cost models

In the highly competitive logistics market, 3PLs are often placed under significant pressure to ensure that their response to RFQs are the most competitive, while at the same time ensuring that they do not engage in business that may run losses during the duration of the contract. In order to manage these pressures, many 3PLs use a number of different cost models.

Cost plus margin

'**Cost plus margin**' is often the preferred model for 3PLs engaging in a new business where the statement of work is not detailed, or where the customer demands complete transparency of all costs.

This model is based on a general assumption that space will be charged at a fixed cost per square or cubic metre, and staff costs will generally be presented as a loaded cost to include base wages and related employer costs including contribution to social taxes, health insurance, pensions and so forth. Materials handling equipment (MHE) such as forklift trucks, racking and any other equipment used would generally be charged as a depreciated annual charge. IT charges would usually be the next item to be listed in a schedule of charges and may be split between user licences, IT support and development, in addition to depreciation for equipment used, including warehouse management systems and office servers and computers.

When all charges are identified, the 3PL will generally then try to negotiate a mark up to cover corporate allocation or management overhead. Finally, the required profit margin will be added.

The main advantages with this type of model are:

- It provides complete transparency for all parties involved
- Risk is reduced for both parties – the customer should be better able to budget and the 3PL will also live in the certainty that its costs should be covered.

The main disadvantages are:

- There may often be reluctance for the 3PL to drive continuous improvement in order to reduce cost as the 3PL's profit margin increases as the total cost increases
- Resources may be fixed at a level that meets the peak season demand, thus resulting in excess cost during quieter periods. Also resources employed may not be adequate to meet business requirements
- From the 3PL's perspective there is little opportunity to make high profits as it will be very difficult to negotiate a margin higher than that quoted by competitors.

Transactional pricing

'Transactional pricing' would generally see a 3PL use all their available re-sources across multiple customers and quote a unit rate for standard warehouse activities:

- Receiving charged per carton or per pallet
- Storage charged per carton or pallet on a weekly or monthly basis
- Picking and handling out at unit, carton or pallet level.

These typical charges would be fully inclusive and include all staffing, space and equipment. IT setup charges would likely be charged as part of the original account project setup costs.

The main advantages of this type of model are:

- Resources are generally not fixed by the customer. Thus during the off-peak period, the customer does not have to pay for space or labour for which they do not have a requirement
- The 3PL will be highly motivated to drive efficiency at all stages of their process as any savings made will result in higher profits. An efficient warehouse operation running to capacity should make it possible for the 3PL to make a larger potential profit with transactional pricing in place with their customers

The main disadvantages are:

- The customer may not always get the customer service that they require unless they separately pay for fixed office resource
- The 3PL needs to ensure that special requests are charged separately as the base rates should in general over-cover a minimum level of service
- The customer does not have transparency to resources employed supporting their business.

Alternative pricing models

As the service offered by 3PLs can include a range of services, some cost models can be highly complex and may include an element of fixed and variable costs that may be billed on cost plus or transactional basis, or indeed any combination of each. Often it is critical for the customer to have certain resources within the 3PL dedicated to them while still ensuring that other resources are only employed as required. For example, the customer may decide to pay for a dedicated account manager, but may only pay space on a pallet or carton basis.

SERVICE LEVEL AGREEMENTS (SLAs)

As well as negotiating and managing LSPs or other suppliers' costs, companies also need to ensure that a mutually arranged and understood agreement is in place between both the company buying the service and the company providing the service. The document that covers this area is commonly known as an **SLA – a service level agreement**. It is typically within the SLA that the selected performance metrics are detailed and elaborated. Typically SLAs will include details of:

- roll-out and duration of the service or process being purchased
- scope of services
- areas of responsibility (i.e. who is responsible for what)
- performance metrics.

LEARNING REVIEW

In this chapter we looked at basic forms of measurement in use in logistics systems, the trend towards measurement of a wider array of activities and the driving forces behind this trend. Customers in particular may attempt to dictate what metrics are used. It is important to remember that although the customer may have specific requirements which should be met, they may be out of touch with the day-to-day operation, and so may not be best positioned to decide how the complete metric set should look. Once the metric set has been decided, we saw that the current practice has evolved to such an extent that metrics are routinely shared with customers.

We saw that metrics are never set in stone, and they can and indeed should change as processes alter and the company's commercial focus changes. Before implementing a set of measures, one must first understand why this task is important, and to determine what type of measures should be implemented, it is important to get a good understanding of what the driving force behind the overall activity is.

Metric development is a complicated activity, but collection of data should nevertheless not be allowed to take too much time. Operational resources must be first prioritised to ensure that operational tasks are completed before data collection and related metrics generation are started. We examined where metric data should come from, which and how many KPIs to track, and importantly who in the organisation should receive the data and reports generated.

We also looked in this chapter at benchmarking of logistics costs and other variables. Commonly used metrics were also reviewed, in particular warehouse/inventory metrics and total landed costs. The various costs associated with using LSPs were also reviewed and the framework for service level agreements outlined.

This chapter concludes our series of chapters (Part Two) that deal with how to 'do' logistics and emphasise the key flows in supply chains. The final part of the book now moves on to deal with strategic issues, such as how to design effective and efficient supply chains and how to deal with important issues such as risk and sustainability.

QUESTIONS

- What are the various driving forces leading to greater use of KPIs in the logistics environment?
- In your view should all metrics be routinely shared with customers?
- Where does the data for metrics come from, and who within the organisation should receive KPI reports?
- Describe the various warehouse/inventory metrics currently in use.
- Why are service level agreements needed in the logistics sector?

PURCHASING 3PL SERVICES

Chapter 4 introduced the whole area of logistics service provision and the role played by 3PLs. In this chapter we looked at how those who purchase the services of 3PLs can manage their performance, and how the 3PLs themselves can manage their own performance.

The 3PL sector, as you will have observed, is now a global business with global players who in turn typically have large, global contracts with leading companies. Search for examples of any large, high profile, global 3PL contracts and endeavour to see what metrics they employ within these contracts (sometimes new contracts are reported in the media with headlines that the new 3PL partner will reduce costs or increase performance in some specific area – metrics will be put in place to track this).

NOTES

1. The terms 'metric' and 'KPI' are usually used interchangeably; in a literal sense, while there may be many metrics, some will be more important than others and more accurate measures of important areas of performance, and would thus be more correctly labelled as 'key performance indicators'.

2. As noted in the previous chapter, the reference for the balanced scorecard is: Kaplan, R. and Norton, D. (1992) The balanced scorecard – measures that drive performance, *Harvard Business Review*, January–February. For further insights into and applications of the balanced scorecard, see also Kaplan's and Norton's various subsequent writings.

FURTHER READING

For a comprehensive series of readings on different aspects of business performance management by various contributors see: Neely, A. (2002) *Business Performance Measurement: Theory and Practice*, Cambridge, Cambridge University Press.

Deutsche Post/DHL

Mike Tayles

University of Hull

DHL (the letters stand for Dalsey, Hillblom and Lynn, the first letters of the last names of the three company founders) started life in 1969. In fact it was one of the first air courier companies in that its original product was the delivery by air of ships' papers from San Francisco to Honolulu (allowing customs clearance of a ship in Honolulu before the ship actually arrived, thus dramatically reducing waiting time in the harbour). Today the company is 100% owned by Deutsche Post World Net, a global organisation with a workforce of over 500 000 employees present in more than 220 countries and territories. Along the way it has acquired a number of logistics companies including Danzas and Exel, making DHL today one of the world's largest logistics companies. The Chairman of the Board of Management declared in the latest annual report 'we are both the market leader and a pioneer in our industry, always a step ahead of the competition. Our next mission is not just to be the biggest logistics company in the world but also the best'. Deutsche Post's accounts are denominated in euros. A brief summary and interpretation of their accounts follows to illustrate issues contained within Chapter 10.

Deutsche Post consists of five business segments, which are shown in the Deutsche Post Revenue by Segment table. In order to examine in an approximate way the accounts of the logistics aspects of the group, certain adjustments have been made to the published accounts in the 2006 annual report. This adjustment particularly removes the implications of the company's activity in financial services (Postbank), which would otherwise distort any appreciation of the accounts of a typical logistics company. Postbank offers financial services facilities to customers in Germany and the nature and content of some aspects of financial reporting in banks would distort the appreciation of what would be the content of the accounts of a typical trading company. It should be stressed that these adjustments are approximate and would be improved with greater access to the companies' accounts, it cannot be claimed therefore that these adapted accounts are detailed and authoritative. The published accounts of Deutsche Post can be located at http://www.dpwn.de. It can be observed that a number of the statistics quoted within the 170 pages of their published accounts are similar to the results presented here.

Deutsche Post Revenue by Segment

	Percentage
Logistics	34.0
Express	25.7
Mail	19.9
Financial Services	14.3
Services	6.1

Deutsche Post Balance Sheet as at 31.12.2006

Assets	Euros M	Euros M
Intangible Assets	14652	
Property, Plant, etc.	9510	
Financial Assets	994	
Other Noncurrent Assets	918	
Total Fixed Assets		26074
Inventories	324	
Receivables	9587	
Financial Services	7164	
Cash and Equivalent	2391	
Total Current Assets		19466
Total Assets		45540
Equity and Liabilities		
Issued Capital[1]	1202	
Reserves and Retained Earnings	10018	
Equity of DP Shareholders	11220	
Minority Interest	2732	
		13952
Noncurrent Provisions	12340	
Noncurrent Liabilities	5285	
Total Noncurrent Liabilities		17625
Current Provisions	1893	
Financial Services Liabilities	1945	
Trade Payables	5069	
Other Current Liabilities	5056	
Current Liabilities		13963
Total Equity and Liabilities		45540

The current market price per share of the company at the year end was 22.84 euros.

[1]This represents 1202 million 'one euro' shares in the company in this case.

Deutsche Post Income Statement – Year to 31.12.2006

	Euros M	Euros M
Revenue		63 366
Material Expenses	34 349	
Staff Costs	18 616	
Depreciation etc.	1 771	
Other Operating Expenses	4 758	
Less Total Operating Expenses		59 494
Net Income		3 872
Less Net Finance Costs		1 030
Profit Before Tax		2 842
Less Taxation		560
Net Profit		2 282
Attributable to DP Shareholders		1 916
Attributable to Minority Interest[2]		366

INVESTOR RATIOS

A common ratio of which investors and analysts take notice is the *earnings per share* (EPS). This is based on the annual total profit after tax divided by the number of shares in issue. A trend of this figure over a number of years is a good indicator of the overall success or otherwise of the company.

$$\frac{\text{Earnings for shareholders } (\in M) \ 1916}{\text{Number of shares (M) } 1202} = 1.60 \text{ euros per share}$$

Another overall value that may be of interest to an outsider is the *market capitalisation* of the company, that is the value the market places on the company as a whole in its present state as a going concern, the number of shares multiplied by its current market price. For Deutsche Post this is:

1 202m $\times$ 22.84 = 27 454m euros

This figure can be contrasted with the value shown in the balance sheet, where for example the equity (shareholders' investment) is valued at €11 220m. This suggests that in addition to their tangible assets the stock market perceives the company has considerable intangibles, for example management ability, good reputation, a brand, etc. This is in addition to intangibles already mentioned in the balance sheet. The balance sheet shows that shares and accumulated profit invested in the company is €11 billion approximately, yet if sold today it would raise €27 billion.

---

[2]The entry in the accounts of a minority interest indicates that Deutsche Post has a majority interest in some companies but does not own them entirely. As a consequence the companies' accounts are incorporated into the results of Deutsche Post (DP), but their total results are not the property of DP shareholders. The minority interest is the sum owed to others outside the company, but because of its majority status DP has to take responsibility in accounting for and reporting this.

Another externally quoted statistic which is used is a *price earnings (PE) ratio,* a relationship between the current market price per share and the EPS quoted above. In this case the calculation is:

$$\frac{\text{Market price } (€)}{\text{EPS } (€)} \quad \frac{22.84}{1.60} \quad 14.3 \text{ times}$$

This reflects the fact that the stock market values the company at over 14 times its current reported earnings. In other words it would take over 14 years to recover the share price based on its current earnings and is a statement about the confidence in the company's ability to continue its earning and future potential. If a PE ratio was about 2 this would be a very low estimate of the potential of the company and the quality of its earnings. In a reasonably healthy mature economy it could be said that a PE of 14 is representative of an upper quartile performance. It needs careful interpretation however, in that the ratio compares an estimate of future performance (market price) with a past measure (last year's profit).

MANAGEMENT RATIOS

Some of the investor ratios featured above are reflected inside the company by measures that relate key components of the profit and loss account or the balance sheet. For example *return on equity* compares the annual net profit with the balance sheet value of shareholder funds, thus:

$$\frac{\text{Net profit after tax (attributable to shareholders)}}{\text{Shareholders' equity}} \quad \frac{1916 \times 100}{11220} = 17.1\%$$

The above figure is after tax but it may be given greater relevance to management by being computed before tax, after all management cannot easily influence the tax burden of the company. If a profit figure before tax and interest charges is used it should be related to investment in the company by both shareholders and lenders, in other words it is a broader measure of financial performance:

$$\frac{\text{Net profit before interest and tax}}{\text{Capital employed (shares and loans)}} \quad \frac{3872 \times 100}{13952 + 17625} = \frac{3872 \times 100}{31577} = 12.3\%$$

A useful indicator of overall profitability of sales is the relationship of net profit to total sales value. It is a key profitability ratio and indicates the average net profit margin being earned on all business undertaken. For Deutsche Post this is:

$$\frac{\text{Net profit before interest and tax}}{\text{Total sales revenue}} \quad \frac{3872 \times 100}{63366} = 6.1\%$$

While profitability is important, the absolute scale of the business is also significant, that is the rate at which this profit is being earned (how busy is the company, is it working its people and its tangible assets hard, is it 'sweating' the assets?). A ratio that displays this aspect is the *turnover of capital employed:*

$$\frac{\text{Total sales revenue}}{\text{Capital employed}} \quad \frac{63366 \times 100}{31.577} \quad \text{2 times approx.}$$

Note that the turnover of capital employed when multiplied by the net profit ratio is equivalent to the return on capital employed (2 × 6.1% = 12.3% approx).

It should be noted that the above illustrates the ratios for the whole company, but they can be broken down by major business segments if this information is available. For example, within Deutsche Post they could produce this for the business segments mentioned above. However, they are not obligated to provide all this detail to outsiders, furthermore some of the analysis may require an arbitrary split of costs, revenues and assets to do it. Some overview of performance by segment is required to be reported to investors and the public so some insight can be obtained for this.

CAPITAL STRUCTURE AND LIQUIDITY

It is important for any reader of accounts to realise that a company can raise funds from both shareholders, who have an ownership interest in the company, and lenders who look only for a reward of regular and contractually agreed interest payments. The balance between these two represents the *gearing* of the company and can have implications for the risk the stock market perceives the company is bearing. There are many alternative formulae for gearing but a common one is the relationship of debt to debt plus equity. Thus for Deutsche Post:

$$\frac{\text{Debt}}{\text{Debt} + \text{Equity}} \quad \frac{17625 \times 100}{17625 + 13952} = 56\%$$

Deutsche Post is funded by 56% of loans and other fixed liability funding, which is perhaps an average level of gearing.

Finally it is important to examine whether the company is likely to be able to pay its way in the future. Does it have sufficient *liquidity*? That is, does it have the funds to meet its bills when they fall due? These bills can be for general trading activities or one-off bills such as taxation, dividend, etc. A financial measure used for this purpose is the *current ratio*, a comparison of current assets and current liabilities, thus:

$$\frac{\text{Current assets}}{\text{Current liabilities}} \quad \frac{19466}{13963} = 1.4 \text{ times.}$$

The fact that current assets exceed current liabilities is reassuring. For some manufacturing businesses a ratio as high as two times is suggested to be appropriate, however this varies with different types of company. In this case, Deutsche Post is not in manufacturing, it holds very little inventory of its own, often it is other people's inventory, the balance sheet shows a very small inventory, so a figure well below two times is acceptable. It is not advisable for a company to carry a high level of current assets because it has to finance this by raising money from shareholders.

It should be noted that the accounts shown here may be distorted by some current assets which relate particularly to the financial services business of Deutsche Post, if these are removed a lower current ratio emerges indicating prudent use of resources.

$$\frac{\text{Current assets}}{\text{Current liabilities}} \quad \frac{19466-7164}{13,963-1945} \quad 0.9 \text{ times}$$

Gate Gourmet: Success Means Getting to the Plane on Time[*]

M. Day

Headquartered at Zurich Airport, Switzerland and Reston, VA, USA, Gate Gourmet is the world's second largest airline catering company, providing catering services to many of the world's major airlines, such as British Airways, Swissair, United Airlines, Delta Airlines, Virgin Atlantic and Cathay Pacific to name just a few. In a very competitive and low margin industry, the company manages to provide 534 thousand meals a day worldwide, on average 195 million every year. It has 115 flight kitchens in 30 different countries, in locations as diverse as Hawaii, Los Angeles, Buenos Aires, New York, Madrid, London, Bangkok, Sydney and Tokyo. However, it is far more than a food preparation operation; most of its activities involve organising all on-board services, equipment, food and drinks, newspapers, towels, earphones and so on. And that's not all. Gate Gourmet also unloads from the aircraft, disposes of waste, cleans the cutlery, trays, and trolleys, stores all these customer-specific accessories for each airline, and makes everything ready for the next time it's needed at the required location. In sum it is, essentially, a specialist logistics operation for the aviation industry.

Gate Gourmet places considerable emphasis on working in unison with cleaning staff, baggage handlers and maintenance crews to ensure that the aircraft are prepared quickly for departure. Normally, no more than 40 minutes are allowed for all these activities in the tight confines of an aircraft cabin and hold, so complete preparation and a well-ordered sequence of working are essential. Eric van den Berg, Director of Business Applications at Gate Gourmet, gives a practical example of the complexity that is involved in servicing an aircraft in a tight schedule: 'For example, a long haul flight from Asia may stop at Zurich Airport for only two to three hours before it returns. In this timeslot, beside un-boarding and re-boarding passengers plus cabin cleaning, we are scheduled to unload the plane of used cutlery and rubbish, and prepare and load about 5 tons of new food, drinks and equipment for the return flight,' explains Eric. 'The process is further complicated by the fact that last-minute passengers can show up shortly before departure and also would like a meal according to the airline's specification. Then there are the passengers that require special meals (e.g. a kosher meal or a low fat meal) and at the same time we try to avoid producing and loading more meals than actual passengers (so-called "over-catering") as this is a loss for the airline and us. People often talk about "just-in-time" delivery, but for us, just-in-time delivery is literally down to minutes.'

These requirements for speed and total dependability would be difficult enough to achieve in a stable environment, but as Eric explained there are wide-ranging uncertainties that have to be managed. Although Gate Gourmet is advised of the likely numbers of passengers for each flight, the actual number of passengers for each flight is only fixed 6 hours before take-off (although numbers can still be increased after this, due to late sales). The agreed menus are normally fixed for six months, but the actual requirements for each flight depend on the destination, the type of aircraft and the mix of passengers by ticket class. Finally, flight arrivals are sometimes delayed, putting pressure on everyone to reduce the turnaround time, and upsetting work schedules.

BUSINESS CRITICAL PROCESSES

Gate Gourmet has chosen to use information technology to assist in the scheduling of food and ancillary goods. The system, called Scala, covers almost all business processes for the company's catering operation. Food cannot be easily produced too far in advance as most of it has to be freshly prepared. Preparation and production for a flight usually starts 12–24 hours before departure, at a time when passenger numbers for this flight often still change both up and down.

The focus for Scala is to make sure that all the meals and all their accessories are delivered at the right time, at the right place and in the right quantities. The flight kitchen's control area monitors all flight operations and responds to any last-minute changes. This is vital, too: every delay, every cancellation, every rebooking and every aircraft reassignment will have a direct and immediate impact on the catering process. Minutes can often be crucial; and Gate Gourmet's dedicated teams need to respond with the utmost flexibility. This is why close contacts are constantly maintained between the purchasing, kitchen and logistics units.

Eric explains more about how Gate Gourmet uses Scala in practice for its internal processes: 'The service contracts we have with the airlines include flight schedules and meal specifications (bill of material), which are pre-set into Scala,' he says. In the days leading up to a flight, the company is kept updated with the latest passenger numbers by the airline. These numbers are either entered or electronically uploaded into Scala where, in conjunction with the flight schedule and bill of material, the daily demand for meals is calculated, and a timetable for production is worked out. Through Scala and additional fax software, the chefs in the kitchen can directly send daily purchase orders for, for example, vegetables to the suppliers. 'You will find Scala terminals everywhere on the shop floor in our flight kitchens.'

When food for a flight is ready to be boarded, a last quality check is made and trolley labels and delivery notes are printed from Scala. Once shipped and confirmed in Scala, invoices are printed either on paper or in electronic form and sent to the airline.

Scala relies on vast databases that store thousands of detailed recipes to ensure consistent ingredients, presentation and taste, even on the largest of scales and stowing modules in which the layout for each aircraft is captured.

HAND-CRAFTED FOOD MANUFACTURING

Yet despite these high-tech inroads into the cooking world, the majority of the food preparation work is still done by hand. The vast range of products for snacks, tasters, starters, main courses, desserts and in-between meals for over 250 airline customers has to be processed and prepared every single day. No conveyor-belt production is possible here: every day, Gate Gourmet prepares over 570 000 hot and cold meals in repetitive batch processes that use a small range of cooking techniques that preserve the quality of the ingredients. On top of this, the group produces a large quantity of special meals, which are also changed daily. All these products need to pay due and full regard to the cultural and culinary features of each specific destination.

Needless to say, the strictest hygiene standards are applied at all Gate Gourmet's production premises, which are regularly inspected by the relevant authorities. One hundred per cent cleanliness is constantly maintained; and the correct handling of foodstuffs is an uncompromising imperative. Gate Gourmet's in-house laboratories and hygiene specialists are a further guarantee of the group's full compliance at all times with the highest quality and hygiene standards.

THE WIDER SUPPLY CHAIN

Gate Gourmet has also invested a great deal of time and money in integrating its supply base into the systems that provide real-time data into the Scala system. Under the banner of 'e-gatematrix', a series of web-enabled systems capture schedule data from Gate Gourmet's airline customers using it to schedule meal deliveries, procure and synchronise deliveries from suppliers, and finally close the purchase to pay loop by managing supplier and airline invoicing.

One of the most testing times for Gate Gourmet and the e-gatematrix system came during the weeks and months following September 11, 2001, when there was an endless stream of changes regarding in-flight services that needed to be communicated and implemented. A number of Gate Gourmet's customers needed to communicate changes about:

- Flight schedules
    - Over 10% of the flights were eliminated
- Meal services
    - The number of flights with meal service was reduced by over 40%
    - Meal service levels were changed on the remaining flights
- In-flight equipment
    - Regulations required that certain equipment could no longer be used during the flight (i.e. knives)
- Supply chain issues
    - Equipment and perishable inventory re-balancing in the network.

The workload involved service scheduling, galley planning and menu specifications. Using e-gatematrix's integrated technology systems, the e-gatematrix team created all the changes necessary to maintain accurate communications to the upstream supply chain about the current in-flight service specifications. Additionally, technology interfaces with the airline's legacy systems allowed Gate Gourmet to communicate new demand expectations to the supply chain by publishing accurate passenger load forecasts and service level demand forecasts, reducing production volumes throughout the supply chain.

As a result Gate Gourmet and their airline partners were able to successfully communicate thousands of individual changes regarding in-flight services to the airline's in-flight supply chain. The changes were created and managed using the e-gatematrix technology systems, providing the supply chain with real-time communication of those changes. Communications were made to the service providers and suppliers who serviced over 140 worldwide stations and encompassed hundreds of flight schedule changes and many more service level, meal and equipment changes. The ultimate result of quickly implementing all of these changes was Gate Gourmet's airline customers realised significant savings and cost avoidances, quickly adapting to the changes in the industry's economic environment.

QUESTIONS

- What supply chain challenges do Gate Gourmet face when dealing with demand fluctuations from airlines? Comment on how their supply chain investments support their overall customer service and resource utilisation objectives.

- What prerequisites are important for the operation of the lean systems that Gate Gourmet has in place?

Managing Supply Chain Information at HBOS:[*]
The SRM (Supplier Relationship Management) initiative

J.-N. Ezingeard

THE MERGER

HBOS was formed on 10 September 2001 when Halifax plc, the UK's largest mortgage lender, merged with the Bank of Scotland, which was Scotland's first bank, having been established by an Act of the Scots Parliament on 17th July 1695. The merger created the UK's fifth largest bank in terms of turnover with assets of £320 bn (€500 bn). Unlike many bank mergers, the deal was presented to investors as a defensive market growth exercise (the two banks had little geographic or sector overlap) rather than an operation aimed at cutting costs and jobs.[1] Each bank kept its high street trading names and no compulsory redundancies were announced. Nonetheless the organisation quickly identified possible synergies that would not damage its market growth strategy. One such synergy was procurement.

Soon after the merger, HBOS was divided into five divisions: Retail Banking, Business Banking, Corporate Banking, Insurance and Investment and Treasury. The divisions operated through branches, by telephone and over the internet as appropriate to their business model. Following the strategy set out at the time of the merger, the company's objective remained to be 'distinctive' and as such the five divisions operated fairly independently. A Services Division provided centralised processing and IT support to these customer-facing divisions. The Services Division included the group procurement team. It was that team that had identified a number of savings that could be made as a result of the merger. Ian Taylor, head of group procurement, would argue soon after the merger: 'The role of procurement has been a key element in delivering cost savings following the HBOS merger.'[2]

Banks have many supply sources, ranging from paper suppliers (of which the companies in the Halifax group alone purchased over 10 500 tons in 2001) to equipment rental companies on which HBOS had spent £24 m (€38 m) in 2001.[3] In addition to these traditional procurement activities Taylor's team also covered more complex purchasing contracts such as the provision of legal

[*]Dr Jean-Noel Ezingeard (2003) Managing Supply Chain Information at HBOS. Reproduced by permission of Dr J.-N. Ezingeard, Dean Faculty of Business and Law, Kingston Business School.

services. Even before the merger, Halifax plc had nearly 8000 suppliers. Following other acquisitions and the merger, this number had grown to just under 30 000 in 2002 with a total procurement spend of more than £1.7 billion (€2.6 bn). This made it essential to start procuring goods and services more strategically, and a target was set to achieve £300 m savings (€469 m) in procurement by mid-2005.

THE SRM PROJECT

From the start it was decided that the target of £300 m could not be achieved without adequate management information. IT would play a major role in delivering these savings and the Supplier Relationship Management (SRM) project was set up in early 2002.

The aims of the SRM project were explained by Taylor:[4] 'We wanted to provide accurate, timely information to decision makers involved in supplier negotiations, and to measure supplier costs and performance across the group. Acquiring management information in procurement was the key to unlocking the cost-savings opportunities presented by a whole range of post-merger procurement projects.' One of the challenges facing him was that each of the merged institutions had its own purchasing information systems. This made it almost impossible to get an integrated view of the information the company had about its suppliers. This left buyers with little management information. They sometimes even found themselves in situations where they had to rely on the suppliers themselves to provide them with total spend figures, for instance. This also made it difficult to combine the 'purchasing weight' of the two pre-merger banks.

THE LEGACY INFORMATION

Most of the information needed by decision makers in the procurement team was available in one of the legacy systems, but obtaining it in a useable form was difficult as purchasers had to rely on skilled IT staff to produce the reports they needed.[5] Not only had the Halifax and the Bank of Scotland had their own procurement systems, but also the Halifax in particular had acquired other financial institutions prior to its merger with the Bank of Scotland. Legacy systems were therefore numerous. Sometimes the same software was used, but different reporting periods were in place or different versions of the same package were still running. In looking for an SRM solution, the first objective was therefore integration, the second objective was data accuracy and the third was useability.

The first option to solve the lack of integration would have been to modify existing systems to make them work together, but an initial study suggested this would be too expensive. Another solution would have been to implement a new, unified system to replace all the legacy systems across the group – this too was ruled out on the grounds of costs. This would also have gone against the bank's 'federal philosophy' where each division has total control over the software required to drive its business.[6]

ETL

Implementation began in January 2002. The solution chosen by the project team for integration is known as ETL (Extract/Transform/Load).[7] The ETL tool was used to bridge the gap between HBOS's legacy systems. Choosing an ETL tool is a complex exercise and the team of consultants advising Taylor opted for a market leader known for its 'ability to execute'.[8] Once extracted from the legacy systems and after initial preparation by the ETL tool, the data would be passed to a data warehouse. The data would be stored without conversion into a single view. It was there that it could be manipulated, allowing for multiple views of the data. According to its vendors, the software 'stored data copied from any number and variety of sources in an application neutral form'.[9]

Reporting would be handled through a well-known, market-leading package. This package was already in use at Halifax prior to the merger, and managers were already comfortable with it. It would allow them to create their own management reports through a user-friendly (web-based) interface, and without the need to rely on the IT department. Soon after the implementation, completed in May 2002, Taylor pointed out: 'There was no resistance to the system whatsoever. We received a lot of positive feedback. It's a common application available to all users with the same user interface, so there is no bias.'

DATA PREPARATION

Although the system made data integration, manipulation and presentation easy, some data cleansing had to be carried out. HBOS chose to involve procurement managers in the process rather than leave the exercise to IT specialists. Much of the data cleansing involved creating 'categories'. At first, the team had 17 000 individual account codes. These were re-ordered into 27 'commodities' split into 142 'categories'. Although the process was lengthy, it was greatly facilitated by the software tools in place and only had to be carried out once. It also meant that purchasers could now view procurement information in numerous ways[10] (by supplier, category of spend or by commodity) and drill down to individual purchase orders if the need arose.

In addition to the benefits of being able to work with 'clean' data presented in reports that met the users, need, the system allowed data to be enriched. Fields had been added to supplier information for instance to indicate the amount of 'influenceable spend'.[4] This was invaluable to help buyers explore medium term opportunities. Ultimately, the data available should enable the bank to have a better idea of the performance of its suppliers.[11] Des Quigley, the bank's procurement systems manager, had recently explained:[12] 'This will move us to a balanced scorecard view of our procurement process, adding more detailed invoice and contract information, which in turn will help us to negotiate better deals with suppliers.'

THE FUTURE

So far, the procurement team had concentrated on gaining leverage with the bank's suppliers. As explained by Taylor, 'Unless purchasing is delivering significant savings, all its other work is devalued.' Now savings were clear, the company was considering extending its use of IT in procurement with three initiatives:

1. More e-procurement could well be on the cards for instance. This was an initial objective of the SRM project[13] but still remains Taylor's next big challenge. This had not yet been fully achieved.

2. HBOS was also considering letting suppliers access data on HBOS's SRM system. This would involve exchanging information with suppliers electronically. Other companies that had implemented SRM solutions for instance allowed suppliers to view procurement schedules and suggest amendments to them, or send email alerts directly from within the application. Tests had been carried out to exchange information electronically with a small number of suppliers, but nothing extensive was yet in place.

3. The use of e-auctions. The bank had auctioned its print requirements for the first time in 2002 and achieved savings of 21%. Although the process had been time consuming, Taylor thought that it had been a significant success, achieving 'well in excess of return on investment.'[14]

Both e-procurement and supplier integration were taking time, but Taylor was not worried: 'We were able to prove each stage internally as we went along and easily adapt things to suit our own needs,' he had recently argued in an interview.[15] 'We also collaborated closely with our suppliers to ensure that they could take the technology on board at each step of the way. We haven't achieved Nirvana in terms of absolute integration with their systems, but we'll get there.'

QUESTIONS

- What challenges are facing HBOS on the road to 'true' Supplier Relationship Management?
- How would you rate the performance it has achieved to date in this regard as outlined in the case?

NOTES

1. English, S. (2001) Merged banks target big four rivals, *The Daily Telegraph*, 5 May.
2. HBOS drives savings with new SRM system, *Finance on Windows*, 15 October, 2002.
3. HBOS plc 2001 accounts.

4. Bring to account, *Financial Sector Technology*, October, 2002.

5. The Information Age interview, *Information Age*, 21 October, 2002.

6. HBOS presentation to Merrill Lynch, 9 October, 2001.

7. Extract/Transform/Load (ETL) refers to three separate functions combined into a single programming tool. First, the extract function reads data from a specified source database and extracts a desired subset of data. Second, the transform function works with the acquired data using rules or lookup tables, or creating combinations with other data to convert it to the desired state. Finally, the load function is used to write the resulting data (either all of the subset or just the changes) to a target database, which may or may not previously exist.

8. Friedman, T. (2002) ETL magic quadrant update: a market in evolution, *Gartner Research Note*, 6 May.

9. Kalido Information Integration Solution – fact sheet for version 7.

10. HBOS merger saves cash, *Technology for Finance*, 11 October, 2002.

11. John, G. (2002) Show me the money, *Supply Management*, 28 August.

12. Watson, J. (2003) *Informatics*, 14 May.

13. Big savings promised by procurement overhaul, *Supply Management*, 15, November, 2001.

14. Cushing, K. (2002) HBOS uses e-auctions to cut spend, *Computer Weekly*, 12 September.

15. E-procurement: myth is as good as a mile, *CFO*, 1 January, 2003.

Supplier Evaluation at EADS[*]

Roger Moser

On 8 March, 2004, John Summers, Head of the supply management strategy at EADS, a company based in Europe, got the assignment from the Procurement Directors Board (PDB) to make suggestions for improving the company's supplier evaluation system. The proposal was to be presented at the PDB meeting the following month.

EADS AND THE AEROSPACE INDUSTRY

EADS was one of the largest players in the aerospace industry. There were only a few other companies in the market and therefore the competition was characterised by oligopolistic structures.

EADS had a sales volume of approximately €30 billion while its biggest competitor sold airplanes and other products for the aerospace industry worth around €40 billion, followed by some other competitors with sales volumes of €10–20 billion. Due to its strong sales position in North America and Europe, but some weaknesses in Asia and South America, EADS was looking for new ways to improve its competitive position on the last-named continents.

EADS's main customers were airlines from all over the world which were using their increasing purchasing power to get price reductions and flexible contracts. Since EADS and its competitors had a degree of value added of only 25–35%, the suppliers were an important source of competitive advantage and a potential leverage for cost reductions, revenue enhancements and risk reduction.

THE SUPPLY SITUATION IN THE AEROSPACE INDUSTRY

Due to long development cycles and extremely long product lives in the aerospace industry, the supplier situation in this industry was determined by some special requirements. The suppliers had to be able to guarantee the durability and quality of their products in a high-tech environment and under extreme conditions. EADS and its suppliers had to fulfil the needs of its global customers on the one

[*]This case was written by Roger Moser, Supply Management Institute (SMI), European Business School. It is intended to be used as the basis for class discussion rather than to illustrate either effective or ineffective handling of a management situation. The case was made possible by the cooperation of European Aeronautic Defence and Space Company (EADS).

hand and very demanding requirements from official bodies, such as the Federal Aviation Administration (FAA) of the United States of America, on the other. Therefore, every supplier for critical parts had to go through a tough and costly quality audit process and had to prove regularly that their products meet the certification requirements.

Due to the outstanding product complexity, EADS and its competitors could not handle all the requirements and necessary activities of airplane manufacturing on their own. Interdependent relationships occurred between EADS and its most important suppliers in terms of innovation and efficiency management. As a consequence, EADS had to buy most of its crucial manufacturing parts from single source suppliers.

THE SUPPLY ORGANISATION OF EADS

The final decision making body for all supply management issues of EADS was the Procurement Directors Board. The PDB consisted of the procurement directors of the eight business units of EADS. On the second level, the corporate supply organisation was divided into PDB subgroups that were responsible for different tasks such as the management of the specific lead-buyers within the organisation, the e-procurement processes or the supply management strategy for which John Summers was responsible. On the third level, there were the different sourcing organisations of EADS's business units with about 1 800 buyers.

THE SUPPLY STRATEGY OF EADS

The supply vision of EADS was to achieve competitive advantage by winning, integrating and developing the world's best suppliers. Therefore, EADS had a supply strategy that aimed at getting the best suppliers possible in order to fulfil the following objectives:

- Procurement marketing: the supply activities of EADS needed to support its sales department because selling airplanes to certain countries required that the airplanes are produced in line with local content requirements.
- Risk and opportunity management: suppliers had to share the risks and opportunities of the aerospace industry with EADS.

THE SUPPLIER EVALUATION SYSTEM OF EADS

When John Summers and his team analysed the supplier evaluation system at EADS they found five common criteria for evaluation:

1. Commercial performance (product cost, delivery cost, quality cost, etc.)
2. Logistics performance (reliability, delivery preciseness, etc.)

3. Customer support (geographical distribution of plants and service stations, etc.)

4. Quality performance (quality level, quality reliability, etc.)

5. Technical performance (product design and development, process development, etc.).

EADS had implemented a system that measured the different evaluation ratings for each supplier on the basis of the delivered commodities on business unit and corporate level (see Figure C6.1). The supplier value was determined on the aggregated performance and future contracts were given to high scoring suppliers. However, the rating measures sometimes bore little relationship to the supply strategy requirements.

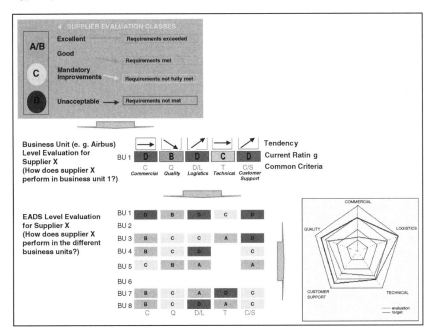

Figure C6.1   The supplier evaluation system at EADS.

THE SUPPLIER STRUCTURE OF EADS

In 2003, EADS had approximately 24 000 suppliers in total. However, it bought almost 65% of its supply volume from only about 250 suppliers. It sourced more than two-thirds of the products and services in Europe and only a quarter in North America. The supply volumes in Asia or South America were almost negligible. Therefore, the supply volume of EADS was even more unequally distributed than its sales volume.

JOHN'S SUGGESTIONS FOR IMPROVEMENT

John knew that the current supplier evaluation system had worked smoothly for more than four years and was well implemented. However, he was not sure whether EADS was really measuring all important dimensions of the supplier value in order to achieve new competitive advantages in the relevant markets.

QUESTIONS

- If you were in the position of John Summers, what problems and weaknesses could you identify?
- Suppose you were John Summers and you had prepared a list of suggested improvements for discussion at the PDB meeting. Discussion of other agenda items at the meeting however took longer than expected, with the result that John now only has 10 minutes (and not 30 minutes) to present his ideas. Given this time constraint what 3 steps would you prioritise for discussion at the meeting?

PART THREE

SUPPLY CHAIN DESIGNS

Supply Chain Vulnerability, Risk, Robustness and Resilience

Helen Peck

Cranfield University

INTRODUCTION

In the mid 1990s the subject of supply chain risk or vulnerability would have been of little interest to anyone but professional logisticians and supply chain managers. Even then they would likely have interpreted risk as simply the financial or competitive disadvantage resulting from a failure to implement 'best practice' SCM concepts. But times have changed. It is no longer unacceptable to acknowledge that bad practice may still flourish elsewhere in the network or that even well managed operations can, and occasionally do, fail. This chapter provides an introduction to the complex, but fascinating subject of supply chain risk, and the related concepts of vulnerability, robustness and resilience.

Chapter 12 comprises five core sections:
- Some working definitions
- Changing times and an uncertain world
- The shortcomings of risk management
- The need for holistic approaches
- A simple framework for a wicked problem

LEARNING OBJECTIVES

- Provide working definitions for key concepts.
- Explain why supply chain risk and conversely robustness and resilience have emerged as important themes in supply chain management.
- Address the problems surrounding interpretations and the treatment of 'risk' in management.
- Highlight the need for a holistic approach to managing supply chain vulnerabilities.
- Provide a structured framework for the identification and management of supply chain risk and resilience.

SOME WORKING DEFINITIONS

Chapter 1 of this book highlighted an enduring problem in logistics and supply chain management – confusion over key terms, even amongst specialists and academics. Things become doubly difficult when we begin to look at matters of supply chain risk, robustness and resilience.

Risk

The main problem stems from multiple meanings of the term *'risk'*. In decision theory it is a measure of the range of possible outcomes from a single totally rational decision and their values, in terms of upside gains and downside losses. The concept tends to be illustrated by examples from gambling. Alternatively, 'risk' is sometimes used to refer to a particular type of hazard or threat, for example technological risk or political risk. Finally, 'risk' may describe the downside only consequences of a rational decision in terms of the resulting financial losses or number of casualties. The latter can be traced back to risk management disciplines, notably the safety and engineering literature.[1] The reasoning behind each of these interpretations and why they matter in a logistics or SCM context will be visited later in this chapter.

Supply chain vulnerability

In the meantime we will use the term 'risk' as it relates to '**vulnerability**' as our point of embarkation; that is, *'at risk*: vulnerable; likely to be lost or damaged'. In Chapter 1 of this book we adopted a definition of a supply chain as 'the network of organisations that are involved through upstream and downstream linkages in the different processes and activities that produce value in the form of products and services in the hands of the ultimate customer'.[2] Given that supply chains comprise many different elements and that SCM embraces many different functions, it is perhaps useful to ask the question 'What is it that is vulnerable, in other words *at risk?'* Is it a product or service, the performance of a process or specific activities, the well-being of an organisation, a trading relationship or the wider networks as a whole? Or is it the vulnerability of one or more of these to some external malevolent force that should be the focus of our consideration? In fact, supply chain vulnerability takes in all of these.

Ideally we should strive to identify and manage known vulnerabilities by asking questions such as:

- What has disrupted operations in the past?
- What known weaknesses do we have?
- What 'near misses' have we experienced?

Recording near misses is something that all organisations should do. Unfortunately, it does not always happen. Sometimes no one was aware that a near miss took place, and often they go unreported because people feel that the incident might reflect badly on them or their department. The willingness to report events of this kind is often dependent on the culture of the department or wider organisation. Forward-thinking organisations recognise that near misses are often warnings of worse to come.

Taking a more proactive stance, a good supply chain manager should also be asking 'effects' based questions, such as:

- What would be the effect of a shortage of a key material?
- What would be the effect of the loss of our distribution site?
- What would be the effect of the loss of a key supplier or customer?

Robust SCM

Whilst individual managers might focus on the effects of a range of eventualities, some argue that everyday SCM strategy also plays a part. In Chapter 3 reference was made to the work of Christopher Tang,[3] who identifies key elements of a **robust** SCM strategy. The dictionary definition of 'robust' is 'strong in constitution, hardy, or vigorous'.[4] Tang suggests that a robust strategy should enable a firm to manage regular fluctuations in demand efficiently under normal circumstances regardless of the occurrence of a major disruption. It might be supposed that any organisation would actively seek to ensure such a position. However, as Tang points out, for a variety of reasons, this is not always the case. What is more, even if your own organisation has implemented the tenets of best practice SCM, does this mean that your supply chain will not fail? Have other organisations in the supply chain all done the same? Even if they have, will that be enough to ensure operations continue? Research by Cranfield University into the UK food and drink industry suggests that there are instances when they will not.[5] A robust strategy has much to commend it, but does not in itself make a resilient supply chain.

Resilience

The term '**resilience**' is used to mean 'the ability of a system to return to its original (or desired) state after being disturbed'. Based on a dictionary definition borrowed from the science of ecosystems,[6] this definition has been adopted in much of the work by Cranfield University into supply chain vulnerability, risk and resilience[7,8] for three reasons:

- It encourages a whole system perspective
- It explicitly accepts that disturbances happen
- It implies adaptability to changing circumstances.

If we are really to embrace the notion of global inter-organisational supply chains within a complex and dynamic environment, then this whole system-wide perspective is the position we should adopt when considering matters of supply chain risk or vulnerability.

CHANGING TIMES AND AN UNCERTAIN WORLD

In a complex inter-organisational supply chain it would of course be difficult if not impossible for anyone to identify every possible hazard or point of vulnerability. Moreover, it must be remembered that 'known' problems are only part of the picture.

Known unknowns, knowable unknowns and unknowable unknowns

To illustrate the point, we will look at some of the high profile events that have propelled supply chain vulnerability, risk and resilience onto the political and corporate agendas. First, though, we turn to the words of former US Secretary for Defence Donald Rumsfeld,[9] whose famous and much derided quote[10,11] brought to wider public attention the idea of 'known unknowns', 'knowable unknowns' and 'unknowable unknowns'. These are useful touchstones to bear in mind when considering the wider subject of supply chain, vulnerability, risk and resilience.

> Reports that say that something hasn't happened are always interesting to me, because as we know, there are known knowns; there are things we know we know. We also know there are known unknowns; that is to say we know there are some things we do not know. But there are also unknown unknowns – the ones we don't know we don't know. And if one looks throughout the history of our country and other free countries, it is the latter category that tend to be the difficult ones.
>
> Donald Rumsfeld, 12 February, 2002

Contrary to popular belief, Rumsfeld did not invent the concepts himself in an off-the-cuff attempt to justify the case for US military action against Iraq. He was in fact drawing directly on concepts used by researchers such as Chris Demchak, who drew on High Reliability Organisations[12] and complex systems theory when working in the field of military logistics.[13] Demchak investigated the underlying thinking behind the technology driven idea of a 'managed battle space' in which all battlefield weapons systems are synchronised in real time with just-in-time logistics and supply. She concluded that this optimistic vision tends to ignore organisational implications and the uncertainties of the battlefield environment.

Y2K: the millennium bug

Y2K highlighted how dependent the societies of the developed world had become on information and communications technologies. In the UK, the Government launched a public information campaign to encourage businesses to take the necessary measures to prevent systems crashes as dates rolled over to the year 2000, and to engage in business continuity planning[14] just in case systems failures arose. Y2K was a 'known known', a discrete, known threat, within engineered systems. Once identified, the 'millennium bug' could be controlled and eliminated. As a result, the widely anticipated disruptions to supply chains never occurred. The Government was delighted, believing that business continuity planning had saved the country from disaster, but the non-event left many managers sceptical as to whether the costly preventative measures had really been necessary.

Y2K highlights one of the intractable problems about proactive measures to improve organisational and supply chain resilience: if successful, preventative measures mean that nothing happens, which inevitably leads to questions of value or cost/benefits justification. Moreover, managers are highly unlikely to be promoted for spending money to prevent a non-event!

> It is very difficult to make a business case for proactive 'just in case' measures to improve resilience.

Creeping crises

Having survived Y2K with minimal problems, the UK economy fared less well in September 2000, when a small number of protestors blockaded some of the country's oil refineries, causing chaos at the petrol pumps. The protests were an outpouring of simmering resentment among farmers and transport operators over rising fuel costs, driven in part by the Government's 'fuel price escalator'. The escalator increased prices annually by 6% over and above the general rate of inflation. Within days the fuel crises escalated, resulting in serious disruptions to the operations of countless companies and to the national economy as a whole. The outbreak of foot and mouth disease in British livestock herds in February 2001 again resulted in damage to whole sectors of the economy.

What made these events so memorable was that even those who were aware of threats did not anticipate the scale of their impact across the UK economy. A survey undertaken by Cranfield University[15] in 2002, involving 137 senior managers from both public and private sector companies, found that 82% of the organisations represented had been affected by the fuel protests, with 49% experiencing some impact from foot and mouth. Both these events could arguably be said to have been caused by 'knowable unknowns'. There were clear warnings that farmers and transport companies were aggrieved over fuel duties and that some form of protest was a real possibility. Foot and mouth was a known threat to livestock, albeit one that had not been seen in the UK for a generation.

The impact of livestock diseases is something that might reasonably be expected to be included in the supplier monitoring activities of companies engaged in the production and distribution of food. But what about car manufacture's or high fashion apparel companies? The shortage of high-quality leather following the foot and mouth outbreak affected automotive manufacturers and fashion houses across Europe. It also had a catastrophic effect on the British tourism industry.

The scale and extent of the disruptions prompted the UK Government to seek a better understanding of what are now sometimes referred to in emergency planning circles as '**creeping crises**'. During the fuel protests and the foot and mouth outbreak it was industry and Government – not the usual 'blue light' emergency services – that found themselves in the unfamiliar role of 'first responders'. These 'creeping crises' were remarkable in one other respect – they represented *systemic supply chain disruptions*.

Creeping crises illustrate the fact that supply chains are more than value-adding mechanisms underlying competitive business models. Supply chains link organisations, industries and economies. They are part of the fabric of society. Back in 1958 Jay Forrester, a Professor at Massachusetts Institute of Technology, predicted that 'there will come a general recognition of the advantage enjoyed by the pioneering management who have been the first to improve their understanding of the interrelationships between separate company functions and between the company and its markets, its industry and the national economy'.[16] Forrester is widely regarded as one of the founding fathers of SCM and of the study of industrial dynamics. SCM has made some progress towards Forrester's vision, but the creeping crises of recent years suggest there is still work to be done.

Few realise that it was the creeping crises of 2000–2001, together with the outbreak of bovine spongiform encephalopathy (mad cow disease) in the 1990s, and increased incidences of flooding (not the threat of international terrorism) that prompted the most extensive review of UK national emergency planning policy since World War II. The inability of civil authorities to overcome the collapse of vital supply chains providing food, water, medicine, money, transport and communications to the citizens of New Orleans following Hurricane Katrina is a clear example of why such work is necessary.

Post 9/11 security matters

More than any other event, the 9/11 terrorist attacks on New York and Washington marked the beginning of a change in attitude towards the whole notion of supply chain vulnerability. The events of 9/11 were so far out of risk managers' field of reference, that they can arguably be classed as 'unknowable unknowns'. It is widely recognised that the terrorist attacks did not themselves cause any significant disruption to global supply chains or even North American industry. But the reaction of the US authorities did.[17] The closure of US borders and the grounding of transatlantic flights dislocated international supply chains making supply chain vulnerability front page news.

Post 9/11, new security measures were hurriedly introduced at US border posts, ports and airports, affecting inbound freight to the USA, including the

Container Security Initiative (CSI) and **customs-trade partnership (C-TPAT)**. CSI looked to new technology to pre-screen 'high risk' containers (those where declared cargoes deviated from usual profiles) before they arrived at US ports. C-TPAT is a 'known shipper' programme, which allows cargoes from companies certified by US Customs to clear customs quickly with minimum inspection. Around the world national or supranational customs authorities adopted similar mindsets and soon tabled rafts of similar measures. The European Union's Approved Economic Operator scheme is an example.

Corporate scandals, operational risk and business continuity

Societies around the globe reeled from the shock of 9/11, but within a few months, supply chain risk was once more synonymous with the perils of poor performance. However, in the world of corporate risk management events were unfolding that would push 'operational risk' (i.e. internal threats to organisational well-being) to the very top of the corporate agenda.

The Enron Corporation, once held up as a model of best practice corporate risk management, collapsed in late 2001. Inadequate internal management controls were blamed. Another North American giant, WorldCom, quickly followed. In Europe Dutch retailer Royal Ahold and Italian dairy conglomerate Parmalat Finanziara did the same. In a bid to protect shareholders and ultimately the well-being of the financial markets, regulators hurried to bring in their own more rigorous reporting requirements. The international banking community had faced the same stark realities only a few years earlier, when the unchecked activities of Singapore-based 'rogue trader' Nick Leeson led to the collapse of London-based Barings Bank, threatening irreparable damage to Singapore's reputation as a financial centre.

These financial scandals highlighted the need for more diligent corporate governance in general. They also increased the appetite for measures to monitor, manage and control operational risk. The Basel Accords in International Banking (1998, 2004), and the introduction of new stock market regulations formalised the requirements.

Among the wave of new regulations, the *Sarbanes–Oxley Act 2002* (SOX) (which you may recall we discussed in Chapter 10) is particularly noteworthy. Applied to all US quoted companies in 2002, and a year later to their overseas suppliers, SOX requires full disclosure of all potential risks to corporate well-being within the business. Importantly it also requires disclosure of potential vulnerabilities that might once have been considered to be beyond the legal boundaries of the firm. Among its many requirements is an obligation to declare all 'material off-balance sheet transactions' including 'contingent obligations' and 'interests transferred to an unconsolidated entity'. These encompass some inter-organisational risk sharing and risk transfer activities, including fixed volume shipping service contracts, VMI and outsourcing agreements.

SOX also demands that providers of outsourced services (including LSPs) must be able to demonstrate the existence of appropriate internal process controls. Finally, it requires consideration to be given to other possible externally induced disruptions. Externally induced disruptions include disruptions to transport and communications. Failure to identify and disclose any of the above may result in a jail sentence for the company's Chief Executive. As a result, board members have became much more interested in identifying 'knowable unknowns' and have turned to risk management and to *business continuity management* (BCM) to help them prove that they have acted with 'due diligence'.

BCM efforts tend to start with the preparation of a **Business Continuity Plan (BCP)**. A business continuity plan is defined as 'a documented collection of procedures and information that is developed, compiled and maintained in readiness for use in an incident to enable an organisation to continue to deliver its critical products and services'.[18] Continuity planning is part of the wider BCM discipline which overlaps SCM, operational risk management, corporate governance and other associated concerns. Current best practice BCM would include an on-going programme of training, rehearsals and reviews of the initial plans to cope with various eventualities as well as careful consideration to the management of an after-the-event recovery phase.

BCM is rooted in IT disaster recovery, but its remit has expanded greatly. In the months before Y2K it focused on protecting 'mission critical computer data'. In more recent years it has moved on to encompass the protection of all 'mission critical corporate assets'. These assets include: data and information; high-value physical items; people and their experience; knowledge; commercial contracts; and, ultimately, corporate reputation. More recently still, best practice BCM has looked beyond asset-based approaches to risk management, to focus on maintaining 'mission critical activities'. This is particularly so for service sectors such as retailing, banking and other financial services. Financial services is also the sector where classical approaches to risk management have been developed over centuries.

THE SHORTCOMINGS OF RISK MANAGEMENT

Earlier in this chapter we mentioned that the term risk has several different meanings. All are used, often indiscriminately in the context of SCM. This is not simply a shortcoming of managers working in SCM. Scholars have been grappling with the nature of risk for centuries, but risk management is a far from mature discipline, with significant disagreements raging over some of its basic tenets.

Decision theory and managerial tendencies

The starting point for many discussions of risk is as it is presented in the gambling-dominated thinking of classical decision theory.[19] Some years ago, researchers James March and Zur Shapira defined risk – from a decision theory perspective – as 'variation in the distribution of possible outcomes, their likelihoods and their subjective values'.[20] In their seminal paper on managerial perceptions of risk and risk taking, the same writers observed that even in financial management circles this much cited interpretation had actually been under attack for many years. Their own research showed that the rational assumptions of classical decision theory do not reflect how managers see risk, nor do they reflect managers' behaviours or the social norms that influence them. March and Shapira cited findings that showed that managers adopt and apply only selected elements of the total risk equation. The managers concerned paid little attention to uncertainty surrounding positive outcomes, viewing risk in terms of dangers or hazards with potentially negative outcomes. Moreover it was the scale of the likely losses associated with *plausible* outcomes, rather than the range of *possible* outcomes, that tended to qualify for consideration.

Furthermore, March and Shapira observed that individual managers' risk-taking behaviour changed with circumstances. 'Attention factors' such as performance targets and questions of survival are likely to have the greatest impact. In comfortable circumstances managers are likely to be risk-averse, but when staring failure in the face – in terms of shortfalls in performance targets – research shows that this tendency reverses and they become risk-prone.

When it comes to the risk appetites and risk strategies of organisations, there is often an assumption that an organisation has a single definable risk appetite, yet more recent research suggests that risk strategies can and do vary between functions within the same business.[21] For example, a propensity for risk taking was found to be acceptable in the areas of core competencies, but much less tolerated in noncore activities within the same firm.

In the real world, where managers routinely deal with imperfect information, these behavioural characteristics may not be as irrational as it might first seem. That is because managers are for the most part making decisions under uncertainty. *Risk* and *uncertainty* are terms that in practice are often used interchangeably, but back in the 1920s Knight made a helpful distinction: 'If you don't know for sure what will happen (e.g. when throwing a dice) but you know the odds, that's risk and if you don't even know the odds, that's uncertainty'.[22] Uncertainty is, according to Knight, 'the realm of judgement'.

- Managers focus on the possible losses associated with plausible outcomes
- Decisions involving risk are heavily influenced by their impact on the manager's own performance targets
- There is unlikely to be a single unified attitude to risk taking within a large organisation

Objective risk and perceived risk

Despite the wisdom of Knight, the words of Rumsfeld, and the canon of research to date, the dominant paradigm in risk management remains that of the cold logic of 'objective risk'. Objective risk reflects a view of risk set out by the engineers and physicists of The Royal Society in a report published in London in 1983.[23] The report stated that risk was 'the probability that a particular (known) adverse event occurs during a stated period of time, or results from a particular challenge. As a probability in the sense of statistical theory, risk obeys all formal laws of combining probabilities.'

Furthermore, the report made a clear distinction between *'objective risk'* as determined by experts applying quantitative scientific means, and *'perceived risk'* – the imprecise and unreliable perceptions of ordinary people. This 'objective' position, combined with the Royal Society's definition of 'detriment' as 'the numerical measure of harm or loss associated with an adverse event' reflects the compound measure of risk widely encountered within the engineering, health and safety literature, and frequently within SCM. It is a position supported by the work of other prestigious institutions such as the National Academy of Sciences and the National Academy of Engineering in the USA in the 1980s and 1990s.[24]

However, it is also a position that has been vehemently contested by social scientists. Social scientists contend that, where people were involved, objective and perceived risk become inseparable. They argue that risk is not a discrete or objective phenomenon, but an interactive culturally determined one, that is inherently resistant to objective measurement. The essential problem is, as distinguished writers such as John Adams point out, that people modify their behaviour and thereby their likely exposure to risk in response to subjective perceptions of that risk, subtly balancing perceived costs and benefits.[25]

Nevertheless proponents of 'objective risk' continue to champion the view that we *should* promote the scientific management ideal, of a rational, predictable world, populated by rational predictable people. As a result Adams observed that 'virtually all the formal treatments of risk and uncertainty in game theory, operations research, economics and management science require that the odds be known, that numbers be attachable to the probabilities and magnitudes of possible outcomes.' In these disciplines, risk management still strives to identify, quantify, control and where possible eliminate specific narrowly defined known threats. The same disciplines continue to underpin much of SCM theory and best practice.

Many of the commonly used tools, techniques and concepts used to identify, evaluate and estimate risk remain rooted in the 'divide and conquer' thinking of engineering and scientific management. Consequently it has been argued that they fail to consider that failures and accidents may be 'emergent properties'; that is, unexpected and often undesirable effects, arising within the wider system as a whole.[26] In this instance the systems we are talking about are the multi-organisational networks that characterise contemporary supply chains.

Even in enterprise risk management, it is clear to some that risk management models have failed to keep pace with the realities of our networked world.

They have been slow to account for operational interdependencies between firms brought about by the trend to outsourcing. Consequently they underestimate the range and severity of risks faced by a company.[27] The Sarbanes–Oxley Act has helped to highlight this shortcoming.

Why this all matters from a practical supply chain risk management perspective, is that if supply chains are only seen from a business process engineering and control perspective, then the selective (downside only) engineering-derived views of objective risk sit quite well. However, if we also accept that supply chains involve relationships that link organisations, populated

> It is important to recognise that 'objective risk' and 'perceived risk' both have places in logistics and SCM.

by people, then there is an equally persuasive argument for perceived risk, with supply chains viewed as open *interactive societal systems*. If we also accept that these may be global supply chains, then those culturally determined perceptions of risk could vary greatly from one region to another. Along the way the forces of nature can demonstrate just how far removed from the controlled environment of the casino this all might be.

THE NEED FOR HOLISTIC APPROACHES

Chapter 1 underlined the fact that SCM is integrative and interdisciplinary, and that logistics is just one of several established sub-disciplines that fall under the SCM umbrella. It is therefore important to recognise that managers from many interacting disciplines as well as from different organisations will have interests in supply chain risk management. Each will likely be viewing risk management decisions in relation to their own performance measures, sometimes using quite different assumptions and interpretations of risk as points of reference. The result is that in practice supply chain risk management is likely to be a patchwork of sometimes complementary, but often conflicting or competing efforts. This means that supply chain risk management can be expected to display all the characteristics of a *'wicked problem'*.

Wicked problems

A *'wicked problem'* is a technical term first coined back in the early 1970s by Horst Rittel and Melvin Webber, two professors from Berkeley, who produced a paper on 'Dilemmas in a General Theory of Planning'.[28] Rittel and Webber's contribution was to produce a lucid explanation of why societal problems are inherently different from the problems that scientists and some engineers tackle in their daily work.

Scientists and engineers deal with discrete identifiable problems (Y2K is a good example), where the desired outcome is known, providing clarity of mission and an easily recognisable desired end state.

Wicked problems are different, because they involve multiple stakeholders, each with slightly different interests and value-sets. As a result, there is no single common definitive goal, no clarity of mission and no universal solution. Rittel and Webber observed that 'with "wicked problems" ... any solution, after being implemented, will generate waves of consequences over an extended – virtually an unbounded – period of time. The next day's consequences of the solution may yield utterly undesirable repercussions ... If the problem is attacked on too low a level, then successful resolution may result in making things worse, because it may become difficult to deal with the higher problems.'

Therefore to understand a wicked problem you must understand the wider context. To that end Rittel and Webber recommend that problems should be considered within 'valuative' frameworks, where multiple and differing perceptions are retained. Such frameworks recognise problems as the links tying open systems into large and interconnected networks of systems, and that the outputs from one become the inputs from another.

A SIMPLE FRAMEWORK FOR A WICKED PROBLEM

Taking Rittel and Webber's advice, Figure 12.1 shows a supply chain broken down into its component parts, hopefully without losing the sense of dynamic interaction. Looking at supply chains in this way enables the inclusion of many different functional and hierarchical perspectives, their respective interpretations of risk, as well as an opportunity to position some of the management tools and techniques currently available.

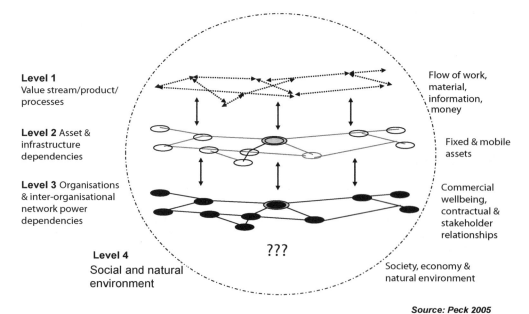

Level 1
Value stream/product/
processes

Flow of work,
material,
information,
money

Level 2 Asset &
infrastructure
dependencies

Fixed & mobile
assets

Level 3 Organisations
& inter-organisational
network power
dependencies

Commercial
wellbeing,
contractual &
stakeholder
relationships

Level 4
Social and natural
environment

Society, economy &
natural environment

???

Source: Peck 2005

Figure 12.1   A supply chain as an interactive system[29]

Level one – process engineering and inventory management

Level one in the figure concentrates on a process engineering or inventory management perspective. It focuses on what is being carried – work and information flows – and process design *within and between* organisations. This perspective underlies lean manufacturing and the 'end-to end' perspective required for the 'agile' supply chain concept. Risk management is largely about improved visibility (of demand and inventory), velocity (to reduce the likelihood of obsolescence and optimise asset utilisation) and control. If processes are tightly monitored and controlled, then nonconformance to plan can be quickly detected. Risk reduction tools are often borrowed from total quality management. Related process improvement and control methodologies such as 'six sigma' are also favoured by some, as are automated event management systems, which readily alert managers to deviations from plan and minimise human intervention.

In the ideal world of scientific management, mastery of process control methodologies would facilitate the identification, management and elimination of risk. Unfortunately we do not live in an ideal world, so levels two, three and four of the model bring in a host of other factors that often intervene.

Level two – assets and infrastructure dependencies

Level two considers the fixed and mobile assets used to source, produce or carry the goods and information flows addressed at level one. When viewed at this level, nodes in the networks may be farms, factories, distribution centres, commercial retail outlets, or public service delivery points such as schools or hospitals. Alternatively they may be facilities housing IT servers and call centres. Links in the network are the transport and communications infrastructure; that is, roads, railways, flight paths and sea lanes, pipelines and grids, plus mobile assets – boats, trains, trucks and planes. The transport and communications networks have their own nodes in the form of ports, airports and satellites.

Well-known asset-based approaches to risk management, developed in insurance, are appropriate and commonly used in this context. These actuarial approaches draw on plentiful historical data to provide some indication of the likelihood of fire, flood and many other eventualities affecting the insured asset. They tend to define risk along the lines of the *Probability* (likelihood of a given event) x *Severity* (negative impact should it occur). In a wider vein it is helpful to explore the impact on operations of the loss of links or nodes in the production/distribution and infrastructure networks, through network modelling.

Mitigating the impacts of potential disruptions to nodes and links is where business continuity planning (BCP) also has a place. More often than not Level two disruptions are not the result of catastrophic failures caused by the phenomena that have exercised generations of actuaries. The disruptions are just as likely to be the results of poorly managed IT upgrades or physical network reconfigurations. Planned site closures and relocations are often to blame, nevertheless it is perhaps worth noting that cross-sector surveys suggest that loss of key skills is actually a more frequently encountered problem than either loss of site or IT systems.[30]

Level two is of course the territory of unglamorous 'trucks and sheds' logistics – an early candidate for outsourcing (along with IT support) in most manufacturing and retail organisations. The increase in global sourcing and supply that we discussed in Chapters 2 and 5 means that, for much of the developed world, the transport element of SCM and the associated resource requirements are increasing. It also means that more shipments are travelling further than ever before, increasing the possibility that assets (and their goods) may be damaged, stolen or simply mislaid along the way. To reduce the likelihood of this happening RFID is starting to be used in asset and consignment tracking.

Naturally, technological solutions, or any other aspect of operations at this level, need appropriately trained personnel, though this simple fact is often overlooked. The case below provides a real example of why consignment tracking matters and why staff training is so vitally important.

RFID AND THE COST OF LOSING TRACK

Hundreds of thousands of people met violent and untimely deaths in Iraq in the years following the invasion in 2003. Few of these individual tragedies have been so well investigated as the death of a British soldier, Sgt Stephen Roberts, who died in action after being hit in the chest by a wayward bullet. A shortage of essential body armour meant that he had been required to hand his over to a fellow serviceman who was judged to be more 'at risk'. The tragedy of this incident was that an investigation by the UK National Audit Office would later reveal that 200 000 components of body armour had been purchased by the Ministry of Defence, but misplaced somewhere within the logistics system. The scandal made an indisputable case for the extension of RFID within the UK defence logistics system.

RFID was used to track consignments by US forces and to a limited extent by UK forces during the 2003 invasion of Iraq. However, even tagged consignments appeared to be going missing. The root cause was a training failure. Back at base, enthusiastic logisticians were aware of the potential benefits of RFID technology and its operating requirements. Unfortunately neither US or UK forces fully recognised the need to inform their front line troops, who had no idea what the tags were, or what should be done with them when they reached their destination. As a result many were simply unclipped and thrown into buckets when the containers were unloaded. Some were shot off the containers by US troops believing them to be improvised explosive devices.

Level three – organisations and inter-organisational networks

Level three looks at supply chain risk at the strategic level of organisations and inter-organisational networks. These are the organisations that own or manage the assets and infrastructure, that make or carry the freight and information flows. At this level risk is likely to be perceived as the financial consequences of an event or decision for an organisation – particularly its impact on budget or shareholders. This is where strategic management concerns, corporate governance requirements and conflicts of interest in risk management become most evident.

From a purely SCM perspective, risk at this level is the downside financial consequences of a specific event. The loss of a sole supplier or customer is the most obvious danger here. The trading relationships that link organisations and power dependencies between them should also be watched carefully.

Low margins are likely to encourage consolidation within industry. Consolidation can change the balance of power between organisations in a supply chain, reversing dependencies, changing service priorities, negotiating positions and risk profiles. Post-takeover or merger, once compliant suppliers may no longer be willing to dance to a customer's tune. They may wish to concentrate on other bigger customers, or have completely different strategic priorities. Consolidation also heralds network reconfigurations and the associated disruptions described at level two.

Partnering, dual sourcing and outsourcing are likely to be put forward as risk management solutions, backed up by contractual obligations. However, anecdotal evidence abounds to suggest that in times of shortage contractual guarantees become unreliable, with suppliers diverting scarce resources to their largest customers, regardless of contractual requirements. Software is available that allows companies to divert supplies automatically to service their most valuable accounts.

Best practice strategic management and corporate governance tend to see risk differently from SCM. Here risk retains the upside as well as downside connotations of decision theory. Strategic management is likely to encourage managers to take 'big bets' to maintain competitive advantage in core competencies. The high-risk big bets are offset by a requirement for lower risk taking in noncore activities. This line of logic encourages strategists and corporate risk managers (few of whom have operational SCM experience) to attempt to transfer risks associated with noncore activities off balance sheets to suppliers. One pitfall associated with this reasoning is that the definition of what is and is not a core capability may be too narrowly drawn, with key elements of SCM falling by the wayside. Outsourcing and contractual means are nevertheless seen as legitimate methods employed to reduce exposure to financial risk. The option is even more tempting if short-term cost savings can be realised. However, when liability for risk management is transferred in this way, the operational consequences of failure remain.

The industrial relations battle between Swiss-based, North American-owned airline catering company Gate Gourmet (you will recall we also studied the operations and logistics processes in this company in the case study at the end of Part Two) and its UK workforce in the summer of 2005 illustrated the point. The Gate Gourmet dispute was a landmark case in that it marked the return of secondary industrial action, not seen in the UK for decades.[31] It also illustrates why supply chains should also be viewed as interactive societal systems.

GATE GOURMET

Gate Gourmet was sole supplier of in-flight catering services to British Airways (BA). Many of the staff had been BA workers until a cost reduction programme prompted the airline to outsource the activity in 1997 to Swiss-owned company Gate Gourmet. The move had been financially beneficial to BA which, in a competitive environment, had continued to pursue further cost reductions through its supply chain. The pressure to continually cut costs was in turn cited by some as the root cause of the Gate Gourmet dispute.

In the post-9/11 climate of fear, demand for transatlantic air travel dropped and oil prices rose. These were hard times for the airline industry and its suppliers. The catering business went into loss. In 2002 Gate Gourmet was sold on to US-based private equity firm Texas Pacific Group (TPG). At this point BA exercised an option within the original outsourcing agreement to renegotiate the contract for more favourable terms. The new owners improved productivity and increased management pay, but continued to lose money on the BA contract. In 2005 the new owners sought to cut its costs with redundancies amongst catering staff, and by imposing less generous terms and conditions on those who remained. At the same time the company took on 130 seasonal workers on lower rates of pay. The resulting dispute and 670 sackings – involving mostly women drawn from the local Asian community – did not on the face of it represent a significant threat to BA. The airline could operate its core business without in-flight meals. However, when about 1 000 BA ground staff – many of them with family ties to the sacked catering workers – decided to walk out in sympathy, the consequences for BA were unavoidable. The four-day strike halted BA flights out of its Heathrow hub, damaging the airline's reputation, and costing BA (and its shareholders) an estimated £40m in cancelled flights and the cost of food and accommodation for 70 000 stranded passengers.

With bankers threatening to move against TPG and TPG threatening to take Gate Gourmet into administration, BA was forced to intervene. The airline agreed to renegotiate its catering contract, and to donate about £7m towards the cost of enhanced redundancy packages, but did so on the condition that Gate Gourmet settled its own labour dispute. On 27 September 2005 an agreement was reached between the trade unions and Gate Gourmet. About 700 catering staff volunteered to accept the new redundancy offer, slightly over the number required. In March 2007, TPG sold its holding in Gate Gourmet to bankers Merill Lynch.

Level four – the macro-environment

The fourth and final level of analysis is the macro-environment, within which the assets and infrastructure are positioned and organisations do business. The 'PEST' (political, economic, social and technological) analysis of environmental changes, used in strategic management, is appropriate here. Sometimes 'green' environmental and legal/regulatory changes are included in the basic analysis or given separate treatment. Socio-political factors, such as action by pressure groups (e.g. environmentalists or fuel protestors) can be identified by routine 'horizon scanning' using specialist or general media sources, allowing measures to be put in place to mitigate the impact. Geo-political factors, such as war, often take time to build, but the extent to which they can influence demand for all manner of goods and services should not be underestimated. For example, the 2003 invasion of Iraq coincided with a drop in business confidence, leading to a fall in advertising, and a marked reduction in demand for high quality paper. The war had the reverse impact on the demand for oil as fears of oil shortages swept the world, and on oil prices, which are critical for the global economy.

Beyond a controlled 'casino' or even factory environment, there are the forces of nature – meteorological, geological and pathological – to contend with. Most are likely to be far beyond the control of supply chain managers, so risk avoidance, or contingency planning are appropriate courses of action. However, one category – pathogens – such as contaminants and diseases – is worth particular attention here. Whether it is BSE, foot and mouth, avian flu, a human pandemic or the computer viruses that mimic them, what makes pathological factors so dangerous is that they are *mobile*. They have the ability to hitch a ride with the flows of goods and information (and people) that logisticians and supply chain managers work so hard to speed around the globe. Once inside the system, they have the potential to bring it down from within. With more goods and information travelling further and faster than ever before the potential for this to happen cannot be ignored.

The creeping crises referred to earlier in this chapter could all be regarded as level four disruptions, but it would be wrong to regard them only as *external* threats to the supply chain. Their potency as disruptive challenges is a reflection of our interconnected, interdependent societies and the efficiency of our supply chains.

LEARNING REVIEW

This chapter has provided an introduction to the complex, but fascinating subject of supply chain risk, and the related concepts of vulnerability, robustness and resilience. It has tackled some of the competing concepts of risk, the shortcomings of risk management and their relevance to a logistics and SCM context. The chapter draws on earlier writings in open systems theory to explain why supply chains should be viewed as open societal systems as well as engineered processes. How, when and why the different concepts of risk fit with some elements of supply chains but not others were explained. Throughout, the chapter has endeavoured to provide a holistic overview of supply chain vulnerability, providing a multi-level framework, based on a simple exploded model of a supply chain. Within this framework appropriate supply chain risk management tools are positioned.

QUESTIONS

- What is meant by supply chain vulnerability?
- Why is a robust supply chain not necessarily a resilient supply chain?
- Distinguish objective and perceived risk.
- Discuss the relevance of the Sarbanes-Oxley Act 2002 (SOX) to logistics.
- Outline how risk might be dealt with in levels 1, 2 and 3 of Peck's model of the supply chain.

THE IMPACTS OF CREEPING CRISES

We discussed above the role of creeping crises in today's uncertain and changing world. Can you think of other creeping crises in addition to the ones mentioned in this chapter?

Taking either your own examples or the ones described in this chapter, outline the impacts these crises had on economies and societies.

NOTES

1. For an explanation of the origins of orthodoxies in risk management see: Adams, J. (1995) *Risk*, Abingdon, Routledge.
2. Christopher, M. (1998) *Logistics and Supply Chain Management* (2nd edn), London, Financial Times/Pitman Publishing.
3. Tang, C. (2006) Robust strategies for mitigating supply chain disruptions, *International Journal of Logistics Research and Applications*, 9(1), 33–45.
4. *Collins English Dictionary* (2000) Glasgow, Harper Collins.
5. Peck, H. (2006) *Resilience in the Food Chain: A Study of Business Continuity in the Food and Drinks Industry*, London, Department for Environment, Food and Rural Affairs.
6. *Collins English Dictionary, op. cit.*
7. Peck, H. (2003) *Supply Chain Resilience*, London, Department for Transport.
8. Peck, H. (2005) Drivers of supply chain vulnerability: an integrated framework, *International Journal of Physical Distribution and Logistics Management*, 35(4), 210–232.
9. Rumsfeld, D. http://www.defenselink.mil/transcripts/transcript.aspx?transcriptid=2636
10. Matthews, R. (2004) QED: science and philosophy, *The Daily Telegraph*, http://www.telegraph.co.uk/connected/main.jhtml?xml=/connected/2004/07/07/ecrqed07.xml
11. BBC News, Rum Remark Wins Rumsfeld an Award, 2 December, 2003.

12. For an introduction to the concept of high reliability organisations see: La Porte, T.R. & Consolini, P. (1991) Working in practice, but not in theory: theoretical challenges for 'high reliability' organizations, *Journal of Public Administration Research and Theory*, 1(1), 19–47.

13. Demchak, D. (1996) Tailored precision armies in fully networked battlespace: high reliability organizational dilemmas in the 'information age', *Journal of Contingencies and Crisis Management*, 4(2), 93–103.

14. For an introduction to business continuity planning and its place within the wider discipline of business continuity management see: Hiles, A. & Barnes B. (1999) *The Definitive Handbook of Business Continuity Management*, Chichester, Wiley and Sons.

15. Peck, H. and Jüttner, U. (2002) Risk Management in the Supply Chain, *Logistics and Transport Focus*, 4(11), December, 17–22.

16. Forrester, J.W. (1958) Industrial dynamics: a major breakthrough for decision makers, *Harvard Business Review*, 38, July–August, 37–66.

17. Sheffi, Y. (2001) Supply chain management under threat of international terrorism, *International Journal of Logistics Management*, 12(2), 1–11.

18. British Standard 25999 Business Continuity, British Standards Institute, 2006. http://www.bsi-global.com/en/Assessment-and-certification-services/management-systems/Standards-and-Schemes/BS-25999

19. Borge, D. (2001) *The Book of Risk,* New York, John Wiley and Sons.

20. March, J.G. & Shapira, Z. (1987) Managerial perspectives on risk and risk taking, *Management Science*, 33(11), 1404–1418.

21. Noy, E. & Ellis, S. (2002) Corporate risk strategy: is it a unified whole or does it vary across business activities? Unpublished paper, Tel Aviv University.

22. Knight, F. (1921, 1965) *Risk, Uncertainty and Profit,* New York, Harper and Row.

23. Royal Society for the Prevention of Accidents (1983) *Risk Assessment: A Study Group Report*, London, Royal Society.

24. National Research Council (1983) *Risk Assessment in the Federal Government: Managing the Process*, Washington DC, National Academy Press.

25. Adams, J. (1996) *Risk*, London, Routledge.

26. White, D. (1995) Applications of systems thinking to risk management: a review of the literature, *Management Decision,* 33(10), 35–45.

27. Martha, J. & Subbakrishna, S. (2002) Targeting a just-in-case supply chain for the inevitable next disaster, *Supply Chain Management Review*, September/October, 18–24.

28. Rittel, H.W.J. & Webber, M.M. (1973) Dilemmas in a general theory of planning, *Policy Sciences*, 4, 155–169.

29. Peck (2005) *op. cit.*

30. Peck, H. & Jüttner, U. (2002) *op. cit.*

31. Arrowsmith, J. (2005) British Airways Heathrow flights grounded by dispute at Gate Gourmet. European Industrial Relations Observatory online (Eironline), 20 September. http://www.eurofound.europa.eu/eiro/2005/09/feature/uk0509106f.html

Integration and Collaboration

INTRODUCTION

Thus far in this book we have alluded to the fact that supply chain integration and collaborative partnerships have a positive effect on supply chain performance. This chapter now discusses each concept in further detail to offer insights into how they can be achieved. In today's world of international trade and global competition, where increasingly supply chains compete more so than individual firms and products, integration and collaboration have become key differentiators of high performing supply chains. In this chapter, we learn about current thinking from research and practice to understand how these important concepts are evolving.

Chapter 13 comprises five core sections:
- Supply chain integration
- Supply chain collaboration principles
- Supply chain collaboration methods
- Collaborative planning, forecasting and replenishment (CPFR)
- Vendor managed inventory (VMI)

LEARNING OBJECTIVES

- Define the terms integration and collaboration in the global SCM context.
- Explain how internal and external integration can be achieved to benefit supply chain performance.
- Discuss collaborative working and partnerships.
- Elaborate on specific methods used to enable collaboration.
- Offer a holistic perspective of SCM to provide an understanding of how supply chains can gain greater integration and collaboration in the future.

SUPPLY CHAIN INTEGRATION

Supply chain integration is a term that embodies various communication channels and linkages within a supply network. However, it should not be confused with **collaboration**. While supply chain integration is the alignment and interlinking of business processes, collaboration is a relationship between supply chain partners developed over a period of time. Integration is possible without collaboration. For example, order processing via electronic data interchange (EDI) (as discussed in Chapter 9) or the Scala system in the Gate Gourmet case are integrated transactions, but do not require the customer and supplier to operate collaboratively. Conversely, integration is an enabler of collaboration. This is discussed further in the section on supply chain collaboration principles below. Hence the terms integration and collaboration should not be confused.

There are four primary modes of integration within a supply chain (also illustrated in Figure 13.1):

1. Internal integration: cross-functional integration within a selected organisation.
2. Backward integration: integration with selected first tier, and increasingly second tier suppliers.
3. Forward integration: integration with selected first tier customers or service providers (e.g. LSPs). Forward integration with second tier customers is uncommon.

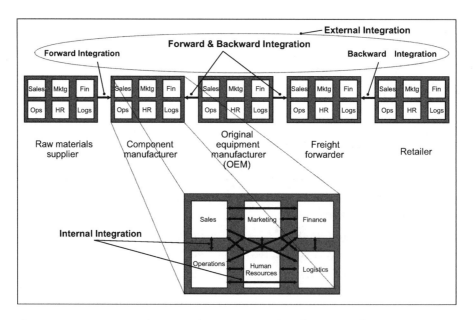

Figure 13.1   Distinctions between the primary modes of integration[1]

4. Forward and backward integration: integration with suppliers and customers. This 'total' integration is rare but theoretically ideal.

The latter three modes listed above can be classified as **external integration** (i.e. extending beyond the confines of a single organisation); compared with **internal integration**, which limits integration to within a particular organisation.

Focusing firstly on internal integration, the aim is to integrate communications and information systems so as to optimise their effectiveness and efficiency. This can be achieved by structuring the organisation and the design and/or implementation of information systems for improved communication and information sharing. In doing so, nonvalue adding activity is minimised (e.g. duplication of effort), costs are reduced (e.g. reduced error rectification), lead times are reduced (e.g. order processing) and service quality is improved (e.g. improved order tracking).

Conventionally, businesses have been organised in **functional silos** such as those illustrated in Figure 13.2(a). This is still a common organisation design, but is no longer viewed as ideal. Each function is usually housed in a distinct department

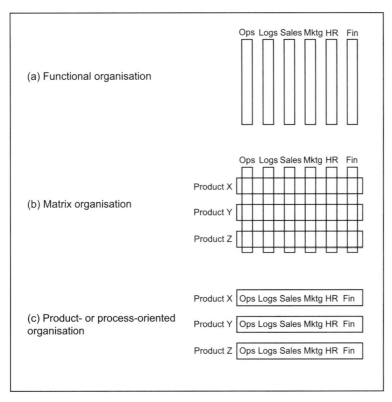

Figure 13.2   Selected generic organisation structures

where specific job roles are defined by their function. This functional design has long been recognised as having the potential to create ineffective and inefficient information processes and communications between departments because each department designs their own silo for their own purposes, without due consideration of the needs of other departments. Examples of inefficiencies include: duplication of effort, processing delays or misdirected information as a result of the distance between silos, and physical and cultural barriers between different departments. Imagine, for example, that you work in the logistics department and you have an empty shelf in the warehouse. You need to understand why this stockout has occurred and know when new stock is due (if it has been ordered). To obtain this information you need to speak to somebody in the procurement department, which is in a different location. Plus any one of 20 people could have (or not have) placed the order! You may never get an answer to your questions.

The fundamental solution to the inefficiencies of functional organisations is to shift to a **product or process orientation**. That is to say that specific people from each functional department are assigned to a particular product, group of products or a process. For example, within the procurement department of an automotive OEM, there would be a dedicated team or individual for each car sub-assembly (for example seats, engines, and so forth). This would be mirrored in each of the other departments. This is commonly referred to as a *matrix organisation*, illustrated in Figure 13.2(b). The **matrix organisation** design enables improved integration between dedicated teams in each department. By having teams or individuals accountable for particular products and processes, communication and information processing between departments is streamlined. However, this does not overcome the issue of distance, which causes long lead times. Furthermore, matrix organisation designs retain functional reporting structures. This can cause conflict of purpose between, and duplication of the roles, of, the functional managers and the process or product managers.

What is currently perceived to be best practice in organisational design is a complete shift away from functional silos to a pure product or process organisation structure (Figure 13.2(c)). In this case, product or process teams are grouped together. Individuals from each relevant function are located together (physically in a single location or virtually) with little or no need to operate outside of that team. Using the empty warehouse shelf example above, you (the logistics coordinator) would be working directly with the buyer for that particular product, enabling you to speak to them immediately to resolve the issue, or in fact eliminate it occurring by informing them in advance of the impending stockout.

How can this reorganisation be achieved? Business process reengineering (BPR) and/ or socio-technical systems (STS) methods are commonly used to analyse existing organisational structures, eliminate nonvalue adding activities, and implement new work structures, as discussed in Chapters 7 and 9.

Information technology has not yet been discussed in this chapter. However, practitioners increasingly view it as the key to improved internal integration. As discussed in Chapter 9, ERP is a key enabler of internal integration. However, for optimal performance of the technology, the organisation must first be optimally aligned. Joint optimisation is a central tenet of both BPR and STS. Indeed, why design an ERP to perform a series of nonvalue adding activities? In fact, ERP implementation will often expose any remaining nonvalue adding activities in the organisation.

As listed above, external integration can take one of three forms. EDI, as discussed in Chapter 9, is a key enabler of supply chain integration. The automated transfer of order data between supply chain partners streamlines information sharing and processing. However, as with ERP, effective and efficient organisational design is a prerequisite. Leading automotive manufacturers work closely with their first tier suppliers to integrate manufacturing, logistics and information processes. This enables just-in-time line-side delivery at their assembly plants. For example, the OEMs use consultants to work with their suppliers to design their work structures and processes to fit with those of the OEMs. By adopting the same practices, a seamless lean supply chain is created. That is to say that the processes up to line-side delivery at the assembly plant are part of one extended operation.

To filter these same principles further upstream, the Japanese automotive OEMs typically adopt a '**keiretsu**' supply chain structure, where the OEMs support their first tier suppliers, their first tier suppliers in turn support the second tier, and so on. Keiretsu was pioneered in Japanese banking and has since been adopted with great success in Japanese SCM. Thus, while information technologies are enablers of supply chain integration, optimal and uniform organisational structures are fundamental to integrating various parties across the supply chain. Nevertheless, the scale and complexity of global supply chains remains the key constraint to integration across multiple echelons.

SUPPLY CHAIN COLLABORATION PRINCIPLES

As discussed at the beginning of this chapter, supply chain integration is an enabler of collaboration. While integration is product and process oriented, collaboration is focused on relationships. formation sharing can be achieved by implementing integrated processes and applications, but may not be of benefit to all supply chain partners, possibly exposing suppliers to their competitors. For example, as discussed in

> While information technologies are enablers of supply chain integration, optimal and uniform organisational structures are fundamental to integrating factors in a supply chain.

Chapter 9, supermarket retail is intensely competitive, as are automotive sales. This drives down consumer prices at the supermarket shelves and car dealers' forecourts, which in turn causes them to 'squeeze' their suppliers to operate with lower profit margins and tighter delivery schedules while maintaining service quality. Consequently, suppliers are forced by these market conditions to behave competitively rather than collaboratively. Collaboration is dependent on the provision of mutual benefit. Clearly in such supply chains, mutual benefit between suppliers is difficult to achieve. Hence trust becomes an issue.

The dynamics of trust and collaboration can be explained via the prisoner's dilemma, an example of Nash equilibrium game theory. Here is the analogy:

You and a partner are suspected of committing a crime and arrested. The police interview each of you separately. The police detective offers you a deal: your sentence will be reduced if you confess! Here are your options:

- If you confess but your partner doesn't: your partner gets the full 10-year sentence for committing the crime, while you get a 2-year sentence for collaborating.
- If you don't confess but your partner does: the tables are turned! You get the full 10-year sentence, while your partner gets the 2-year sentence.
- If both of you confess: you each get a reduced sentence of 5 years.
- If neither of you confess: you are both free people.

The dilemma you face is 'do you trust your partner to make the same decision as you?'

As we can see in Figure 13.3, the best strategy is based on trust, and results in a 'win-win' situation. Yet, if neither partner trusts each other, it is most likely that both will confess and spend time in prison.

Traditionally, business relationships have been built on open market negotiations (i.e. gaining the lowest priced products and/or services). From this common 'competitive' starting point, a trust-based win-win situation in a supply chain partnership takes time. Trust needs to be built up step-by-step. The journey towards a collaborative supply chain can be long and arduous. This is illustrated in Figure 13.4.

Collaboration has two dimensions: **vertical collaboration** between suppliers and customers, and **horizontal collaboration** between competitors and other supply

	You	
	Confess	Don't confess
Your partner — Confess	5,5	2,10
Your partner — Don't confess	10,2	0,0

Figure 13.3   The prisoner's dilemma

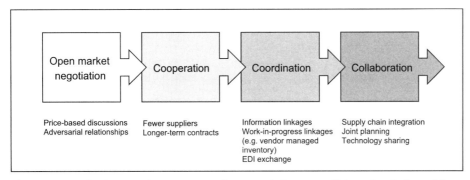

Figure 13.4   The journey from open market negotiations to collaboration (adapted from Spekman *et al.*, 1998)[2]

chain actors. This is illustrated in Figure 13.5. As per our discussion thus far, vertical collaboration is more common and easier to implement than horizontal collaboration. However, supply networks that achieve both will gain significant business benefit. In the context, for example, of transport management, the combination of vertical and horizontal collaboration can achieve reduced inventory-carrying costs, reduce unproductive waiting time, reduce overall transport costs, improve integration of the transportation network, reduce empty running times and improve lead time performance by adopting collaborative methods such as joint planning and technology sharing.[3] Imagine the benefits of two major high street retailers sharing transport capability in and out of London to their stores. This reiterates the prisoner's dilemma. Both retailers would benefit from improved logistics performance, but the fact that they compete directly for consumers' business is a

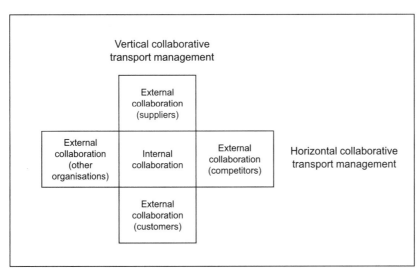

Figure 13.5   The two dimensions of collaboration applied to transport management (adapted from Mason *et al.*, 2007)[4]

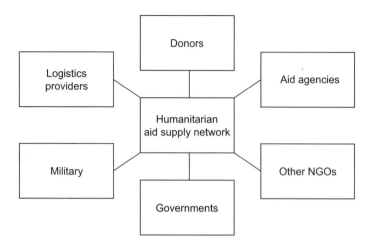

Figure 13.6   Actors in humanitarian logistics (Kovács, 2007)[5]

significant barrier. Indeed we will see in the next chapter, which deals with sustainability, that retailers are in fact adopting solutions such as this.

So far, the focus of our discussion has been in the business context. But what, for example, of the **humanitarian logistics** context? In a humanitarian disaster, competition between supply chain actors could have potentially devastating consequences. For example, two or more nongovernment organisations (NGOs) attempting to deliver the same aid to a particular location could overstock one area and understock another! Figure 13.6 identifies the actors in humanitarian logistics.

In humanitarian logistics, vertical coordination and collaboration between representatives/governors of a disaster-struck region and actors from outside of that region, such as the national government or United Nations, is essential for preparation, immediate response and reconstruction; as illustrated in Figure 13.7. Nevertheless, horizontal collaboration is uncommon. While some NGOs may share warehouse facilities, this is not the norm.[6] Yet, if achievable, it is arguable that significant benefits could be gained. For further insights into the important and growing area of humanitarian logistics, see the case study on this topic at the end of Part Three.

SUPPLY CHAIN COLLABORATION METHODS

As discussed above, global supply network complexity is a major constraint of both integration and collaboration. In networks such as those of the major retailers and automotive and aerospace OEMs, there are multiple echelons with many suppliers competing for the same business. Hence **supply base rationalisation** is periodically a key focus of such organisations. For example, in 2002 Nissan cut its supply base by half to reduce complexity and therefore costs. This resulted in record profits for Nissan that year.[7] This was in part a response to market pressures. However, upstream in such

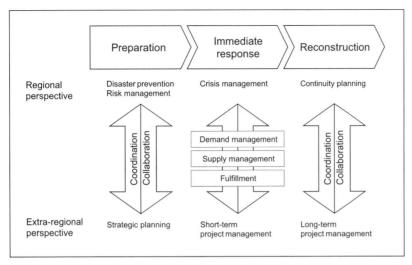

Figure 13.7   A framework for humanitarian logistics (Kovács, 2007)[8]

a supply chain it is not uncommon to find two companies with the same capabilities (for example engineering SMEs manufacturing cylindrical engine components) competing for the same orders handed down from their first tier customer. This traditional competitive behaviour creates supply chain inefficiencies. If small-scale suppliers with limited resources are continually competing for business, they will inevitably drive down their prices, promise unrealistic lead times and lose their focus on product and service quality. While we are conventionally led to believe that competition in business is good, in this case it is destructive. From our discussion of keiretsu above, it is far easier for a company such as Nissan to work with a few selected suppliers, than to work with many suppliers. Furthermore, from our discussion of horizontal collaboration, suppliers who are not directly competing against each other for individual orders are more likely to collaborate. Supply chain rationalisation and horizontal collaboration are also discussed in the Aerogistics case below.

Coupled with the inevitable periodic supply base rationalisation should be a supplier development activity (you may recall we introduced this topic in Chapter 5 in the context of our discussion on procurement and outsourcing). As discussed in the context of keiretsu above, supplier development can enable improved integration and also collaboration. In the Aerogistics example (see below) they employ supplier development to shift their suppliers' mindsets from thinking competitively to collaboratively. This enables them to utilise their integrated order processing application for **aggregated procurement**. That is to say, rather than individual suppliers tendering for particular orders, specific suppliers are selected by a supplier selection software package based on their capabilities. In the previous *competitive* environment some suppliers would win orders while others would not. In the new *collaborative* environment each supplier gains a share of the total orders based on their ability to deliver the order on time and to specification. Consequently, the overall supply base incrementally improves, reducing the likelihood of future rationalisation.

AEROGISTICS HOLDINGS LTD

The UK has a strong aerospace industry with a number of market-leading original equipment manufacturers (OEMs). Hence a number of UK-based manufacturers exist to supply aerospace components to these OEMs. Meanwhile these suppliers also supply to maintenance, repair and overhaul companies (MROs) who maintain in-service aircraft. A typical existing UK aerospace supply chain is illustrated in Figure 13.8

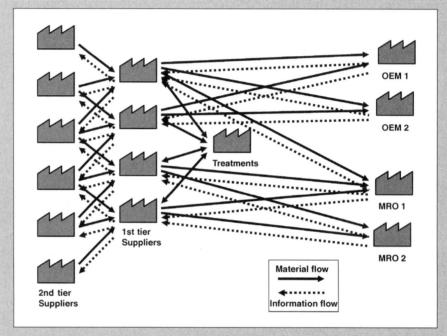

Figure 13.8   An existing UK aerospace supply chain

A significant issue in this existing supply chain is the late delivery of components to OEMs and MROs. Late delivery is caused by demand fluctuations from a mixture of three types of order: steady state production orders (i.e. components required to build new aircraft, which can be forecast from OEM production order data); spares orders (i.e. components required for scheduled maintenance of in-service aircraft, which can be forecast from MRO maintenance schedule data); AoG (Aircraft on Ground) orders (i.e. components urgently required for unscheduled maintenance of in-service aircraft that cannot be used until repaired, which cannot be forecast).

Upstream suppliers are typically SMEs (small and medium sized enterprises) operating with low profit margins. Hence, these suppliers bid for any orders that are offered, regardless of whether they have sufficient capability to fulfil those orders to the customers' requirements. Furthermore, they neither have the time nor the finances to implement best practice processes and information systems to improve their responsiveness to this complex and difficult-to-forecast overall market demand. These suppliers are therefore locked into a vicious cycle of competing for orders that they cannot effectively fulfil. Likewise, OEMs and MROs have the burden of chasing unfulfilled and late orders, and typically receive individual components (for example, an undercarriage axle shaft) at irregular intervals from each supplier rather than consolidated kits of parts from a single source (for example a complete kit of undercarriage axle parts for assembly/replacement).

Aerogistics Holdings Ltd specialises in integrating aerospace supply chains, and has developed a solution to this problem. It has purchased the treatments plant[1] in the supply chain represented above. The treatments plant is both positioned close to the downstream end of the supply chain and is conventionally viewed as a 'bottleneck' where a number of component batches from various suppliers converge simultaneously. It is therefore a key position to gain visibility and control of both upstream and downstream processes. Yet this alone is not enough to improve the supply chain. It has also developed three new businesses to improve supply chain agility, namely:

An order processing business

Using a bespoke suite of software, order processing operatives (1) receive orders from OEMs and MROs, (2) select suppliers based on their capabilities (e.g. experience of producing that component, lead time, dependability, etc.), and (3) forward orders to the selected suppliers. Orders are then tracked via software through to fulfilment. OEMs and MROs therefore benefit from aggregated procurement and order processing by a third party. Suppliers receive fewer (but more focused) orders, enabling them to avoid wasting resources on competing for orders that they could not fulfil, and instead to focus on their core competences.

A supplier development consultancy

Supplier development consultants work with suppliers to improve their capability via initiatives aimed at lead time reduction, product and service quality improvement, delivery reliability and cost reduction.

A kitting warehouse

When orders have completed all manufacturing and treatment operations they are consolidated and packaged (i.e. kitted) before being shipped to the OEM or MRO as a complete order.

---

[1] Many of the components are metal. Metal components require protection from corrosion, hardening and non-destructive testing. These specialist processes are commonly known as treatments.

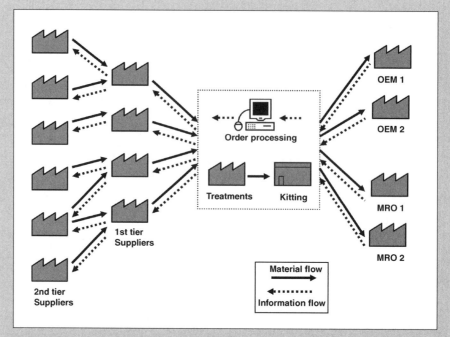

Figure 13.9 The redesigned supply chain

This supply chain redesign is represented in Figure 13.9. Thus Aerogistics has integrated the supply chain and enabled supplier collaboration by: aggregating procurement and offering single source supply to OEMs and MROs; matching orders to suppliers' capabilities to rationalise the number of transactions; and supporting suppliers in improving their internal processes.

COLLABORATIVE PLANNING, FORECASTING AND REPLENISHMENT (CPFR)

Further downstream, less drastic measures are employed. As discussed in Chapter 9 (p.155), collaborative planning, forecasting and replenishment (CPFR) is more than just another IT application. The CPFR process is illustrated in Figure 13.10.

Conceptually, CPFR should enable significant scope and depth of collaboration across a supply chain. However, as discussed above, scale and complexity are significant constraints. Fundamentally, it is difficult to forge close partnerships with many partners.[9] Hence some CPFR solutions will have greater scope and/or depth than others. As such, three modes of CPFR can be identified: basic CPFR, developed CPFR and advanced CPFR.[10]

Basic CPFR involves a limited number of business processes integrated between a limited number of supply chain partners (e.g. a supermarket retailer and a selected

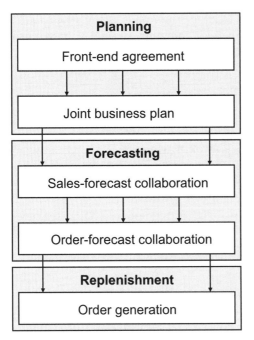

Figure 13.10   The CPFR process (adapted from Cassivi, 2006)[11]

first tier supplier). There is usually a lead partner, who selects those processes where CPFR is adopted (e.g. exchange of stock holding data). This basic CPFR implementation is commonly the starting point of a data sharing collaborative arrangement, which can potentially lead to developed CPFR.

As is implied, developed CPFR has greater scope and depth than basic CPFR. This will typically involve a greater number of data exchanges between two partners, and may extend to suppliers taking responsibility for replenishment on behalf of their customer (i.e. vendor managed inventory, discussed further below).

Advanced CPFR goes beyond data exchanges to synchronise forecasting information systems and coordinate planning and replenishment processes. Hence product development, marketing plans, production planning and transport planning are seamlessly integrated with forecasts based on actual consumer demand extracted from point-of-sale data.[12] Hence, through this high level of integration and collaboration close to the consumer interface, retailers and their first tier suppliers enable the agility to respond to ever more erratic consumer market demand fluctuations.

As illustrated in Figure 13.4, to make the transition to an advanced CPFR solution first requires a long-term relationship to have built up. Hence, time, complexity, scale and the substantial financial investment required are considerable constraints. Nevertheless, for large-scale multinational organisations such as the leading supermarkets and their first tier suppliers, the benefits of CPFR outweigh the initial investment. For organisations without the same economies of scale, the development of an advanced CPFR solution is obviously considerably more difficult to achieve.

VENDOR MANAGED INVENTORY

Although introduced in Chapter 9, which dealt with technology, vendor managed inventory (VMI) is also more than just an IT solution. A holistic view of inventory levels is taken throughout the supply chain with a single point of control for all inventory management. By enabling a vendor to manage stock replenishment at their facilities, a customer (e.g. a supermarket retailer) is effectively eliminating an echelon in the supply chain. In doing so, upstream demand visibility is improved to reduce the impact of demand fluctuations (i.e. the bullwhip effect).[13] Hence VMI can enable supply to more accurately and precisely meet demand.

Although VMI is today centred around an IT solution, the concept of a customer merely defining their requirements and their supplier being accountable for fulfilling them predates contemporary IT.[14] A simplified VMI scenario is illustrated in Figure 13.11.

By providing improved supply and demand information visibility via centralised control, VMI can specifically reduce the impact of the following sources of the bullwhip effect: price variation (e.g. three items for the price of two promotions), rationing and gaming (i.e. customers over-ordering due to stock shortages; the Houlihan effect), demand signal processing (i.e. the Forrester effect), and order batching (i.e. ordering in batches; the Burbidge effect), as discussed in Chapter 7. As with ERP, the implementation of just a software application will not derive the full benefits of VMI. By essentially eliminating an echelon, certain logistics activities

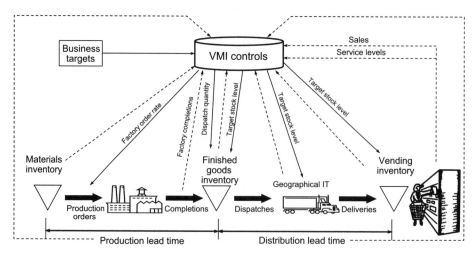

Figure 13.11   A simplified VMI scenario (adapted from Matthias *et al.*, 2005)[15]

Table 13.1   Types of vendor managed inventory in supply chains[16]

Configuration	Description of collaborative or vendor managed functions
Type 0	Traditional supply chain
Type I	Replenishment only
Type II	Replenishment and forecasting
Type III	Replenishment, forecasting and customer inventory management
Type IV	Replenishment, forecasting, customer inventory management and distribution planning

and information processes will either become redundant or be redesigned. Business process reengineering (BPR) is again necessary to eliminate the nonvalue adding activities created and to align the IT with the business processes. As with CPFR, significant investment in developing an appropriate collaborative relationship is a prerequisite to operating VMI.

> Supply chain collaboration cannot be achieved through IT solutions alone. Substantial investment in building resilient, long-term relationships is a prerequisite.

Disney *et al.* (2007)[16] have suggested four types of VMI as given in Table 13.1. Type I and Type II have been implemented in supply chains in various sectors, whereas Type III and Type IV are more advanced and require further research and development.

LEARNING REVIEW

This chapter discussed integration and collaboration in contemporary supply chains. We discussed integration and collaboration separately, and distinguished these two separate but interlinked concepts.

In discussing integration, we introduced different modes of integration, illustrating that it extends beyond the integration of computer systems to the integration of business processes, both within a single organisation and between supply chain partners. We then went on to discuss how organisational design can improve integration.

We discussed both the principles and practices of supply chain collaboration. The prisoner's dilemma illustrates how collaborative behaviour can be more beneficial than competitive behaviour. This is further illustrated by the Aerogistics case, enabling the whole supply chain to improve. In practice, collaboration between supply chain partners takes a great deal of time and effort. Methods such as CPFR and VMI are currently best practice, but require substantial investment in nurturing a collaborative, 'win-win' relationship.

The next chapter continues to focus on supply chain design issues and will focus on sustainability.

QUESTIONS

- Consider the three work organisation designs in Figure 13.2. How might a multinational organisation evolve from a functional organisational design to a product-oriented organisational design?
- How might a response to a humanitarian disaster be improved through vertical and horizontal collaboration between the various actors?
- Redraw Figure 13.11 to include multiple echelons and map the information and material flows onto it. What are the potential constraints of a multi-echelon VMI system?
- Table 13.1 refers to four types of VMI system. While types I and II are well-established, types III and IV are yet to gain widespread adoption. What are the barriers to moving to types III and IV?

COLLABORATION IN HUMANITARIAN LOGISTICS

Review our discussion of collaboration in humanitarian logistics (Figures 13.6 and 13.7 above; also see the case 'Humanitarian Aid Supply Chains' at the end of Part Three of the book). In any humanitarian disaster, a quick and effective response is essential. Logistics operations typically involve the many actors illustrated in Figure 13.6. Hence this complex network of actors should collaborate to deliver the relief and support required in a timely and accurate fashion.

How can the various actors in humanitarian logistics work together to ensure fast and effective disaster relief in any location, at any time in the world?

NOTES

1. Fawcett, S. & Magnan, G. (2002) The rhetoric and reality of supply chain integration, *International Journal of Physical Distribution and Logistics Management*, 32(5), 339–361.

2. Adapted from Spekman, R., Kamauff, J. & Myhr, N. (1998) An empirical investigation into supply chain management: a perspective on partnerships, *Supply Chain Management*, 3(2), 53–67.

3. Mason, R., Lalwani, C. & Boughton, R. (2007) Combining horizontal and vertical collaboration for transport optimisation, *Supply Chain Management: An International Journal*, 12(3), 187–199.

4. *Ibid.*

5. Kovács, G. (2007) The humanitarian supply chain: challenge or role model? Centre for Logistics Research Seminar, Hull University Business School, Hull, 4 July 2007.

6. *Ibid.*

7. BBC (2002) Nissan results shine, http://news.bbc.co.uk/1/hi/business/1976931. stm, accessed 4 July 2007.

8. Kovács, *op. cit.*

9. Holmström, J., Främling, K., Kaipia, R. & Saranen, J. (2002) Collaborative planning forecasting and replenishment: new solutions needed for mass collaboration, *Supply Chain Management: An International Journal*, 7(3), 136–145.

10. Skjoett-Larsen, T., Thernøe, C. & Anderson, C. (2003) Supply chain collaboration: theoretical perspectives and empirical evidence, *International Journal of Physical Distribution and Logistics Management*, 33(6), 531–549.

11. Cassivi, L. (2006) Collaboration planning in a supply chain, *Supply Chain Management: An International Journal*, 11(3), 249–258.

12. *Ibid.*

13. Disney, S. & Towill, D. (2003) Vendor-managed inventory and bullwhip reduction in a two level supply chain, *International Journal of Operations and Production Management*, 23(6), 625–651.

14. *Ibid.*

15. Adapted from Matthias, H., Disney, S., Holmstrom, J. & Smaros, J. (2005) Supply chain collaboration: making sense of the strategy continuum, *European Management Journal*, 23(2), 170–181.

16. Disney, S., Farasyn, I., Lambrecht, M., Towill, D., Van De Velde, W. (2007) Controlling bullwhip and inventory variability with the golden smoothing rule, *European Journal of Industrial Engineering*, 1(3), 241–265.

Sustainable Logistics and Supply Chain Systems

You turn over an iPod and there are six words that are a metaphor for the global economy: 'designed in California, made in China

Professor Gary Hamel, London Business School

INTRODUCTION

The above quote comes from one of the world's most respected management thinkers and aptly sums up the way the world's economy increasingly works today. We already looked in-depth in Chapter 2 at globalisation and international trade, and how both shape today's logistics systems. We also saw in Chapter 2 that increased outsourcing and offshoring to lower cost locations, in particular, have generated huge flows of international freight. Many of the preceding chapters in this book have given various insights into how effective and efficient logistics and SCM can influence the success of organisations. Success, however, has different interpretations which go beyond consideration of only economic success. The purpose of this chapter is to look beyond how logistics and SCM can influence organisational success and to consider the issue of sustainability as it applies to logistics and SCM.

Often, people regard sustainability as just referring to 'green' issues. This however is just one (albeit very important) dimension and in this chapter we will also consider the issue of economic sustainability; that is, how can the firm itself survive and grow in a sustainable manner without having adverse impacts on future generations, and specifically what is the role of logistics and SCM in this context. The important, and growing, area of reverse logistics (both in terms of return of end-of-life products and packaging, as well as return of defective and unwanted products) is also covered in this chapter. Kleindorfer *et al.* (2005)[1], for example, use the term sustainability to include 'environmental management, closed-loop supply chains [we will consider these in the section below on 'Reverse logistics'], and a broad perspective on triple-bottom-line (3BL) thinking, integrating profit, people and the planet into the culture, strategy and operations of companies.'

Sustainable logistics is concerned with reducing the environmental and other disbenefits associated with the movement of freight. Sustainability seeks to ensure that decisions made today do not have an adverse impact on future generations. Sustainable supply chains seek to reduce these disbenefits by *inter alia* redesigning sourcing and distribution systems so as to eliminate any inefficiencies and unnecessary freight movements.

Later in the chapter we consider two caselets that describe the significant increases in scale that have occurred in global container shipping. The facts in these caselets go to the heart of the sustainability debate: some argue that by enjoying such scale as is evidenced in the examples cited is the only way to ensure that global trade can continue by helping to further reduce unit transport costs, others argue that scale is not the solution and that the answer must lie in local sourcing and production.

It is important to also note that the movement of freight is not responsible for all of the environmental disbenefits associated with transportation: the movement of people also creates disbenefits and some logisticians argue that freight takes an unfair share of the blame.

In our discussion in this chapter we draw on examples from maritime transport, air transport and road haulage to highlight issues of sustainability.

Chapter 14 comprises five core sections:
- The 'green revolution' and supply chain redesign
- The link between economic growth and transport growth
- The role of 'scale' in logistics and SCM
- Efficiency solutions
- Reverse logistics

LEARNING OBJECTIVES

- Understand what sustainability involves in the context of logistics and SCM.
- Understand key terms such as carbon footprints, food miles, reverse logistics, etc.
- Illustrate best practice examples of attempts to reduce environmental footprints.
- Understand the link that exists between growth in logistics and concomitant growth in the demand for transport.
- Examine the different aspects of the two key dimensions used in logistics to reduce environmental impacts, namely scale and efficiency.
- Explain the different aspects of reverse logistics.

THE 'GREEN REVOLUTION' AND SUPPLY CHAIN REDESIGN

Recent years have seen a dramatic increase in what have come to be known as 'green' issues, which can generally be regarded as encompassing respect for the world's natural environment (including its atmosphere) so as to ensure that actions taken today do not hinder future generations. Figure 14.1 summarises the key drivers behind the increased emphasis on green issues.

A key concern centres in particular around the use of fossil fuels for power generation and the resultant carbon emissions. The international Kyoto Protocol has called for a 60% reduction in carbon emissions by 2050. This is a steep target with many commentators pessimistic it will ever be achieved (the Deutsche Post World Net case at the end of the chapter, however, conveys a less pessimistic view). 'Emissions trading' has now come into fashion whereby companies and countries engage in environmentally positive activities (for example, planting trees) in order to offset the deleterious effects of carbon emissions.

The term '**carbon footprint**' has come into use to describe the environmental disbenefits associated with economic activities such as the movement of freight. Consumers are becoming increasingly aware of the impact of purchasing goods that may have been sourced over long distances. It may generally appear to be the case that such goods have a larger carbon footprint, although we would caution that this view is over-simplistic. For example, if locally produced goods are manufactured and distributed in an environmentally damaging manner, then this may be worse than procuring goods from overseas where they are manufactured and distributed in an environmentally sustainable manner.

Another term that has come to be increasingly used is what are referred to as '**food miles**': this refers to the distance by which the various components of a particular

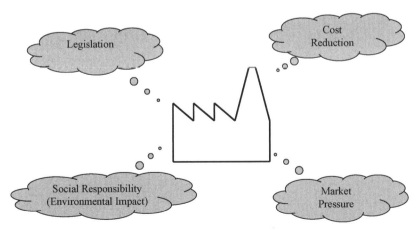

Figure 14.1   The drivers behind the increased emphasis on green issues. Source: Kevin Ord, Scarborough Campus, The University of Hull.

food item have to travel before final consumption. In time it may be the case that ingredients labels on foodstuffs will also include such food miles data.

It is difficult to know exactly how *green* a supply chain actually is, and there is no industry standard to measure it. What is accepted, however, is that greening a supply chain is largely about forward planning, with some commentators noting that over 80% of carbon savings are achievable only at the supply chain design stage.[2] While various initiatives such as, for example, switching to hybrid fuel vehicles are obviously welcome, and generate publicity benefits for companies, it is the (often unnoticed in the public eye) *supply chain design* decisions, such as deciding where to locate warehouses and distribution centres and deciding which transport modes to use, that have the greatest impact. In Europe, for example, there is something of a *renaissance* in short sea shipping, where goods are increasingly moved over short sea routes (a more environmentally friendly mode of transport) rather than along congested (and environmentally more harmful) roads.

Other examples of sustainable supply chain redesigns include reconfiguring distribution networks so as replace small deliveries direct to all end customers with centralised deliveries to a hub from where end customers retrieve their goods. London's Heathrow Airport, for example, has developed a retail consolidation centre adjacent to the airport which receives deliveries on behalf of the various retailers within the airport. Deliveries from different suppliers for these retailers can then be grouped together and delivered to the retailers. The key principle at play here is that it is, other things being equal, more environmentally sustainable when freight moves *in bulk* as far downstream as possible; conversely we can envisage a delivery truck with a small consignment going to a single customer as having relatively high environmental costs. It is important to add that other benefits can also accrue with such an initiative; for example in the airport environment freight could be security checked and rendered safe to be delivered 'airside' once it passes through the hub, thus cutting down on the need for other security checks. Another example is DHL's PACKSTATION initiative illustrated in the Deutsche Post World Net case at the end of the chapter.

As was noted in the chapter outline section above, a possibly more environmentally friendly scenario is local sourcing. One should not, however, underestimate the role of the various factors we discussed in Chapter 5 (such as cheaper labour and materials costs), combined with the fact that many companies have made substantial investments in overseas lower cost locations which they will want to recoup. These factors can thus still render locally sourced goods more expensive. The key then is to ensure that if goods are sourced overseas, that this is done in an environmentally sustainable manner. Furthermore, as many businesses have profit as their primary objective, the key is to ensure that they see the business benefits of environmentally sustainable activities, which may include, for example, reduced

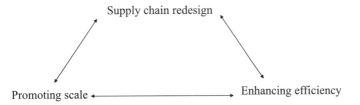

Figure 14.2 Sustainable logistics and SCM

energy bills and enhanced consumer loyalty (although we know that there is a limit to how much more customers will be willing to pay for goods with a low carbon footprint).

We can conclude at this juncture that there are in effect three ways in which to improve the sustainability of logistics and supply chain systems (Figure 14.2):

- Redesigning supply chains
- Using *scale* to reduce the negative environmental effects of logistics activities (i.e. by moving freight in larger single loads, thus cutting down on both unit costs and disbenefits)
- Similarly promoting various *efficiency* solutions (by transporting and handling freight more effectively).

It is important to note that these three solutions are not mutually exclusive: a smart, environmentally sensitive supply chain will combine all three.

We have already considered supply chain redesign; in the following sections we will look at the role of scale and efficiency in the context of sustainable logistics and SCM, but first we will look at the link between economic growth and transport.

THE LINK BETWEEN ECONOMIC GROWTH AND TRANSPORT GROWTH

It can generally be shown that there is an inexorable link between economic growth (as measured usually by GDP) and transport; that is, as economies grow, more transport is required to move the freight that economic growth inevitably generates. A core issue for

> Economic growth and growth in transport are closely linked.

policy makers is to endeavour to *decouple* economic growth and transport growth, in other words to find ways of allowing economic growth without comparable growth in transport (see the caselet 'Decoupling road freight transport and economic growth' below). There are a multiplicity of factors behind such decoupling as the analysis in the caselet illustrates.

DECOUPLING ROAD FREIGHT TRANSPORT AND ECONOMIC GROWTH

In the UK in recent years research by Professor Alan McKinnon at Heriot-Watt University in Edinburgh has shown a partial decoupling between road haulage growth and economic growth.[3] On the surface this looks like a very positive outcome. However, as Professor McKinnon's research shows, the reasons behind this decoupling are varied. Between 1997 and 2004, GDP in the UK increased by one-fifth, while the volume of road freight movement remained stable. His analysis showed that about two-thirds of the decoupling is due to three factors which can be quantified: more non-UK hauliers operating in the domestic market (the relevant UK road haulage statistics just capture the freight tonne-kilometres of UK based hauliers), a decline in road transport's share of the freight market (i.e. freight is shifting from road to other more environmentally friendly modes such as rail and coastal shipping, which obviously is a positive development), and real increases in road freight rates.

Professor McKinnon cites several other factors as having a significant effect, though these cannot be measured on the basis of available statistics. These factors include the relative growth of the service sector (i.e. an increased share of nonmanufactured products in economic growth), the diminishing rate of centralisation, and the offshoring of manufacturing. Professor McKinnon concludes that, while the decoupling is in the right direction from a public policy standpoint, the net environmental benefits are likely to be modest.

The world economy is likely to continue to grow in the medium term, and a feature of such economic growth will be increased demand for transport and distribution. It will be essential that logisticians seek to reduce as much as possible the environmental disbenefits associated with such growth. We already saw that one way they can do this is by reconfiguring supply chains; we will now look in turn at two other approaches, namely *scale* and *efficiency*.

The role of 'scale' in logistics and SCM

THE EMMA MAERSK: 'SANTA'S SHIP'

In Chapter 4 we introduced the global shipping and logistics company A.P. Moller – Maersk (www.maersk.com). Established in Denmark in 1904, today the group employs more than 110 000 people in over 125 countries. The group's shipping subsidiaries operate some of the world's largest container vessels. Maersk Line's new flagship vessel the 'Emma Maersk', which won the title of ship of the year at the 2007 Lloyd's List awards in London, is said to be the world's largest container vessel with an operating capacity of some 11 000 TEUs (20 foot equivalent units). The Emma Maersk is one of five such sister vessels and their actual maximum potential capacity is said to be up to 14 500 TEUs.

Emma Maersk received widespread media interest during her inaugural visit to the UK port of Felixstowe.[4] Media reports noted that the ship is a quarter of a mile long, 200 ft high and as wide as a motorway. The vessel can be operated by a crew of just 13. Other notable facts include the weight of the anchor (29 tonnes) and that the accommodation and bridge area are as high as a 12-storey building. The welcome for the vessel, however, was not universal with the Green Party Member of the European Parliament for South East England, Dr Caroline Lucas MEP, suggesting that the environmental costs of long-distance trade need to be properly taken into account. She was quoted as saying that 'we must manage international trade in a way which is socially and environmentally sustainable, working towards global agreement on a raft of measures such as taxation on fuel and import tariffs designed to support home-grown businesses.'[5]

According to the global shipping and logistics company A.P. Moller – Maersk:[6]

- If all the containers in the world were lined up, it would create a container wall with a length of 108 000 kilometres. This is a third of the way to the moon, equivalent to 18 times the length of the Great Wall of China, or 2.7 times around the earth at the equator.
- The volume of freight that can be held in one standard 40 ft container is quite significant: 200 dishwashers, 350 bicycles or 5 000 pairs of jeans.
- The shipping cost per unit is thus quite low: Maersk estimates for freight coming from Asia to Europe it costs £9 per dishwasher, £5 per bicycle and just £0.35 per pair of jeans.

Only certain ports can handle such ultra large vessels like the Emma Maersk, however, and many container vessels in routine operation are much smaller than this. With fewer ports able to handle larger vessels, there is growing traffic concentration at certain ports. Increasingly, many mid-sized ports are playing a feeder role to the very large ports as hub and spoke networks have emerged. In these networks the larger vessels ply between the major transhipment hubs, with the result that the prosperity of the smaller ports is increasingly dependent on the route strategies of the major shipping lines. This then is the impact of increasing scale on global shipping and port operations. Regardless of the impact of these developments on ports and shipping, important as they are, the question we need to address is: are these patterns of trade sustainable going forward?

Given the increasingly integrated nature of the global economy, some commentators argue that such developments are both inevitable and necessary. Others argue that the frequent movement of low value products around the world is unnecessary, deleterious to the environment, and not sustainable in the long term (especially in the context, for example, of some of the risks that were outlined in Chapter 12). A cursory analysis of the Moller – Maersk figures quoted above, however, shows that container shipping costs are only a fraction of end product value; unless then there is a dramatic rebalancing between regions of other costs in the global economy (such as raw materials and labour costs) it is likely that these patterns of trade are set to continue. If they are, our concern from a logistics standpoint must be how to facilitate them while reducing as much as possible their negative consequences on the environment.

IKEA PROVES ITS GREEN CREDENTIALS [7,8]

In Christmas 2006, the Swedish retailer Ikea gave its 9 000 employees a free bicycle as a Christmas present. They also offered staff a 15% subsidy on public transport. Ikea has long been regarded as a very environmentally conscious company and these initiatives were part of many wider efforts to evidence the company's commitment to sustainability and which are detailed in its 'Social and Environmental Responsibility Report'. One example is where Ikea worked with a supplier to reduce by one centimetre a package containing a sofa from 91 cm wide to 90 cm. As a result, four extra sofas could now be fitted onto each trailer. This in turn reduced the transport costs and environmental penalties associated with moving each sofa.

EFFICIENCY SOLUTIONS

As well as looking to an increased scale, many logistics operators are also seeking efficiencies with how they move and store freight so as to reduce the environmental impact of their activities. The caselet on 'Port centric logistics' below gives insights into how for example logistics companies are seeking to reduce unnecessary road haulage movements for imported maritime freight, and in turn reducing the carbon footprint of such freight movements. Table 14.1 lists some of the many ways in which logistics efficiencies can be generated, and simultaneous environmental penalties reduced, in the case of road haulage. You will recall that we also looked at the efficiency of transport services and asset utilisation in Chapter 8 (p.144). We noted then that the issue of supply chain strategy can impact the efficiency of the transport services demanded, with JIT strategies, for example, leading to inefficient transport utilisation with frequent small loads. Whether JIT systems are sustainable from an environmental perspective going forward is an important question.

PORT CENTRIC LOGISTICS: ONE POSSIBLE SOLUTION?

Some ports are actively encouraging companies to locate distribution centres at ports rather than in their traditional locations, which tend to be in geographically central, inland locations. These ports argue that current patterns of (inland) distribution centre location ignore the fact that most of the freight that passes through these distribution centres first transits through a port. Therefore they argue that it is logical (and often easier in terms of land cost, lack of congestion, etc.) to site such distribution centres at ports. The term **'port centric'** is sometimes used to refer to this approach.[9]

One advantage of port centric logistics is that it cuts down on the number of empty (return) containers on roads by 'stripping' (i.e. emptying) imported containers at the port. This also allows faster repositioning of containers to another port where they are required (we saw in Chapter 2 the significant directional imbalances that exist on global shipping corridors, consequently shipping lines endeavour to reposition empty containers to where they are next needed as quickly as possible).

In the port of Felixstowe in the UK, for example, the BAP Group operates half a million square feet of on-port warehousing and is a major logistics provider for the retailer Sainsbury's. It cites a variety of examples where port centric logistics has been effectively employed:[10]

- Sainsbury's previously took imported containers to an inland RDC, but now the containers are stripped at the port, eliminating a return leg of empty containers. They estimate that this saves 700 000 road miles for every 5 000 TEUs handled.
- Many imported containers are not completely full because of weight restrictions on UK roads. However, if the containers are to be emptied at the port, and not travel on the roads, then the containers can be filled to capacity, which they estimate can in some instances be up to 40% more.

In transportation, it is not just the road haulage sector that is seeking to reduce its environmental footprint. With the growth of air travel, spurred on in particular by rapid growth in the so-called low fares category of air travel, many commentators are looking towards the air transport sector to reduce its impact on the environment. The European low fares airline easyJet, for example, recently unveiled its 'easyJet ecoJet' concept (i.e. a next generation aircraft design, which it believes aircraft manufacturers should be seeking to create). Its concept aircraft would be 25% quieter, emit 50% less CO_2 and 75% less NO_x than today's newest aircraft. To achieve these aims it would comprise *inter alia* rear-mounted 'open-rotor' engines and an airframe built from advanced weight-reducing materials. The aircraft would also be slightly slower than some of today's aircraft, a small price to pay perhaps for a lower environmental footprint. The Chief Executive of easyJet is

Table 14.1 Improving road haulage logistics efficiency and reducing environmental penalties[11]

- Reducing empty running, pooling and sharing capacity, obtaining 'backhaul' loads (a number of websites have been developed that match carriers who have available capacity with shippers seeking capacity – see the case below on electronic logistics markets).
- Increasing vehicle payload capacity (by weight and/or by cubic volume) – double deck and higher trailers, single tractor unit and multiple trailer combinations, etc.
- Improved vehicle routing using GPS and other systems.
- More efficient use of packaging and loading of containers.
- Improved vehicle driving (in-cab computer monitoring of driving style, even examining the benefits of air conditioning versus open windows!).
- Enhancing vehicle operating efficiency (for example using hybrid fuels, ensuring correct wheel alignment and enhanced aerodynamic styling of trucks).

quoted as saying that 'the aviation industry has an excellent record in reducing the environmental footprint of aircraft … Today's aircraft are typically 70% cleaner and 75% quieter than their 1960s counterparts'.[12]

In logistics, efficiency solutions are not just restricted to transportation. The area of green warehouse design is also growing in popularity. Many warehouses are vast structures and their environmental footprints can be reduced by, for example, more efficient lighting and heating/refrigeration systems.

ELECTRONIC LOGISTICS MARKETS[13]

As we noted in Table 14.1 above a number of websites have been developed which match LSPs who have available capacity with shippers seeking capacity. These *electronic logistics markets* (ELMs) provide opportunities both for the LSPs and for those companies using them: the LSP can offer excess capacity within its fleet to a greater potential client base, thus maximising its loaded miles and leading to an ability to reduce freight charges; for shippers, ELMs enable them to increase the number of LSPs, and their concomitant services, that they can reach. Various ELMs provide services ranging from matching of one-off backhaul loads through to managing complex tendering processes for consignors.

REVERSE LOGISTICS

Reverse logistics encompasses a number of streams of activity:

- Return of end-of-life products
- Return of defective, damaged and unwanted products
- Return of packaging and recovery of returnable equipment such as containers, pallets and barrels.

Sometimes the abbreviation **RMA (return material/merchandise authorisation)** is used to refer to such materials; an RMA is in fact strictly speaking a number or form that accompanies the returned product.

We will consider these sets of activities together as they effectively involve material moving back up the supply chain. The term '**closed-loop supply chain**' is usually used to refer to supply chains that also comprise reverse/return flows. Moving material back up a supply chain is not necessarily a simple activity: imagine a motorway largely designed for one-way traffic and occasionally a vehicle has to move in the opposite direction against the flow of traffic. In the same way, materials moving up a supply chain can cause considerable difficulties when that supply chain is designed largely around moving goods downstream to customers.

The frequency and cost of reverse logistics activities is summarised in research by Stock *et al.* (2006):[14]

- Average return rate for online retail sales is 5.6% (varies by product and time of year)
- Cost of processing a return can be 2–3 times that of an outbound shipment
- Average cost of processing per return for items bought on the internet is $30–$35
- Liquidators and outlet stores buy returned/unsold goods at only 10–20% of their original value.

However, it need not all necessarily be negative. Jayaraman and Luo (2007),[15] for example, suggest that if product flow in the reverse direction is managed properly, it can lead to greater profitability and customer satisfaction, and be a boost to the environment. They add that a good reverse logistics programme can be a differentiator and provide a means of gaining market advantage.

With regard to end-of-life products, interest has grown in reverse logistics as a result of growing awareness of and desire for recycling (the maxim 'reduce, reuse and recycle' is becoming ever more popular). In some regions this is also being driven by new legislation, such as in Europe where the recently introduced 'WEEE Directive' now controls the destiny of end-of-life electrical and electronic products. In Chapter 1 we used terminology such as 'farm to fork' and 'cradle to grave' to illustrate the end-to-end nature of SCM. With regard to recycling, we can extend this logic further by referring to 'cradle to reincarnation'. We saw earlier that it is at the supply chain design stage that the most contribution can be made to reducing a supply chain's environmental footprint. In a similar vein, it is at the product design stage that the most contribution can be made towards reducing a product's environmental footprint (this is sometimes referred to as *green product design*).

DEUTSCHE POST WORLD NET AND SUSTAINABILITY[16]

Deutsche Post World Net, one of the world's largest logistics companies, comprises three core divisions: Deutsche Post, Postbank and, its most well-known division, DHL. According to the company's Chairman, 'during the last few years we have become the global leader in our industry. This leadership entails great responsibilities toward society, the environment and our employees, as well as with respect to our continued sound financial performance.'[17]

In its first sustainability report, the company outlines some of the initiatives it is currently undertaking. One chapter of the report is aptly titled 'Creating problems or offering solutions' and reflects the company's proactive approach to reducing its environmental footprint. It states, for example, that the company supports the realisation of the Kyoto Protocol's emission reduction targets, and that the company does this through improving the efficiency of its network, implementing technological solutions and introducing new sustainable products and services for its customers.

Some of the company's initiatives include: a partnership with the UN in the area of disaster management, reducing the amount of paper used in airwaybills (with a potential annual saving of 207 tonnes of paper, and other savings such as reduced fuel consumption from the transportation of lighter airwaybills; in addition the company has long been regarded as a pioneer in the use of electronic airwaybills), and its PACKSTATION initiative whereby parcels are sent to a central collection point where consignees can retrieve them from an automated storage unit using an emailed password.

LEARNING REVIEW

The chapter sought to investigate the important, and rapidly growing, area of sustainable logistics and supply chain systems. We first looked at the growth of interest in environmental and sustainability issues, the so-called 'green revolution'. We also saw that there is a link between economic growth and growth in the demand for transport, although policy makers are endeavouring to weaken this link so that economic growth does not always have to be accompanied by concomitant growth in the demand for transport. Some commentators argue that the solution to reduce the environmental impact of current logistics systems is to source more freight locally, as opposed to overseas, but we saw that the issues surrounding this are more complex than first appear. We also touched on the impact of prevalent JIT systems and whether these are sustainable from an environmental perspective going forward.

We then reviewed the three key (and not mutually exclusive) ways in which the environmental footprint of logistics and SCM can be reduced: by redesigning supply chains, by exploiting the benefits of scale (for example, using larger ships), and by seeking out efficiencies in terms of how we move freight. Finally, we looked at the area of reverse logistics which encompasses end-of-life products, packaging, returnable equipment and also the often necessary process of getting defective, damaged and unwanted products back upstream in the supply chain.

Having studied the critically important area of sustainability, we now move to the final chapter of this book, which seeks to look towards the future and consider new supply chain designs for tomorrow's business environment.

QUESTIONS

- What are the pertinent sustainability issues in the context of logistics and SCM?
- What are the different ways by which the environmental footprint of logistics and SCM can be reduced?
- What is meant by the term 'port centric logistics'?
- How might we 'decouple' economic growth and transport growth?
- Why might JIT inventory management approaches not be sustainable from an environmental perspective?
- What is meant by the term 'carbon footprint'?

LOCAL VERSUS OVERSEAS SOURCING?

Some commentators argue that the solution to reduce the environmental impact of current logistics systems is to source more products locally, as opposed to overseas.

In your view what factors militate against this? It may be helpful to consider specific products and markets, and to consider the *price elasticity* of demand for those products (i.e. how will demand for the product change as the market price for the product changes).

NOTES

1. Kleindorfer, P., Singhal, K. & Wassenhove, L. (2005) Sustainable operations management, *Production and Operations Management*, 14(4), 482–492.
2. French, E. (2007) Green by design, *CILT Focus*, June, gives an excellent insight into the issues discussed in this paragraph.
3. McKinnon, A. (2007) Decoupling of road freight transport and economic growth trends in the UK: an exploratory analysis, *Transport Reviews*, 27(1), 37–64.
4. 'Giant Christmas goods ship docks', *BBC News online*, 5 November 2006.
5. *Ibid.*
6. www.maerskline.com
7. Ikea gives staff a chance to get on their bikes, *The Independent*, 20 June 2007.
8. Ikea 'Social and Environmental Responsibility Report', available at www.ikea.com
9. Falkner, J. (2006) A better place to do logistics?, *Logistics Manager*, May.
10. 'Port-centric logistics', *Ship2Shore* (customer magazine of Hutchinson Ports UK), Issue 1, June 2007.
11. Many of the ideas in this table have been elicited from www.freightbestpractice.org.uk

12. www.easyjet.com

13. See, for example, Wang, Y., Potter, A.T. & Naim, M.M. (2007) Evaluating the reasons for using electronic logistics marketplaces within supply chains, Proceedings of the Logistics Research Network Conference, Hull, September 5–7, pp.137–142.

14. Stock, J., Speh, T. & Shear, H. (2006) Managing product returns for competitive advantage, *Sloan Management Review,* 28(1), Fall.

15. Jayaraman, V. & Luo, Y. (2007) Creating competitive advantages through new value creation: a reverse logistics perspective, *Academy of Management Perspectives*, May.

16. *Facing the challenges of global logistics*, DHL Sustainability Report 2006, available from www.dhl.com

17. *Ibid.*

FURTHER READING

For further reading in the area of sustainable logistics and SCM, see a special issue of the *International Journal of Production Economics* (2007) edited by Piplani, Pujawan and Ray. Also, a paper by Srivastava (Green supply chain management: a state of the art literature review, *International Journal of Management Reviews*, 9 (1), 2007) provides an exhaustive literature review of the whole field of green SCM and also provides a helpful timeline in terms of how the field has developed within the academic literature.

The website of the IMRC at Cardiff University's Sustainable Logistics programmes (www.cuimrc.cf.ac.uk) is a valuable source of up-to-date research in the area, as is the website of the 'Green Logistics Project' (www.greenlogistics.org), which is a four-year EPSRC funded programme involving six UK universities: Heriot Watt, Leeds, Cardiff, Lancaster, Westminster and Southampton.

To celebrate its 80th anniversary in 2006, the CILT in the UK (www.ciltuk.org.uk) published a special report on sustainable logistics titled *Back to the Future: the next 80 years of joined up thinking and joined up journeys*. The report comprises a range of highly informative expert views of what logistics and SCM might look like over the next 80 years given the growing interest in and importance of environmental sustainability issues.

New Supply Chain Designs

INTRODUCTION

This concluding chapter of the book endeavours to bring together many of the key issues discussed in the preceding 14 chapters. The particular focus of this chapter is to elaborate how various trends are shaping logistics and SCM, and in turn how supply chains can be best designed to meet these challenges. As we noted in Chapter 3, and reiterated throughout the book, increasingly it is supply chains that compete more so than individual firms and products. A company can have the best and most sophisticated product in the world, but if it doesn't have a good supply chain behind it then it will likely not be able to compete, especially in terms of cost and speed, and indeed many other attributes also. The design of appropriate supply chains is thus a critically important factor for many organisations today.

Chapter 15 comprises six core sections:
- Strategies and practices in SCM
- The ever changing context
- Synchronising product design and supply chain design
- Determining supply chain costs and value
- Modelling supply chain designs
- The supply chain manager of the future

LEARNING OBJECTIVES

- Review the many strategies and practices employed in logistics and SCM today.
- Appreciate the emerging and changing context within which logistics and SCM exists.
- Understand the need to synchronise the design of supply chains with the design of products.
- Understand the disparate costs that exist across supply chains.
- See how modelling approaches can assist in supply chain design.
- Detail the skills and knowledge areas required of logistics and supply chain managers in the future.

STRATEGIES AND PRACTICES IN SCM

In Chapter 3 we discussed the wide and important area of strategy, and in particular the role of logistics/supply chain strategy, and we noted the current focus on adopting strategies based around lean and agile principles, and various combinations of both. A particular focus in this regard was choosing strategies appropriate to various demand and lead time characteristics. In Chapter 3 we also elaborated some key principles in supply chain planning, namely: that a 'one size fits all approach' doesn't always work, to again quote Gattorna[1] that companies need to use a process of 'dynamic alignment' to match changing customer needs and desires with different supply chain strategies; the need to focus on processes and flows, rather than getting stuck in a functional/silo mentality; the need to focus on high level objectives; and the importance of people in SCM, a topic we will discuss further in the section on 'The supply chain manager of the future' below.

We have described a variety of different strategies and practices throughout the book; these are all detailed in the glossary. The common strategies and practices that logistics and supply chain managers usually need to consider are summarised in the list below. This extensive list illustrates the diverse and multifaceted areas of activity with which logistics and supply chain managers need to be concerned. This in turn requires a particular skills mix, as noted above something we will discuss further below.

- Pursuit of strategies based around lean and agile principles, and varying combinations of both
- Mass customisation/postponement
- Time compression – faster order to delivery cycles and elimination of non value-adding time
- Developing value-adding activities
- Managing reverse logistics flows
- Operating in a more sustainable fashion, especially by exploiting scale and seeking out greater efficiencies
- Operating 'own account' transport versus using LSPs; and with regard to the latter identifying and selecting LSPs, and determining whether or not to employ a 4PL approach
- Coordinating and managing transport flows and directional imbalances; selecting modes and routes
- Use of electronic logistics markets
- Integration of systems, business processes, etc.
- Collaboration with supply chain partners, use of strategies such as CPFR and VMI
- Managing distribution centres and cross docking facilities
- Application of factory gate pricing and consolidation

- Managing outsource and offshore activities
- Procurement (sourcing and purchasing)
- Supplier rationalisation and development
- Determining how much inventory to hold, in what location(s) to hold it, and what inventory control system to use
- Increasing visibility and information enrichment in supply chains
- Determining costs – activity based costs, generalised costs, landed costs, and whole life costs
- Selecting tracking and materials handling technologies
- Use of WMS, MRP, MRPII and ERP systems
- Identifying and tracking appropriate metrics, ensuring compliance with SLAs
- Coordinating and managing upstream and downstream materials flows
- Business continuity planning
- Maximising capacity utilisation and efficiency
- Assessing risks and complying with security, customs, food safety and other requirements.

THE EVER CHANGING CONTEXT

The plethora of strategies and practices listed above make the logistics/supply chain manager's job complex and wide ranging. Added to this is the rapidly changing context within which these managers, and their organisations, have to operate. Professor Martin Christopher from Cranfield University has identified seven major business transformations that must be undertaken for competitive success in tomorrow's marketplace and these are detailed in Table 15.1.

Table 15.1   Christopher's key business transformations[2]

Business transformation	Leading to:
1. From supplier-centric to customer-centric	The design of customer-driven supply chains
2. From push to pull	Higher levels of agility and flexibility
3. From inventory to information	Capturing and sharing information on real demand
4. From transactions to relationships	Focus on service and responsiveness as the basis for customer retention
5. From 'trucks and sheds' to end-to-end pipeline management	A wider definition of supply chain cost
6. From functions to processes	The creation of cross-functional teams focused on value creation
7. From stand alone competition to network rivalry	More collaborative working with supply chain partners

The seven transformations in the table provide a good insight into the new and emerging context within which logistics and supply chain managers increasingly have to operate. Professor John Gattorna from the University of Wollongong lists 13 strategic issues likely to have an impact on supply chains in the future, these can be summarised as:[3]

- Sustainability
- The impact of oil prices on cost-to-serve
- Outsourcing
- The adoption of supply chain principles by service organisations
- Vulnerability of supply chains; designs with embedded resilience
- The rise of genuine collaboration in supply chains
- Increased use of talent
- Learning to design and manage multiple organisation formats
- Increased geographical spread of supply chain networks
- Adopting whole-of-enterprise mindset in managing supply chain operations
- Collaborating with the enemy
- Innovation, product design and product life cycles
- Learning to manage inherent complexity in supply chains.

Again, the ever changing and challenging context within which logistics and supply chain managers have to operate is evidenced from this wide-ranging list of issues. Indeed some countries have an exciting vision of the future of logistics and the opportunities available, as illustrated by the case at the end of the book on 'Dubai Logistics City'.

SYNCHRONISING PRODUCT DESIGN AND SUPPLY CHAIN DESIGN

Simchi-Levi *et al.* (2003) describe the advent in the 1980s of *design for manufacturing* where designers and engineers moved from focusing solely on designing products to a focus on including consideration of the actual manufacturing process when designing products; that is, not only designing good products, but also ones that can be manufactured cheaply and efficiently. They note that recently a similar transformation has begun in SCM, whereby managers have started to realise that 'by taking supply chain concerns into account in the product and process design phase, it becomes possible to operate a much more efficient supply chain'.[4] Mass customisation for example can be enabled by designing postponement into the production process – this can be something straightforward, such as delayed product differentiation enabled by downstream supply chain partners.

Notwithstanding all of this it is of course important to note that no matter how well designed a supply chain is, it cannot overly compensate for poor products. You will recall that in Chapter 3, in the context of our discussion on supply chain strategy, we quoted Christopher *et al.* who state that 'responsive supply chains … cannot overcome poor design and buying decisions which fail to introduce attractive products in the first place'.[5]

Synchronising product design and supply chain design is, as we saw in the previous chapter, also important from a sustainability perspective. We noted then that greening a supply chain is largely about forward planning, with some commentators noting that over 80% of carbon savings are only achievable at the supply chain design stage.[6] We also noted that while various initiatives, such as, for example, switching to hybrid fuel vehicles are obviously welcome, and generate publicity benefits for companies, it is the (often unnoticed in the public eye) *supply chain design* decisions, such as deciding where to locate warehouses and distribution centres and deciding which transport modes to use, that have the greatest impact.

From a societal perspective, supply chain design is not just concerned with sustainability issues, important as they are. Sustainability is one part of the wider framework of CSR, a topic already discussed in Chapter 5. Increasingly, ethical shareholders, regulators and customers are using their power to ensure organisations act responsibly, and the implications of this need to be considered at the supply chain design stage.

It is often the case that supply chains are not as it were designed *ab initio*, often an extant supply chain is already in place, but may need for a variety of reasons to be modified or redesigned. A good example of this is in many countries the supply chain for blood transfusion products, which needed to be redesigned following on from some very significant concerns in terms of product traceability and integrity (many countries have witnessed in recent years awful scandals around the issue of contaminated blood products infecting already ill people). Indeed, more generally the area of pharmaceutical SCM has undergone significant transformation in recent years and this area, together with what has become known as *Good Distribution Practice* (GDP), is detailed in the case study on 'Good Distribution Practice and Pharmaceutical Supply Chain Management' at the end of the book.

DETERMINING SUPPLY CHAIN COSTS AND VALUE

In designing or modifying any supply chain, one of the key considerations is to know what costs are incurred, where they are incurred, and how can they be managed. Conversely, we need to understand where cost can be minimised and where value can be maximised. We met the various categories of costs in different parts of the book, and it is worthwhile to summarise them here.

Generalised costs (Chapter 4)

The concept of generalised costs is often used in transport and includes all of the disparate costs that form the overall *opportunity costs* of a trip. Thus, in addition to the actual rate charged by the LSP, other costs are also taken into account such as packaging costs, insurance costs, costs associated with transit time (the longer the trip takes, the longer the value of the freight is 'tied' up in transit, etc.).

Total landed costs (Chapter 11) and total cost of outsourcing (Chapter 5)

Total landed costs incorporate the various costs associated with sourcing from different suppliers in different places (actual material costs, generalised transport costs, import duties, etc.). The total cost of outsourcing extends this to also incorporate the costs associated with identifying and managing suppliers.

Inventory costs (Chapter 6)

Chapter 6 described in detail the various costs associated with inventory and how inventory can be both controlled and minimised. We saw, for example, that inventory can be *hidden* at multiple points in the supply chain and that as well as the costs associated with carrying inventory, there are also costs associated with ordering and receiving inventory.

Financial accounting, financial management, management accounting (Chapter 10)

A wide variety of financial issues pertinent to supply chain design was discussed in Chapter 10. These included issues such as ensuring sufficient cash flow for the business to survive, financial risk and exposure to currency fluctuations, how much debt to carry, whether to employ transfer pricing, and how to cost various activities (for example activity based costing on a per SKU basis, which was also discussed in Chapter 11, and whole life costing). Ensuring the supply chain is designed to accord with whatever financial objectives are to be prioritised is obviously a primary objective of supply chain design.

Once the various costs are understood, the issue of monitoring performance, discussed in detail in Chapter 11, needs to be considered and supply chains need to be designed to take cognisance of such performance measurement requirements.

MODELLING SUPPLY CHAIN DESIGNS

In order to assess if a supply chain configuration accurately reflects the intended design, modelling techniques can be used.[7] Some of the applications and modelling tools have already been discussed in Chapters 7 and 8. These can generally be divided into two categories: *optimisation techniques* and *simulation techniques*.[8]

Optimisation techniques

Optimisation techniques can be used to determine the supply chain networks that will produce minimum total transport cost solutions. In applications where the data on transport costs are not available, these techniques can be used to determine minimum total tonne kilometres solutions. Optimisation techniques used for modelling network designs are *static* and model only a given set of origins and destinations. The optimal solution consists of which supplier should supply to which distribution centre/warehouse to achieve minimum total cost for a single product. If new suppliers/warehouses are added in the network, the model needs to be rerun with a new formulation and a new data set.

One of the frequently used optimisation techniques is the 'transportation model' discussed in Chapter 8. Transportation models used for allocation of suppliers to distribution centres or warehouses can also be used to assist in determining the optimal number of distribution centres/consolidation centres needed for a total minimum cost solution for a distributor.[9] These models are used with route planning software to include actual travelling distance between an origin and a destination. One of the frequently used software packages is 'CAST-dpm' developed by Radical Ltd (http://www.radical.co.uk/cast/), which can be used with transport route planning software such as 'Paragon' developed by Paragon Software Systems plc (http://www.paragonrouting.com). Transportation models use linear programming for problem formulation and numerical methods for finding the optimal solution.

One of the other optimising techniques used for network design applications is integer programming. Integer programming formulation uses binary variables and is considered suitable for applications in network design where a variable can take only one of the two states such as 'yes' or 'no'. Integer programming has been used for design of production, distribution and vendor network supply chains.[10]

Simulation techniques

Simulation techniques are used for modelling *dynamic* systems as they include variables that could change with time. Two types of models commonly used for supply chain simulation are 'system dynamics (SD) models' and 'discrete event simulation (DES)'.

System dynamics models capture physical flows of freight and information flows, and the factors affecting the responses of the design, in a causal-loop diagram. The causal-loop diagrams are used to draw closed-loop block diagrams clearly depicting the linkages and feedback loops in the system. The linkages and feedback loops represent a supply chain in terms of inputs, transformation and outputs, capturing the dynamics of order policies, lead times, difference between target and actual output and correction mechanism. SD simulation has been extensively used to model supply chain designs, for example to assess the impact of new inventory management strategies such as VMI on supply chain performance.[11] SD models have been used to identify suitable strategies for minimising demand amplification (the bullwhip effect) in supply chains as discussed in Chapter 7.

SD simulation can be developed using Excel spreadsheets or using specialised SD simulation software such as 'STELLA' and 'iThink' developed by isee systems (http://www.iseesystems.com) that assists the decision maker in understanding complex relationships in supply chain operations. The decision maker can also add new linkages, feedback loops, new components and additional information such as forecasts by supply chain players. This facility helps in modelling various supply chain scenarios and in studying the performance under dynamicconditions.

Discrete event simulation (DES) can replicate existing supply chain systems very closely and can assist a decision maker to assess how performance will be affected if the system is modified. DES attempts to create a real world process simulating the operating characteristics of the supply chain being modelled and can include the decision making mechanism. DES requires real life, accurate data on the supply chain system operations and seeks the estimated data on the proposed operations. DES models are generally developed using a process map flow chart of the system based on operations events and activities. For model development, historical time based data and statistical distributions for both actual data sets and estimates are required. DES application requires computer simulation for model development, validation and application. Simulation packages such as ARENA have been used to simulate supply chains.[12]

DES places considerable demands on operational data. In addition, its development, validation and application require good understanding of simulation methodology and the software to be used for this purpose. Once a DES model for a particular application has been validated, however, it is a valuable tool for a decision maker to apply, experiment with, and compare performance of a supply chain over a range of alternative design strategies.

THE SUPPLY CHAIN MANAGER OF THE FUTURE

In Chapter 1 we defined SCM as the management across a network of upstream and downstream organisations of material, information and resource flows that lead to the creation of value in the form of products and/or services. We considered in this book different aspects of each of the three flows (material, information and resource); to again note what was pointed out in Chapter 1, none of these flows are more important, and all are interdependent. The challenge then for the logistics/supply chain manager is to operate with such complexity and competing demands.

Christopher added requisite skills for each of the seven business transformations outlined above in Table 15.1 and these are detailed in Table 15.2 below. As the table illustrates, the skills required are wide-ranging and challenging.

Table 15.2 Christopher's key business transformations and the implications for management skills[13]

Business transformation	Leading to:	Skills required
1. From supplier-centric to customer-centric	The design of customer-driven supply chains	Market understanding; customer insight
2. From push to pull	Higher levels of agility and flexibility	Management of complexity and change
3. From inventory to information	Capturing and sharing information on real demand	Information systems and information technology expertise
4. From transactions to relationships	Focus on service and responsiveness as the basis for customer retention	Ability to define, measure and manage service requirements by market segment
5. From 'trucks and sheds' to end-to-end pipeline management	A wider definition of supply chain cost	Understanding of the 'cost-to-serve' and time-based performance indicators
6. From functions to processes	The creation of cross-functional teams focused on value creation	Specific functional excellence with cross-functional understanding. Team working capabilities
7. From stand alone competition to network rivalry	More collaborative working with supply chain partners	Relationship management and win-win orientation

As we noted in Chapter 3, the aim of SCM is to take a cross-functional, process perspective as distinct to a functional or silo based perspective. The implication of this re-orientation is that the supply chain manager of the future will require a 'T-shaped' skills profile (see Figure 15.1).

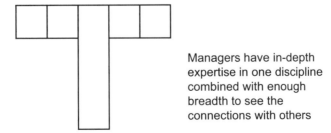

Effective process management requires significant cross-functional skills.

Creating the 'T-shaped' skills profile:-

Managers have in-depth expertise in one discipline combined with enough breadth to see the connections with others

Figure 15.1 Skills profile[14]

The idea is that as well as bringing specific logistics management skills to the job (the vertical bar) supply chain managers need to have a wide understanding of related areas such as, for example, business process reengineering, asset management and activity based costing (the horizontal bar). Research into the development of future logistics and supply chain managers identified the pertinent knowledge areas and competencies/skills illustrated in Table 15.3.

Table 15.3   Key knowledge areas and competencies/skills required by logistics and supply chain managers[15]

Knowledge areas	
General	Finance
	IT
	Management/Strategy
Logistics/SCM specific	Operations/SCM
	Focus on processes/flows
	Legal, security and international trade
	Multimodal logistics
	Logistics in emerging markets
Competencies/skills	
	Analytical
	Interpersonal
	Leadership
	Change management
	Project management

People, with the right skills and knowledge, are thus critical to effective SCM. As we noted in Chapter 3, via a quote from Professor John Gattorna, 'it's people who drive the supply chain, both inside and outside your business, not hard assets or technology'.[16] We also quoted James Quinn who stated that to achieve any measure of supply chain success, three critical elements (people, process and technology) need to be kept in balance.[17] He added that there is no single answer as to which of these three is the most important to supply chain success, although in his view 'you can't do *anything* without the right people'.

This is an appropriate topic with which to conclude the book; essentially supply chains are all about people. As a student of this fascinating subject, by equipping yourself with the appropriate knowledge and skills, an exciting and rewarding career hopefully awaits you. We hope this book will be of help to you on your journey.

LEARNING REVIEW

This chapter served to bring together the material developed in the preceding 14 chapters. The many strategies and practices employed in logistics and SCM today were detailed and illustrated the wide-ranging demands on logistics and supply chain managers. We also identified appropriate trends and the changing context within which logistics and SCM exists.

The point was developed that it is important, when designing supply chains, to endeavour to synchronise the design of supply chains with the design of products. We also reviewed the disparate costs that exist across supply chains (cost and value being key criteria in the context of supply chain design) and saw how modelling approaches (in particular optimisation and simulation) can assist in supply chain design.

The chapter concluded with a discussion of the skills and knowledge areas required of logistics and supply chain managers in the future. Logistics and SCM are ever changing and demanding disciplines, but provide attractive and rewarding opportunities to people who wish to work in these areas. The purpose of this book has been to equip you, the reader, to do this.

QUESTIONS

- Table 15.1 listed a wide-ranging number of common logistics/supply chain strategies and practices. In your view are all of these undertaken regularly by all organisations, or are some of them specific to certain types of organisations?
- Why is it important to synchronise product design and supply chain design? What are the implications of this from an environmental perspective?
- Summarise the various costs incurred in a typical supply chain.
- How might a supply chain be redesigned to allow for transfer pricing?
- Describe the various approaches for modelling supply chains.
- To what extent do you believe a supply chain can be redesigned to compensate for poor product design or poor product quality?
- Why do you think logistics and supply chain managers require a 'T-shaped' skills profile?

THE EVER CHANGING CONTEXT AND SKILLS REQUIRED OF LOGISTICS AND SUPPLY CHAIN MANAGERS

Look at the general business literature and try and identify various pertinent trends (in addition to those detailed in this chapter) which you believe are shaping the areas of logistics and SCM today.

What are the implications of these trends in terms of skills requirements?

You could, for example, review online and other job advertisements for the logistics and related sectors and try and identify skills requirements. If you can look at past advertisements you will be able to identify various trends such as an increased requirement for skilled logisticians; in addition it should be apparent that logistics and supply chain managers are being appointed at higher levels within organisations.

NOTES

1. Gattorna, J. (2006) *Living Supply Chains*, London, Financial Times/Prentice Hall.
2. Christopher, M. (2005) *Logistics and Supply Chain Management* (3rd edn), London, Financial Times/Prentice Hall.
3. Gattorna, J. (2006) *op. cit.*
4. Simchi-Levi, D., Kaminsky, P. & Simchi-Levi, E. (2003) *Designing and Managing the Supply Chain* (2nd edn), New York, McGraw-Hill, p.212.
5. Christopher, M., Peck, H. & Towill, D. (2006) A taxonomy for selecting global supply chain strategies, *International Journal of Logistics Management*, 17(2), 277–287.
6. French, E. (2007) Green by design, *CILT Focus*, June.
7. Mason, R. & Lalwani, C. (2006) Transport integration tools for supply chain management, *International Journal of Logistics: Research & Applications,* 9(1), 57–74.
8. See, for example, Schary, P. & Skjott-Larsen, T. (2001) *Managing the Global Supply Chain*, Copenhagen, Copenhagen Business School Press, p.394.
9. Potter A., Mason, R. & Lalwani, C. (2007) Analysis of factory gate pricing in the UK grocery supply chain, *International Journal of Retail and Distribution Management*, 35(10), 821–834.
10. Simchi-Levi, D. *et al.*, *op. cit.*
11. Disney, S. & Towill, D. (2003) Vendor-managed inventory and bullwhip reduction in a two level supply chain, *International Journal of Operations and Production Management*, 23(6), 625–651.
12. Kelton, W., Sadowski, R. & Sturrock, D. (2004) *Simulation with ARENA*, New York, McGraw-Hill; for an example of application see: Potter, A., Yang, B. & Lalwani, C. (2007) A simulation study of dispatch bay performance, *European*

Journal of Operational Research, 179 (they demonstrated the application of DES for improving dispatch bay performance in a steel products manufacturing company in the UK).

13. Christopher, M. (2005) *op. cit.* (p.289)

14. Mangan, J. & Christopher, M. (2005) Management development and the supply chain manager of the future, *International Journal of Logistics Management,* 16(2), 178–191.

15. *Ibid.*

16. Gattorna, *op. cit.,* p.xiii.

17. Quinn, F. (2004) People, process, technology, *Supply Chain Management Review,* January/February, 3.

Humanitarian Aid Supply Chains

Graham Heaslip

Institute of Technology, Carlow, Ireland

A fundamental issue of management of any supply chain is evaluating the trade-off between efficiency and effectiveness. In the commercial world, one strategy to success is to realise cost reduction built on forecasted demand without compromising the increased capacity that is needed to meet the unexpected. Supply chain managers in the humanitarian field face the challenge of successfully managing irregular demand patterns and unusual constraints. As a result, there is an increasing acknowledgement that disaster response has much to gain from commercial SCM thinking[1] and this, in turn, is leading to greater interest amongst academics[2] as well as politicians and the general public.

Humanitarian logistics, the function that is charged with ensuring the efficient and cost effective flow and storage of freight and materials for the purpose of alleviating the suffering of vulnerable people, came of age during the tsunami relief effort in Asia.[3] There are clear parallels between business logistics and relief logistics, but the transfer of knowledge between the two has been limited and the latter remains relatively unsophisticated, although, more recently, greater effort has been put into understanding and developing systems that can improve the relief supply chain.[4] Outside the world of business, logisticians in many other fields face the challenge of successfully managing the transition between steady state and surge situations.[5] This is particularly true for humanitarian logisticians preparing and executing their organisations' response to a rapid onset disaster where the price of failure can be counted in lives rather than lost profits.[6]

THE IMPORTANCE OF HUMANITARIAN SUPPLY CHAINS

When disasters strike, relief organisations respond by delivering aid to those in need. Their supply chains must be both fast and agile, responding to sudden-onset disasters which may occur in cities such as New Orleans, or on the other side of the globe in areas such as rural Pakistan. Since 2004, two large-scale natural disasters have captured the attention of the international media: the 2004 tsunami and the 2005 earthquake in South Asia. Disasters of this magnitude cause donors, beneficiaries, and the media to closely monitor how quickly and efficiently relief organisations are able to respond.

One of the notable aspects of the relief efforts following the Asian tsunami in 2004 was that logistics was publicly acknowledged to play an extremely important role in the relief effort.[7] The Asian tsunami placed humanitarian aid provision under greater stresses than ever before with the sheer scale of the disaster leaving more than 220 000 dead. Aid distribution had to be coordinated on an unprecedented scale amongst a number of governments and a wide range of NGOs, UN bodies, ICRC and military players.[8] As a European Ambassador at a post-tsunami donor conference said, 'We don't need a donor's conference, we need a logistics conference'.[9] Similarly, a spokesman for Médécins sans Frontières (Doctors without Borders), announcing their decision not to accept any more money for the relief operations, said, 'What is needed are supply managers without borders: people to sort freight, identify priorities, track deliveries and direct the traffic of a relief effort in full gear'.[10]

HUMANITARIAN AID SUPPLY CHAINS IN PRACTICE

Practical provision of humanitarian aid generally has to take place in locations where sophisticated logistics techniques are difficult to implement and in situations that are often subject to military conflict.[11] The provision of humanitarian aid in such circumstances has led to many organisations developing inadequate logistics systems and concentrating on funding relief rather than on the processes that support the delivery of that relief.[12] The problem has been exacerbated by environmental factors, funding issues, employee turnover, weak use of technology and poor manual processes.[13] Awareness of such problems has received a higher profile and in the recent past greater effort has been put into understanding and developing systems that can improve the relief supply chain.[14]

Central to any relief operation is the establishment and management of an emergency supply chain, which is often fragile and volatile. The provision of humanitarian aid and the complex logistics systems which enable that aid to be delivered are more intricate than simply providing disaster relief, for example securing humanitarian aid and protecting the supply chain are important issues.[15] Provision of humanitarian aid generally, although not exclusively, takes place in locations where sophisticated logistics techniques are difficult to implement (e.g. major natural disaster or military conflict) and which therefore require some form of coordination between individual NGOs or between military and NGOs but where there is little agreement on the status of the relationships between them.[16] Responses to both natural and man-made crises are generally multi-faceted and involve governments, NGOs, UN agencies, military bodies and private sector organisations.[17]

CONCLUSION

The graphic images broadcast to the living rooms of the West opened the wallets of individuals and governments. Emergency funding became big business and the number of NGOs grew. Unfortunately, disaster relief is, and will continue to be, a growth 'market'. Both natural and man-made disasters are expected to increase another five-fold over the next 50 years due to environmental degradation, rapid urbanisation and the spread of HIV/AIDS in the developing world.[18] According to the Munich Reinsurance Group, the real annual economic losses have been growing steadily, averaging US$75.5 billion in the 1960s, US$138.4 billion in the 1970s, US$213.9 billion in the 1980s and US$659.9 billion in the 1990s.[19]

Business logistics usually deals with a predetermined set of suppliers, manufacturing sites, and stable or at least predictable demand – all of which factors are unknown in humanitarian logistics.[20] Humanitarian logistics in contrast is characterised by large-scale activities, irregular demand and unusual constraints in large-scale emergencies.[21] In terms of the strived for end-result, business logistics aims at increasing profits, whereas humanitarian logistics aims at alleviating the suffering of vulnerable people.[22]

NOTES

1. Thomas, A. (2004) *Humanitarian Logistics: Enabling Disaster Response*, Fritz Institute; Thomas, A. & Kopczak, L.R. (2005) *From Logistics to Supply Chain Management – The Path Forward in the Humanitarian Sector*, Fritz Institute; Kovács, G. & Spens, K. (2007) Humanitarian logistics in disaster relief operations, *International Journal of Physical Distribution and Logistics Management*, 37(2), 99–114; Tatham, P. & Kovács, G. (2007) An initial investigation into the application of the military sea-basing concept to the provision of immediate relief in a rapid onset disaster, Proceedings of *POMS 18th Annual Conference*, Texas, 4–7 May.
2. Kovács & Spens (2007) *op. cit.*; Oloruntoba, R. & Gray, R. (2006) Humanitarian aid: an agile supply chain? *Supply Chain Management – An International Journal*, 11(2), 115–120; Van Wassenhove, L.N. (2006) Humanitarian aid logistics: supply chain management in high gear, *Journal of the Operational Research Society*, 57(5), 475–589; Heaslip, G., Mangan, J. & Lalwani, C. (2007) Integrating military and non governmental organisation (NGO) objectives in the humanitarian supply chain: a proposed framework, *Proceedings of the Logistics Research Network Conference*, ILT, Hull, 5–7 September.
3. Thomas (2004) *op. cit.*; Heaslip *et al.* (2007), *op. cit.*
4. Tatham & Kovács (2007) *op. cit.*
5. *Ibid.*
6. Thomas & Kopczak (2005) *op. cit.*
7. Marlowe, L. (2005) Ahern plans disaster response team, *Irish Times*, January.
8. *New York Times* (2005) January, 6.

9. Economist.com global agenda, 5 January, 2005.

10. Oloruntoba, R. & Gray, R. (2002) *Logistics for humanitarian aid: a survey of aid organisations,* Proceedings of the Logistics Research Network Conference, pp. 217–222.

11. Pettit, S.J. & Beresford, A.K.C. (2005) Emergency relief logistics: an evaluation of military, non military and composite response models, *International Journal of Logistics: Research and Applications,* 8(4), 313–332.

12. Thomas, A. (2003) Why logistics?, *Forced Migration Review,* 18, 4.

13. United Nations Joint Logistics Centre (2006) *Logistics Support Systems Pipeline Tracking,* http://www.unjlc.org/supply_chain

14. Fritz Institute (2004) *Humanitarian Logistics Software,* Fritz Institute; United Nations Joint Logistics Centre (2006) *op. cit.*

15. Byman D., Lesser, I., Pirnie, B., Bernard, C. & Wazman, M. (2000) *Strengthening the Partnership: Improving Military Coordination Relief Agencies and Allies in Humanitarian Operations,* Washington DC, Rand.

16. Pettit, S.J. & Beresford, A.K.C. (2006) Modelling humanitarian supply chains, *Proceedings of the Logistics Research Network Conference,* CILT, Newcastle, September, pp.323–328.

17. *Ibid.*

18. Thomas & Kopczak (2005) *op. cit.*

19. *Ibid.*

20. Cassidy, W.B. (2003) A logistics lifeline, *Traffic World,* 27 October, 1.

21. Beamon, B.M. & Kotleba, S.A. (2006) Inventory modelling for complex emergencies in humanitarian relief operations, *International Journal of Logistics: Research and Applications,* 9(1), 1–18.

22. Thomas & Kopczak (2005) *op. cit.*

Good Distribution Practice and Pharmaceutical Supply Chain Management

Ciaran Brady

PLS Pharma Logistics

Optimising the supply chain has become a competitive necessity for companies across the globe including those in the pharmaceutical sector. The pharmaceutical supply chain is somewhat unique in that compliance at every point along the supply chain is essential.

It might be tempting to imagine that a manufacturer's responsibility for a pharmaceutical product lies only within the 'four walls' of a manufacturing facility, but of course, this has never been the case. Whether through legislation and guidelines or simple common sense, it is clear that at any point along the supply chain the integrity of all pharmaceutical products must be assured and not compromised. In short, a manufacturer's responsibility extends to sourcing materials from approved suppliers, continues through manufacturing under Good Manufacturing Practice (GMP), and on to delivery of the product to the final customer or patient under Good Distribution Practice (GDP).

Hence, Good Distribution Practice remains an essential aspect of compliance for all pharmaceutical companies as products are stored, transported and delivered on a global and local basis. Assuring supply chain integrity and patient safety has never been so important.

Moreover, as global supply chains are becoming more complex, combined with increasing commercial pressures and the global growth of counterfeiting, it is likely that GDP has never been more critical. Coupled with a global increase in temperatures, the need to carefully manage cold chain, frozen and ambient/controlled temperature products from receipt, storage, transportation and distribution is a significant challenge for all firms who move pharmaceutical products along more complex and compliant supply chains.

GOOD DISTRIBUTION PRACTICE

GDP can be defined as 'that part of quality assurance that ensures that the quality of a pharmaceutical product is maintained by means of adequate control of the numerous activities which occur during the distribution process'.[1] This definition could reasonably be extended to include sourcing, receipt, storage and transportation, looking at the full supply chain that is necessary to make and sell pharmaceutical products. The critical need is to establish controls at all points along the supply chain so that all partners handling and transporting pharmaceuticals do so within compliance. According to the European Parliament: 'The main purpose of any regulation on the manufacture and distribution of medicinal products for human use should be to safeguard public health.'[2]

The importance of GDP is elaborated in for example the EU Guidance on Distribution Practice. Although hugely paraphrased, the following summary of that Principle does reliably reflect its observations:

> The Community pharmaceutical industry operates at a high level of quality assurance ... and this level of quality should be maintained throughout the distribution network so that authorised medicinal products are distributed to retail pharmacists and other persons entitled to sell medicinal products to the general public without any alteration of their properties.[3]

AREAS FOR CONCERN

Recent information available from the main regulators suggests there are many areas throughout the pharmaceutical supply chain where deficiencies can be found. Recently the Medicines and Healthcare Products Regulatory Agency (MHRA) in the UK stated that '32% of all critical and major deficiencies recorded at inspections related to the control and monitoring of storage and transportation temperatures'. Other deficiencies include inadequate systems for dealing with returns and establishing *bona fides* for all stakeholders. There is no reason to suppose that the incidents highlighted are in any way restricted to the UK and statistics from other countries and regulators suggest many of the findings are similar. Worryingly, temperature control and monitoring is a recurring theme. With the growth of biotechnology products and the increasing need to ship more products under cold chain conditions (2–8°C), more and more pharmaceutical companies are now refocusing efforts and resources in ensuring that temperature controls in their transportation/supply chain are correct. Global warming is also contributing to the challenges faced by the pharmaceutical industry and the industry needs to take care to address this sensitive issue correctly for all products no matter what their temperature requirements are.

COUNTERFEITING

One of the biggest challenges for the pharmaceutical industry and one of the main reasons why GDP/good SCM is critical is because of the growth of counterfeit medicines on a global basis. The US based Centre for Medicines in the Public Interest predicts that counterfeit drug sales will reach US$75 billion globally in 2010, an increase of more than 90% from 2005. The EC recently reported a five-fold increase in the seizure of counterfeit pharmaceutical items for 2006 compared with 2005. The World Health Organisation website suggests that counterfeits account for around 1% of sales in developed countries to over 10% in developing countries, and medicines purchased over the internet from sites that conceal their physical address are counterfeit in over 50% of cases.

Counterfeit medicines are part of the broader phenomenon of substandard pharmaceuticals – medicines manufactured below established standards of quality and therefore dangerous to patients' health and ineffective for the treatment of diseases.

The difference is that counterfeits are fraudulent and may be deliberately mislabelled with respect to identity, composition and/or source. Counterfeiting occurs both with branded and generic products, and counterfeit medicines may include products with the correct ingredients but fake packaging, with the wrong ingredients, without active ingredients or with insufficient active ingredients and may even contain harmful or poisonous substances.

Counterfeit medicines represent an enormous public health challenge. Anyone, anywhere in the world, can come across medicines seemingly packaged in the right way, in the form of tablets or capsules that look right, but which do not contain the correct ingredients and in the worst case scenario, may be filled with highly toxic substances. In some countries counterfeiting is a rare occurrence, in others it is an everyday reality. In developing countries the most disturbing issue is the common availability of counterfeit medicines for the treatment of life-threatening conditions such as malaria, tuberculosis and HIV/AIDS.

Good SCM coupled with best in class GDP is a minimum requirement in helping to stem the flow of counterfeit products into legitimate distribution channels and pharmaceutical supply chains. The need for all stakeholders in the pharmaceutical industry to work in partnership to ensure supply chain integrity and that only *bona fide* suppliers and customers are allowed to buy and sell pharmaceutical products is a must. Regulators across the world are working with manufacturers, distributors and all stakeholders in pharmaceutical supply chains to enhance compliance standards.

Both manufacturers and distributors need to fully understand their obligations when it comes to managing supply chain and product integrity under GMP/GDP and to be vigilant where noncompliance could compromise patient safety. Without doubt GDP is a minimum requirement for successful pharmaceutical SCM and necessary to stem the flow of counterfeit products into legitimate distribution chains.

CONCLUSION

Optimising the supply chain is a competitive necessity but product integrity, compliance and patient safety is non-negotiable in the pharmaceutical supply chain. Manufacturers, distributors and partners who transport and distribute product must ensure that the high level of product quality achieved by observing good manufacturing practice is maintained throughout the distribution network as products are transported and delivered on a global and local basis.

GDP is as essential to the continued success of the pharmaceutical industry as GMP. All pharmaceutical companies and partners who transport and distribute product on their behalf must ensure best practice is in place to ensure that no counterfeit products enter legitimate supply chains and that patient safety is protected at all times.

While the regulators are doing all they can to heighten awareness and compliance in the management of pharmaceutical supply chains, all stakeholders must go the extra mile to ensure compliance with all regulations and guidelines so that patient safety is assured from manufacturer to patient – delivering the right product on time every time.

Efficient and compliant SCM should have well-trained staff who will ensure GDP (and GMP) are managed successfully and that pharmaceutical products are handled, transported and delivered with best in class standards and full compliance.

NOTES

1. World Health Organisation (2006) World Health Organisation Technical Report Series 937, WHO Expert Committee on specifications for pharmaceutical preparations, Geneva, WHO.
2. Directive 2004/27/EC of the European Parliament.
3. Rules and Guidance for Pharmaceutical Manufacturers and Distributors (2007) MHRA, Pharmaceutical Press.

Dubai Logistics City:
A Quantum Leap in Logistics*

S. Walter & L. Eiermann

'…it was just amazing! They plan to build a tower that will be even higher than the Tokyo Millennium Tower'. Peter Winter, assistant to Mr Schmidt, CEO of Schmidt & Partner Logistics Solutions Inc headquartered in Munich, nodded in a friendly manner and looked at the clock on the wall. His boss had been describing his impressions from his holidays with his wife in Dubai for almost 15 minutes now. 'But now the most impressive thing: I heard about a new logistics project called Dubai Logistics City'. Mr Schmidt continued. 'They say it will be a quantum leap in logistics!' He made a dramatic pause. 'So, you know what your task is for the next week: find out what this project is all about, and whether it could be beneficial for our company!'

One hour and some holiday stories later, Peter Winter was sitting at his desk again. Dubai … the first thing that came to his mind was that one of the world's most exclusive hotels, the Burj Al Arab, was located in the city. In fact, he had seen some documentary films about the amazing development of the location showing the Palm Island resorts, the car collections of the wealthy sheikhs, and the extremely hot, desert-like climate of the region (Figure C9.1). With these pictures in mind, he was sure that his knowledge was not sufficient to give his boss a reasonable appraisal and recommendation concerning the Dubai Logistics City project.

Burj Al Arab Hotel

One of the four Palm Islands

Dubai skyline

Figure C9.1 Impressions of Dubai. Photographs provided courtesy of the Government of Dubai, Department of Tourism and Commerce Marketing. Reproduced by permission (ECCH Ref.: 606-033-1).

*This case study was written by Professor Dr Stefan Walter and Lars Eiermann, Supply Management Institute, ebs European Business School, with the support of Roger Moser and under the supervision of Professor Dr Christopher Jahns. It was prepared solely to provide material for class discussion and does not intend to illustrate either effective or ineffective handling of a managerial situation. Copyright © 2006 by Supply Management Institute.

DUBAI: AN AMAZING CITY

Peter's initial thought was to have a look at the map in order to find out exactly where Dubai is located in the world (Figure C9.2). Next, he started extensive internet research about the region and its historical development. With great satisfaction, he looked at the notes he had made throughout the day.

With its 1.2 million inhabitants, the emirate Dubai is the second largest and second wealthiest of the seven emirates that form the United Arab Emirates. Its historical development had started slowly but had accelerated enormously during the second half of the last century. In the late nineteenth century, trade grew and included pearl trading. As a result of tax concessions and the development of the harbour, the city of Dubai encouraged foreign traders to use the city as a link between the West, Persia and India. In the 1930s, English aircraft carriers were deployed in the city, further extending the harbour and adding to Dubai's importance as a trading point. Demand dictated the need for new wharfs, warehouses and port facilities. In 1967, construction began on a deep-water harbour, initially planned for four berths, but after completion it was able to harbour 35 berths. Later, a second port was developed in the southern part of the city, which has become the world's largest man-made port. In 2004, both harbours together handled 6.42 million 20 ft Equivalent Units (TEUs).

The discovery of oil in 1966 led to rapid growth and infrastructure development, but Dubai's rulers have always been aware that this resource will be depleted one day. Consequently, the royal family pays close attention to the diversification of their country's economic foundations. In order to keep Dubai as independent as possible from its oil sources, the development of the trade and tourism sector was encouraged early on. In 2005, only 12 per cent of Dubai's gross domestic product (GDP) still depended on oil sources, and this percentage is still decreasing.

Figure C9.2   Dubai location

During the 1990s, the country presented and marketed itself as a premium tourist destination, characterised by its internationality and 'easy-living' atmosphere. In addition, religious issues are handled liberally and English is widely spoken, which adds to the attractiveness of Dubai to foreigners. Construction was booming until the present because of the growth in tourism. The latest mega-project is the 'Burj Dubai', planned to become the highest tower in the world on completion. It is located on a man-made island, similar to the Burj Al Arab Hotel. Together tourism and conferences made up approximately 4.9% of current annual GDP, mainly from travellers attracted by duty-free shopping and world-class accommodation. One of the largest projects was the Dubai Palm Island development – man-made islands in the shape of a palm tree, which are so large that they are visible from outer space, offering hotels, villas and apartments.

Regarding business opportunities, Dubai's main focus so far has been on trade, manufacturing and processing, as well as on transport and distribution. Over the years, it has become a leading regional trade hub, serving about two billion customers worldwide. Docking, road and airport facilities, as well as concessionary zones, such as the Jebel Ali Free Zone, Dubai Internet City and Dubai Media City, were very favourable for foreign investors because foreign companies could set up free of local ownership and benefit from a renewable 15 year guarantee of no taxation. These conditions attracted a growing number of foreign direct investments, and even more tax-free zones are planned for the future. The country is already a gateway to a $150 billion import-export market and its economy is still growing rapidly. Dubai's imports have more than doubled since 1989 and the ongoing liberalisation is expected to further boost demand.

After having collected these basic facts about the country, Peter decided to call his friend Karl Huber who worked for an agency helping German companies to set up a business in Dubai. He would surely be able to give him some information about the political situation and the culture of the emirate.

Mr Huber told him that Dubai is known as the 'Switzerland of the Arabian countries'. This title seemed adequate considering its largely neutral and stable role in its external political environment and its internal political stability, and makes the emirate stand out against other states of the region. Like other Gulf States, Dubai's politics are dominated by clans. The Al-Maktoums hold the important positions in the country's government and possess absolute power. However, their decisions are largely popular among the citizens of Dubai since they have overseen a long period of prosperity. The official head of the family is Sheikh Maktoum bin Rashid al-Maktoum, the oldest son of Sheikh Rashid bin Saeed al-Maktoum, who started modernising Dubai in the 1970s. After Sheikh Rashid's death in 1990, Sheikh Maktoum inherited his position. In 1994, he appointed his brother, Sheikh Muhammad bin Rashid al-Maktoum, as crown prince of Dubai. Since then, Sheikh Muhammad has been the main driving force behind Dubai's current boom. For more than 10 years, Sheikh Muhammad bin Rashid al-Maktoum of the royal family has been the ruler of Dubai and has guaranteed stable political and economic conditions.

The main focus of all decisions has always been the sustainable growth and development of the country. Due to the monarchic system, long-term planning and co-ordination of projects and policies is possible. One point that really surprised Peter was the overall fiscal and trading conditions in Dubai. In fact, there are no corporate taxes or income taxes; there are no foreign exchange controls and no trade barriers. In addition, labour and energy costs are at an internationally competitive level. Even if Peter had expected labour costs to be far under the level of Western countries, he was amazed by the excellent start-up conditions in Dubai.

However, Mr Huber emphasised that adapting to the Arabian way of doing business could be difficult for foreign investors. In many negotiations, Arab partners do not have open discussions about the advantages and disadvantages of a certain project in question. Instead, they withdraw from the negotiation, consider the issue in private and inform their foreign business partners about their decision afterwards.

Nevertheless, life in Dubai – with its mixture of different cultures and as a model of tolerance – is characterised by friendliness and kindness but also by the superficiality of those just 'doing business' and 'shopping'.

In fact, there are some differences in the treatment of foreigners in comparison to natives: one in point case is that expatriates – whether they are Asian labourers or wealthy Western executives – do not have any political representation. In the same way, they do not have the right to request an audience with the Sheikh at the 'majils' (meeting places that provide an informal system of popular representation) as natives do.

When Peter asked Mr Huber about more facts on the country's culture, Mr Huber pointed out that religion plays an important role in daily life. The official religion of the city-state is Islam, and Muslims make up about 50 per cent of the population. However, the emirate's commercial ethos and its international inhabitants obviate a stringent enforcement of religious rules. Equally, Dubai's high standard of living seems to preclude radicalism to the effect that the risk of terrorist attacks is considered relatively low.

THE CURRENT LOGISTICS ACTIVITIES IN DUBAI

After having found all the information about Dubai and its amazing development, Peter now wanted to know what Dubai Logistics City (DLC) is all about. But before starting to explore the concept behind the Dubai Logistics City project, he was curious how the logistics activities were handled at present and what the main triggers were that initiated the development of Dubai Logistics City.

In this context, he remembered his boss talking about the Dubai International Airport (DXB), which had been established in 1959 when Sheikh Rashid bin Saeed al-Maktoum ordered the construction of the first airfield. Hence, he started his research by gathering information about the Dubai International Airport and the corresponding Dubai Cargo Village (DCV). The first obvious challenge of this airport was its location in the middle of the city. This was mainly caused by the fast development of the city. Currently, approximately 25 million passengers fly to and from the Dubai International Airport. Compared to large international airports, such as Frankfurt or London which handle about 60 million passengers per year, the Dubai International Airport is still of manageable size. It is also possible to expand the passenger area to a capacity of up to 75 million passengers. Another interesting aspect concerning the passenger flow at the Dubai International Airport is the extreme peaks in the number of passengers between midnight and 1 am and between 7 am and 8 am. These peaks are primarily a result of the regulations at the departure and arrival airports in Europe and Asia. There are only specific time slots when airplanes may land and take off from most international airports. Additionally, this phenomenon is further influenced by the fact that Dubai is used as a hub for long-distance flights.

So far, Peter had realised that the passenger business sector was not responsible for the development of the Dubai Logistics City. Hence, Peter expected the main problems to be found in the Dubai Cargo Village. To find out more about the Dubai Cargo Village, he looked through the intranet of Schmidt & Partner Logistics Solutions Inc, hoping to find a colleague who could provide him with more information concerning the Dubai Cargo Village. Half an hour and a few unsuccessful phone calls later, Peter was finally talking to Mr Reinhardt. He had been working for the Frankfurt Airport Cargo City for almost 15 years before he joined Schmidt & Partner Logistics Solutions Inc. As a result of his long work experience, he knew most of the international airports quite well and had developed a good sense for the strengths and weaknesses of the different worldwide operating airports. As Mr Reinhardt was very interested in the education of young employees, he was more than willing to help Peter and started explaining right away that the Dubai International Airport has experienced very strong growth in terms of air freight. Since 1999 the amount of air freight has more than doubled from approximately 480 000 tonnes in 1999 to approximately 1.2 million tonnes in 2004. Figure C9.3 shows the air freight development from 1999 to 2003 of the Dubai International Airport in comparison to two other important airports in the United Arab Emirates (UAE), the Sharjah International Airport (SHJ) and the Abu Dhabi International Airport (AUH).

The existing facilities in the Dubai Cargo Village are considered to be the best in the region, because they are very flexible and enable a fast handling of goods. Peter started to wonder why Dubai actually saw the need to build the Dubai Logistics City, because, so far, the situation for the logistics activities seemed to be satisfactory. However, as Mr Reinhardt had just recently visited the Dubai International Airport, he reported two significant problems, which he had realised during his visit. Firstly, the logistics service providers face significant operational constraints in cargo handling. Secondly, there is no, or only limited, capability to meet the growing demand for value-added services in logistics. These problems result from

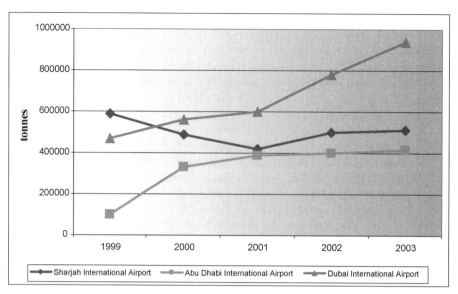

Figure C9.3 Airfreight tonnage in the United Arab Emirates. Reproduced by permission of Dubai Logistics City

the airport's unusual location in the middle of the city and the resulting space limitations. In this context Mr Reinhardt remembered a situation that he experienced three months ago. As it is generally very hot in Dubai and it only rains a couple of times a year, a large amount of pallets are stored outside. Therefore, on the last day of his visit, he saw numerous pallets with personal computers standing in the rain, obviously damaged. Such an incident is characteristic for the current situation at the Dubai Cargo Village. Concerning the airside, there are no constraints for growth in volume because they have accounted for it in their long-term planning. However, there is no more space to increase agents' warehouse capacity on the landside. Due to the bordering highway, there is only a very small amount of space available for an enlargement of the airport. Such an expansion would also reach capacity in five years at the latest and is therefore not an optimal solution. Figures C9.4 and C9.5 show the expected space requirements based on surveys with the logistics service providers. The figures clarify that even at present the companies could use more than twice as much space as they currently have at their disposal. Furthermore, the survey found that the forwarders wished to increase their turnover as well as their range of value-added services.

THE IDEA OF 'DUBAI LOGISTICS CITY'

So far, Peter understood the difficult situation because of the considerable expected growth and the significant space constraints. Mr Reinhardt, still very enthusiastic, continued to explain the development of Dubai Logistics City. The initial thought to solve the problem was to look for space as close as possible to the Dubai International Airport. However, this idea was finally discarded because

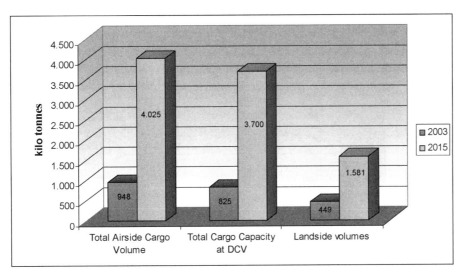

Figure C9.4   Dubai air cargo projections. Reproduced by permission of Dubai Logistics City

it was expected to reach capacity in the near future and would not be an optimal solution. As a result, the sheikhs decided to go a big step further and build Dubai Logistics City next to the existing Jebel Ali Port as another free zone and part of the future Dubai World Central which would also host an all-new airport (JXB) (see Figure C9.6). The airport will start operation at the end of 2007 with the first runway. Ultimately, a capacity of 120+ million passengers and 12 million tonnes of airfreight are expected to be handled per year.

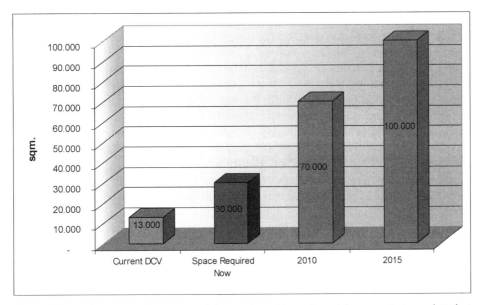

Figure C9.5   Space requirements of forwarders. Reproduced by permission of Dubai Logistics City

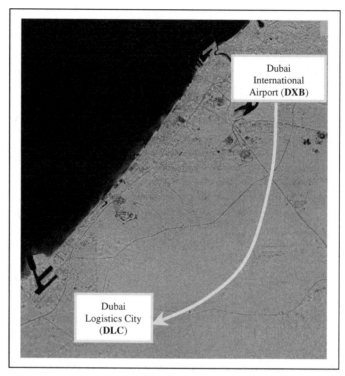

Figure C9.6   New location for Dubai Logistics City. Reproduced by permission of Dubai Logistics City

The decision for such a radical solution instead of an expansion near the Dubai International Airport was based on the following arguments. A principal advantage for developments in Dubai compared with European countries is that the sheikhs are in the position to focus on a long-term investment horizon. This influenced their decision-making process since they do not have to focus on short-term success (e.g. to guarantee a re-election) but can instead focus on the long term and decide which solution is most beneficial for Dubai in the long run. In accordance with the general boom of Dubai and the amazing projects already realised, such as the Burj Al Arab Hotel and the Palm Islands, the sheikhs decided to dare such a quantum leap in logistics to further contribute to the outstanding image of Dubai. Another fact that facilitated the concept development of the Jebel Ali International Airport and Dubai Logistics City was that it will be constructed in the desert. For this reason, vast expansion possibilities are available even though space in closer proximity to the city is limited. The location in Jebel Ali was chosen to be best for Dubai Logistics City because of its direct proximity to the Jebel Ali Port. This will enable companies to benefit from perfect tri-modality within a single customs bonded zone. It will be very easy to change freight from air, sea or land transportation. Goods arriving at Dubai Logistics City could easily be transported to the neighbouring countries, as well as to further locations. The transportation could be done by ships from the Jebel Ali Port, by trucks or by another flight. In the case of a shipment to a neighbouring country, the use of junks instead of bigger container vessels is not uncommon because for some destinations tank ships are simply too big. An important advantage of Dubai's location in comparison to its neighbouring countries, Oman and Yemen, is that no mountains constrain inland transportation. One of the especially important advantages for air freight is that all European airports can be easily approached. In addition, the location of Jebel Ali as a free zone has no regulatory obstacles for logistics services providers.

Figure C9.7 shows the Dubai World Central site (with Dubai Logistics City and the Jebel Ali International Airport) adjacent to the Jebel Ali Port.

'As you can see,' continued his colleague, '… this is really a very big and cost-intensive project'. To guarantee the success of the Dubai Logistics City project, the current master plan, which entails a time plan until 2050, has to be re-evaluated, analysed and advanced on a continuous basis. This is necessary to react in the most efficient way to external changes and new developments in the logistics sector. The implementation of new technologies or improved security systems are examples of the challenges in the future. Another critical aspect which had to be considered was that the amount of space that is directly on the border of the airport is limited. Therefore, the infrastructure has to be very well structured to make efficient transporting and easy handling of the goods possible. The free zone will be built in modules as a result of these challenges. This development will depend on the demand for spaces. Besides Dubai Logistics City, there will also be offices, research and development buildings, and residential areas among other things. Figures C9.8, C9.9 and C9.10 illustrate the main elements of the master plan for Dubai World Central.

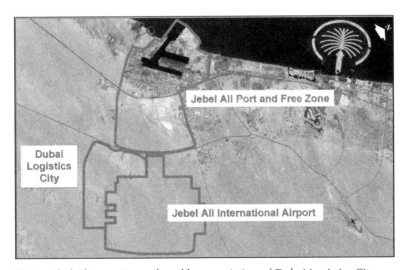

Figure C9.7   Jebel Ali area. Reproduced by permission of Dubai Logistics City

> Dubai Logistics City (2007)
> Jebel Ali International Airport (2007)
  - One runway
  - Executive flights
  - Passenger terminals
> Residential City (2007)
> Exhibition City
  - Dubai World Trade Center (2008)
  - Dubai Air Show (2009)
> Master Planning reaches into 2050 and includes
  - Commercial city
  - Aviation city
  - Technology park
  - Golf resort
  - Full passenger airport

Figure C9.8   Elements of the master plan. Reproduced by permission of Dubai Logistics City

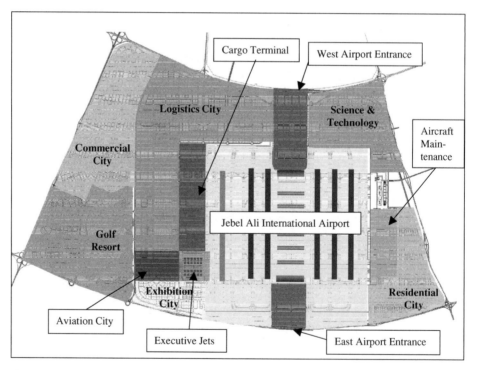

Figure C9.9   Master plan: sub-sections of Dubai World Central. Reproduced by permission of Dubai Logistics City

> ➤   25 km² in total
> ➤   More than 800 plots of land from 3,500 m² to 40.000+ m² for industry/trade distribution centres and contract logistics businesses
> ➤   More than 200 plots of land of 10,000 m² dedicated for forwarders
> ➤   More than 50,000 m² of handling space for forwarders in shared facilities
> ➤   Up to 16 air cargo terminals of 30,000 m² each for a total of 12 million tons of air cargo annually
> ➤   Numerous office, amenity and labour residence facilities

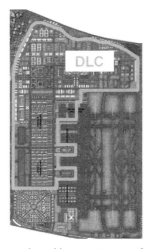

Figure C9.10   Dubai Logistics City: summary of key figures. Reproduced by permission of Dubai Logistics City

Principally, the target companies for the Dubai Logistics City (DLC) project are logistics service providers and manufacturers with high transport volumes. Companies cannot buy, only rent land long-term at DLC if they operate in the logistics sector. Especially for tri-modal logistics service providers, Dubai Logistics City offers a range of opportunities. Tri-modal logistics service providers use three different ways of transportation: air, sea and land transportation. Potential industries that could primarily take advantage of Dubai Logistics City are consumer electronics, pharmaceutical products, high-tech products, spare parts and products which make use of value-added services within the supply chain.

With his acquired knowledge about the location of Dubai and the broad range of advantages offered by the Dubai Logistics City project, Peter was then curious if it would be beneficial for Schmidt & Partner Logistics Solutions Inc. Therefore, he took a closer look at the company and their clients.

SCHMIDT & PARTNER LOGISTICS SOLUTIONS INC: AN INTEGRATED LOGISTICS SERVICE PROVIDER

Schmidt & Partner Logistics Solutions Inc was founded in 1955 by Wolfgang Schmidt. The headquarters is in a small town close to the Alps, 15 km south of Munich. The most important event in the history of the company was in 1975 when the major competitor, Gohlke Logistics, was acquired. This led Schmidt & Partner Logistics Solutions Inc to become a dominant player in the German logistics market. In 1981, Wolfgang Schmidt's son, Dieter Schmidt, became the new CEO. After having worked for his father for almost 20 years, his goal was to become a global player in logistics. Nowadays, Wolfgang Schmidt, who is still participating in some board meetings, could be very proud of his son, as he has reached his goal and

Schmidt & Partner Logistics Solutions Inc has become one of the leading providers of integrated logistics solutions in the world. The 35 000 employees work in 200 different locations, mostly in Europe. The 2004 turnover reached an all-time high of almost $6 billion and increased 6% compared with 2003. The turnover is expected to grow further in the near future by an average rate of approximately 5% per year. To guarantee the ongoing success of Schmidt & Partner Logistics Solutions Inc, the company considers the key factor to be in the successful worldwide flow of goods in integrated logistics solutions. Therefore, networked warehouse and transportation concepts are needed and have been developed. Furthermore, the company emphasises the wide range of services offered by Schmidt & Partner Integrated Logistics Solutions Inc. As this company is still growing, it is very open to new and innovative solutions in the field of logistics.

To reach further insight into the business of the company, Peter analysed three of their biggest clients. In this way, he could better understand the challenges and problems the company and their clients were facing. The customer perspective was an important aspect that needed to be taken into account for the evaluation of the Dubai Logistics City concept.

One of the important clients is an international clothing company. Its production sites are primarily in East Asia and India. They sell their products worldwide but the main market is Central and Western Europe. The clothes are mostly seasonal and located in the higher price segments. The company had significant problems in the past with the quality of its products. Many stores complained that they did not get the clothes in a proper condition and therefore better handling was needed.

Another representative client is a fruit supplier from India. The fruits are primarily sold in Germany. The fruits are mostly transported by ship and trucks, and only under special circumstances with airplanes. The company faces some problems with the durability of a few kinds of fruits because of significant temperature differences during the transportation.

A third client is a producer of medical equipment. The products are produced at different production sites in Asia. Some of the produced machines have to be gathered and customised before they are sold to the end customers, such as hospitals in Europe or the United States of America. The crucial aspect for this company is reliable and short-term delivery. However, the company also focuses on cost optimisation and therefore tries to do most of the transportation by sea freight instead of air freight.

PETER'S CHALLENGE

Over the past days, Peter had worked hard and had compiled a great deal of information. His internet research and his phone calls provided a range of facts about the emirate of Dubai, the Dubai Logistics City project and the cultural as well as socio-economic aspects of the region. The only thing that was left to do was to come to a conclusion whether the idea of the Dubai Logistics City project was beneficial for the company or not.

QUESTIONS

- What factors have led to the development of the Dubai Logistics City project?
- What issues should be considered when deciding to set up a branch of Schmidt and Partners Logistics Solutions Inc. in Dubai?
- What are the possible advantages and disadvantages of establishing a branch at Dubai Logistics City?
- What are the opportunities and risks to be considered both for the Dubai Logistics City project as a whole, and also for the proposal of Schmidt and Partners Logistics Solutions Inc. to set up a branch in Dubai?

Morning365: An Online Bookstore's Strategy to Grow in the Constantly Changing Market*

B. Kim

In August 2003, Mr Ji Soo Park, CEO of Morning365, looked very much concerned about the future of his company, which was the second-largest online bookstore in Korea. Since the company was formally founded in September 2000, Morning365 has experienced a remarkable growth for the previous three years. It recorded 156% sales growth from 2001 to 2002, and its market share increased from 5.4% to 8.5% during the same period.

The Korean book market, with sales of over $2.5 billion in 2002, had been long dominated by large-scale offline bookstores. Riding the unprecedented internet boom in Korea, however, online bookstores like Morning365 entered the book market in the late 1990s and grew steadily to become a formidable force in the market: total sales of the internet bookstores combined was about $258 million in 2002. Since online bookstores did not have to retain inventory, they could afford to offer deep discounts to book buyers, which enabled them to be more competitive vis-à-vis their offline competitors. Compared with other online bookstores, moreover, Morning365 had been able to enjoy further advantage derived from its creative logistics system, which utilised the well-connected subway networks in the Seoul metropolitan areas.

But now the two important competitive advantages – steep book discounts and the subway-based logistics system – seemed to be slipping away from the company. For the last several years, offline bookstores contended that discounting by online bookstores was an unfair business activity and demanded that the government intervene. The government finally gave in and promulgated a 'fixed price rule', which prohibited the online bookstores from discounting books published within one year. The law became effective in March 2003. Still worse, Morning365's exclusive contract with the Seoul Metropolitan Subway Corporation (SMSC), which had been the backbone of the company's logistics strategy, would expire in about two years.

*Copyright © 2004 KAIST Business School. Professor Bowon Kim wrote this case based on the one developed by Ji Yeon Kim, Yoon Hee Hwang (MS students), and Eunjun Bae (an MBA student) under his supervision at KGSM. Reproduced by permission of KAIST (Korea Advanced Institute of Science and Technology) Business School.

The weather was hot. But what actually made Mr Park perspire was not the summer weather. It was this reality he had to face very soon. He knew that the traditional dominant players in the market, the online giants, had been waiting for this moment to take revenge on small guys like Morning365. In addition, he could not afford to allow other online bookstores to eat away at its competitive advantage because of the imminent expiry of a contract with SMSC. He had to design a new strategy to overcome these huge obstacles amid one of the most prolonged economic recessions in Korea. There was only one thing for sure: there would not be a single thing he could afford to take for granted.

THE ONLINE BOOKSTORE INDUSTRY

In 2003, Korea was one of the most advanced countries in the world in terms of internet technology and its subscription level.

The country boasted the widest access to broadband in the world (see Table C10.1). With this rapidly expanding internet infrastructure, e-commerce in Korea had been growing fast as well: internet shopping malls grew at about 12% per quarter from late 2000 to early 2003. The internet book market constituted about 5% of internet shopping mall sales during the same period (see Table C10.2).

Table C10.1   Broadband access per 100 inhabitants, June 2003

Korea	Canada	Denmark	Sweden	Japan	US	Germany	France	UK	Australia
23.17	13.27	11.11	9.16	8.60	8.25	4.84	4.13	3.63	2.65

Source: OECD [www.oecd.org/sti/telecom]

THE TRADITIONAL BOOK MARKET

The Korean book market had grown steadily, except for a steep decline in the late 1990s primarily because of the currency crisis in Asia. Before the advent of online bookstores, there were three types of bookstores in Korea: mega, general retail, and specialised (see Table C10.3). Mega bookstores like Kyobo, Youngpoong, and Chongro sold a variety of books, retaining huge inventories. In fact, these mega bookstores provided customers with a one-stop shopping experience centred on books. For instance, Kyobo sold not only books but also fancy items, stationery,

Table C10.2   Korea's internet shopping mall market size ($ million)

Year	2000	2001				2002				2003
Quarter	**4**	**1**	**2**	**3**	**4**	**1**	**2**	**3**	**4**	**1**
Market	571	617	689	752	861	1,167	1,276	1,334	1,469	1,545
Quarterly growth rate (%)		8.06	11.67	9.14	14.49	35.54	9.34	4.55	10.12	5.17

Table C10.3   Shares of major product categories in the internet shopping mall sales (%)

Year	2000	2001				2002				2003
Quarter	4	1	2	3	4	1	2	3	4	1
Electronics	18.3	21.8	23.3	20.0	19.1	17.9	18.1	19.0	19.4	17.0
Computers	30.2	29.4	28.6	23.7	20.5	16.9	14.8	13.6	13.8	13.7
Conveniences	6.3	5.6	5.6	7.8	8.0	10.5	12.4	12.2	12.3	11.5
Clothes	3.3	3.3	3.9	5.3	7.5	8.2	8.3	8.7	10.5	10.3
Reservation	5.6	5.1	5.2	7.1	7.5	5.6	5.7	6.2	7.1	6.8
Cosmetics	3.1	2.5	1.9	2.2	2.8	3.7	4.3	5.1	5.4	6.5
Books	4.6	5.6	5.4	5.5	5.3	5.7	4.8	4.9	4.5	5.8
Grocery	1.3	1.6	1.6	3.3	4.8	5.4	5.3	5.8	4.2	4.2
Others	27.3	25.1	24.5	25.1	24.5	26.1	26.3	24.5	22.8	24.2

movies and concert tickets, and CDs and DVDs, and even operated fast food restaurants, all inside one *gigantic* place: in the Kyobo Insurance Building at the heart of downtown Seoul.

Retail bookstores were in general small or medium-sized. They were located in small neighbourhoods in cities, towns, and villages. On the one hand, these stores could not afford to maintain a large inventory for a variety of books, therefore their product lines were limited and they lacked cost competitiveness vis-à-vis the mega stores. On the other hand, though, they offered easy access to their customers and they were able to build close personal relationships with them. Thus, customers whose needs were not comprehensive or complicated were usually satisfied with their neighbourhood bookstores.

Specialised bookstores focused on particular types of books, and tailored their services to a small group of customers such as medical doctors, lawyers, accountants, or other professionals. These bookstores constituted a small portion of the book market in Korea (see Table C10.4).

In general, the traditional book market was characterised by two attributes – an inefficient book distribution system and high inventory managing costs. Except for the mega bookstores, most of the retail or specialised bookstores were small; that is, the book market was very fragmented. Even the book publishing industry consisted of relatively small companies. It was also fragmented – these small publishing companies could not afford to maintain their own distribution channels, and therefore had to rely on regional intermediaries. Mega bookstores were able to open accounts directly with publishing companies, but other small and medium-sized bookstores had to go through regional intermediaries. The problem was that the

Table C10.4   The Korean book market ($ billion)

Year	1992	1993	1994	1995	1996	1997	1998	1999	2000	2001	2002
Market	1.70	1.84	2.17	2.39	2.85	3.56	3.29	1.88	2.02	2.11	2.45

intermediaries themselves were small businesses and each intermediary was able to maintain exclusive distribution contracts with only a few publishing companies. This mechanism forced the retail bookstores to deal with more than 40 different intermediaries for only a very basic assortment of books. This complex distribution system caused great inefficiency, which translated directly into a reduction in the profit margins of the bookstores. In addition, the excessively long distribution channel and its associated inefficiency made it difficult to forecast the demand accurately. Inaccurate demand forecast, in turn, forced the bookstores to hold excessive inventory levels that further deteriorated their profitability.

THE ONLINE BOOK MARKET

Riding the unprecedented internet boom in Korea, e-commerce activity increased drastically. In order to facilitate cyber transactions, it was better for the goods to be standardised – it must be easy for the customers to evaluate the quality of the product. Therefore, books were ideal candidates for e-commerce, and it was natural for the internet book market to grow fast (see Table C10.5).

Online bookstores had two major advantages vis-à-vis their offline counterparts. First, unlike large offline bookstores, the online stores were able to offer their books at prices 20–50% lower than regular ones. They directly contacted a large number of publishers, and eventually were able to get deals as favourable as those given to the large offline bookstores: the internet gave them access to a market as large as that accessed by the large offline bookstores, and therefore they were able to enjoy a reasonable scale economy. Compared with the mega bookstores, however, the online stores had an additional advantage: they did not have to keep huge inventories since their operations strategy was 'order-to-order'. The online bookstore placed an order with an appropriate publisher only when the end-customer (the reader of that book) placed an order via the internet.

The second major advantage was defined from the customer's viewpoint. Many customers who were usually busy office workers couldn't find time to physically visit bookstores during the day, and many local bookstores were not able to meet their busy time schedule. Internet shopping opened a whole new way of buying books for internet-savvy customers: it was very convenient for them to buy books online. Moreover, there was the additional advantage that their books were delivered directly to them. Thus, it was this convenience that gave the online bookstores another competitive advantage vis-à-vis their offline counterparts.

Table C10.5   Korea's internet book market size ($ million)

Year	2000	2001				2002				2003
Quarter	4	1	2	3	4	1	2	3	4	1
Market	26.15	34.00	37.49	41.85	46.21	66.26	61.03	64.52	66.26	87.18
Quarterly growth rate (%)		30.02	10.26	11.63	10.42	43.39	−7.89	5.72	2.70	31.57

Table C10.6   Market share (%): June 2002

Yes24 + Wowbook	Kyobobook	Morning365	Aladdin	Others
40	14	10	9	27

Yes24 – In June 1998, Mr Kang In Lee started WebFox as the first internet bookstore in Korea by benchmarking Amazon.com. It was soon renamed Yes24. At that time, publishers were reluctant to give him favourable pricing since they didn't want to see their books discounted deeply in the market. Like most small and mid-sized bookstores, however, most publishers were themselves small and mid-sized and didn't want to forgo an opportunity to boost their own sales. Mr Lee eventually succeeded in signing favourable contracts with several major publishers and started his online bookstore business. After that, many publishers followed suit and Yes24 grew fast to become the market leader that even threatened the large offline behemoths. In 2002, Yes24 merged with Wowbook, and enjoyed a 40% market share in the online book market (see Table C10.6). Its goal was to become a specialised online portal for selling not only books, but also a wide variety of cultural goods from DVDs to cartoon characters.

Kyobobook – Amid astoundingly rapid change in the Korean book market, many traditional offline bookstores faltered. It was shocking to observe Chongro Bookstore, which was once the largest and most profitable store in Korea, go bankrupt due to its inability to adapt to the new environment. Facing the tragic demise of one of their own kind, offline bookstores were ready to enter the internet arena. Kyobo, the largest offline bookstore, formally established its own online bookstore, Kyobobook. Its strategy was to leverage its offline prowess not only to win the online market, but more importantly to protect its offline territory from being eaten away by the online bookstores. Even the publishers tried jumping on the bandwagon following the move by the offline bookstores into the net.

Morning365 – Although it was a relatively late entrant into the online book market, Morning365 grew quite rapidly. Established in September 2000, Morning365 became the second-largest player in the market only 10 months after its opening.

In addition, there were many relatively small online bookstores. Although each one of these small players was insignificant, collectively they represented almost 40% of the market, which was still pretty much fragmented.

MORNING365

Morning365 was founded in 2000, using the unique technology patented by Woori Technology, which was listed on KOSDAQ (equivalent to NASDAQ in Korea) as a manufacturer of nuclear power plants and industrial control equipment. Mr Duck Woo Kim, president of Woori Technology, was the largest shareholder with a 21.79% share of the company. Mr Kim was a very attentive and inventive person, and conceived an idea of using the subway system as a logistical mechanism for burgeoning e-commerce in Korea. Incessantly congested roads in Seoul prompted Mr Kim to develop such an idea; in fact, most of the people whose offices were in Seoul used the city's metropolitan subway system to commute, which virtually guaranteed on-time departures and arrivals. Although in retrospect it seemed a very simple idea, it was rather novel at the time when Mr Kim conceived it. In 1999, Mr Kim applied for patents and got two separate patents for his idea of using the subway system as a logistical option: they were for a *logistics system in the metropolitan area* and for a *logistics system using the subway network*. Both were approved in 2002 (see Table C10.7).

The patents would enable the company to utilise the metropolitan subway network in two interrelated ways. First, it could use the subway stations as the posts where customers could pick up the books they ordered via the internet. Second, it could use the subway network as the physical transportation system, which was inexpensive and almost always on time.

In 2000, with these unique patents pending, Duck Woo Kim approached two public corporations that were in charge of the subway network in the metropolitan areas, Seoul Metropolitan Subway Corporation (SMSC) and Seoul Metropolitan Rapid Transit Corporation (SMRTC), and eventually succeeded in signing exclusive contracts with them. Under these contracts, Woori Technology obtained exclusive rights for six years to use the entire subway infrastructure for its business operations and in return had to pay fixed annual fees to the corporations. When signing the contracts, the corporations asked Mr Kim not to extend the use of the subway logistical system to other business areas such as newspapers and food courts, for which they already had separate contracts.

Initially, Mr Kim wanted to form strategic alliances with existing e-commerce companies to capitalise on the contracts, but those companies turned down his offer on the basis that the subway logistical system was not yet a proven technology. Without any willing partners, Woori Technology decided to establish its own e-business, which was the beginning of Morning365 in 2000.

Table C10.7   Patents owned by Woori Technology

Patent code	Registration number	Application date	Registration date	Inventor	Patent title
B65G1/00	1003638710000	1999-09-30	2002-11-25	D. W. Kim	Logistics system in the metropolitan area
G06F17/60	1003481220000	1999-04-27	2002-07-26	D. W. Kim	Logistics system using the subway network

Patent rights expire 20 years after their application date in Korea.

MORNING365'S DISTINCTIVE COMPETITIVE ADVANTAGE – SUBWAY LOGISTICAL SYSTEM

Besides being cost competitive, online shopping provided customers with one additional valuable service, *delivery*, which was usually free with a purchase over a certain dollar amount. The most widely used was 'door-to-door' delivery. Most of the online shopping mall companies did not have their own delivery means. Instead, they employed either integrated logistics companies such as FedEx or DHL, governmental post services, or the so-called 'quick service companies', which were in general very small private firms. Although delivery was considered as a key element early on, few online companies believed that *the specific delivery method they used* would affect their competitive advantage in the market.

Morning365 used three different delivery methods for its customers: the subway delivery system, convenience store pickup, and door-to-door delivery. Door-to-door delivery was the same as that used by many online companies. Both subway delivery and convenience store pickup required customers to visit physical distribution points and take the books they ordered via the internet. The difference between these two options was the types of physical distribution points. Morning365 ran kiosks, called 'Happy Shop', inside subway stations for subway delivery, whereas for its convenience store pickup it signed contracts with convenience stores such as LG25, Buy-the-way, and FamilyMart, which were among the largest convenience store chains in Korea.

The subway delivery system consisted of logistics centres and Happy Shops at subway stations. Logistics centres functioned as distribution hubs for orders, and Happy Shops operated as terminals where customers could receive their orders. The success of this subway logistics model was dependent on the subway population. Considering that the main customers in e-commerce were young people in their 20s and 30s (see Table C10.8), and most of them preferred the subway as their transportation means, the subway delivery system seemed to be an ideal strategy for an online bookstore.

Table C10.8   Percentage of internet shopping mall users: distribution of age

Age bracket	2002	2003
6–19	16.2	13.5
20–29	32.3	51.0*
30–39	27.5	40.1
40–49	19.9	25.6
50–59	15.4	21.0
Over 60	13.4	17.1

*51% of the total internet users at age 20–29 used the internet shopping mall at least once in 2003.

Source: Korea National Statistical Office (http://www.nso.go.kr)

Customer incentives – From the customer's perspective, Happy Shops were best. Except for an order over $26.16, the customer had to pay $1.74 for door-to-door delivery, and $1.31 for convenience store pickup. Should the customer use a Happy Shop, she could get an additional discount depending on the order size. If the order was $17.40 to $26.16, the customer got a $0.87 refund, and if the order was $26.16 to $34.87, $1.74 was refunded (see Table C10.9).

Table C10.9   Morning365's delivery fee schedule ($)

Order size	Happy Shop	Convenience store	Door-to-door
Less than $8.72	0.44	1.31	1.74
$8.72 to $17.40	0	1.31	1.74
$17.41 to $26.16	− 0.87	1.31	1.74
$26.16 to $34.87	− 1.74	0	0

The traditional door-to-door delivery service had several pitfalls. First, it was very hard to deliver the books if there were no recipients at home. If the recipient received the wrong order, it was cumbersome to return the book. The customer would have to use either another delivery service or the post office. Moreover, it was difficult to guarantee the quality of delivery services provided by individual delivery clerks, many of whom were non-professional employees at small quick service companies. Another difficulty was related to the complex and inefficient mail address system in Korea. It was difficult to match a mailing address with a physical location because the mail address system had not been updated frequently and systematically enough to keep up with the rapidly expanding suburbs in Seoul over the previous decades.

On the contrary, the subway delivery system had several advantages vis-à-vis the door-to-door delivery system (see Figure C10.1). When taking the subway, customers could visit one of the Happy Shops to pick up their orders: they could reduce their waiting time, easily exchange or return books, and get refunded. The delivery time was much shorter, too. Customers could get their orders within eight hours if they lived in the Seoul metropolitan areas, not 2–3 days as it was via the door-to-door system. This was possible because the subway could avoid the notorious traffic jams in Seoul. In addition, Morning365 had an IT system to track orders and control deliveries.

Morning365's subway logistics – The subway logistics system helped Morning365 reduce delivery costs because delivery was made to the designated Happy Shops instead of individual customers' homes, thus the delivery distance as well as complexity could be reduced significantly. Morning365 delivered books every two hours, five times a day by subway. Trucks were only used to deliver books from logistics centres to subway stations. The usual delivery system used by other internet shopping malls was faced with numerous different delivery destinations; for example, each individual customer's home. Consequently, it was very hard for the delivery workers to accumulate relevant logistical experience. On the contrary, under the subway delivery system, the delivery workers moved between fixed delivery points and thus became capable of accumulating relevant logistical knowledge

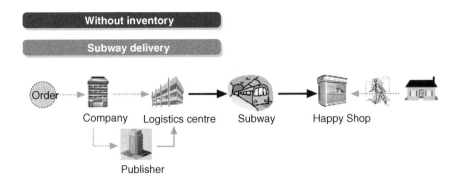

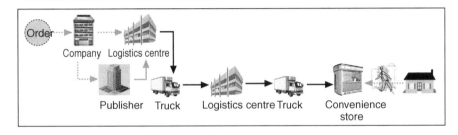

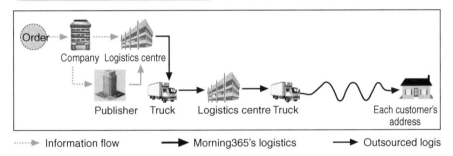

Figure C10.1   Comparison between 'door-to-door' and subway delivery

and experience, which enabled the company to reduce delivery costs. As a result, the delivery cost using the subway logistics system was equivalent to only 35% of the cost of the door-to-door delivery (see Table C10.10).

Table C10.10   Cost structure of respective delivery methods

	Average purchase amount	Sales proportion	Average delivery cost*
Door-to-door	$41.85	40%	100
Convenience store	$41.85	10%	78
Happy Shop	$21.76	50%	35

*Assuming the door-to-door costs 100.
Source: based on Morning365 company data, first half of 2003.

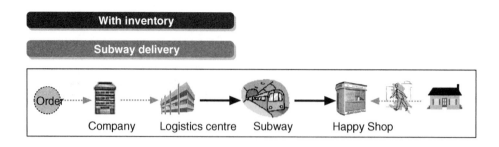

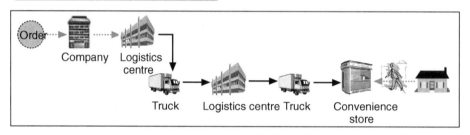

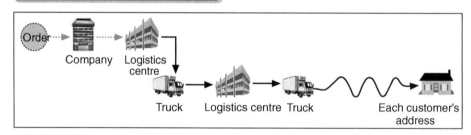

Figure C10.1 *(Continued)*

Almost half of the orders the company received were delivered via the subway system, which was the least expensive option. Thus, the cost advantage from using the subway logistics system directly affected the company's bottom line. Mr Sung Mo Kim, a marketing manager at the company, said:

'Thanks to our big saving in delivery, the operating cost of Morning365 was just 12% of sales, whereas that of other online bookstores was 17% [see Figure C10.2]. It was this 5% advantage in operating cost that gave Morning365 overall competitive advantage vis-à-vis our online competitors.'

Delivery cost and process – Each of the three delivery options cost Morning365 different amounts (see Table C10.11). The subway delivery system incurred fixed

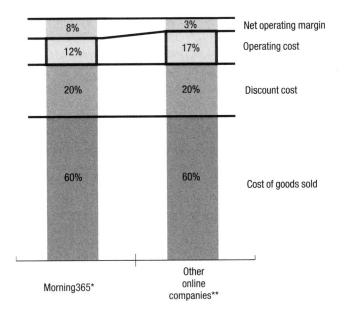

* Morning365 company data (July 2003).

**Percentage based on average purchasing amount of $40.

Figure C10.2 Cost structure comparison

costs in addition to variable costs: fixed costs for running a Happy Shop are $2,000 a month, and variable costs are 1% of sales. On the contrary, there were no fixed costs involved in using convenience store or door-to-door delivery systems. But, the two delivery options cost more in terms of variable costs than the subway delivery system. The convenience store delivery system cost $1.64/order plus 3% of sales, whereas door-to-door delivery cost $2.18/order plus 3% of sales. Another

Table C10.11 **Delivery cost structure**

	Fixed costs	Variable Delivery	Costs Other**
Subway***	$2,000/month/shop* Itemised ($/month/shop) – Fees to SMSC: $455 – Salary: $910 – Administrative cost: $455 – Miscellaneous: $180	None	1% of sales
Convenience store****	None	$1.64/order	3% of sales
Door-to-door****	None	$2.18/order	3% of sales

   *Total fixed costs to run a Happy Shop per month. Currently, there are 25 Happy Shops.

  **Other costs such as handling, packaging, and tracking.

 ***Average purchase per order using subway delivery = $23.

****Average purchase per order using convenience store or door-to-door delivery = $44.

factor to consider was that the average purchase amount was different across delivery options: the average purchase amount per order using the subway system was $23, whereas that using convenience store or door-to-door delivery systems was $44.

The delivery process was slightly different, depending on whether the ordered books were currently in inventory or not (see Figure C10.1). If the books ordered by customers via the internet were currently in inventory, Morning365 informed one of its five logistics centres to locate the books and directly make the deliveries to appropriate Happy Shops for customer pickup (subway delivery) or it asked third-party delivery companies to visit the logistics centre, pick up the books, and deliver them to either convenience stores (convenience store delivery) or to the customers' houses (door-to-door delivery). If the books were not in inventory, one additional step was needed. Once Morning365 received an order and found that it wasn't in stock, it asked the publishers to send the ordered books to an appropriate Morning365 logistics centre. After the centre got the books from the publishers, it followed the same procedure as when the books were in inventory.

Managing Happy Shops – The subway system in the Seoul metropolitan areas was very comprehensive and well built. As of 2003, there were eight subway lines, Line 1 to Line 8, which covered almost every neighbourhood in each of the areas of Seoul (see Figure C10.3). In 2001, Morning365 built 20 Happy Shops on lines 1–4 and another 20 shops on lines 5–8. After operating them for a year, they analysed the sales from each shop, and decided to build 10 additional shops on lines 1–4 while closing some of the shops on lines 5–8. Most of the Happy Shops were located at the transfer points where two subway lines met. This limited market coverage was one critical shortcoming of subway delivery.

Morning365's plan was to gradually expand its market coverage to various provinces, which constituted the outer boundary of the Seoul metropolitan areas. To do this, they built extra delivery spots by adding nine new Barota Zones – the new name of Happy Shops for the provinces – in August and six in September 2003 (see Figure C10.3).

Managing the inventory – One of the important advantages online bookstores had over their offline counterparts was the low cost of managing the inventory. The most ideal situation might be 'zero inventory'. However, in reality, keeping zero inventory would be a daunting task, even for the nimble online bookstores. Morning365's goal was to keep four days' inventory: on average, Morning365 delivered 15 000 books a day, and thus the target inventory level was at about 60 000 books.

For the last three years, Morning365 sold 100,000 different book titles, and estimated that 1 000 titles of top bestsellers amounted to over 80% of the company

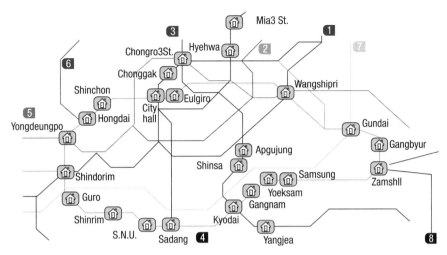

Figure C10.3 Subway lines and Happy Shops

sales. Thus, a sort of 'rule of thumb' used by Morning365 was to retain inventory only for the best-selling books. Morning365 believed that its arch-rival, Yes24, retained about one million books in inventory.

ENVIRONMENTAL CHANGES

The fixed price policy

Following the economic slump in the global market, the Korean economy has been in recession for the last few years. When living on a tight budget, people usually cut back their spending on items related to non-essential activities; for example, recreational items including books. Thanks to an unanticipated macroeconomic hardship, book sales fell by as much as 14%. Fearing the worst possible scenario, Mr Ji Soo Park, CEO of Morning365, wrote an article in one of the most influential newspapers in Korea, expressing his concern over severe contraction of the internet book market and encouraging readers to continuously invest in their future by buying and reading more books.

What made matters worse was the Korean government's enforcement of a new rule, the *fixed price policy,* which would prohibit bookstores from selling books published within the current year at discounted prices. This policy had been constantly suggested by the Offline Bookstore Association. Since they couldn't afford to give steep discounts to their customers, offline bookstores were complaining about discounting by online bookstores, arguing that such behaviour of the online bookstores was destroying the book market as a whole. The government gave in. As feared by many online bookstores, the effect was immediate and direct – book sales via the internet fell significantly (see Table C10.12). The ability to give steep discounts to their customers enabled the online bookstores to enjoy formidable competitive advantage over offline players. But now a large chunk of that competitive advantage

Table C10.12   Sales ($ millions)

	2000	**2001**	**2002**	**Febuary 2003**	**March 2003**	**April 2003**
Yes24	105.87	37.76	870.1	12.55	9.15	7.85
Kyobo	105.78	120.59	451.16	N/A	N/A	N/A
Morning365	—	8.59	22.08	4.80	3.84	N/A

Sources: Yes24 Performance Dashboard Analysis, February 2003, Kong-Myong Ha (Yes24 sales);
Kyobo Book Center Audit Report, http://dart.fss.or.kr (Kyobo sales including offline sales);
Morning365 Company Data (Morning365 sales); Electronic Times, May 2003; Yes24 Performance
Dashboard Analysis, February 2003, Kong-Myong Ha

evaporated, and there remained very little incentive for the customers to buy books
online.

Reaction of the online bookstores – A delivery war

The initial reaction from the online bookstores to the fixed price policy was
literally 'shock'. But, very soon they realised there was only one way, at least in
the short run, to cope with this colossal change in the market – doing away with
the delivery fees! First, Bookpark, the online bookstore run by Interpark, one
of the largest internet shopping malls in Korea, announced that when the order
amount was over $34.87, they would not charge any delivery fee, which usually
was about $1.74 per order, from July 2003. Soon after it eliminated the condition
'purchase over $34.87', and started charging no delivery fee for any order regard-
less of its size. Since then, sales soared by 30% and daily sales reached averages
of over $60 000.

Yes24 quickly responded to the market change as well, by introducing 'convenience store pickup' services. Thanks to this new delivery scheme, Yes24 was able
to reduce its payment to the logistics companies from $2.18 to $1.57 per order on
average. The company believed in the effectiveness of the new delivery method.
On average, customers using the convenience pickup system could receive their
orders in 1–2 days, whereas it usually took 2–3 days using door-to-door delivery.
Moreover, there were over 2 000 convenience stores throughout the metropolitan
areas, which made it very easy for office workers to pick up their orders during
their lunchtime or on their way home. In order to induce more customers to use
the convenience store pickup system, Yes24 decided to offer its customers a $0.87
discount on their order until the end of 2003.

NEW STRATEGY FOR THE NEXT 10 YEARS

The weather was still too hot for Mr Park. Over the past few years, the business
environment had been very favourable to Morning365, but now the situation seemed
rather hostile. Mr Park felt that he was being forced to make a critically hard decision

Table C10.13   Market size for each book category in 2002 (estimated)

Rank	Category	Estimated number of copies published	Average price ($)
1	References	23,592,869	25
2	Kids	19,957,670	8
3	Cartoon	35,944,520	3
4	Social sciences	6,149,686	16
5	Literature	12,787,892	7
6	Technical sciences	5,882,748	15
7	Language	4,363,811	11
8	Art	2,019,200	14
9	Religion	3,302,663	8
10	History	1,681,628	14
11	Philosophy	898,140	12
12	Pure science	623,430	12
13	Others	295,290	9
	Total	117,499,547	12

on the future of his company. Before finalising his new strategy, he wanted to cool down a little bit and reconsider the still evolving conditions in the market.

New development in the fixed price policy

Facing the hard criticism from the online bookstores in a weak economy, the government decided to allow a little flexibility in the fixed price policy. Although the rule still prohibited the bookstores from discounting books published within one year, now an exception was allowed for two categories of books: (1) those addressing 'practical knowledge' such as gardening, cooking, sporting, and so on, which would be exempted from 2005; and (2) reference books for elementary school students, exempted from 2007 (see Table C10.13). There was a very delicate connotation associated with this new rule: it was very difficult to define 'practical knowledge.' Should the bookstores be successful in persuading the government to interpret it in a very comprehensive manner, it would become equivalent to nullifying the fixed price policy itself completely from 2007.

Contract expiry

Mr Park was also concerned with the expiry of the exclusive contracts Morning365 signed with the Seoul Metropolitan Subway Corporation and Seoul Metropolitan Rapid Transit Corporation, both of which would expire in 2006. Although the patents that enabled Morning365 to design the subway delivery system would be valid for about 15 years from 2005, the company would find it very difficult to enjoy actual competitive advantage vis-à-vis its competitors without the real 'mediums' – Happy Shops at the subway stations, which made the subway delivery system complete as a logistical option. After a contract expires, the corporations can request an open

Table C10.14   Price comparison*

	Morning365	Yes24	Kyobo	Aladdin	Interpark
Tag price	$43	$43	$43	$43	$43
Discounted price	$33.65	$34.94	$33.43	$34.13	$36.43
Mileage points**	$3.01	$2.31	$3.05	$3.41	$2.35

 * Average prices of books for novels, business, nonfiction, and language.
** Customers can use mileage points as cash when they order next time.

bidding from qualified companies. Mr Park felt relieved to know that the public cor-porations funded by the government had a tendency to renew their contracts unless a serious mishap occurred during the contract period. After discussing this issue with the company's financial advisors, he estimated that there was a 50–70% chance of winning the contracts again in 2006, assuming no serious calamity would happen before that.

Good news or bad news – Conflicting reports from the field

Recently, Mr Park asked his marketing manager to collect market survey data and to analyse it. He found that the market responses were not always as favourable as the company had hoped for. As expected, Morning365 did not have price com-petitiveness over its rivals in the market (see Table C10.14).

The CEO was not surprised by the data. He had known it from the beginning, and that was why he had been emphasing the company's strategy to utilise the subway delivery system. While reviewing other data, Mr Park was transfixed by the market survey results that seemed to contradict his long-held belief. The customers an-swered that they were not satisfied with Morning365's delivery performance (see Table C10.15). Moreover, their overall satisfaction level with Morning365 was not at all better than those with other bookstores (see Table C10.16). Data about how

Table C10.15   Market survey – customer satisfaction

	Web design search function	Web contents	Ease of payment via internet	Price	Delivery	Return
Yes24	B+	B	B	C	B+	D+
Aladdin	A	C+	C+	C+	B+	C
Interpark	D+	D+	B	D+	A+	C+
Kyobo	B+	D+	D+	D+	A	C
Youngpoong	D+	D+	D	D+	A	D+
Books4U	B	D+	E+	D+	B+	D+
Morning365	C+	E+	C+	D+	C	B
Lotte.com	D+	D	C	E+	B+	C
Bandibook	B+	D	D+	D+	C+	E+

Table C10.16   Index of recognition, utilisation, and satisfaction (relative scores)

	Recognition	Utilisation	Satisfaction
Yes24	83.0	76.8	72.8
Kyobo	47.2	24.5	70.8
Morning365	16.2	17.0	68.7
Aladdin	19.6	14.7	68.6

frequently the company's web site was visited by its customers in comparison with others confirmed Mr Park's concerns over dismal customer satisfaction outcomes (see Table C10.17).

Despite these adverse observations, Mr Park wanted to remain optimistic and tried to concentrate on how to leverage the company's unique logistics system. However, he was disappointed once again when he glanced at the most recent market data on the delivery methods used by the online shopping mall businesses (see Table C10.18): it indicated that door-to-door was becoming more and more widely used. This trend was completely contradicting Morning365's strategy, which was dependent on the subway delivery system.

Mr Park became even more confused than before. He hoped to find encouraging evidence in the field data. Instead, he had to become more serious about the original strategy Morning365 had worked with so far. But first he wanted to understand why there was so much contradiction between what he had believed and what the market said. What was really the truth? Should the overall market trend be differentiated from that specific to the internet book market? What long-term strategy should he design for his company? Could it be based on the subway logistical system as the core competence in the future? How should Morning365 be prepared to respond to the significantly changing market conditions such as the fixed price policy, expiration of exclusive contracts, and potential imitation by its competitors? Should Morning365 try to find M&A partners to survive in the market, or could it stand alone like it had been doing so far? Should Mr Park gather more information before making further decisions?

Table C10.17   Share of user session visit (%)*

	May 2003	June 2003	July 2003
Yes24	39.7	39.3	38.1
Morning365	14.5	13.7	13.7
Kyobo	13.8	13.1	12.8
Aladdin	10.7	10.7	10.5
Libro	6.3	6.5	6.2
Interpark	0.5	2.5	4.9

* Assuming there are 100 customers visiting the internet bookstores' sites, it shows how many of them visit each internet bookstore.

Table C10.18 **Proportion of the internet shopping mall delivery methods (%)**

Year	2000	2001				2002				2003
Quarter	4	1	2	3	4	1	2	3	4	1
Door-to-door	61.6	71.8	71.8	73.1	80.8	82.8	82.2	82.7	83.5	84.2
Self logistics*	26.0	19.2	17.6	15.2	10.2	10.2	11.1	10.1	8.9	7.2
Postal service	3.2	4.1	4.2	3.8	3.1	3.0	3.0	3.2	2.9	3.3
Post logistics**	4.6	3.1	4.9	5.2	3.7	2.8	2.7	2.8	3.1	3.5
Other	4.7	1.9	1.5	2.7	2.1	1.2	1.1	1.1	1.6	1.8

* Using the internet shopping mall company's own logistical operations.
** Includes convenience store pickup and subway delivery.

He soon became swamped with too many questions with too few clues. Now he really wanted to cool down. He was gazing at the August sun in Seoul through his office window. The stifling heat seemed to be trying to give Mr Park a taste of coming competition in the internet book market. The CEO murmured, 'OK. Now it's time for me to do some serious internet surfing, perhaps start with Yes24's homepage.'

QUESTIONS

- What would you recommend Mr Park do in order to sustain Morning365's position in the Korean retail book market?
- Morning365's use of the Seoul subway system for its logistics (book distribution and pick-up) was quite innovative and unique. Do you think this approach would work elsewhere and for other types of products?

NOTES

1. Fisher, M.L. (1997) 'What is the right supply chain for your product?' *Harvard Business Review,* March–April, 105–116.
2. In fact, modularity has its own significance. See Baldwin, C.Y. and Clark K.B. (2000) *Design Rules: The Power of Modularity,* The MIT Press, Cambridge, MA.
3. Fisher, M. Hammond J. Obermeyer, W. and Raman A. (1998) 'Configuring a supply chain to reduce the cost of demand uncertainty,' POM Series in *Technology and Operations Management, vol. 1* (Global Supply Chain and Technology Management), 76–90. Production and Operations Management Society, Miami, Florida.
4. Narus, J.A. and Anderson J.C. (1996) 'Rethinking distribution: adaptive channels,' *Harvard Business Review,* July–August, 112–120.

SCM: *The Past is Prologue**

Donald J. Bowersox

A PIONEER IN THE FIELD SHARES HIS HISTORICAL PERSPECTIVE ON THE BIRTH OF THE DISCIPLINE AND OFFERS SOME THOUGHTS ON THE DIRECTION IT MIGHT TAKE IN THE FUTURE

When asked to contribute an article for the inaugural issue of *CSCMP's Supply Chain Quarterly*, I felt honoured and, to a significant degree, intimidated by the challenge of writing about my perspective on the history of the discipline we call supply chain management.

Well, I do have a perspective, which has quite often been shared at professional meetings and in numerous classrooms. To the best of my ability (and memory), I will present in this article my thoughts on how supply chain management got to where it is today. As a lifelong educator, I can't resist also including a few comments concerning where I think we are going as we deal with globalisation in the Information Age.

Before I begin, let me say that two ground rules are in order. First, I will not name specific individuals who made the events I've chosen to discuss a reality, thereby assigning neither fame nor blame. And second, I've borrowed Walter Cronkite's trademark 'And that's the way it is' closing to his nightly news broadcast – but my version is 'And that's the way I see it.' That is to say, my interpretation is only one perspective concerning what happened.

There have been many men and women who have contributed to the development of the discipline of supply chain management. It is to them I dedicate this bird's-eye view of history.

WHAT IS A DISCIPLINE?

I remember sitting in an undergraduate political science class when the professor asked each of us to write an essay defining a 'discipline'. As I recall, I never did get it right to his satisfaction. Some 50 years later, at the 2006 CSCMP Doctoral Consortium, I once again faced that question when a doctoral candidate asked, 'Is supply chain management a discipline?' Since by that time I had both grey hair and tenure, I felt confident in answering, 'Yes'.

*This article was written by Donald J. Bowersox. Reprinted from CSCMP's *Supply Chain Quality* with permission from Supply Chain Media LLC. © 2007 www.supplychainquarterly.com.

In my opinion, a discipline is an integrated body of knowledge that defines the theory and practice of a field of study. A discipline explains interrelationships between knowledge and practice in the form of constructs, which ideally are supported by empirical research and documentation. Perhaps most importantly, the totality of a discipline provides a framework to help anticipate or predict outcomes.

Supply chain management is a discipline because it offers an integrated body of knowledge to guide research and practice. To support this conclusion, I have used a time line that captures the sequence of events leading to the development of the body of supply chain knowledge.

A VIEW ACROSS TIME

The roots of the discipline of supply chain management can be traced back to the Great Depression, World War II, and the post-war economic boom of the late 1940s. Following World War II, we lived in a world that had survived deep despair and deadly conflict. Consequently, we were immersed in an economy driven by pent-up demand and characterised by unprecedented growth.

At that time, some of the most complex business problems were directly linked to distribution. But the war effort had made people aware of a possible solution to those problems: logistics. Primarily a military concept, logistics was defined as the science of supporting global operations.

At the heart of logistics was transportation. The rapidly growing economy couldn't get enough of it, and by 1950 we were experiencing what one might call transportation's heyday.

THE 1950S: TRANSPORTATION MANAGERS GAIN CONTROL

Among the most powerful corporate executives in those days were a select few who had been ordained vice president of corporate transportation. Executives at this and many other levels of the transportation hierarchy controlled the movement of freight in a transportation industry that was highly regulated by both state and federal governments. This was the era of traffic clubs that served as both professional and social strongholds.

The traffic manager of the 1950s was expected to continuously reduce the cost per hundredweight (CWT) to move products and materials. This single yardstick was the barometer of success.

But doubt was beginning to cloud the horizon. Many managers began to challenge the accepted definition of the total cost to serve. What about the cost of inventory, they wondered. Could a business reduce its total cost by spending more for transportation if it achieved faster and more dependable delivery?

The best practices of the day were being called into question – and those asking the hard questions were not necessarily senior leaders. They were most often middle managers and a few educators who felt that there were better ways to utilise business resources. This growing group began to talk about 'total landed cost'. Borrowing from the logic of electrical systems theory, they created a framework for quantifying total logistics costs, and they structured examples of cost-to-cost trade-offs, such as transportation for inventory. Their surprising conclusion: A combination of individual, lowest-cost activities didn't always equate to the lowest total cost.

Clearly, change was in the wind. In fact, the first course in physical distribution management, a combined undergraduate and graduate seminar, was offered on an experimental basis in 1958. The curriculum explored a combination of real estate, facility location, inventory management, warehousing, and transportation, all loosely linked by a systems-theory framework. I was one of a half-dozen students who enrolled in the initial seminar – wild stuff for those times! We all came away from that seminar fully committed to one of the supply chain's first constructs: total cost.

THE 1960S: A NEW ORGANISATION EMERGES

As the 1960s unfolded, more practitioners and academics were attracted to the mysteries of total cost and its far-reaching ramifications. Forums for discussing such 'out-of-the-box' ideas were few and far between. The American Marketing Association dabbled a little with the concept but soon turned its attention exclusively to marketing. In 1962, the American Management Association facilitated a forum on the topic of total cost in Saranac Lake, New York. What happened next was truly an unexpected consequence of that meeting.

Within weeks, eight disciples of the total cost concept began to organise their own forum. Following two preliminary meetings in 1962, an expanded organisational session took place in St Louis, Missouri, in January of 1963. Others joined the original group in St Louis to discuss forming an organisation that would serve as a platform for dialogue about the new concept. One of the main debates was what to call the emerging organisation. Some argued that the name should include 'logistics', while others argued that logistics was 'too militaristic' to be adopted by industry. Finally, the group coined and adopted the term 'physical distribution management'.

That movement became the basis of a new organisation – the National Council of Physical Distribution Management (NCPDM) – that was formed in December 1963. The fact that we were thinking at a national level conveys a great deal about our vision. I don't, however, recall anyone at those meetings talking about a global organisation.

During the 1960s, the doctrines of physical distribution management slowly but surely emerged. As time would prove, the concept of physical distribution was here to stay.

As the discipline started to emerge, so did literature expressing varied approaches to cross-functional management. Universities began to explore new course structures, and curricula rapidly expanded. In 1968, the first physical distribution textbook joined the growing arsenal of teaching materials.

The discipline received a great boost on April 6, 1965, when the late Peter F. Drucker addressed the annual meeting of the fledgling organisation. Dr Drucker's address was titled 'Physical Distribution: The Frontier of Modern Management'. His remarks contained many nuggets of encouragement, but two in particular stood out. Early in his address, he defined physical distribution this way: 'Physical distribution is simply another way of saying "the whole process of business." I can assure you, that comment turned some heads! In his closing remarks, Dr Drucker put the ball in play with the following statement:

'The only model of a business we can so far truly design – the only operational system, in other words – is that of the business as physical distribution, as a flow of materials. And because our new tools are particularly adept at handling such physical phenomena, we can have powerful results as soon as we study, analyse, and reshape this system. Physical distribution is thus today's frontier in business. It is the one area where managerial results of great magnitude can be achieved. And it is still largely virgin, a largely unsettled frontier.'

Following resounding applause, we all departed the hall in quiet anticipation.

THE 1970S: A BODY OF KNOWLEDGE BEGINS TO MATURE

With the benefit of hindsight, the decade of the '70s is best viewed as a period of conceptual consolidation. The concept of total cost gained legitimacy as more businesses began to recognise, adopt, and implement its logic.

Companies found their proof of performance in the dramatic, cross-functional cost savings they achieved by applying the principles of physical distribution. Managers redesigned their finished-goods distribution strategies. Many of these strategies began to explore different levels of customer service performance.

Soon the domains of the emerging discipline began to focus on measuring cost-versus-service trade-offs. The logic went something like this: Once the total cost to serve had been identified, it became possible to increase and decrease service levels as a means of determining and quantifying customer sensitivity. Bingo! The focus of physical distribution quickly shifted from purely cost to include a concurrent focus on customer service. Thus, the focus was on a combination of top-line revenue growth and bottom-line profitability.

Looking back, the 1970s were among the most prolific of the early decades of supply chain management. The maturing discipline was creating a growing body of knowledge. Attention was focused on both profitability and customer satisfaction. And the groundwork was already being laid for gaining the boardroom's respect and acceptance.

THE 1980S: INTEGRATED MANAGEMENT TAKES SHAPE

The 1980s saw progress on multiple fronts. I like to remember this decade as the period when practitioners made theory work.

New developments came quickly in two distinct tracks. The first followed the original orientation of physical distribution, looking 'downstream' from the end of the manufacturing line to the final consumers. A second track, typically referred to as materials management, looked 'upstream', backward from manufacturing and out across the supply base.

Both of them took an integrated approach to management that extended beyond the scope of a firm's traditional managerial concern, with a focus on cooperation and coordination across either the supply base or the go-to-market structure. The physical distribution concept was mainly attractive to companies in lower-value, consumer goods industries. The process of moving consumer products from the point of manufacturing or processing to retail stores, moreover, was similar across a great variety of industries. The materials management concept of integrating the supply base, on the other hand, had appeal for industries with a strong commitment to supplier innovation and valueadded performance. Research into this focal separation between inbound and outbound physical flow identified what is often called the 'Great Divide': that point of separation between managing what is being sold and what is being made.

What was lacking, however, was the fusion of these two approaches into a broader concept of integrated management. In many companies, both types of organisations existed as separate entities. And even though gains were being made, many believed that some key benefits were being left on the table.

In 1985, NCPDM dropped the term physical distribution in favour of logistics, and it officially became the Council of Logistics Management (CLM). While there were many different motivations behind this move, at least some of the people involved saw the change as supporting a broader view of the physical movement of goods and materials from suppliers through to customers. The functional components of logistics were equally relevant to managing both inbound and outbound inventory movement and positioning. Few fully understood that we were on the threshold of developing the concept of supply chain management.

THE 1990S: COLLABORATION EXTENDS THE ENTERPRISE

For the emerging discipline of supply chain management, the decade of the 1990s was something like the first moon landing: a great breakthrough followed by a period of great achievement. Senior leaders embraced the challenges and opportunities of end-to-end integration by adopting the supply chain business model. Within that model, three important characteristics emerged:

1. The decade witnessed a head-on attempt to close the 'Great Divide'. Supply chain integration was positioned and extended to include customers and suppliers.

2. The concept of supply chain collaboration sparked an unprecedented level of integration that extended beyond traditional enterprise boundaries.

3. Supply chain alignment became a global concept extending across geographically separated customer and suppliers.

Integration across the total supply chain began to achieve the end-to-end efficiencies that many had anticipated. There were also some unintended, but positive, consequences. For one thing, increased connectivity allowed suppliers to become involved in new-product innovation. Moreover, companies that gained more end-to-end visibility began to tap expertise that previously had been excluded from activities that affected consumers. The result was not only greater supply chain efficiency but also major increases in effectiveness and customer relevancy.

As the decade unfolded, technologies that supported enterprise extension enabled senior leaders to develop new business models to guide supply chain integration. The earlier focus on cooperation and coordination was expanded to include collaboration.

Companies that collaborate for successful supply chain execution have three characteristics in common. First, they acknowledge their dependency. Second, they are willing to share strategic information. And third, they acknowledge and comply with cross-organisational leadership. As such, the supply chain organisation that emerged by the late 1990s was clearly a new business model. In fact, it was everything Dr Drucker had hypothesised and something more: it was a union of organisations collaborating in pursuit of shared goals.

In many ways, the conceptual framework of the supply chain business model developed faster than did its implementation. As the new millennium approached, concerns over Year 2000 (Y2K)-related technical performance raised dark clouds of concern. Many companies tried to leapfrog the technology challenge by adopting enterprise resource planning (ERP) systems. Their goal was to achieve integrated financials and end-to-end operating systems that would be capable of guiding supply chain globalisation. Most got the financials they were after; few achieved end-to-end operational integration. The decade closed with serious questions concerning our ability to meet the global connectivity challenge.

2000 AND BEYOND: PUSH COMES TO PULL

A great deal has changed since 2000. The Y2K technology challenge was met. We learned the hard way what ERP is and, perhaps more importantly, what it is not. It also has become clear that the 21st century is characterised by disruptive technology; that is, technology that disrupts and puts in question what is considered to be best practice in a particular field.

This is also a period when event visibility and networked business structures are creating real-time connectivity that transcends the most complex supply chain structure. In addition, business leaders are increasingly aware of the challenges associated with digitisation, or the reinvention of an enterprise in order to take full advantage of current and future technology. Most believe that such a transformation is far more extensive than traditional business process reengineering.

This is not ordinary change management. Global supply chain management requires traditional 'brick and mortar' firms to reinvent how they operate. Earlier standards of performance are giving way to new mandates, such as 'perfect order' execution, rapid cash-to-cash conversion, and total product lifecycle management.

In fact, the whole time posture of business operations is quickly shifting from a forecast, or anticipatory, model to a highly interactive business model that is designed to rapidly fulfil precise customer expectations. This model, which responds to the 'pull' of customer demand rather than 'push' inventory out, is best viewed as a connected network of collaborating customer and business entities. These collaborative networks are devoted to achieving unprecedented levels of customer satisfaction through last-minute product and service accommodations. And they are increasingly exploiting technology to facilitate highly responsive business solutions.

Given the magnitude of the changes taking place around us, it was no surprise when CLM's leadership decided to once again seek a new name to better reflect what was happening around the globe. In 2005 CLM officially became the Council of Supply Chain Management Professionals (CSCMP).

NEW FRONTIERS IN SUPPLY CHAIN MANAGEMENT

So we return to our original question. Is supply chain management a discipline? In my view, the answer clearly is 'yes'. Supply chain management today is a highly developed discipline that is being taught and researched at almost all major universities. What's more, it is something companies test daily in the laboratory of global commerce.

As it stands now, in the 2007–2008 time frame, six imperatives combine to create the supply chain discipline. They are: (1) customer-centricity, (2) operational excellence, (3) integrative management, (4) real-time responsiveness, (5) network leveraging, and (6) collaboration. In combination, these imperatives frame the integrated supply chain business model.

In that supply chain business model we have a logical body of knowledge based on experience and experimentation. It provides a framework for predicting outcomes. But we are not finished constructing that framework; as happens in any emerging discipline, the frontiers of what constitutes supply chain management will continue to expand. New concepts and theories will emerge to replace old paradigms, and those that are capable of withstanding the challenges of time will form working constructs.

It is hoped that both research and prevailing practice will expand and, from time to time, modify our best thinking. As the Information Age continues to play out, we can expect new and more revealing insights into the structural framework – the genome, if you will – that makes a supply chain work best.

Where will this new discipline go next? How will it develop? Have we seen our greatest hour? These are questions with unclear answers. But more than 40 years later, I still agree with and believe Dr Drucker's comments. And while I do not feel comfortable making specific predictions, I am convinced that the 'Golden Age of Supply Chain Management' is still to come.

As we move more deeply into the Information Age, I foresee a day when we will fully capture the potential of many-to-many, real-time communication networks in the design of supply chain systems. Our attention will increasingly shift to implementing responsive supply chain solutions capable of exploiting extreme postponement strategies. I also believe we will continuously discover and implement environmentally friendly supply chain solutions based on our growing understanding of the importance of netzero environmental impact.

I will close by expressing one major concern. As an educator, I have concerns regarding what appears to be the growing separation of the academic and practitioner communities. The origins of our discipline were founded and grew on the strength of close bonds between industry and academia. Trust between these two important constituencies opened the doors of business to teachers and researchers, who were then able to gain a practical understanding of prevailing best practices and real-world needs. The research that followed was grounded in applied relevancy. Over the past decade, this has begun to change.

In a May 2005 *Harvard Business Review* article, 'How Business Schools Lost Their Way', Warren Bennis and James O'Toole warn that academia has failed to meet the professional needs of managers who are dealing with the challenges of the Information Age. A great deal of the Bennis–O'Toole criticism can be traced to demands that professors publish in 'select' academic journals, which some believe reflect proper academic rigor. Those teaching and researching the developing supply chain discipline have faced this dilemma for years. In the current 'publish or perish' environment, even books that report groundbreaking research rank behind a 'properly placed' academic article. Unfortunately, 'proper' placement often results in articles that emphasise abstract issues and excessive quantification. These articles are published in obscure academic journals that most practitioners never see – or if they do see them, they do not read them.

I know full well that the state of academic publication is unlikely to change very soon. Thus there is a need for sponsoring, participating in, and supporting other, quality outlets for relevant academic research. I applaud CSCMP, which was founded on and grew from active collaboration between campus and industry, for launching *Supply Chain Quarterly*. This new publication, in combination with the *Journal of Business Logistics* and a few other respected journals, will offer our discipline a respected forum.

Educator Donald J. Bowersox is uniquely qualified to write about the history of the supply chain management profession. He helped launch the National Council of Physical Distribution Management, the forerunner of the Council of Supply Chain Management Professionals (CSCMP), and served as the group's second president. One of the best-known academics in this field, Bowersox taught courses in distribution, logistics, and supply chain management at Michigan State University from the late '60s until his recent retirement. He now holds the title of University Professor and Dean Emeritus of MSU's Eli Broad Graduate School of Management.

Glossary

Chapter	Term	Definition
6	ABC – stock classification system	An inventory management system that separates out the most important inventory items so that more attention can be focused on those items
10	ABC – activity based costing	Where organisations examine in detail the activities they carry out in the production and delivery of a product, and subsequently identify a number of activities (for example number of orders processed, number of quality inspections or machine setups, and number of deliveries) which may be used to apply overhead to products more appropriately
11	Advanced shipment notification (ASN)	Advance notification to a WMS of an arriving shipment
13	Aggregated procurement	A method for selecting suppliers based on their capabilities rather than individual suppliers tendering for particular orders
3	Agile	Ability to cope with volatility in demand
4	Air trucking	Moving freight, which will be carried by air at some stage on its journey, by road (often air freight rates will be applied for the *full* journey).
7	Automated guided vehicle (AGV)	A mobile robot used to move materials between locations in a warehouse or factory
9	Automatic identification and data capture (AIDC)	Technologies that automatically identify assets and freight, capturing specific data to enable traceability and security amongst other benefits
10	Balanced scorecard	A tool which seeks to include other factors, and not just financial factors, in measuring organisation performance
10	Balance sheet	A snapshot of the financial position of the organisation at that date and consisting of a list of assets and liabilities
4	Bill of lading	A document that contains all of the key information in relation to a consignment being transported (referred to as an airwaybill in air transport)

6	Buffer stock	Also known as safety stock, it is inventory held to meet demand in the event that unforeseen issues lead to insufficient inventory being available to meet demand
7	Bullwhip effect	The distortion of orders along the supply chain, where small fluctuations in end customer demand result in amplification of demand upstream
12	Business continuity plan (BCP)	A documented collection of procedures and information that is developed, compiled and maintained in readiness for use in an incident to enable an organisation to continue to deliver its critical products and services
9	Business process reengineering (BPR)	A management technique commonly used to realign business processes with new technology implementations such as ERP
7	Capacity efficiency	A measure of capacity utilisation that factors in planned downtime, and is derived from the actual output achieved at that process divided by the effective capacity
7	Capacity utilisation	A measure of the capacity utilised by a process derived from the actual output achieved at the process divided by the design capacity
14	Carbon footprint	A term that has come into use to describe the environmental disbenefits associated with economic activities such as the movement of freight
10	Cash flow statement	Illustrates for an organisation where funds have come from and where the funds go to
4	CFR	cost and freight
4	CIF	cost, insurance and freight
4	CIP	carriage and insurance paid
14	Closed-loop supply chain	Term used to refer to supply chains that also comprise reverse/return flows
13	Collaboration	A relationship between supply chain partners developed over a period of time
9, 13	Collaborative planning, forecasting and replenishment (CPFR)	Fundamentally a collaborative method of scheduling logistics between suppliers and customers, commonly implemented as a software package or add-on to ERP
4	Consignee	Recipient of a consignment
1	Consignment	A shipment of freight which is passed on, usually to some type of logistics service provider, from a manufacturer or other source
4	Consignor	Originator of a consignment

4	Consolidated shipment	Where smaller shipments from various consignees are grouped into one single, full load
12	Container Security Initiative (CSI)	The use of IT to pre-screen high risk containers prior to their arrival at the destination port
5	Contract manufacturer (CM)	First tier suppliers who manufacture products for OEMs
5	Corporate social responsibility (CSR)	A term used to refer to a multitude of activities and issues, and in essence concerns how 'ethical' a company's activities are
11	Cost plus margin	A charging mechanism used by 3PLs which incorporates actual incurred costs plus an agreed margin
10	Cost, volume, profit (CVP) analysis	Identification of likely revenue, cost and profit at different levels of output
4	CPT	carriage paid to
12	Creeping crisis	Systemic supply chain disruptions that arise usually from unexpected sources and with widespread consequences
7	Cross docking	Transfer of inventory between two vehicles without the inventory going into storage
12	Customs-trade partnership (C-TPAT)	An agreement that allows freight from companies certified by US Customs to clear customs quickly with minimum inspection
4	DAF	delivered at frontier
4	DDP	delivered duty paid
4	DDU	delivered duty unpaid
3	Decoupling point	The point in the production process at which the base product is customised to become the end product
7	Demand amplification	The amplification of demand upstream in the supply chain, where downstream activities create fluctuations in demand, causing suppliers to overproduce
7	Dependent demand	Products with dependent demand are part of an order for multiple interrelated items
1	Deregulation	Reduction/removal of various government imposed barriers that hinder competition in markets
8	Derived demand	The fact that people or freight do not travel for the sake of making a journey, they/it/travel for some other reason
4	DEQ	delivered ex quay
4	DES	delivered ex ship

2	Directional imbalances	Mismatches in the volumes or types of freight moving in opposite directions in a freight market (leading to different freight rates being charged in opposite directions)
8	Distribution centre (DC)/regional distribution centre (RDC)/national distribution centre (NDC)/consolidation centre (CC)	Terms used to describe different types of warehouses depending upon their particular role and geographic coverage
1	Downstream	Customer end of the supply chain
11	Dropped delivery	A consignment that is not delivered for any of a variety of reasons (for example insufficient address details or consignee not present)
9	e-Business	A term to define business methods that include all electronically mediated information exchanges across a supply chain that support various business processes
6	Economic order quantity	That order quantity which seeks to balance two important sets of costs associated with inventory: the costs associated with ordering and receiving freight, and the costs associated with actually holding the freight
7	Effective capacity	The capacity of a process allowing for planned downtime, which includes scheduled maintenance and changeovers
9	Electronic data interchange (EDI)	Intercompany, computer-to-computer transmission of business data in a standard format
3	Electronic point of sale (EPOS) data	Electronically available data that captures, usually real time, sales to customers
7, 9	Enterprise resource planning (ERP)	An enterprise-wide planning and control software, which plans and controls all resources required from receipt of an order to delivery of freight
5	Environmental separation index (ESI)	An index that measures the difference between the working environments of outsourcer and outsourcee companies
2	Ethnocentricity	Thinking only in terms of the home country environment
13	External integration	Integration of business processes across more than one organisation in the supply chain
4	EXW	ex-works

8	Factory gate pricing	The use of an ex-works price for a product plus the organisation and optimisation of transport by the purchaser to the point of delivery
4	FAS	free alongside ship
4	FCA	free carrier
8	FCL	Full container load
2	FDI	Foreign direct investment – financial flows from a company in one country to invest (for example in a factory) in another country
10	Financial accounting	Using the balance sheet, the profit and loss account and the cash flow statement, largely for reporting to and meeting the requirements of parties outside of the organisation
10	Financial management	The management of its funds by a company over the longer term
4	FOB	free on board
14	Food miles	Term used to refer to the distance by which the various components of a particular food item have to travel before final consumption
4	Fourth party logistics (4PL®)	Invented and trade-marked by Accenture in 1996 who originally defined it 'as a supply chain integrator that assembles and manages the resources, capabilities and technology of its own organisation, with those of complementary service providers, to deliver a comprehensive supply chain solution'
8	Freight tonne kilometre (FTK)	Volume of freight measured in tonnes multiplied by the distance the freight travels measured in kilometres
13	Functional (silo based) organisation	A conventional organisational structure based on business functions (e.g. finance, operations, human resourses, etc.)
4	Generalised costs of transport	A single, usually monetary, measure combining, generally in linear form, most of the important but disparate costs which form the overall opportunity costs of a trip
2	Geocentricity	Acting completely independent of geography and adopting a global perspective
2	Globalisation	An umbrella term for a complex series of economic, social, technological, cultural and political changes which continue to take place throughout the world
2	Glocalisation	Thinking on a *global*, world market scale, but adapting to *local* wants as appropriate

14	Green product design	Seeking to reduce a product's environmental impact by making appropriate design decisions at the product design stage
4	Groupage	The provision of freight transport using consolidated shipments
13	Horizontal collaboration	Collaboration between suppliers who would conventionally be viewed as competitors
13	Humanitarian logistics	Logistics to deliver humanitarian aid
4	Incoterms	Abbreviation for international commercial terms that are now commonly accepted standards in global trade
7	Independent demand	Products with independent demand are those that are ordered independently of any other products
9	Information visibility	The ability to see information at the various points across the supply chain as and when required
8	Intermodal transport	Where freight moves within a loading unit (known as an ITU – intermodal transport unit), this unit may move upon a number of different transport modes, but the freight remains within the unit at all times
13	Internal integration	Integration between business functions within a single organisation
1	Intersectionist view	Suggests that there is overlap between parts of both logistics and SCM, but also that each has parts that are separate and distinct
6	Inventory	Any material that a firm holds in order to satisfy customer demand (and these customers may be internal and/or externalto the firm).
6	Inventory centralisation	Holding inventory in one, or few, locations rather than in multiple locations
6	Inventory turnover	A measure of a firm's performance in inventory management which compares the annual sales a firm achieves with the amount of average inventory held throughout the year
8	ITU	Intermodal transport unit – see 'intermodal transport'
3, 6	Just-in-time inventory management (JIT)	A production philosophy and set of techniques which has many components and principles, but at its core is the idea of making do with the minimum possible level of inventory holding. Inventory is thus kept to a minimum and replenished only as it is used
13	Keiretsu	A Japanese term, which translates literally as 'system' or 'series'. Used to define a series of relationships in a supply chain that promote unified best practice and continuous improvement

11	Key performance indicator (KPI)	Specific metrics used to monitor performance on an ongoing basis
9	Knowledge worker	A knowledge worker is defined by Peter Drucker as someone who knows more than anyone else about their job role
8	LCL	Less than full container load
6	Lead time	The time between placing an order and receiving inventory
3	Leagile supply chain	A supply chain that combines both lean and agile logistics philosphies
3	Lean	Elimination of waste and 'doing more with less'
10	Lifecycle costing/ whole life costing	Determining the costs associated with a product or service over its entire life
1	Logistics	Logistics involves getting, in the right way, the right product, in the right quantity and right quality, in the right place at the right time, for the right customer at the right cost
4	Logistics service provider (LSP)	The various types of companies (hauliers, freight forwarders, etc.) that provide logistics services
3	Make-to-order (MTO)	Producing product only to meet actual customer demand
3	Make-to-stock (MTS)	Producing product which is subsequently put into storage
10	Management accounting/cost accounting	The use of detailed internal information with which to manage the development of the enterprise on a more short-term basis, undertaken to ensure that the long-term financial management of the enterprise is on track
7	Manufacturing resource planning (MRPII)	A planning and control software, which plans and controls all manufacturing resources required to source, manufacture and deliver products
3	Mass customisation	Customisation into various different finished products of what are often largely mass produced products
1	Material substitution	Replacement of physical product by virtual product
7	Materials handling equipment (MHE)	A term used to describe the various types of equipment for handling inventory
7	Materials requirements planning (MRP)	A planning and control software, which plans and controls the manufacture and assembly of products
13	Matrix organisation	An organisational structure that maintains a conventional functional management reporting system, but also has a process/product/project reporting structure

11	Metric	A measurement of an activity; specific important metrics are usually referred to as 'key performance indicators' (KPIs)
2	MNCs	Multinational companies – companies with operations in areas beyond their home country
4	NVOCC	Non-vessel-owning common carrier: refers to companies who consolidate smaller shipments from various consignees into full container loads which the NVOCC then takes responsibility for
2, 5	Offshoring	Offshoring is the transfer of specific processes to lower cost locations in other countries
6	Opportunity cost	In the case of inventory management this is the amount of money the firm would have earned if the money was invested elsewhere other than in inventory
5	Order losing sensitive qualifiers	Order qualifiers that are more critical than other order qualifiers in terms of the outsourcer's requirements
5	Order qualifier	Those criteria and/or performance expectations that a company must meet for a customer to even consider it as a possible supplier
5	Order winner	One or more criteria that lead to the selection of a particular outsourcee by an outsourcing company
5	Original equipment manufacturer (OEM)	Companies that produce final, branded products (with the components often produced by CMs)
2, 5	Outsourcing	Outsourcing involves the transfer to a third party of the management and delivery of a process previously performed by the company itself
4	Own account transportation	Where a company does not use an LSP to transport its freight, but instead transports the freight using its own vehicles
6	Part commonality	An approach which seeks to reduce the number of different components in a product
6	Periodic inventory control system	Inventory levels, and order requirements, are reviewed periodically, not continuously
2	Polycentricity	Adopting the host country perspective
14	Port centric	The co-location of various logistics activities at a sea port rather than at inland locations
3	Postponement	The reconfiguration of product and process design so as to allow postponement of final product customisation as far downstream as possible. Other names for this approach are simply 'delayed product configuration', 'delayed product differentiation', and 'late stage customisation'

5	Procurement	Procurement includes sourcing and purchasing and covers all of the activities from identifying potential suppliers through to delivery from supplier to the customer
13	Product/process-oriented organisation	An organisational structure with teams or organisational groupings being defined by products or processes rather than business function
10	Profit and loss account/income statement	An account of the trading activity of the business for a defined period of time
3	Pull philosophy	Materials are only produced and moved when they are required
5	Purchasing	The specific functions associated with the actual buying of goods and services from suppliers
3	Push philosophy	Materials are produced according to a planned forecast (which may or may not be accurate) and moved to the next stage of the supply chain
9	Radio frequency identification (RFID)	A radio frequency-based technology used for automatic identification and data capture
2	Regional trade agreement	Agreements between neighbouring countries that allow free trade between those countries
1	Re-labelling view	Contends that logistics has been relabelled by the more recent term SCM
6	Reorder point	The inventory level at which an order for more inventory is placed
6	Reorder point inventory control system	A system where inventory levels are continuously monitored, and orders are issued when the inventory is depleted to a predetermined level (the reorder point)
12	Resilience	The ability of a system to return to its original (or desired) state after being disturbed
5	RFQ/RFT/RFI/RFP (request for quote/tender/information/proposal)	A document containing all requisite information pertaining to an outsourced service
14	RMA	Return material/merchandise authorisation: usually used to refer to returned products and packaging; in fact strictly speaking an RMA is a number or form that accompanies the returned product.
12	Robust	Used in a supply chain context to imply a strong or vigorous capability to for example manage regular fluctuations in demand
6	Safety stock	See buffer stock

10	Sale and lease back	The sale, usually for tax and other reasons, of valuable assets to financial intermediaries from whom the assets are subsequently leased back
10, 12	Sarbanes–Oxley Act 2002 (SOX)	Legislation enacted in the US to improve the oversight of accounting and reporting practices
11	Service level agreement (SLA)	A mutually agreed and accepted document that defines agreed KPIs and other issues between two contracting parties
13	Silos	A term used to describe teams or business functions operating in isolation to others
7, 9	Socio-technical systems (STS)	A management philosophy that promotes: joint optimisation of the technical and social system; quality of work life; employee participation in system design; and semi-autonomous work groups
5	Sourcing	Identifying and working with appropriate suppliers
6	Square root rule	An approximation which states that the inventory buffer needed is proportional to the square root of the number of locations in which inventory is held
3	Stock keeping unit (SKU)	A unique version in terms of size, packaging, etc. of a particular product type
5	Supplier development	Activities led by buyers which seek to assist their suppliers in improving the services or products which their suppliers provide to them
13	Supply base rationalisation	The process of reducing or rationalising the number of suppliers in a supply network, typically to reduce complexity and therefore cost
1	Supply chain	The supply chain is the network of organisations that are involved, through upstream and downstream linkages, in the different processes and activities that produce value in the form of products and services in the hands of the ultimate consumer
13	Supply chain integration	The alignment and interlinking of business processes
9	Supply chain knowledge management	A term used to describe those knowledge management processes that span a supply chain
1	Supply chain management (SCM)	The management across a network of upstream and downstream organisations of material, information and resource flows that lead to the creation of value in the form of products and/or services.
11	Tachograph	A device typically fitted to a truck and used to record the speed of the truck, distance travelled and any breaks taken by the driver

4	Third party logistics company (3PL)	LSPs that provide multiple logistics services, often in an integrated fashion
2	TNCs	Transnational corporations – companies that trade across many borders, with operations in multiple countries
11	Total landed costs	The total costs associated with sourcing and receiving products from another location
3	Toyota Production System (TPS)	A production system designed by Toyota to eliminate waste in seven key areas
1	Traditionalist view	Regards SCM as a subset of logistics, as if it were an add-on to logistics
10	Transaction exposure	Exposure to potential financial loss as a result of trading in another currency
10	Transfer price	The value attributed to goods or services when they are transferred between divisions of the same company
10	Translation exposure	Variation in asset value arising from currency fluctuations
1	Transport cost sensitivity	The relationship of transport costs to freight value: high sensitivity implies minor changes in transport rates will have a major impact on transport choice decisions
8	Transportation model	A model used to work out a minimum total transport cost solution for the number of units of a single commodity that should be transported from given suppliers to a number of destinations
1	Unionist view	Logistics is seen as part of a wider entity, SCM
1	Upstream	Supplier end of the supply chain
7	Value-adding activities	Supply chain activities that enhance products to increase the customer's perceptions of those products' benefits
9, 13	Vendor managed inventory (VMI)	An inventory management system that takes a holistic view of inventory levels taken throughout the supply chain with a single point of control
13	Vertical collaboration	Collaboration between suppliers and customers along the supply chain
1	Vertical integration	Ownership, or at least control, of upstream suppliers and downstream customers
2	Virtual organisation	Companies which outsource most, if not all, major functions
8	Volumetric charging	Charging for freight based on the dimensions of the consignment

12	Vulnerability	The likelihood of a supply chain or logistics system being exposed to damage, disruption or failure
7	Warehouse management system (WMS)	A software that manages materials and freight movement throughout the warehouse. This may interact directly with automated handling equipment or provide work instructions for operatives
10	Whole life costing	See lifecycle costing

Index

Note: Page numbers in **bold** relate to glossary entries. 'n.' after a page reference indicates the number of a note on that page.

3PLs *see* third party logistics companies
4PLs® (fourth party logistics companies)
    65–66, **349**
8 Rs definition of logistics   9
9/11 terrorist attacks   234–35
80/20 rule   103

A B Barr   118, 125, 128, 130
A.P. Moller – Maersk Group   65, 272–73
A.T. Kearney/FOREIGN POLICY
    Globalization Index   23
ABC (activity based costing)   178–80, **345**
ABC stock classification system   103–4,
    345
  warehousing   116
absolute variance   198
Abu Dhabi International Airport
    (AUH)   307, 308
academia   342
Accenture   66
accountability, corporate governance   167
accounting profession   167–68
Acer   28
activity based costing (ABC)   178–80,
    345
Adams, John   238
adjusted inventory accuracy   198
adjustments below the line   171
advanced collaborative
    planning, forecasting and
    replenishment   261–62
advanced shipment notification
    (ASN)   196, **345**
Aerogistics Holdings Ltd   258–59
aerospace industry   223–26

Dubai   306–11
  UK   258
  see also air transport
aged stock reports   198
aggregated procurement   257, **345**
agile strategies   38, 42, 44, **345**
  combined logistics strategies   45–48
  radio frequency identification   156, 160
AGVs (automated guided vehicles)   115,
    345
AIDC (automatic identification and data
    capture)   154, **345**
air transport
  relative costs and operating
    characteristics   134
  sustainable logistics   275–76
  see also aerospace industry
air trucking   69, **345**
airlines   61
airwaybills (AWBs)   66
  Deutsche Post/DHL   277
Aladdin   321, 332–33
American Management Association   337
American Marketing Association   337
annual accounts   168, 186
Apple Inc   188
ARENA   288
Arthur Anderson   168
ASEAN (Association of South East Asian
    Nations)   20
Asian tsunami   296
ASN (advanced shipment
    notification)   196, **345**
asset perspective, risk management
    241–42

Association of South East Asian
        Nations   20
Audi   44, 55
auditors   168–69
automated guided vehicles (AGVs)   115,
        345
automatic identification and data capture
        (AIDC)   154, **345**
automobile manufacturing industry
    mass customisation   45, 54
    mass production   38–39
avian flu   245
AWBs (airwaybills)   66
        Deutsche Post/DHL   277

BA (British Airways)   244
backhaul loads   275–76
backward integration   250–51
balance sheets   168–70, **345**
    Deutsche Post/DHL   206
    international business   173
balanced scorecard (BSC)   181–82, **345**
    HBOS   219
    metrics   195
Bandibook   332
Bank of Scotland   217–18
bankers   167
BAP Group   275
Barbie   23
Barings Bank   235
Barota Zones   328
base flow inventory   104–5
Basel Accords in International
        Banking   235
basic collaborative planning, forecasting
        and replenishment   260–62
BCM (business continuity
        management)   236
BCPs (business continuity plans)   233,
        236, 241–42, **346**
benchmarking   191–92
Benetton   55
Bennis, Warren   342
bills of lading   66, **345**
bills of materials   123–24
        Gate Gourmet   212
blood transfusion products, supply chain
        for   285
book market, Korea   317–34
Bookpark   330

Books4U   332
borrowing   175–76
bottom–up perspective on strategy   36, 37
bovine spongiform encephalopathy
        (BSE)   234, 245
BPO (business process outsourcing)   29
    failures   81
BPR *see* business process reengineering
British Airways (BA)   244
brokerage   62
BSC *see* balanced scorecard
BSE (bovine spongiform
        encephalopathy)   234, 245
budgeting   180
buffer stock (safety stock)   92–93, 98–99,
        106, **346**
    delayed product differentiation   100
    inventory centralisation   99–100
    outsourcees   81
bulk
    breaking   112, 114
    creating   112, 114
    sustainable logistics   270
bullwhip effect   122–23, **346**
    vendor managed inventory   262–63
Burbidge effect   122
    vendor managed inventory   262–63
Burj Al Arab Hotel, Dubai   303, 305, 310
Burj Dubai   305
business contacts   167
business continuity management
        (BCM)   236
business continuity plans (BCPs)   233,
        236, 241–42, **346**
business process outsourcing (BPO)   29
    failures   81
business process reengineering
        (BPR)   252, **346**
    enterprise resource planning   154–55
    information visibility and
        transparency   151–53
    vendor managed inventory   262–63
business risk, international
        environment   173
business transformations   283–84
    implications for management
        skills   288–89
business unit strategy   36–37
Button, K.   70
BX Shoes   87

Cannon, Michael   55
capacity efficiency   119, 120, **346**
capacity management   116–21
capacity utilisation   119, 120, **346**
capital allowances   183n1
capital structure, Deutsche Post/
    DHL   209–10
carbon emissions   269, 278
carbon footprint   269, 270, 274, 279,
    346
cargo, definition   7
carrying costs   199
cash flow   171
cash flow statements   168, 171, **346**
cash-to-cash cycle   171
CAST-dpm   287
CCs (consolidation centres)   138, **348**
    factory gate pricing   140–41
Centre for Medicines in the Public
    Interest   301
Chairman's Statements   168
Chartered Institute of Logistics and
    Transport (CILT)   9
chase demand plans   120, 21
China
    exports   20–21
    offshoring   79
    outsourcing   79
    trade corridors   30, 31
Chongro Bookstore   318, 321
Christopher, Martin
    business transformations   283, 288–89
    supply chains   10, 49, 285
        agility   42, 44
        competing   50
CILT (Chartered Institute of Logistics and
    Transport)   9
circular routings   32
Citroën   43–44
CLM (Council of Logistics
    Management)   339, 341
closed-loop supply chain   276, **346**
CMs (contract manufacturers)   78, **347**
    increased reliance on   188
Colin, J.   50
collaboration   249, 250, 263–64, 340,
    346
    methods   256–60
    principles   253–56
    vendor managed inventory   262–63

collaborative planning, forecasting and
    replenishment (CPFR)   153, 155,
    260–62, **346**
Combined Code of Best Practice, financial
    accounting   167
combined logistics strategies   45–48
combining freight   112, 114
competition, as driver for performance
    measurement   189
competitive stage, outsourcing
    relationships   85
competitive supply chains   50–51
confidentiality issues, outsourcing
    relationships   82
conservatism   169
consignee   60, **346**
consignment   **346**
    definition   7
consignor   60, **346**
consolidated shipments   62, **347**
consolidation   243
consolidation centres (CCs)   138, **348**
    factory gate pricing   140, 141
consultative stage, outsourcing
    relationships   85
Container Security Initiative (CSI)
    234–35, **347**
containerised transport
    directional imbalances   30–31
    Emma Maersk   272–73
    evolution   6
    port centric logistics   274, 275
    scale   273
contract manufacturers (CMs)   78, **347**
    increased reliance on   188
corporate governance   167–68, 235
    risk   243
corporate report   168
corporate scandals   167–68, 235–36
corporate social responsibility (CSR)   84,
    285, **347**
corporate strategy   36, 37
cost accounting *see* management
    accounting
cost issues
    determining supply chain costs   285–86
    logistics costs performance
        3PL cost models   200–202
        total landed costs   198–200
    outsourcing relationships   82

cost object   177
cost plus margin   200–201, **347**
cost, volume, profit (CVP) analysis   180, **347**
costing   177–78
  activity based   178–80
costs at the margin   180
Council of Logistics Management (CLM)   339, 341
Council of Supply Chain Management Professionals (CSCMP)   341, 343
  definition of logistics management   8–9
counterfeit medicines   300–301
couriers   62
CPFR (collaborative planning, forecasting and replenishment)   153, 155, 260–62, **346**
craft production   38, 39
creeping crises   233–34, 245, **347**
cross docking   49, 114, 115–16, **347**
CSI (Container Security Initiative)   234–35, **347**
CSCMP (Council of Supply Chain Management Professionals)   341, 343
  definition of logistics management   8–9
CSR (corporate social responsibility)   84, 285, **347**
C-TPAT (customs-trade partnership)   235, **347**
cultural issues
  information visibility   151
  outsourcing relationships   81
currency exposure   173–74
current ratio   209–10
customer satisfaction, as performance measurement driver   189
customs
  carrier responsibilities   66, 67
  freight forwarders   62
customs-trade partnership (C-TPAT)   235, **347**
CVP (cost, volume, profit analysis)   180, **347**
cycle counts   197

Danzas   65, 205
Davies, G.J.   69
DCs (distribution centres)   137–38, **348**
  factory gate pricing   144, 145

debt   175
decoupling economic and transport growth   271, 272
decoupling point   43, 48, **347**
  leagile supply chain   47–48
defects   41
delayed product configuration/ differentiation *see* postponement
Dell   53–55
  cash-to-cash cycle   171
  competitive supply chain   48, 55
  contract manufacturers   188
  cost savings and service enhancements   13
Dell, Michael   53, 55
demand amplification   122, **347**
demand fluctuations   118–19
demand signal processing   122
  vendor managed inventory   262
Demchak, Chris   232
Deming, W. Edwards   39
dependent demand   123, **347**
depreciation   169, 175
derived demand   **347**
  transport   136
deregulation   **347**
  of transport   5
design capacity   119, 120
design for manufacturing   284–85
Deutsche Post World Net
  DHL   65, 205–10, 270, 277–78
  financial management   172
  sustainable logistics   277–78
developed collaborative planning, forecasting and replenishment   261
developing countries
  counterfeit medicines   301
  international trade   20–21
  merchandise exports   20–21
  transnational corporations   27–28
DHL   62, 63, 65, 205
  ABC system   179
  information technology   6
  mergers and acquisitions   189
  PACKSTATION   270, 278
  sustainable logistics   277–78
direct costs   177
directional imbalances   30–32, **348**
  port centric logistics   274
Directors' Reports   168

disaster relief (humanitarian logistics)   256, 257, 264, 294–95, **351**
discipline, nature of a   335–36
disclosure, corporate governance   167
discrete event simulation (DES)   287, 288
dispatch   115
distribution centres (DCs)   137–38, **348**
   factory gate pricing   140, 141
dividends   170, 175
downstream   10, **348**
dropped delivery   163, 187, **348**
Drucker, Peter F.   6, 338, 340, 342
Dubai   303–15
Dubai Cargo Village (DCV)   307, 308
Dubai Exhibition City   312
Dubai International Airport (DXB)   306–9
Dubai Internet City   305
Dubai Logistics City (DLC)   303–15
Dubai Media City   305
Dubai Residential City   312
Dubai World Central   309, 312
duty   199
DYNAMO simulation   122

EADS, supplier evaluation at   223–26
earnings per share (EPS)   207
easyJet   275–76
e-auctions   77
   HBOS   220
e-business   154, **348**
   FloraHolland   152
   see also internet
echelons in the supply chain   11
Economic and Social Research Institute   137
economic growth and transport growth, link between   271–74
economic order quantity (EOQ)   92–96, **348**
EDI *see* electronic data interchange
effective capacity   119, 120, **348**
efficient supply chains   45
EFT (electronic funds transfer)   154
e-gatematrix system, Gate Gourmet   213–14
electronic data interchange (EDI)   154, **348**
   integration   249
   supply chain integration   253
electronic funds transfer (EFT)   154
electronic logistics markets (ELMs)   276

electronic point of sale (EPOS) data   46, **348**
ELMs (electronic logistics markets)   276
emissions trading   269
Emma Maersk   272–73
employees
   key performance indicators, designing   192–93
   motivation   190
   as source of performance data   193–94
empowerment practices   190
end-of-life products   277
Enron   167, 235
enterprise resource planning (ERP)   124, 153, 154–55, **348**
   Gate Gourmet   211–14
   history   340, 341
   supply chain integration   253
environmental separation index (ESI)   84, **348**
EOQ (economic order quantity)   92–96, **348**
EPOS (electronic point of sale) data   46, **348**
e-procurement, HBOS   217–20
EPS (earnings per share)   207
ERP *see* enterprise resource planning
ESI (environmental separation index)   84, **348**
ethnocentricity   25, **348**
ETL (Extract/Transform/Load) tool, HBOS   219
European Union
   Approved Economic Operator scheme   235
   pharmaceutical distribution guidance   300
   regional trade agreements   20, 33n1
   trade corridors   31
   transport
      Irish infrastructure   136
      modal split for goods transport   135
   Waste Electrical and Electronic Equipment (WEEE) Directive   116, 277
event management systems   241
evolution
   of grocery distribution   138–39
   of logistics and SCM   4–7
   of manufacturing   38–39

exceptional items   170
Exel   65, 205
explicit knowledge   161
external integration   250, 251, **348**
Extract/Transform/Load (ETL) tool,
    HBOS   219
extraordinary items   171

Fabbe-Costes, N. 50
factory gate pricing (FGP)   49, 137,
    138–39, 140–41, **349**
fairness, corporate governance   167
fashion industry, mass customisation   47,
    55
FCLs (full container loads)   145, **349**
    factory gate pricing   140
FDI (foreign direct investment)   25–26,
    349
Federal Express (Fed Ex)   62, 64
    deregulation of transport   5
    information technology   6
Ferdows, Kasra   47
FGP (factory gate pricing)   49, 137,
    138–39, 140–41, **349**
financial accounting   167–72, 286,
    349
financial analysts   167
financial barriers to information
    visibility   151
financial management   165–66, 172–73,
    182, 286, **349**
    borrowing   175–76
    Deutsche Post/DHL   205–10
    international business   173–75
financial planning and control   180
financial reporting standards (FRS)   168
finished goods   90
Fisher, Marshall   45
fixed costs   180
Flextronics Inc   188
flooding, UK   234
FloraHolland   152, 160, 163
flows, focus on   48–49
food miles   269–70, **350**
foot and mouth disease   233–34, 245
Ford, Henry   38–39
Ford Motor Company   28, 38–39
foreign direct investment (FDI)   25–26,
    349
Forrester, Jay   122, 234

Forrester effect   122
    vendor managed inventory   262
forward and backward integration   251
forward integration   250
fossil fuels   269
fourth party logistics companies
    (4PLs®)   65–66, **349**
Foxconn   188
France, exports   21
freight
    definition   7
    total landed costs   199
freight agents   62
freight brokers   62
freight forwarders   62
freight receiving area, warehouses   114
freight tonne kilometres (FTKs)   135, **349**
FRS (financial reporting standards)   168
FTKs (freight tonne kilometres)   135, **349**
fuel protests, UK   233, 234
full container loads (FCLs)   145, **349**
    factory gate pricing   140
functional operations, metrics for   194,
    195
functional products   45
functional (silo based) organisation   49,
    251–52, **349**
functional strategy   36, 37
future, supply chain managers of
    the   288–90

gaming   122–23
    vendor managed inventory   262
Gate Gourmet   211–15, 244–46, 250
Gateway   28
Gattorna, John
    4PLs®   66
    inventory flow types   104
    living supply chains   48
    people, importance of   49, 290–91
    strategic issues affecting future supply
        chains   284
    supply chain strategies   46, 282
GDP (Good Distribution Practice),
    pharmaceuticals   299, 300–301,
    302
'gearbox' approach to inventory
    management   101
gearing   175
    Deutsche Post   209

generalised costs of transport   69, 70–71, 102, 286, **349**
geocentricity   25, **349**
Geodis   193
Germany, exports   20, 33–34n3
global logistics performance index (LPI)   21–22
global perspective   14
global warming   300
globalisation   19, 22–28, 32–33, **349**
  manufacturing sector   80
  see also international trade
glocalisation   23, **349**
GMP (Good Manufacturing Practice), pharmaceuticals   299, 301, 302
GNI (gross national income) per capita   21, 22
Gohlke Logistics   313
Good Distribution Practice (GDP), pharmaceuticals   299, 300–301, 302
Good Manufacturing Practice (GMP), pharmaceuticals   299, 301, 302
Government, financial accounting   167
green product design   277, **350**
green revolution   269–71
green waehouse design   276
grocery sector
  evolution of distribution   138–39
  factory gate pricing   138, 139, 140–41
gross national income (GNI) per capita   21, 22
gross profit   170
groupage   62, **350**
Gunton, C.E. 69

Halifax plc   217, 218
Hamel, Gary   267
Happy Shops, Korea   323–29, 331
hauliers   61
HBOS   217–20
healthcare services   13
  triage   14
Heathrow Airport   270
hedging risk   173
Hewlett Packard (HP)   55, 188
hierarchy of needs for freight purchasing   69–70
high-level objectives, focus on   49
history of SCM   335, 341

1950s   336–37
1960s   337–38
1970s   338–39
1980s   339
1990s   340
2000   341
holistic view of strategy formulation   37
horizontal collaboration   254–55, 257, **350**
  humanitarian logistics   256
Houlihan effect   122
  vendor managed inventory   262
house airwaybills   66
HP (Hewlett Packard)   55, 188
hub and spoke networks   64
  ports   273
Huber, Karl   305, 306
humanitarian logistics   256, 257, 264, 295–97, **350**
Hurricane Katrina   234

IBM   28, 53, 193
Ikea   13, 274
income statements *see* profit and loss accounts
incoterms   71, **350**
independent demand   123, **350**
India
  offshoring   79
  outsourcing   79, 87
indirect costs (overheads)   177, 178
information
  flows   15, 59, 149–52, 163–64
    warehousing value-adding services   114
  replacing inventory by   100
  role in global supply chains   150–51
  visibility and transparency   151–53
information superhighway   61
information technology   150
  applications   153–56
  evolution of logistics and SCM   6
  factory gate pricing   139, 140, 141
  HBOS   219–20
  RFID *see* radio frequency identification
  warehouse automation   124–26, 128
information visibility   151–52, **350**
infrastructure dependencies, risk management   241–42
innovative products   45

intangible assets   170
integer programming   287
integration *see* supply chain integration
integrators   62–63
   hub and spoke networks   64
intellectual property (IP) rights   82
intermodal transport   135, **350**
intermodal transport units (ITUs)   135, **350**
internal integration   250, 251, **350**
International Chamber of Commerce   67
international commercial terms
      (incoterms)   67, **350**
international logistics   14
International Motor Vehicle
      Programme   41
international reporting standards
      (IRS)   168
international trade   19, 32
   directional imbalances   30–32
   growth   20–22, 78–80
   offshoring   29–31
   outsourcing   28–29
   see also globalisation
internet
   counterfeit medicines   301
   Dell   54
   information superhighway   61
   Korean book market   317–34
   Korean infrastructure   318–320
   reverse logistics   277
   supplier selection auctions   77
      HBOS   220
inter-organisational network perspective,
      risk management   242–44
Interpark   330, 332
intersectionist view   12, **350**
inventory   90, **350**
   costs   286
   metrics related to   196–98
   outsourcing relationships   85
   pooling   106
   reduction   90
      emphasis on   6–7
      principles   106–7
      strategies   99–102
   unnecessary   40
   see also warehousing
inventory accuracy   197–98
inventory centralisation   99–100, 106, **350**
inventory control systems   96–98

inventory flow types   104–5
inventory management   89, 107–9
   control systems   96–98
   economic order quantity model   92–96
   importance   90–92
   inventory reduction principles   106–7
   matching inventory policy with inventory
      type   103–5
   risk management   241
   supply chain   98–102
inventory policy, matching with inventory
      type   103–5
inventory turnover   90–91, 187, 198, **350**
investor ratios   207–8
investors   167
IP (intellectual property) rights   82
Iraq war   242, 245
Ireland, Republic of   136–37
IRS (international reporting
      standards)   168
isee systems   288
ISO certification   82, 189
iThink   288
ITUs (intermodal transport units)   135, **350**

Japan
   exports   21
   keiretsu   253
   total quality management   39
Jayaraman, V.   277
Jebel Ali Free Zone, Dubai   305, 311
Jebel Ali International Airport (JXB)
      309–10, 311, 312
Jebel Ali Port   309, 310, 311
JIT *see* just-in-time inventory management
job design, warehousing   126–28
Journal of Business Logistics   343
just-in-time inventory management
      (JIT)   39, 106–7, 171, **350**
   and bullwhip effect   122
   evolution of logistics and SCM   7
   Gate Gourmet   212
   performance management, 3PLs   189
   sustainable logistics   274
keiretsu   253, 257, **350**
key performance indicators (KPIs)   188,
      351
   designing   192–93
   empowerment practices   190
   see also metrics

Kim, Duck Woo   321–22
Kim, Sung Mo   326
Knight, F.   237
knowable unknowns   232
    creeping crises   233
    Sarbanes–Oxley Act   235–36
knowledge management   161–62
knowledge workers   161–62, **351**
known knowns   232
    millennium bug   233
Korea
    book market   317–34
    internet infrastructure   318, 319
KPIs *see* key performance indicators
Kuehne and Nagel   63, 65
Kyobo/Kyobobook   318–19, 321, 330,
    332–3
Kyoto Protocol   269, 278

'L' flow operation   117
Lalwani, C.   71
landed costs   85, 198–200, 286, **357**
    historical perspective   335
late delivery
    failed outsourcing relationships   81
    safety stock   98
late stage customisation *see* postponement
LCLs (less than full container loads)   145,
    352
    factory gate pricing   140
lead time   92, **352**
    Forrester effect   122
    reducing   106
    transit inventory   101
leagile supply chain   48, **352**
lean consumption   41
lean strategies   38, 39–41, 42, 45, **352**
    combined logistics strategies   45, 46,
        47, 48
    cross docking   116
    performance management, 3PLs   189
Lee, Hau   49
Lee, Kang In   321
Leeson, Nick   235
Lenovo   27–28
less than full container loads (LCLs)   145,
    352
    factory gate pricing   140
level capacity plans   120, 121
Levitt, Theodore   23

Liberia   21
Libro   333
Lieb, Robert   64
lifecycle costing   179, **352**
limited liability   173
liner routings   32
links in the supply chain   11
liquidity, Deutsche Post/DHL   209–10
living supply chains   48
local sourcing, sustainable logistics   270,
    279
localisation, costs of   199
logistics   8–9, **352**
    evolution   4–7
    role in national economies   7–8
    and SCM, distinguishing between
        11–12
logistics performance index (LPI)
    21–22
logistics service providers (LSPs)   59–60,
    69–71, **352**
    acquisitions and mergers market   192
    classifying   61–65
    fourth party   67–66, **349**
    multinational   189
    responsibilities   66–68
    selecting   68–71
    strategic importance to supply chain
        success   189
    third party *see* third party logistics
        companies
logistics strategies *see* supply chain
    strategies
Lotte.com   332
LPI (logistics performance index)
    21–22
LSPs *see* logistics service providers
Lucas, Caroline   273
Luo, Y.   277

macro-environment perspective, risk
    management   244–45
mad cow disease (BSE)   234, 245
Maersk   65, 272–73
mail   7
make-to-order (MTO)   40, 41, **351**
make-to-stock (MTS)   40, 41, **351**
Maktoum bin Rashid al-Maktoum,
    Sheikh   305
manage demand plans   120, 121

management accounting 176–77, 286, **353**
 costing 177–78
  activity based costing 178–80
  nonfinancial information 180–82
management ratios, Deutsche Post/
  DHL 208–9
managers' attitude to risk 237
manufacturing resource planning
  (MRPII) 124, 153, 155, **353**
 superseded by ERP 155
manufacturing sector 13
 evolution 38–39
 flow of funds 172
 globalisation 80
 international trade 20–21, 79
 management principles 189
 offshoring 29–30
 order processing 107
 outsourcing 79, 80
  failures 81
  performance measurement 188
 sourcing patterns 79
 suppliers 29
March, James 236
marginal costs 180
maritime transport *see* water transport
market capitalisation 207
marketing 119, 122
Marks & Spencer 158, 159
Maslow's hierarchy of needs 69
mass customisation 39, 42–44, 45, **353**
 Dell 54
 metrics 195
 synchronising design of products and
  supply chains 284
mass production 38–39
master airwaybills 66
master production schedule (MPS) 123
master–servant stage, outsourcing
  relationships 85
matching, financial accounting 170
material flows 15, 59
 see also inventory; inventory
  management
material substitution 5, **353**
materials handling equipment (MHE) 125,
  353
 cost plus margin 200
materials management 111, 123–24,
  129, 339
 in global supply chains 112

warehouse management systems
  and automation 124–26
materials requirements planning
  (MRP) 123–24, 153, **353**
matrix organisation 251, 252, **353**
McDonald's 23
McKinnon, Alan 272
McLean, Malcolm 6
Medical Devices Company (MDC) 56
Medicines and Healthcare Products
  Regulatory Agency (MHRA) 300
merchandise exports 20–21, 33n2
Merrill Lynch 244
metrics 188, 202–3, **353**
 commonly used 194–95
 employee motivation 190
 inventory/warehouse related 196–98
 logistics cost performance 198–202
 optimum number of 192
 selecting 191
 see also key performance indicators
Metro 159
MHE (materials handling equipment) 125,
  353
 cost plus margin 200
Microsoft 188
military logistics 8
millennium bug (Y2K) 232–33, 239, 340,
  341
 business continuity management 236
Mintzberg, Henry 38
MNCs *see* multinational companies
modelling supply chain designs 286–88
Morning365 317–34
motion, unnecessary 40–41
motivation, employee 190
Motorola 189
MPS (master production schedule) 123
MRP (materials requirements
  planning) 123–24, 153, **353**
MRPII (manufacturing resource
  planning) 124, 154, 155, **351**
 superseded by ERP 155
MTO (make-to-order) 40, 41, **351**
MTS (make-to-stock) 40, 41, **351**
Muhammad bin Rashid al-Maktoum,
  Sheikh 305
multinational companies (MNCs) 24, **352**
 logistics service providers 189
 supply networks 79
multiple sourcing 78

National Council of Physical Distribution
    Management (NCPDM)   337, 339
national distribution centres (NDCs)   138,
    348
NCPDM (National Council of Physical
    Distribution Management)   337,
    339
NDCs (national distribution centres)   138,
    348
net profit before interest and tax   208
net variance   198
network modelling   241
New Orleans   234
new supply chain designs   281, 291–92
    determining supply chain costs and
        values   285–86
    ever changing context   283–84
    future, supply chain managers of
        the   288–90
    modelling supply chain designs
        286–88
    strategies and practices in SCM   282–83
    synchronising design of products and
        supply chains   284–85
Nissan   256, 257
nodes in the supply chain   11
Nokia   200
nonfinancial information, use in
    management accounting   180–82
non-vessel-owning common carriers
    (NVOCCs)   62, **352**

objective risk   238–39
objectives, focus on   49
OEMs (original equipment
    manufacturers)   78, **354**
Offline Bookstore Association, Korea   329
offshoring   29–30, **352**
    growth   78–80
Ohno, Taiichi   39
open book costing   166
operating profit   170
operational risk   235–36
operations management xii–xiii
    metrics for   194–95
opportunity costs   286, **354**
    generalised costs of transport   70, 71
    inventory   93
optimisation techniques, modelling supply
    chain designs   286–87
order batching   122

vendor managed inventory   262
order losing sensitive qualifiers   84, **354**
order picking and packing   115
    pick-to-voice   128
order qualifiers   77, 82–84, **354**
order winners   77, 84, **354**
ordinary shares   173
organisational barriers to information
    visibility   152
organisational perspective, risk
    management   242–44
original equipment manufacturers
    (OEMs)   78, **354**
O'Toole, James   342
outsourcing   28–29, 75, 86–87, **354**
    activity based costing   179
    BX Shoes   87
    capacity management   121
    distribution   139
    evaluating and selecting
        outsourcees   82–85
    evolution of logistics and SCM   7
    failures   81–82
    fourth party logistics providers   66
    growth   78–80
    outsourcer and outsourcee relationship
        development   85–86
    performance measurement   191
        total landed costs   85, 198
    as risk management solution   243
    sustainable logistics   279
    third party logistics providers   65
    total cost   85, 286
overdrafts   175
overheads (indirect costs)   177, 178
overproduction   40
own account transportation   61, **354**

packaging
    postponement   43
    total landed costs   199, 200
packing orders   115
PACKSTATION initiative, Deutsche
    Post   270, 278
paint, mass customisation   45
Palm Islands, Dubai   303, 305, 310
Paragon   287
Paragon Software Systems plc   287
Pareto rule   103
Park, Ji Soo   317, 318, 329, 330–34
Parmalat Finanziara   235

part commonality   100, **354**
pathogens   245
PE (price earnings) ratio   208
peer-to-peer relationship stage, outsourcing
 relationships   85
people, importance of   49
perceived risk   238–39
performance measurement and
 management   185–86, 202–3
 basic measurement   186
 contemporary viewpoint   187
 cost performance   198–202
 costs of   286
 driving forces for measurement   188–90
 metrics
  commonly used   194–95
  inventory/warehouse related   196–98
 selecting the best measures   191–94
period costs   170
periodic inventory control system   97–98,
 354
PEST analysis   244–45
Peugeot   43–44
pharmaceutical supply chain
 management   285, 299–302
Phillip Morris   159
picking orders   115
 pick-to-voice   128
pipelines   134
politeness issues, outsourcing
 relationships   82
political risk, international business   173
polycentricity   25, **352**
port centric logistics   274–75, **352**
post   7
Postbank   205
postponement   42–43, 100, **352**
 Dell   54
 inventory management   100
 synchronising design of products and
  supply chains   284
 warehousing role   112
PPP GNI (purchasing power parity gross
 national income)   34n6
price earnings (PE) ratio   208
price elasticity of demand   279
prices
 falling product   5
 variable
  for demand stimulation   122

vendor managed inventory   262
prisoner's dilemma   254, 255–56
process engineering perspective, risk
 management   241
processes, focus on   48–49
processing, inappropriate   40
process-/product-oriented
 organisation   251, 252, **355**
Procter & Gamble   159
procurement   75, **353**
 HBOS   217–20
 sourcing and purchasing   76–78
product design, synchronisation with
 supply chain design   284–85
product lifecycle concept   179
productivity improvements   6
product-/process-oriented
 organisation   251, 252, **355**
profit and loss accounts (income
 statements)   168, 170–71, **355**
 Deutsche Post/DHL   206
 international business   174
 loan interest   175
prospective investors   167
Public Company Accounting Oversight
 Board, USA   168
public limited companies   167
published accounts   168
pull philosophy   40, 41, **353**
purchasing   76–78, **353**
purchasing power parity gross national
 income (PPP GNI)   34n6
push philosophy   40, 41, **353**
put away   114, 115
 metrics   196–97

qualitative metrics   191, 198
quality issues
 outsourcing relationships   81–82
 performance management, 3PLs   189
 pharmaceutical supply chain   300, 301
 safety stock   106
 see also total quality management
quantitative metrics   191, 198
Quigley, Des   219
Quinn, James   49, 290

Radical Ltd   287
radio frequency identification (RFID)   154,
 156–61, **353**

risk management 242
  STS theory 127
rail transport 135
  relative costs and operating
      characteristics 134
'rapid fire fulfilment' 47
Rashid bin Saeed al-Maktoum,
      Sheikh 305
rationing 122
  vendor managed inventory 263
ratios, financial management 176
  Deutsche Post/DHL 207–8
raw materials 90
RDCs (regional distribution centres) 137,
  348
receiving metrics 196
receiving on-time delivery 196
receiving time 196
recycling 277
regional distribution centres (RDCs) 137,
  348
regional trade agreements 20, **353**
Registrar of Companies 167
re-labelling view 12, **353**
reliability issues, outsourcing
      relationships 81
reorder point (ROP) 92, 93, 96, **353**
reorder point inventory control
      system 96, **353**
replenishment, warehouse 115
request for quote/tender/information/
      proposal (RFQ/RFT/RFI/RFP) 76,
  353
reserves 170
resilience 229–30, **353**
  definition 231–32
resource flows 15, 59
resources, underutilisation of 41
responsibility accounting 180
responsive supply chains 45
responsiveness issues, outsourcing
      relationships 81
return material/merchandise authorisation
      (RMA) 276, **353**
return on equity 208
Revenue and Customs 167
revenue passenger kilometres (RPKs) 135
reverse auctions 77
reverse logistics 276–78
  warehousing 116

RFID *see* radio frequency identification
RFQ/RFT/RFI/RFP (request for quote/
      tender/information/proposal)
      76–77, **353**
risk 229–30, 245–46
  definition 230
  financial management 173, 175–76
  management 236
    holistic approaches, need for
        239–40
    shortcomings 236–39
    wicked problems 239–45
Rittel, Horst 239, 240
RMA (return material/merchandise
      authorisation) 276, **353**
road transport 135
  and economic growth, decoupling 272
  port centric logistics 275
  relative costs and operating
      characteristics 134
Roberts, Sgt Stephen 242
robustness 229–30, **353**
  definition 231
ROP (reorder point) 92, 93, 96, **353**
Royal Ahold 235
RPKs (revenue passenger kilometres)
      135
Rumsfeld, Donald 232, 237

safety stock *see* buffer stock
Sainsbury's 275
sale and lease back 169, 175, **354**
Sarbanes–Oxley Act 2002 (SOX) 168,
      235–36, 239, **354**
satisficing decision-making behaviour 70
Scala system, Gate Gourmet 212–14, 250
scale, role in sustainable logistics 272–73
Schmidt, Dieter 313–14
Schmidt, Wolfgang 313
Schmidt & Partner Logistics Solutions
      Inc 303, 313–14
SCM *see* supply chain management
SD (system dynamics) models 287–88
seasonality 118, 121
Seat 44, 55
senior management, metrics for 194
Seoul Metropolitan Rapid Transit
      Corporation (SMRTC) 322, 331
Seoul Metropolitan Subway Corporation
      (SMSC) 317, 318, 322, 331

September 11 terrorist attacks   234–35
   Gate Gourmet   213–14
service level agreements (SLAs)   77, 202,
   354
service sector   13
   costing   177–78
   growth, UK   272
   international trade   20, 79
   offshoring   30
   sourcing patterns   79
Shapira, Zur   236–37
shareholders   167, 170, 173, 175
shares   173
Sharjah International Airport (SHJ)   307
shipping *see* water transport
shipping companies   61
silo based (functional) organisation   49,
   251–52, **349**
silos   37, 251–52, **354**
   financial management   165
   management accounting   178
Simchi-Levi, D. 284
simulation techniques, modelling supply
   chain designs   286, 287–88
Singapore   25
single sourcing   78
six sigma
   performance management, 3PLs   189
   wicked problems   241
skills requirements, future supply chain
   managers   288–90
Skoda   44, 55
SLAs (service level agreements)   77, 202,
   354
smart fridges   159
Smith, Frederick   64
smoothing supply to meet demand   112,
   114
socio-technical systems (STS) theory
   126–28, 252, **354**
   information visibility and
      transparency   152
Sony   188
sourcing   76–78, **354**
South Asian earthquake   296
South Korea
   book market   317–21, 329, 333–34
   internet infrastructure   318, 319
SOX (Sarbanes–Oxley Act   2002)   168,
   235–36, 239, **356**
square root rule   100, **354**

SRM (Supplier Relationship Management)
   project, HBOS   218, 220
STELLA   288
Stock Exchange   168
straight flow operation   117
strategy   36–38
   see also supply chain strategies
STS (socio-technical systems) theory
   126–28, 252, **356**
   information visibility and
      transparency   152
Summers, John   223, 224, 226
supplier development   77–78, **354**
   integration and collaboration   257
   Volvo Trucks India   79
supplier evaluation at EADS   223–26
Supplier Relationship Management (SRM)
   project, HBOS   218, 220
supply base rationalisation   256, 257, **354**
supply chain   10, **354**
supply chain business model   340,
   341–42
supply chain integration   249–53, 263–64,
   354
   evolution   10
supply chain inventory management
   98–103
supply chain knowledge
   management   161–62, **354**
supply chain management (SCM)   9–11,
   354
   evolution   4–7
   and logistics, distinguishing
      between   11–12
Supply Chain Quarterly 343
supply chain revolution   7
supply chain strategies   35, 50–51
   agile supply chains   42, 44
   combined logistics strategies   45–48
   critical factors   48–50
   evolution of manufacturing   38–39
   lean production   39–41
   mass customisation   42–44, 45
   strategy   36–38
surge flow inventory   104, 105
sustainable logistics   268–69, 277–78, 342
   economic and transport growth, link
      between   271–74
   efficiency solutions   274–76
   'green revolution' and supply chain
      redesign   269–71

reverse logistics 276–78
synchronising design of products
and supply chains 284
system dynamics (SD) models 287–88

tachographs 186, **357**
tacit knowledge 161
tax avoidance 175
tax evasion 175
taxation, international business 174
transfer price 174
Taylor, Ian 217, 218, 219, 220
technical barriers to information
visibility 151
technology *see* information technology
Tesco
factory gate pricing 140
RFID 156
Texas Pacific Group (TPG) 244
third party logistics companies (3PLs)
63–64, 66, **355**
'asset unencumbered' 72
performance measurement and
management 188
competition 189
cost models 200, 202–4
growth of companies 193
manufacturing management principles,
adoption of 189
purchasing 3PL services 203
selecting 68
tiered supplier structures 78
TNCs (transnational corporations) 24,
26–27, **355**
top–down perspective on strategy 36–37
total landed costs 85, 198–200, 286, **355**
historical perspective 335
total quality management (TQM) 39, 41
performance management measurement,
3PLs 189
wicked problems 241
total sales value 208
touch points 62
Toyoda, Kiichiro 39
Toyota
just-in-time inventory system 106
mass customisation 43–44
supplier development 77
Toyota Production System (TPS) 39–41,
355
TPG (Texas Pacific Group) 244

TPS (Toyota Production System) 39–41,
355
TQM *see* total quality management
trade contacts 167
traditional routines 32
traditionalist view 12, **355**
train companies 61
transaction exposure 174, **355**
transactional pricing 201
transfer price 174–75, **355**
transit inventory 90, 100–102
translation exposure 174, **355**
transnational corporations (TNCs) 24,
355
transport 131–32, 145–46
decision making 69
deregulation 5
development of logistics 336–37
efficiency 144–45
evolution of logistics and SCM 4–7
generalised costs 69–71, 102
growth, link with economic
growth 271–74
infrastructure planning 136–37
lean production 39
modes 132–35
operations 137–41
reduced transport intensity of freight
4–5
transit inventory 90, 101–2, 103
Transport 21 project, Republic of
Ireland 137
transport cost sensitivity 5, **355**
transport mobility 21
transportation model 139, 141–44, 287,
358
triage 14
trucking companies 61
trust, and collaboration 254
'T-shaped' skills profile 289–90
tsunami, Asian 295, 296
turnover of capital employed 209

'U' flow operation 118
unadjusted inventory accuracy 198
uncertainty 232–36, 239
unionist view 12, 15, **355**
unit based costing 200
United Arab Emirates
airfreight tonnage 307, 308
Dubai 304–15

United Kingdom
  aerospace industry 258–60
  creeping crises 233–34
  exports 21
  Gate Gourmet dispute 243–44
  Heathrow Airport 270
  Iraq war 242
  Medicines and Healthcare Products
    Regulatory Agency (MHRA) 300
  millennium bug 232–33
  road transport and economic growth,
    decoupling 272
  size of logistics sector 7
United Parcels Service (UPS) 6, 61, 62
United States of America
  Centre for Medicines in the Public
    Interest 301
  exports 22, 33–4n3
  Iraq war 242
  productivity growth 7–8
  Sarbanes–Oxley Act 168, 235–36, 239,
    354
  September 11 terrorist attacks 234–35
  Wal-Mart 7–8
unknowable unknowns 232
  September 11 terrorist attacks 234
UPS (United Parcels Service) 6, 61, 62
upstream 10, **358**

value, determining 285–86
value-adding activities 112, 114, **355**
value stream 41
van den Berg, Eric 211–12
variable costs 180
variance analysis 180
variation, and safety stock 98–99, 106
vendor managed inventory (VMI) 153,
  156, 262–63, **355**
vertical collaboration 254–55, **355**
  humanitarian logistics 256
vertical integration 10, 28, **355**
virtual organisations 28, **355**
VMI (vendor managed inventory) 153,
  156, 262–63, **355**
Volkswagen Group 44, 55
volumetric charging 132, **355**
Volvo Trucks India 79
vulnerability 229–30, **356**
  changing times and an uncertain
    world 232–36

definition 229–30
see also risk

waiting time 40
Wal-Mart 7–8, 34n16
  CPFR 156
  RFID 160
Walters, D.W. 104
warehouse management system
  (WMS) 124–26, 153, 155, **356**
warehouse related metrics 196–99
warehousing 111, 129–30
  bullwhip effect 122–23
  capacity management 116–22
  generic functions 114, 115
  in global supply chains 112–14
  layout and design 114–16, 117
  total landed costs 199
  work organisation and job design
    126–29
Waste Electrical and Electronic Equipment
  (WEEE) Directive 116, 277
water transport 135
  Dubai 310
  relative costs and operating
    characteristics 134
  shipping companies 61
  sustainable logistics 270, 273–74
    port centric logistics 274–76
wave flow inventory 104–5
Webber, Melvin 239, 240
WebFox 321
whole life costing *see* lifecycle costing
wicked problems 239–40
  framework 240–46
Winter, Peter 303, 305, 306–8, 313, 314–15
WMS *see* warehouse management system
Woori Technology 321–22
work-in-progress 90
work organisation, warehousing 126–28
World War II 336
WorldCom 168, 235
Wowbook 321

Y2K 232–36, 239, 340, 341
  business continuity management 236
Yes24 321, 329, 330, 332–33
Youngpoong 318, 332

Zara 46–47, 55